2451

3-50

Emotions in History

General Editors

UTE FREVERT   THOMAS DIXON

The Emotions of Internationalism

Feeling International Cooperation in the Alps in the Interwar Period

ILARIA SCAGLIA

OXFORD
UNIVERSITY PRESS

OXFORD
UNIVERSITY PRESS

Great Clarendon Street, Oxford, OX2 6DP,
United Kingdom

Oxford University Press is a department of the University of Oxford.
It furthers the University's objective of excellence in research, scholarship,
and education by publishing worldwide. Oxford is a registered trade mark of
Oxford University Press in the UK and in certain other countries

First Edition published in 2020

Impression: 1

Published in the United States of America by Oxford University Press
198 Madison Avenue, New York, NY 10016, United States of America

British Library Cataloguing in Publication Data
Data available

Library of Congress Control Number: 2019946149

ISBN 978-0-19-884832-5

DOI: 10.1093/oso/9780198848325.001.0001

Printed and bound by
CPI Group (UK) Ltd, Croydon, CR0 4YY

To Steven, the great belayer

Acknowledgments

I wish to express my gratitude to the institutions that have made this volume possible. Between 2011 and 2018, Columbus State University in Columbus, GA, USA, offered me first a job and later tenure, together with serene working conditions. The Graduate Institute of International and Development Studies in Geneva hosted me as a Visiting Fellow during a crucial phase of my research in the summer 2014. The Mellon and Volkswagen Foundations have sponsored me during the bulk of the writing process. The Dahlem Humanities Center and the John F. Kennedy Institute for North American Studies at the Free University Berlin provided me with an ideal writing environment and enabled me to organize a workshop essential for the development of my argument. The Research Center "History of Emotions" at the Max Planck Institute for Human Development in Berlin offered me incomparable library and intellectual resources. Aston University in Birmingham, UK, allowed me time to complete revisions on my manuscript. Finally, the Coordinating Council for Women in History (CCWH) gave me a powerful network, precious wisdom, and inexhaustible sources of inspiration. None of these pages could have been written without generous support from all of these bodies.

I struggle to find words to thank the extraordinary people that I have encountered throughout this journey. Daniel Gullo, my mentor at CSU, has never ceased to motivate me in this and other projects. The members of CSU's Women Research and Writing Group encouraged me to fulfill my goals every week, keeping my research alive during times of high teaching and service loads. My colleagues in the Department of History and Geography made work a place of collegiality and friendship, intelligence and humor. My CSU students also provided me with a cozy scholarly home: I am especially thankful to the participants in my seminars in the "History of Internationalism" and in the "History of Emotions," who have always commented on my drafts without fears of my "retaliating" while grading theirs.

My mentors outside of my institution also served as remarkable models of scholarship, kindness, and generosity. Davide Rodogno guided me at the Graduate Institute in Geneva in 2014 and never stopped sustaining me ever since. Jessica C. E. Gienow-Hecht has been an incomparable model of scholar and Chair. The entire History Department at JFKI made it a true pleasure for me to be there during the 2016–17 academic year. Ute Frevert and her team at the MPI "feel tank," as Jan Plamper aptly called it, overwhelmed me with their kindness and generosity. Never will I forget how much I have received both intellectually and emotionally during the time I spent in their company. My colleagues at Aston University and the members of our History Colloquium helped me greatly during the completion phase of this book.

An army of archivists has made available to me the most disparate primary sources. Jacques Oberson and Lee Robertson at the League of Nations Archives never tired of addressing my—seemingly endless—questions and requests. The librarians, archivists, and staff of the Geneva Library System, the UNOG library, the International Labor Office Archives, the Archives de la Ville de Geneve, the Bern Federal Archives, the Bern National Library and Archives, the Archives can-tonales vaudoises, the Olympic Studies Center in Lausanne, the UNESCO Archives in Paris, and the Max Planck Institute for Human Development in Berlin also went above and beyond the call of duty to ensure that I could access the materials I needed.

I am deeply grateful to the people who have welcomed me to peruse collec-tions normally not open to the public: Stephanie Stettbacher and the staff of the UIAA (Union Internationale des Associations d'Alpinisme, or International Mountaineering and Climbing Federation) in Bern, Dominique Pillonel of La Manufacture in Leysin, Jacques Auroy of the Club Alpin Suisse, the staff of the Muir S. Fairchild Research Information Center (MSFRIC) at the Maxwell Air Force Base in Montgomery, AL, and the President of APES (L'Association de la Presse Etrangère en Suisse) Emilia Nazarenko. Maria Elena Ingianni and Alessandra Ravelli made it possible for me to access manuscripts housed at the Biblioteca Nazionale del Club Alpino Italiano in Turin. The Municipality of Chamonix and the Alpine Club (UK) have scanned and sent important papers, which I have also included in my work. Riitta Puukka of the Permanent Mission of Finland in Geneva also sent me valuable information. Véronique Bernard of the Leysin Tourist Office welcomed me warmly in Leysin and offered precious help afterwards. Dr. Auguste Rollier's granddaughter, Martine Gagnebin, met with me and later gave me permission to publish photographs from her grandfa-ther's works. Each of these acts of kindness has added much richness to this book, and also made my research experience a real pleasure.

Numerous colleagues within and outside of my institution have provided vital support during the writing process. Stefania Benini, Véronique Bernard, Pierre-Etienne Bourneuf, Daniel Crosswell, Jessica C. E. Gienow-Hecht, Georg Iggers, Wilma Iggers, Barbara J. Keys, Paul A. Kramer, Sönke Kunkel, Daniel Laqua, Stefan Manz, Jon Mathieu, Susan J. Matt, Stefano Morosini, Margrit Pernau, Volker Prott, Amanda Rees, Davide Rodogno, Barbara H. Rosenwein, Patricia Schechter, Brian Sudlow, and Joseph Yannielli provided helpful comments on various parts and drafts of this book. Series editors Ute Frevert and Thomas Dixon, OUP's anonymous reviewers, editors Christina Wipf and Stephanie Ireland, and Senior Assistant Commissioning Editor for Academic History Cathryn Steele have given me invaluable guidance and made this work much stronger than it would have otherwise been. OUP's production and graphic teams have also exceeded my highest expectations. Any mistakes and shortcomings of course remain mine.

If my academic and professional debts are steep, my personal ones are even heavier. I mention here only a few people whose presence in my life has directly affected this book. The late Georg Iggers gave me honest and sincere advice on how to approach this topic, as well as an inspirational model of scholar, citizen, and friend. My mother, Dilva Viocca, never stopped embodying integrity, resilience, and a healthy dose of humor. My children, Rebecca and Damian (along with our puppy, Warwick) added precious disruptions and smiles. My husband, Steven Andrew Gill, has done so much for me that any attempt at crafting a list would be futile. This book belongs to him as well.

Out of all realms, I found that academia—and the historical discipline in particular—offers the best opportunity to spell out an articulate train of thought. Although it is seldom praised, its community remains a fair, intelligent, and attentive readership by all standards, one whose members most often resist the urge of boiling down complex narratives into an easy punchline. The same cannot be said about the public conversations about politics, current events, and culture during the years in which I have researched and written this book. Well aware that objectivity is a "noble dream" at best, and cheap disguise at worse, I did my best to capture subtleties and to spell them out as clearly as possible, addressing colleagues and fellow historians whose constant quest for a more complex answer I can only aspire to match.

This study was inspired by them, and by all those people—within and outside of academia—who have the skill and the stamina to walk a steep path with a steady foot while trying to reach peaks of excellence, and do so without compromising their integrity. Among them, Steven Andrew Gill stands out not only as an exceptionally supportive academic partner but also as the most engaged colleague, activist, and fellow world citizen. In alpine talk: he is a great belayer, who tirelessly facilitates and safeguards the ascent of others with intelligence, skill, wit, and love. *Grazie*.

Contents

List of Illustrations

List of Charts

List of Maps

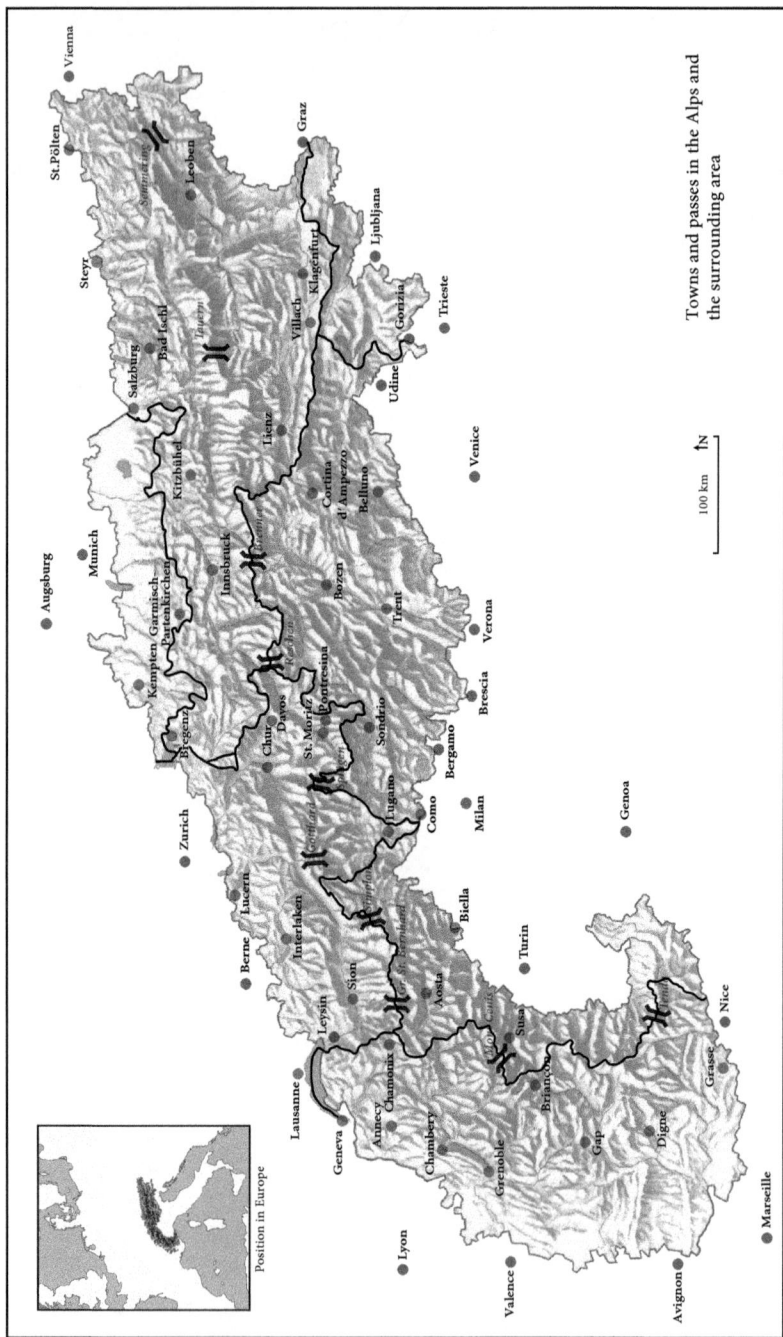

Map 1 'Cities, Passes, and Tunnels across the Alps

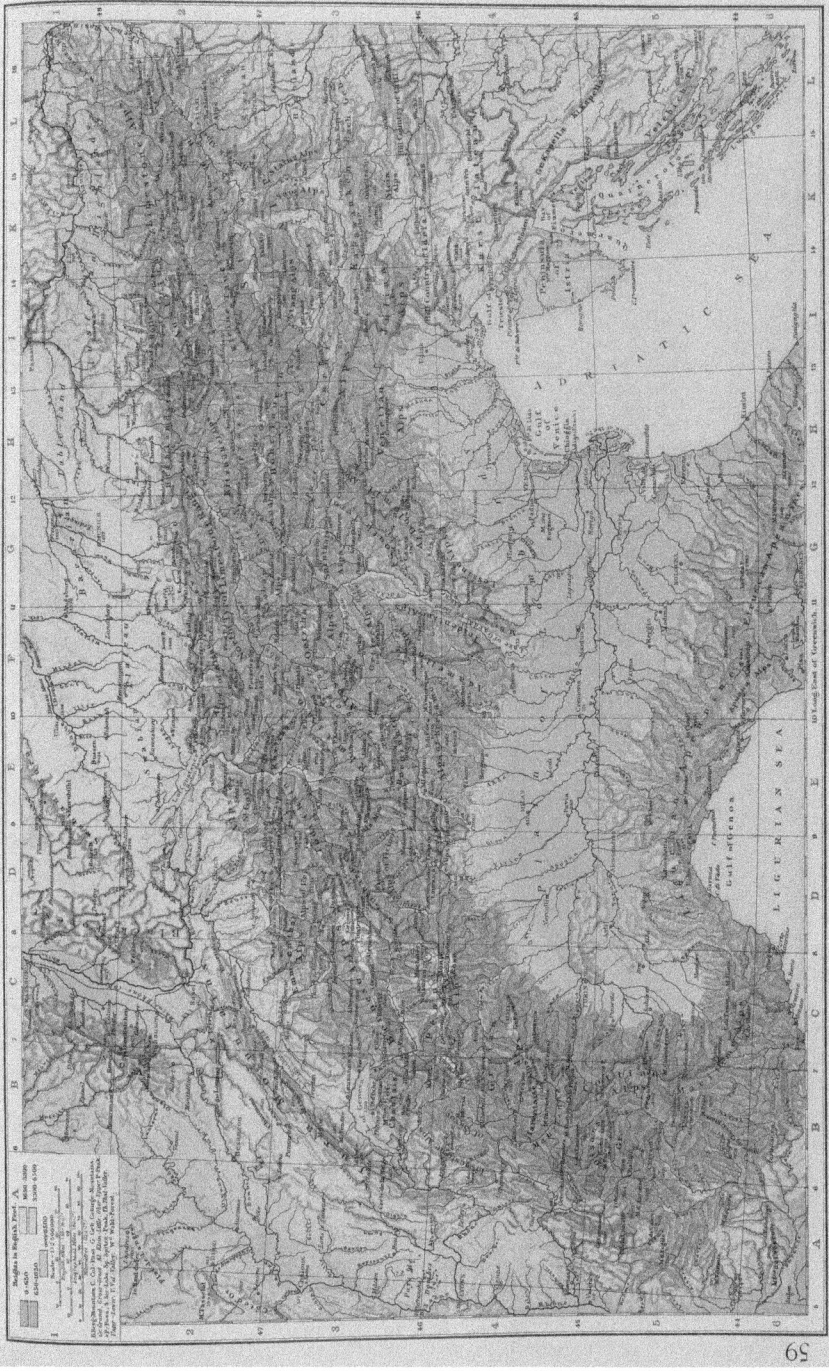

Map 2 The Alps in 1900, political boundaries

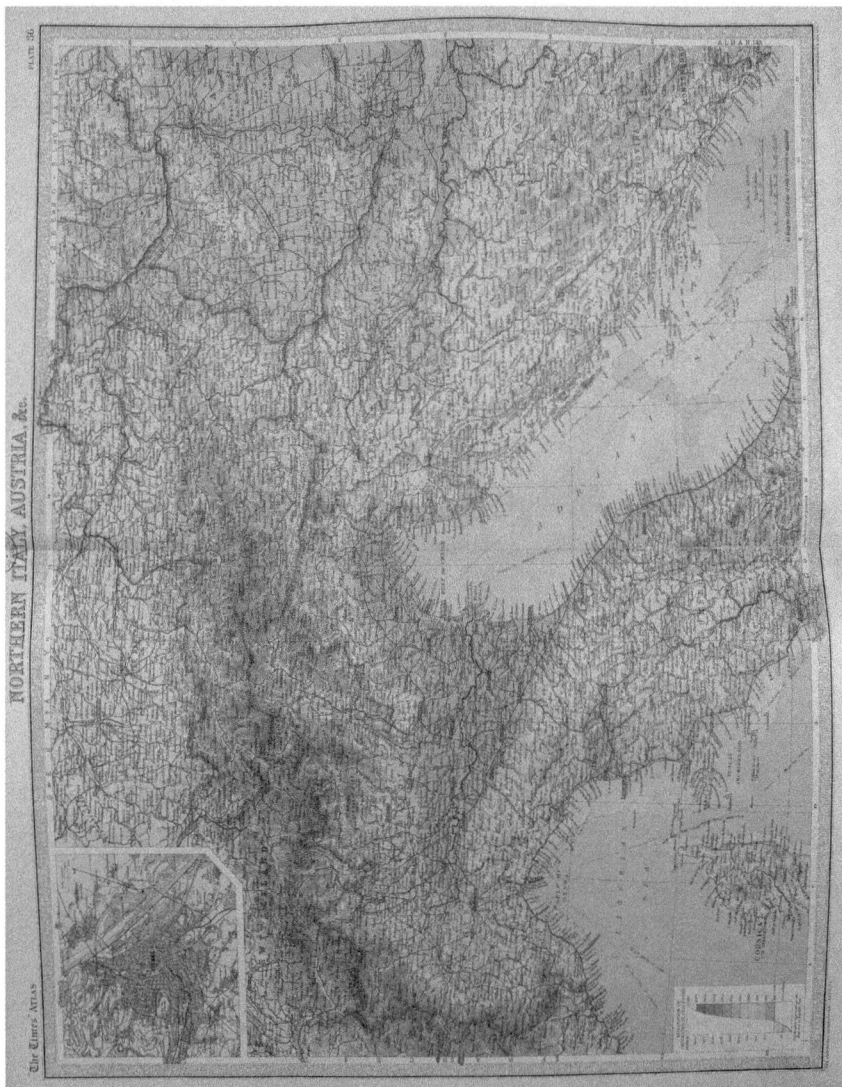

Map 3 The Alps in 1920, political boundaries

Introduction

The Emotions of Internationalism

I saw the monument erected in Turin in honor of the portentous Cenisio tunnel and I imagined this choreographic composition

Luigi Manzotti*

In Luigi Manzotti's famed 1881 ballet *Excelsior*, the climax comes when the French and the Italian teams perforating the first alpine tunnel under the Mont Cenis meet in the "viscera of the earth" (*viscere della terra*).[1] Having marveled at the invention of the steamship, the discovery of electricity, and the opening of the Suez Canal, spectators now anticipate "the last mine" to shatter the remaining barrier between Italy and France. Yet, following a loud bang, alpine rock still dominates the scene, seemingly unmoved. Despair ensues: "so much work, so much sweat, so much gold, all is lost." Then comes the sound of pickaxes, first faint, then louder at every beat. The men dig feverishly, "eager to hug their brothers from the other side of the Alps (*fratelli d'oltralpe*)" whom they can hear but not yet see. Finally, "engineers and workers...throw themselves in the others' arms, while at the Italian salute in homage of this great work the French respond." In this poignant moment, "love" and "brotherhood" triumph, as the "Genius of Humanity" fulfills its promise to unite people "in brotherly embrace."[2]

---

* The epigraph is drawn from Luigi Manzotti, *Excelsior: azione coreografica, storica, allegorica, fantastica in 6 parti e 11 quadri*, musica di Romualdo Marenco (Milan: Regio Stabilimento Ricordi, 1881), 1. The Italian original reads: "*Vidi il monumento innalzato a Torino in gloria del portentoso traforo del Cenisio/ ed immaginai la presente composizione coreografica.*" Unless otherwise noted, all translations to English are my own.

[1] The Ballo Excelsior opened at Milan's La Scala Theatre in 1881 and has toured the stages of theatres across the world ever since. Most recently, it was performed at La Scala in conjunction with the universal exhibition Expo 2015. As ethnomusicologist Roberto Leydi pointed out, "never had a show as much public and critical success as did the ballo Excelsior." Roberto Leydi, "Il 'Ballo Excelsior' e la sua fortuna" in *Excelsior* (Milan: Edizioni del Teatro alla Scala, 1978), quoted in Vittoria Crespi Morbio, ed., *...E guarnizioni spiccantissime. Figurini e schemi coreografici per la rappresentazione del ballo Excelsior all'Eden di Parigi* (Milan: Edizioni Amici della Scala, 1993), 16.

[2] Manzotti, *Excelsior*, 17–20; 7.

The Emotions of Internationalism: Feeling International Cooperation in the Alps in the Interwar Period. Ilaria Scaglia, Oxford University Press (2020). © Ilaria Scaglia.
DOI: 10.1093/oso/9780198848325.001.0001

Like this iconic ballet scene, this book takes readers up in the Alps,[3] a national, international, and transnational[4] "region" which many individuals, institutions, and governments often selected for their activities and emotionalized for political purposes (see Map 1).[5] It undertakes a journey through the most diverse terrains and venues, from the international art exhibitions and congresses organized by the Union Internationale des Associations d'Alpinisme (also known as UIAA, or International Mountaineering and Climbing Federation), to the international schools run by transnational bodies such as the League for Open-Air Education, to the international sanatoria for students, workers, and soldiers healing from tuberculosis in the Swiss village of Leysin. Along the way is a broad spectrum of state and non-state actors involved in all sorts of cross-border endeavors, from large-scale infrastructure projects akin to the tunnel under the Mont Cenis, to the League of Nations and its propaganda efforts, to the plethora of smaller international organizations emulating the League's work in fields such as leisure, health, and education. Through this metaphorical travel, this study argues that starting from the nineteenth century and accelerating in the interwar years emotions such as the ones described in *Excelsior* became a fundamental feature of internationalism, long shaped its development, and constitute an essential dimension of international history to this day.

Internationalists, which I define as individuals and groups who deemed it necessary to involve people from other countries to achieve their goals, expressed emotions profusely and tenaciously chased them because they considered them an essential part of their work. They inextricably linked emotions with their own rhetoric, publicity, and reputation. They treated feelings as a realist goal, as they sought to suppress some (such as the "resentment" lingering after military conflict) and engender others (like "friendship" among individuals from various

---

[3] By the Alps, I mean the mountain range at the frontier between (in alphabetical order) Austria, France, Germany, Italy, Switzerland, and the former Yugoslavia, including also places like the "Pre-alps" and the "Piedmont." I use the term "mountains" to include a diverse spectrum of natural terrains and landscapes (from valleys to peaks, and everything in between), which often hosted initiatives of international cooperation, as well as the multiple artifacts added by humans. For an overview of the history of the Alps as a whole, see Jon Mathieu, *The Alps: An Environmental History* (Oxford: Polity Press, 2019). On the construction of mountains in general, see Bernard Debarbieux and Gilles Rudaz, *The Mountain: A Political History from the Enlightenment to the Present* (Chicago, IL: University of Chicago Press, 2015).

[4] I use the term "transnational" to refer to both non-state actors and cross-border dynamics and communities. For a conceptual framework on "transnational" approaches see Patricia Clavin, "Defining Transnationalism," *Contemporary European History* 14, no. 4 (November 2005), 421–39. On the evolution of transnationalism in historical writing, see "AHR Conversation: On Transnational History," *The American Historical Review* 111, no. 5 (December 2006), 1441–64.

[5] In Europe in particular, "regions" have been entrusted by many to provide at once "tolerant cosmopolitanism" and "warm, personal localism," acting as shields against extreme worldism or radical nationalism. Celia Applegate, "AHR Forum: A Europe of Regions: Reflections on the Historiography of Sub-National Places in Modern Times," *American Historical Review* 104, no. 4 (October 1999), 1158. See also Paul A. Kramer, "Region in World History," in Douglas Northrup, ed., *A Companion to World History* (Chichester, UK: Wiley-Blackwell, 2012), 201–12.

nations and "trust" in the internationalist enterprise). They devoted much energy to managing emotions by rehearsing, testing, and staging friendship rituals. They made emotional "experiences" and "atmospheres" necessary ingredients of their endeavors, emphasizing the feelings they produced in themselves and others. They documented emotional expressions through writings and images, using them to assess and foster their own work. And they created cultural productions of the likes of *Excelsior* to publicize and elicit specific emotions—e.g., "love" and "brotherhood"—and to connect them to larger political projects.

More broadly, internationalists constructed a transnational "emotional community"[6] made of people and institutions that valued international contacts and established a set of specific and acceptable "emotional styles" in which to conduct them.[7] They also attributed moral values to their beliefs and behaviors, presenting them as superior to others (notably, extreme nationalism) and using them to downplay their shortcomings and justify their contradictions.[8] Their ideas and practices were defined by their emotional aspects and by their ability to make people *feel* international cooperation. And, in an age of anxiety and mass politics, their successes and failures were determined by their handling (or mis-handling) of emotions in the eyes—and hearts—of the public.

The consequences of the internationalists' engagement with emotions proved deep and long lasting. As this study sets out to demonstrate, in the 1920s and 1930s, concerns about what people felt came to drive virtually every aspect of international life, from politics to leisure, from education to health. Interwar assumptions about the benign interplay of feelings and international cooperation became normative in international relations in subsequent decades and remain in force today. A glance at any advertisement for corporate team-building activities or for study abroad programs reveals that the inherent virtue of shared experiences and international travel—as well as their supposed effectiveness in instilling "mutual understanding"—have become mainstream social values.[9] "Cosmopolitan"

[6] In a landmark study, Barbara Rosenwein defined "emotional communities" as "groups in which people adhere to the same norms of expression and value—or devalue—the same or related emotions." Barbara H. Rosenwein, *Emotional Communities in the Early Middle Ages* (Ithaca, NY: Cornell University Press, 2007), 2.
[7] In light of recent multidisciplinary debates over the complex nature of emotions (particularly on their individual and their collective aspects, and also on their being rooted in discourses and/or in the body), I find useful Benno Gammerl's concept of "emotional styles" that "encompass instead the experience, fostering, and display of emotions, and oscillate between discursive patterns and embodied practices as well as between common scripts and specific appropriations." Benno Gammerl, "Emotional Styles: Concepts and Challenges," *Rethinking History* 16, no. 2 (May 2012), 163.
[8] On this point, see Ilaria Scaglia, "The 'Hydrologist's Weapons': Emotions and the Moral Economy of Internationalism, 1921–1952," in Sara Graça Da Silva, ed., *New Interdisciplinary Landscapes in Morality and Emotion* (London: Routledge, 2018), 140–52. See also Chapter 3.
[9] In contrast, academic discussions on this subject are more complex. In a landmark study, Emmanuel Sigalas noted that after spending a year abroad, the students' sense of European identity had actually been undermined. Emmanuel Sigalas, "Cross-border Mobility and European Identity: The Effectiveness of Intergroup Contact during the Erasmus Year Abroad," *European Union Politics* 11, no. 2 (June 2010), 241–65. Later works, however, pointed out that other factors—particularly openness

people and emotions too are presumed to be benevolent.[10] As a result, practices such as study abroad increased at an unprecedented scale in the twentieth century, as "the 50,000 studying in Britain, France, the United States and Russia in 1950 increased almost 20-fold by 2000."[11] Several factors contributed to this trend: many governments employed international education to attract skilled workers and to generate revenue, or to pursue "imperialist and quasi-imperial interests." Meanwhile, they continued to follow "a mutual understanding approach" either to justify their policies, or to buttress their efforts in other areas, or as an end in itself.[12] It is therefore imperative to investigate the assumptions on which notions such as "mutual understanding" were based and the complex processes through which these were formed. This book explains how the interplay of emotions and internationalism came to affect these historical developments, demonstrating that emotions became an important part of the internationalist framework and of various forms of "power," and came to define what was possible in the twentieth century and beyond.[13]

Surprisingly, the foundational role of emotions in creating and defining internationalism lack systematic academic study. In recent years, the history of internationalism has experienced a resurgence, as it has become clear that international organizations (and the League of Nations in particular) influenced key historical entities and dimensions—such as the world economy or empire—whose relevance is now undisputed.[14] International cooperation per se has garnered much

---

to mobility and the overall cultural outlooks developed during the study abroad experience—still made it a worthwhile investment for the European Union. Christof van Mol, "Intra-European Student Mobility and European Identity: A Successful Marriage?," *Population, Space and Place* 19, no. 2 (March/April 2013), 209–22, and Viktoria Kaina, Ireneusz Paweł Karolewski, and Sebastian Kühn, eds., *European Identity Revisited: New Approaches and Recent Empirical Evidence* (New York: Routledge, 2016).

[10] On this point, see Robert Fine, *Cosmopolitanism* (London: Routledge, 2007). On the development of a "taste for the world" see Vincenzo Cicchelli and Sylvie Octobre, *Aesthetico-Cultural Cosmopolitanism and French Youth: the Taste of the World* (London: Palgrave Macmillan, 2018).

[11] Hilary Perraton, "Foreign Students in the Twentieth Century: A Comparative Study of Patterns and Policies in Britain, France, Russia and the United States," *Policy Reviews in Higher Education* 1, no. 2 (2017), 164–5.

[12] Perraton, "Foreign Students in the Twentieth Century," 182–3. On study abroad and empire, see also Paul A. Kramer, "Is the World Our Campus? International Students and U.S. Global Power in the Long Twentieth Century," *Diplomatic History* 33, no. 5 (November 2009), 775–806.

[13] I am indebted to Barbara Keys who shed light on the importance of words and frameworks in shaping long-term "moral aspirations" and "behaviors" in her contribution to the "Making a Case of Internationalism Workshop," which I organized at the Free University Berlin in June 2017. On issues of causality and relevance connected to these themes, see also Frank A. Ninkovich, *Global Dawn: The Cultural Foundation of American Internationalism, 1865–1890* (Cambridge, MA: Harvard University Press, 2009).

[14] See Patricia Clavin, *Securing the World Economy: The Reinvention of the League of Nations, 1920–1946* (Oxford: Oxford University Press, 2013); Susan Pedersen, *The Guardians: The League of Nations and the Crisis of Empire* (Oxford: Oxford University Press, 2015). See also Susan Pedersen, "Back to the League of Nations: Review Essay," *American Historical Review* 112, no. 4 (October 2007), 1091–117.

attention as a subject of study, as many authors have noted that both state and non-state actors (such as individuals, networks, and non-governmental organizations) did much to shape both domestic policies and international relations.[15] Histories of humanitarianism have unveiled the centrality of affective links in both moving and justifying various kinds of interventions.[16] Yet the functions that emotions performed in international cooperation have been largely overlooked.

Scholars in many disciplines, and social scientists especially, have long recognized the importance of emotions.[17] International relations theorists have amply demonstrated that feelings touch virtually every aspect of international relations.[18] Most notably, Roland Bleiker and Emma Hutchison have written extensively about "emotions in world politics" and the formation of "affective communities" after traumatic events such as wars; and Todd H. Hall has theorized "emotional diplomacy" among states.[19] Yet the prominence of emotions in the study of international relations has not yet been matched by similar inquiries into their history.

Such omission is striking because emotions are now routinely analyzed from comparative and global perspectives in prominent institutes and departments worldwide.[20] In contrast, they have only begun to be incorporated in international

[15] A useful overview is Daniel Laqua, ed., *Internationalism Reconfigured: Transnational Ideas and Movements Between the World Wars* (New York: I.B. Tauris, 2011).

[16] See for instance Johannes Paulmann, ed., *Dilemmas of Humanitarian Aid in the Twentieth Century* (London: OUP/German Historical Institute, 2016); Michael N. Barnett, *The Empire of Humanity: A History of Humanitarianism* (Ithaca, NY: Cornell University Press, 2011); Bruno Cabanes, *The Great War and the Origins of Humanitarianism, 1918–1924* (Cambridge: Cambridge University Press, 2014); Brendan Simms and D. J. B. Trim, eds. *Humanitarian Intervention: A History* (Cambridge: Cambridge University Press, 2011). On the aesthetic aspects of humanitarianism, see Heide Fehrenbach and Davide Rodogno, eds., *Humanitarian Photography: A History* (New York: Cambridge University Press, 2015).

[17] For an overview of this literature, see Lisa Feldman Barrett, Michael Lewis, and Jeannette M. Haviland-Jones, eds., *Handbook of Emotions*, 4th edition (New York: The Guildford Press, 2016). See also Jan Stets and Jonathan H. Turner, eds., *Handbook of the Sociology of Emotions*, vol. II (New York: Springer, 2014); Jack Barbalet, ed., *Emotions and Sociology* (Oxford: Blackwell, 2002). Outside of the social sciences, emotions have especially attracted the attention of experts in media and advertisement. For an overview, see Katrin Doveling, Christian von Scheve, and Elly A. Konijn, eds., *The Routledge Handbook of Emotions and Mass Media* (New York: Routledge, 2011).

[18] For an overview, see Yohan Ariffin, Jean-Marc Coicaud, and Vesselin Popovski, eds., *Emotions in International Politics: Beyond Mainstream International Relations* (New York: Cambridge University Press, 2016). See also Hanna Samir Kassab, *The Power of Emotion in Politics, Philosophy, and Ideology* (New York: Palgrave Macmillan, 2016).

[19] Roland Bleiker and Emma Hutchison, "Introduction: Emotions and World Politics," *International Theory* 6, no. 3 (November 2014), 490–1, and "Theorizing Emotions in World Politics," *International Theory* 6, no. 3 (November 2014), 491–514; Emma Hutchison, *Affective Communities in World Politics: Collective Emotions after Trauma* (Cambridge: Cambridge University Press, 2016); Todd H. Hall, *Emotional Diplomacy: Official Emotion on the International Stage* (Ithaca, NY: Cornell University Press, 2015).

[20] Among the most prominent hubs are the Research Center "History of Emotions" at the Max Planck Institute for Human Development in Berlin, the Queen Mary Centre for the History of the Emotions of the University of London, and the Australian Research Council Centre of Excellence for the History of Emotions.

history; and when they have been, the focus has been on moments of competition and conflict in the period after 1945—rather than on international cooperation in the previous decades.[21] Emotions have started to be included in the histories of fascism and other political movements in the 1920s and 1930s, often in connection with aesthetics (i.e., in performances, ceremonies, monumentalizations, and also in ritual exchanges and displays of symbols, bodies, objects, and ideas).[22] But, despite this "emotional turn" in many disciplines and historical subfields, we know little about how feeling affected doing, and how emotions came to shape internationalist ideas and practices in the interwar period.

This study opens this new and important line of inquiry by examining how various internationalist groups—which included liberal, proletarian, Catholic, and nationalist individuals and associations—organized events, trips, and long-term stays in the Alps, and devoted much energy to constructing them as sites for "amity" and "solidarity." Meanwhile, governments and private entities involved in building major infrastructure projects presented their work as a means to express and produce "friendship." A substantial body of literature defined "mountain people" as a separate, a-national community, using eugenic and racial categories to label them at once as sick and healthy, "inferior" but threatening to other "superior" groups, withdrawn yet capable of deeper, more "authentic" feelings; and a broad range of cultural productions (film especially) reinforced these images and disseminated them to eager audiences.

Like nationalists, internationalists in the 1920s and 1930s built on these imageries and transposed existing notions of mountains as places for experiencing "the sublime" to the current political situation; in contrast to extreme nationalists, however, they constructed the Alps as ideal sites for feeling and expressing longings for peace.[23] Tales of international friendships formed while climbing

---

[21] A turning point has been the inclusion of essays on the "senses" and on emotions in international history in the latest edition of Frank Costigliola and Michael J. Hogan, eds., *Explaining the History of American Foreign Relations*, 3rd edition (New York: Cambridge University Press, 2016). See Andrew J. Rotter, "The Senses," and Frank Costigliola, "Reading for Emotions," in Costigliola and Hogan, eds., *Explaining the History of American Foreign Relations*, 317–33 and 356–74. See also Barbara Keys, "Emotions in Intercultural Relations," in R. D. Johnson ed., *Asia Pacific in the Age of Globalization* (New York: Palgrave Macmillan, 2015), 212–20; "AHR Conversation: The Historical Study of Emotions," *The American Historical Review* 117, no. 5 (December 2012), 1487–531; Jessica C. E. Gienow-Hecht, ed., *Emotions in American History: An International Assessment* (New York: Berghahn Books, 2010); Jan Lewis and Peter N. Stearns, eds., *An Emotional History of the Unites States* (New York: New York University Press, 1998); Susan J. Matt and Peter N. Stearns, eds., *Doing Emotions History* (Urbana: University of Illinois Press, 2014); Rob Boddice, *The History of Emotions* (Manchester: Manchester University Press, 2018).

[22] One of the first works to examine the interplay of emotions and nationalism was Simonetta Falasca-Zamponi, *Fascist Spectacle: The Aesthetics of Power in Mussolini's Italy* (Berkeley: University of California Press, 2000). See also essays by Giulia Albanese, Alessandro Pes, and Daniela Baratieri in Penelope Morris, Francesco Ricatti, and Mark Seymour, eds., *Politica ed emozioni nella storia d'Italia dal 1848 ad oggi* (Rome: Viella, 2012), 113–67.

[23] On mountains and nationalism, see Alice Travers, *Politique et représentation de la montagne sous Vichy: la montagne éducatrice, 1940–1944* (Paris: L'Harmattan, 2001); Tait Keller, *Apostles of the Alps: Mountaineering and Nation Building in Germany and Austria, 1860–1939* (Chapel Hill: The University of North Carolina Press, 2016).

alpine peaks appeared in publications by a broad range of authors from Pope Pius XI Achille Ratti, to journalist and alpinist Egmond d'Arcis, to countless mountain enthusiasts whose texts peppered specialized journals and popular magazines alike. Stories of soldiers fraternizing across borders evoked images of Christmas-time truces at the front, engraining the idea that amicable feelings could be stronger than conflict. Dramatic scenes of selfless acts—giving up one's sweater in the midst of a blizzard, or risking one's life in dangerous rescue missions—filled novels and films, stirring the imagination of a growing number of readers, viewers, and voters. Through these cultural productions, mountains increasingly appeared as sites of harmonious international cooperation. Against this backdrop, internationalists charged the collaborations and exchanges taking place on the Alps with meaning and presented them to the public as essential moments in international relations.

At a time when they often served as sites of violence and conflict, mountains also provided a crucial milieu for various forms of international cooperation in which nationalist regimes were involved as well.[24] As such, they allow us to see not only where but also *how* internationalism happened in ways that traditional frameworks centered on the nation-state do not.[25] Because mountains marked many of the political and administrative boundaries that divided peoples and nations, numerous international initiatives took place either right on or through them (see Maps 2 and 3).[26] These included not only the opening of tunnels but also the construction of new roads, the creation of electrical, telegraphic, and telephonic lines, as well as the erection of antennas for radio diffusion, all of which were presented in emotional terms with the argument that they drew people closer. Also, the Alps in particular became a preferred space for staging international encounters ranging from assemblies and conferences organized

---

[24] See Judith Matloff, *No Friends but the Mountains: Dispatches from the World's Violent Highlands* (New York: Basic Books, 2017); James C. Scott, *The Art of Not Being Governed: An Anarchist History of Upland Southeast Asia* (New Haven: Yale University Press, 2009). For an overview of this complex past, see also Fiammetta Balestracci and Pietro Causarano, eds. *Al confine delle Alpi: culture, valori sociali e orizzonti nazionali fra mondo tedesco e italiano (secoli XIX–XX)* (Milan: FrancoAngeli, 2018).

[25] This is not to exclude alternative spaces (e.g., seashores or beaches) in principle, though their centrality as a combat zone during the First World War and their longstanding associations with the "sublime" made mountains a preferred site for aesthetic and emotional experiences that could serve a political purpose. On spaces as "contact zones" and as sites where "power" sought to employ emotions to shape the dynamics taking place in them see Madeleine Herren, Martin Rüesch, and Christiane Sibille, eds., *Transcultural History: Theories, Methods, Sources* (Heidelberg: Springer, 2012). See also the extensive literature on seas and oceans as spaces for human interaction. For an overview, see Jennifer L. Gaynor, *Intertidal History in Island Southeast Asia: Submerged Genealogy and the Legacy of Coastal Capture* (Ithaca, NY: Cornell University Press, 2016).

[26] On the geopolitical and imperialist aspects, see Reuben Ellis, *Vertical Margins: Mountaineering and the Landscapes of Neoimperialism* (Madison: University of Wisconsin Press, 2001); Maurice Isserman and Stewart Weaver, *Fallen Giants: A History of Himalayan Mountaineering from the Age of Empire to the Age of Extremes* (New Haven: Yale University Press, 2008). On cultural aspects, see Ann C. Colley, *Victorians in the Mountains: Sinking the Sublime* (Burlington, VT: Ashgate, 2010); Sean Moore Ireton and Caroline Schaumann, eds., *Heights of Reflection: Mountains in the German Imagination from the Middle Ages to the Twenty-first Century* (Rochester, NY: Camden House, 2012).

by the League of Nations to sporting events (most notably the modern Winter Olympics, which began in 1924), to open-air schools and summer camps, to sanatoria for people of all ages and social strata.[27] Mountains thus served as important tools for legitimizing and disseminating political messages and offered a meaningful backdrop and foreground for them.

In this context, the Swiss alpine landscape assumed political significance. To be sure, Switzerland served as an internationalist center not simply because of its topography but because of its long history of neutrality, its geographical location in the heart of Europe, its multilingual character, and especially its long history as a site for internationalist institutions—dating back to the establishment of the International Red Cross in Geneva in 1863—which, in turn, defined its own identity-building process.[28] Swiss neutrality and internationalism at times served to cover the country's own responsibilities, duplicities, and darker sides. There were economic interests attached to international cooperation, which private actors embraced for their own benefit while adopting the rhetoric of international cooperation. A certain luster and prestige accompanied international involvements and events. And bringing together people from different nations often underlined differences and reinforced stereotypes. Still, it is relevant that many people and institutions placed much emphasis on the mountains that surrounded them, connected their internationalism with alpine atmospheres and aesthetics, and inspired many others to do the same.

Most notably, the League of Nations tried to gain people's trust by branding itself as capable of easing the emotional toll of the "Great War." In the words of Belgian representative and League President Paul Hymans, it responded to

---

[27] On the social environment of mountains, see Olivier Hoibian, ed., *L'invention de l'alpinisme: la montagne et l'affirmation de la bourgeoisie cultivée (1786–1914)* (Paris: Belin, 2008); Claudio Ambrosi and Michael Wedekind, eds., *L'invenzione di un cosmo borghese: valori sociali e simboli culturali dell'alpinismo nei secoli XIX e XX* (Trent: Museo Storico di Trento, 2000); Luciano Senatori, *Compagni di cordata: associazionismo proletario, alpinisti sovversivi, sport popolare in Italia* (Rome: Ediesse, 2010); Stefano Morosini, *Sulle vette della patria: politica, guerra e nazione nel Club alpino italiano (1863–1922)* (Milan: FrancoAngeli, 2009); Dagmar Günther, *Alpine Quergänge: Kulturgeschichte des bürgerlichen Alpinismus (1870–1930)* (Frankfurt am Main: Campus Verlag, 1998). On sport and the negotiation between national and international, see Barbara J. Keys, *Globalizing Sport: National Rivalry and International Community in the 1930s* (Cambridge, MA: Harvard University Press, 2006).

[28] On this point, see Madeleine Herren and Sacha Zala, *Netzwerk Aussenpolitik. Internationale Organisationen und Kongresse als Instrumente der schweizerischen Aussenpolitik 1914–1950* (Zürich: Chronos, 2002). See also Harald Fischer-Tiné, "The Other Side of Internationalism: Switzerland as a Hub of Militant Anti-colonialism c. 1910–1920," in Patricia Purtschert, and Harald Fischer-Tiné, eds., *Colonial Switzerland: Rethinking Colonialism from the Margins* (Basingstoke: Palgrave Macmillan, 2015), 221–58. From a cultural standpoint, internationalists constructed Geneva as a site for reconciliation, humanism, and social justice, emphasizing the importance of figures such as Calvin and Rousseau. See for instance Robert de Traz, *L'esprit de Genève* (Paris: Grasset, 1929). On alternative internationalist centers, most notably Belgium, see Daniel Laqua, *The Age of Internationalism and Belgium, 1880–1930: Peace, Progress and Prestige* (Manchester: Manchester University Press, 2013). On international/global cities, see Pierre-Yves Saunier and Shane Ewen, eds., *Another Global City: Historical Explorations into the Transnational Municipal Moment 1850–2000* (New York: Palgrave Macmillan, 2008).

"a need (*besoin*), a sentiment...of justice, harmony, and peace."[29] The League also constructed its main site, Geneva, as a mountain city imbued with ideals and emotions closely linked to internationalism, evoking feelings such as "nobility" through the design of its headquarters (the Palais des Nations) and the adoption of a tempered, alpine emotional style in its publicity.[30]

The League's technical sections dealing with health and intellectual cooperation fostered the internationalization of mountains by encouraging initiatives—ranging from summer camps to school exchanges—based on the notion that "while it is difficult to love someone who has never been seen, it is much easier and fruitful (*fécond*) to love the fellow man (*le prochain*) whom one sees, touches, and with whom he can communicate sorrows and joys."[31] Numerous organizations followed the League's lead and carefully staged international experiences—many focused on the youth—in which every participant, while on foreign land would thrive "in an atmosphere of good camaraderie" while being treated "like a son."[32]

Moved by this emotional peace-building approach, many groups made it a point to operate in the Alps while charging their work with a higher political meaning. Among the most prominent were the protagonists of this book: the aforementioned International Mountaineering and Climbing Federation (UIAA) and the international sanatoria in Leysin, which hosted people of all provenances while they were undergoing treatments for tuberculosis—the international crowd inhabiting Thomas Mann's *Der Zauberberg* (*The Magic Mountain*), which was inspired by the author's sanatorium experience in Davos, immediately comes to mind.[33] Throughout their time of activity—and even later, in their recollections— internationalists promoted images quite different from the ones immortalized in this landmark novel: they spoke of amicable international encounters amid alpine peaks and put forth "Our Peace, Up High" ("Notre Paix, là-haut," to cite one of the most poetic depictions published by an UIAA alpinist during the Second World War) as a formula to avoid future conflicts.[34]

[29] *Journal de Genève*, November 16, 1920, 2–3.

[30] On internationalism and nation-branding, see Ilaria Scaglia, "Branding Internationalism: Displaying Art and International Cooperation in the Interwar Period," in Carolin Viktorin, Jessica C. E. Gienow-Hecht, Annika Estner, and Marcel K. Will, eds., *Nation Branding in Modern History* (New York: Berghahn Books, 2018), 79–100. On nation-branding, see also Jessica C. E. Gienow-Hecht, "Nation Branding," in Costigliola and Hogan eds., *Explaining the History of American Foreign Relations*, 232–44.

[31] M. Gradel, "Les Colonies d'Echange Internationales," 7–8. League of Nations Archives, Box R 3094, folder 11C/9518/9518.

[32] *L'entente des peuples par la jeunesse: études sur les voyages et les échanges scolaires internationaux* (collection des dossiers de la coopération intellectuelle). Société des Nations, Institut International de Coopération Intellectuelle, 1933, 11–18.

[33] Thomas Mann, *Der Zauberberg* (Berlin: S. Fischer Verlag, 1924). After publication, the book soon appeared in English, French, and Italian. See *The Magic Mountain* (New York: Alfred A. Knopf, 1927); *La Montagne magique* (Paris: Fayard, 1931); *La montagna incantata* (Milan: Modernissima, 1932).

[34] *Bulletin du Club Alpin Suisse, Section Genevoise*, September 1940, 133. Detailed explanations of the differences between contemporary literary depictions of sanatoria and the ones put forth by internationalists in this period are included in Chapters 4 and 5. I thank Daniel Laqua and Jessica C. E. Gienow-Hecht for helping me to reason through this fascinating and complex novel.

At a time of emerging mass tourism and expanding social programs, people of all ages and classes participated in such groups or learned about their activities through a growing number of publications and cultural productions, deeply influencing one another in terms of what they thought, did, and felt in this period. In virtually every realm of life, mountains thus became a rich milieu for defining a set of shared feelings and associations that shaped internationalism for decades to follow.

This study postulates that emotions do not have either a positive or a negative value in and of themselves. This is because individual feelings—a term that I use interchangeably with emotions to avoid unnecessary complications—did not exist without their opposites (e.g., notions of "amity" were defined against the "enmity" they were supposed to counter). Especially after the First World War, "brotherhood" was underlined by "mourning" for the losses caused by the previous war, "fear" of the next, and overall "insecurity" about the present. Also, seemingly "positive" emotions often included a "darker" side: as previously mentioned, "friendship" at times concealed internal divisions, questionable partnerships, and ulterior motives. Therefore, the focus is not on the quality of feelings but on their effects on people's behavior.

From a theoretical standpoint, emotions in this study are not mere "imagined" cultural constructs but instead *make people do things* and are *continuously made* by them. Therefore, I conceptualize them as multifaceted entities that are both constructed through language and derived from individual and collective aesthetic and sensorial experiences.[35] I also see them as linked to "space," both inside the body and through its interaction with different kinds of environments.[36] I therefore subscribe to an "interactional" approach to emotions, which—without forgoing biological aspects—emphasizes the importance of social interactions

---

[35] On the limits of language and of individual terms as the basis for historical inquiry, see Ute Frevert et al., *Emotional Lexicons: Continuity and Change in the Vocabulary of Feeling 1700-2000* (Oxford: Oxford University Press, 2014). On how emotions changed through time, see also Ute Frevert, *Emotions in History: Lost and Found* (Budapest: Central European University Press, 2011). On the history of the term "emotion" as a category and a concept, and on the differences with "appetites," "passions," "affections," and "sentiments" see Thomas Dixon, "'Emotion': The History of a Keyword in Crisis," *Emotion Review* 4, no. 4 (October 2012), 338–44. See also Thomas Dixon, *From Passions to Emotions: The Creation of a Secular Psychological Category* (Cambridge: Cambridge University Press, 2003).

[36] For an overview, see discussions on the journal *Emotion, Space and Society* (2008–present). Particularly relevant are debates on "emotional geographies." See also Kay Anderson and Susan J. Smith, "Editorial: Emotional Geographies," *Transactions of the Institute of British Geographers* 26, no. 1 (March 2001), 7–10; Joyce Davidson, Liz Bondi, and Mick Smith, eds., *Emotional Geographies* (Burlington, VT: Ashgate, 2005). For an overview of "personal geographies" within and outside of the body, see Joyce Davidson and Christine Milligan, "Editorial: Embodying Emotion Sensing Space: Introducing Emotional Geographies," *Social & Cultural Geography* 5, no. 4 (December 2004), 523–32. On the various ways in which emotions affect interaction with different environments, see Mick Smith, Joyce Davidson, Laura Cameron, and Liz Bondi, eds., *Emotion, Place and Culture* (London: Routledge, 2009).

in defining what people feel.[37] I draw in particular from Erving Goffman's "dramaturgical" conception of emotions, which explains feeling as one's performance in front of others and as an exchange with the public;[38] and from Monique Scheer's concept of "emotional practices" such as mobilization (trying to elicit, or "chase" emotions in oneself or in others), naming (expressing and talking about feeling), communicating, and regulating emotions, which did not simply reflect, accompany, or follow other forms of doing but rather had a dynamic function in themselves.[39]

From a historical point of view, emotions effected change not only because people felt one thing or another and therefore acted in a certain way but also because many individuals and institutions used them strategically to attain particular goals and shaped their behavior accordingly. This is especially significant when taking into account that in the 1920s and 1930s emotions gained currency as a subject of scientific investigation and of artistic representation, and also as essential ingredients for political ideologies seeking to unite people by creating emotional bonds among them.

From the point of view of emotions, the period after the First World War represented a defining moment. To be sure, by evoking concepts such as "friendship," "fraternity," and "brotherhood" while pursuing political goals, internationalists built on rich traditions that had long intertwined feelings with political thought.[40]

[37] For an overview of "organicist" vs. "interactional" approaches, see Appendix A in Arlie Russell Hochschild, *The Managed Heart: Commercialization of the Human Feeling* (Berkeley: University of California Press, 1983), 201–22. On the notion that structures and agents continuously shape one another see Anthony Giddens, *The Constitution of Society: Outline of the Theory of Structuration* (Berkeley: University of California Press, 1984). On how people's circumstances and experiences affect the ways they function in different settings (in Pierre Bourdieu's terms, their "habitus," "dispositions," and interactions in and with various "fields"), see Pierre Bourdieu, *Distinction: A Social Critique of the Judgement of Taste*, translated by Richard Nice (Cambridge, MA: Harvard University Press, 1984), and *Outline of a Theory of Practice*, translated by Richard Nice (New York: Cambridge University Press, 1977). On emotions as "structures of feelings" made not only of "fixed," "past" aspects but also of "subjective," "present" elements that are constantly generated see Raymond Williams, *Marxism and Literature* (Oxford: Oxford University Press, 1977), 128–35.

[38] Erving Goffman, *The Presentation of Self in Everyday Life* (New York: Anchor Books, 1959), and *Interaction Ritual: Essays on Face-to-face Behavior* (New York: Anchor Books, 1967).

[39] Monique Scheer, "Are Emotions a Kind of Practice (and Is That What Makes Them Have a History)? A Bourdieuian Approach to Understanding Emotion," *History and Theory* 51, no. 2 (May 2012), 193–220. On emotions as "emotives" that at once describe and trigger feelings see William M. Reddy, *The Navigation of Feeling: A Framework for the History of Emotions* (New York: Cambridge University Press, 2001).

[40] See Gilles Bertrand, Catherine Brice, and Gilles Montègre, eds., *Fraternité: pour une histoire du concept* (Grenoble: Cahiers du CRHIPA, 2012); Antonio Maria Baggio, *Il principio dimenticato: la fraternità nella riflessione politologica contemporanea* (Rome: Città Nuova, 2007); Simon Koschut and Andrea Oelsner, eds., *Friendship and International Relations* (Basingstoke: Palgrave Macmillan, 2014); Maximillian Thompson, "Making Friends: Amity in American Foreign Policy," Ph.D. Dissertation, University of Oxford, 2015. On thinkers and groups who engaged in friendship across borders and political boundaries, see for instance Jon Nixon, *Hannah Arendt and the Politics of Friendship* (London: Bloomsbury Academic, 2015); Graham M. Smith, *Friendship and the Political: Kierkegaard, Nietzsche, Schmitt* (Charlottesville, VA: Imprint Academic, 2011); Elora Halim Chowdhury and Liz Philipose, eds., *Dissident Friendships: Feminism, Imperialism, and Transnational Solidarity* (Urbana: University of Illinois Press, 2016).

Since the eighteenth century, ideas of "empathy" across borders accompanied the emergence of "human rights";[41] and, as Jessica C. E. Gienow-Hecht has pointed out, well before 1919, "emotional elective affinity" in fields such as music had drawn peoples and nations closer in ways that transcended and at times even contradicted political interests and calculations.[42] However, the "Great War" caused unprecedented trauma, anxiety, and also hope, and increased the value that people placed on feeling. Between 1914 and 1918, not only did millions of people endure exceptional violence, but, in the words of Paul Fussell, an overall "ambience of mortal irony" made the gap between expectations and reality harder to bear.[43] Furthermore, nationalist propaganda dehumanized "the other" while sentimentalizing people's experience; and "honor" and "sacrifice" increasingly played a central role in defining ideas and behaviors.[44]

This emotional current became funneled directly into nationalist movements; meanwhile, the emotions of internationalism acquired a new urgency as many considered them to be the only way out of a war they experienced through—and often blamed on—mismanaged feelings.[45] Internationalists found inspiration in contemporary discussions about "solidarity" and "Christianity," and also set themselves against notions of comradeship based on the exclusion of others.[46] At a time when emotions were paramount, they based their decisions on what they believed their effect would be on people's feelings.

Like extreme nationalism, internationalism placed much emphasis on youth education, and great energy and planning were devoted to ensuring that all participants would feel camaraderie and become convinced of the viability of internationalism in the political realm. In this context, the importance of health cannot be overestimated: stemming from the centuries-old metaphor that connected the strength of the human body to that of the state/nation, mountains were now looked to for improving the physiology of the international system as

---

[41] Lynn Hunt, *Inventing Human Rights* (New York: W.W. Norton, 2007).

[42] Jessica C. E. Gienow-Hecht, *Sound Diplomacy: Music, Emotions, and Politics in Transatlantic Relations, 1850–1920* (Chicago: University of Chicago Press, 2009).

[43] Paul Fussell, *The Great War and Modern Memory*, 3rd edition (Oxford: Oxford University Press, 2013), 3.

[44] Ute Frevert, "Wartime Emotions: Honour, Shame, and the Ecstasy of Sacrifice," in Ute Daniel, Peter Gatrell, Oliver Janz, Heather Jones, Jennifer Keene, Alan Kramer, and Bill Nasson, eds., *1914–1918-online. International Encyclopedia of the First World War.* https://encyclopedia.1914-1918-online.net/article/wartime_emotions_honour_shame_and_the_ecstasy_of_sacrifice (accessed on August 1, 2018). A useful overview of the emotional aspects of the First World War can be found in Jane Redlin and Dagmar Neuland-Kitzerow, eds., *Der gefühlte Krieg/Feeling War: Emotionen im Ersten Weltkrieg* (Berlin: Verlag der Kunst, 2014).

[45] Most notably, these arguments appeared in Woodrow Wilson's speeches, which are analyzed in Chapter 2.

[46] See Hubert Herbreteau, *La fraternité: entre utopie et réalité* (Paris: Atelier, 2009); Thomas Kühne, *The Rise and Fall of Comradeship: Hitler's Soldiers, Male Bonding and Mass Violence in the Twentieth Century* (Cambridge: Cambridge University Press, 2017). See also Eliah Matthew Bures, "Fantasies of Friendship: Ernst Jünger and the German Right's Search for Community in Modernity," Ph.D. Dissertation, University of California, Berkeley, 2014.

well. The alpine landscape thus turned into a stage for public displays and consumption of internationalism, and emotions played a crucial role as a binding agent and a legitimizing circuit for a new "common sense" rooted in healthy bodies, healthy activities, and a healthful environment.[47]

In their attempt to use emotions in order to attain their goals, internationalists imagined feelings to be collective and shared. They also thought of them as manageable—possible to suppress or instill in other people through rhetoric, the creation of specific "atmospheres," or the staging of aesthetic and sensorial experiences.[48] They valued open displays of emotions (i.e., showing and sharing one's feelings) and considered them as reliable evidence of the success of the internationalist project. Moreover, they saw them as transferrable from the personal to the professional to the political realms, and they deemed them indispensable for internationalism to succeed.

In order to explain this dynamic, this book examines contemporary cultural products to shed light on which emotions became associated with the space under consideration (the Alps); speeches and propaganda to explain how the League of Nations sought to deploy feelings to legitimize itself and its own work; institutional minutes and correspondences to identify how internationalist groups active on the Alps used emotions to mitigate their own contradictions and to assert themselves as important political agents by staging occasions for international encounter; medical writings and photographs—specifically those related to the quintessential disease of this age, tuberculosis—to reveal how these put forth not only scientific but also political arguments; charters of international schools (i.e., the international University Sanatorium in Leysin), memoires by both patients and visitors, and unrealized plans for future international organizations to capture what people thought emotions could do, what and how they tried to make themselves and others feel, and, more generally, how their ideas influenced their actions.

---

[47] The literature on nations, bodies, and nature is extensive. An example of a book that links bodies with eugenics and national efficiency is Ina Zweiniger-Bargielowska, *Managing the Body: Beauty, Health, and Fitness in Britain 1880–1939* (New York: Oxford University Press, 2010). See also Chad Ross, *Naked Germany: Health, Race and the Nation* (New York: Berg, 2005). On how nature was appropriated by various sides of the political spectrum see John Alexander Williams, *Turning to Nature in Germany: Hiking, Nudism, and Conservation, 1900–1940* (Stanford: Stanford University Press, 2007); Laura Lee Downs, *Childhood in the Promised Land: Working-Class Movements and the Colonies de Vacances in France, 1880–1960* (Durham, NC: Duke University Press, 2002). On how therapeutic discourses were transferred to institutions, and on how these began to serve as an emotional sphere in this period, see Eva Illouz, *Saving the Modern Soul: Therapy, Emotions and the Culture of Self-Help* (Los Angeles: University of California Press, 2008).
[48] On "atmospheres" and their particular place between "affect" and "emotion" see Ben Anderson, "Affective Atmospheres," *Emotion, Space and Society* 2, no. 2 (December 2009), 77–81. See also Mikkel Bille, Peter Bjerregaard, and Tim Flohr Sørensen, "Staging Atmospheres: Materiality, Culture, and the Texture of the In-Between," *Emotion, Space and Society* 15 (May 2015), 31–8. In this case, also, internationalists built on contemporary attempts at managing emotions (e.g., in psychology and psychoanalysis), and on their applications in a broad variety of fields from advertisement to corporate culture. I review this literature in Chapters 4 and 5.

As with emotions, this book assumes internationalism to be neither benevolent nor malevolent by definition. This is not to shy away from providing historical assessment: borrowing Mark Mazower's words, international cooperation took place in "no enchanted palace";[49] and, as Glenda Sluga noted, it often espoused assumptions about racial difference and imperial superiority that make obsolete E. H. Carr's old—yet still influential—characterization of it as naively benign.[50] Yet, the focus of this study is on the internationalists' practices—regardless of their qualities—and how these influenced both contemporary and subsequent historical developments.

Much confusion derives from the differing uses of the term "internationalism." Some scholars of US history employ it as synonymous with "interventionism" or "imperialism."[51] Other historians associate it instead with the League of Nations, often emphasizing its realist concerns as well as its relationship with imperialism and nationalism.[52] Overlapping discussions on transnationalism at once enrich and complicate the picture.[53] Moreover, debates about various yet seemingly disconnected kinds of internationalism (e.g., black, communist, conservative, fascist, feminist, and humanitarian) suggest that these many formulations existed separately, or parallel to one another, rather than as different parts of a single integrated movement developing at the same time, in the same place, and often

[49] Mark Mazower, *No Enchanted Palace: The End of Empire and the Ideological Origins of the United Nations* (Princeton: Princeton University Press, 2009).

[50] Glenda Sluga, *Internationalism in the Age of Nationalism* (Philadelphia: University of Pennsylvania Press, 2013); E. H. Carr, *Twenty Years' Crisis, 1919–1939: An Introduction to the Study of International Relations* (London: Macmillan, 1939).

[51] See for instance Andrew Johnstone, *Against Immediate Evil: American Internationalists and the Four Freedoms on the Eve of World War II* (Ithaca, NY: Cornell University Press, 2014); David F. Schmitz, *The Triumph of Internationalism: Franklin D. Roosevelt and a World in Crisis, 1933–1941* (Washington, DC: Potomac Books Inc., 2007).

[52] See the aforementioned works by Patricia Clavin, Susan Pedersen, and Glenda Sluga. See also Daniel Gorman, *The Emergence of International Society in the 1920s* (New York: Cambridge University Press, 2012); David Long and Brian C. Schmidt, eds. *Imperialism and Internationalism in the Discipline of International Relations* (Albany, NY: State University of New York Press, 2005). Among US scholars, some connect the history of wilsonianism and the League of Nations with later forms of American interventionism. See for instance Lloyd E. Ambrosius, *Woodrow Wilson and American Internationalism* (New York: Cambridge University Press, 2017).

[53] On the intersection of internationalism and transnationalism, see Daniel Laqua, ed., *Internationalism Reconfigured*, and "Transnational Intellectual Cooperation, the League of Nations, and the Problem of Order," *Journal of Global History* 6, no. 2 (July 2011), 223–47. See also Patricia Clavin, "Europe and the League of Nations," in Robert Gerwarth, ed., *Twisted Paths: Europe, 1914–1945* (Oxford: Oxford University Press, 2007), 325–54; Akira Iriye, *Cultural Internationalism and World Order* (Baltimore, MD: Johns Hopkins University Press, 1997); Martin H. Geyer and Johannes Paulmann, eds., *The Mechanics of Internationalism: Culture, Society, and Politics from the 1840s to the First World War* (London: German Historical Institute, 2001); Emily S. Rosenberg, *Transnational Currents in a Shrinking World, 1870–1945* (Cambridge, MA: The Belknap Press of Harvard University Press, 2012); Andrew Preston and Douglas C. Rossinow, eds., *Outside In: The Transnational Circuitry of US History* (New York: Oxford University Press, 2017); Daniel Gorman, *International Cooperation in the Early Twentieth Century* (London: Bloomsbury Academic, 2017).

within the same peoples and institutions.[54] Meanwhile, E. H. Carr's interpretation of internationalism as characterized by benevolent but naive idealism—and the interwar period as an age of "crisis"—continues to make its way into discussions both within and outside of academia.[55] One reason is that internationalist rhetoric was imbued with emotional—and, on the surface, idealist and "weak"— images and language.

I put forth an alternative interpretation and redefine the term "internationalism" to refer to a broad set of ideas and practices based on the notion that the success of any given cause was contingent upon involving individuals, groups, and institutions from other nations. Internationalists often disagreed on many issues as their causes differed greatly and, at times, even contradicted one another. Yet, they all engaged in the same practices (e.g., organizing events and long-term stays in the Alps to create and reinforce emotional bonds among people) while trying to strike a balance between two extremes: universalism on the one hand and a vision where people would come together peacefully while remaining proud of their differences on the other.[56]

Internationalism was based on the acceptance of national differences and on the rejection of a form of "cosmopolitanism" perceived as void of identity.[57] In the mountains, too, internationalists took nationality quite seriously: they inevitably accompanied individuals' names with nation-states of provenance, even when people did not serve as official representatives. They also showcased rosters with participating nations, legitimizing them as the fundamental building blocks of the international community. At the same time, universalist discourses and rhetoric often entered their vocabulary, though these were tempered by their own skepticism and fear of being accused of "one-worldism." Feelings thus served as a useful tool to balance these extremes and contradictions.

Emotions also played a significant part in the relationship between internationalists and radical nationalists active in internationalist circles in this period. As this book demonstrates, fascist people and regimes remained involved with internationalist groups until the late 1930s. While pursuing some form of "fascist

---

[54] For an overview of these various formulations see Glenda Sluga and Patricia Clavin eds., *Internationalisms: A Twentieth-Century History* (New York: Cambridge University Press, 2016). See also Steven Parfitt, Lorenzo Costaguta, Matthew Kidd, and John Tiplady, eds., *Working-class Nationalism and Internationalism until 1945: Essays in Global Labour History* (Newcastle upon Tyne: Cambridge Scholars Publishing, 2018); Miguel Bandeira Jerónimo and José Pedro Monteiro, eds., *Internationalism, Imperialism and the Formation of the Contemporary World: The Pasts of the Present* (Cham: Palgrave Macmillan, 2018).
[55] See for instance Richard J. Overy, *The Inter-war Crisis*, 3rd edition (London: Routledge, 2017).
[56] On the coexistence of these elements, see Daniel Laqua, "Internationalisme ou affirmation de la nation? La coopération intellectuelle transnationale dans l'entre-deux-guerres," *Critique Internationale* 52, no. 3 (2011), 51–67. On the centrality of practice in internationalism, see Talbot C. Imlay, *The Practice of Socialist Internationalism: European Socialists and International Politics, 1914–1960* (Oxford: Oxford University Press, 2018).
[57] Sluga, *Internationalism in the Age of Nationalism*, 43–4.

global governance," they also enjoyed the pragmatic gains and the prestige that derived from keeping such connections.[58] In turn, internationalists employed emotions to justify continuously maintaining fascist associations until late 1939 and promptly resuming contacts with the same people after the Second World War—as illustrated for instance by the references to "alpinistic friendship" in the context of the UIAA.[59] In other cases—for example in the political discussions deliberately staged in international sanatoria—internationalists hailed the presence of fascist representatives as evidence of their own success at connecting with people who disagreed, thus protecting themselves from accusations of appeasement. The emotions of internationalism served them well in this endeavor.

Looking at transnational actors such as the ones analyzed in this book helps to illuminate the complex relationship between internationalist institutions and the various forms of nationalism with which they coexisted. These individuals and groups gravitated toward the League of Nations without serving in a formal position or being directly linked to it; in the words of Susan Pedersen, they formed a "League around the League" whose importance has thus far been overlooked.[60] Even if one were to apply the concept of a "global civic society" or of a "Third United Nations" *avant la lettre*, institutions such as these would be excluded on the ground that they did not "work closely" or explicitly enough with or for the League.[61] Yet they mirrored and often emulated the League's structure, vocabulary, and vision, and they pursued many of the League's objectives—particularly in the fields of health and international cooperation—by promoting international exchanges and standardization with the explicit goal of fostering peace.[62] As

---

[58] Madeleine Herren, "Fascist Internationalism," in Sluga and Clavin, eds., *Internationalisms*, 199–212. Fritz Georg von Graevenitz has noted a similar dynamic in the agrarian field, where both state and non-state actors pushed nationalist and protectionist measures while supporting international institutions. Fritz Georg von Graevenitz, *Argument Europa. Internationalismus in der globalen Agrarkrise der Zwischenkriegszeit (1927–1937)* (Frankfurt am Main: Campus Verlag, 2017).

[59] See for instance UIAA Archives, Club Alpino Italiano, AVST, FISI, letter dated September 1, [1945], from Eugenio Ferreri to Egmond d'Arcis, and letter dated November 14, 1945, from Egmond d'Arcis to Eugenio Ferreri. This correspondence is analyzed in detail in Chapter 3.

[60] Pedersen, *The Guardians*, 426. See also Thomas Davies, *NGOs: A New History of Transnational Civil Society* (New York: Oxford University Press, 2014).

[61] According to the most comprehensive research tool currently available, the League of Nations Search Engine (lonsea.de), many of the international organizations examined in this book were not affiliated with the League and none of their officers were connected to it. The International Union of Mountaineering Associations is listed together with the members of its Executive Committee. A search both by people and by organization, however, reveals no connections outside of the organization itself. "League of Nations Search Engine," www.Lonsea.de (accessed on July 26, 2016). On the importance of networks see Davide Rodogno, Bernhard Struck, and Jakob Vogel, eds., *Shaping the Transnational Sphere: Experts, Networks, and Issues from the 1840s to the 1930s* (New York: Berghahn Books, 2014); Madeleine Herren, ed., *Networking the International System: Global Histories of International Organizations* (Heidelberg: Springer, 2014).

[62] This is not to downplay the importance of contemporary forces (e.g., businesses) that pushed in the same direction. I thank Daniel Immerwahr for raising this point and for discussing it with me. Andrew Arsan, Su Lin Lewis, and Anne-Isabelle Richard, "Editorial: The Roots of Global Civil Society and the Interwar Moment," *Journal of Global History*, 7, no. 2 (July 2012), 157–65; Thomas G. Weiss, Tatiana Carayannis, and Richard Jolly, "The 'Third' United Nations," *Global Governance* 15, no. 1

evidenced in this study, they shared the same space (mountains) with nationalists; they competed for the same constituencies (especially the working class and the youth); they endeavored in similar practices (e.g., organizing summer camps); and they emphasized health as a key ingredient for success.

Internationalists active in and around the League built an "emotional community" that shared a different "emotional style" than the one adopted by extreme nationalists. They valued a separate set of feelings, arousing "internationalist friendship" rather than a bond limited to one's own group. They evoked the "nobility" of their cause—in contrast to national "pride." They also shied away from bold symbols such as flags, insisting that if they adopted them, "it would be said 'here is the Super State'." Therefore, they allowed their fear of what people would feel to dictate their decisions on such issues.[63] This emotional management—or mismanagement—proved most influential: because of their reluctance to embrace "strong" symbols and emotions interwar internationalists failed to elicit "trust" in their constituents; at the same time, their emotional style became a synonym of internationalist benevolence, cooperation, and compromise, leaving internationalism and emotions inextricably intertwined.

In terms of trajectory, this book moves outward from the League of Nations to the numerous public and private international institutions and networks that surrounded it. It thus analyzes the largest international organizations dealing with the issues that the functional sections of the League of Nations in the fields of intellectual cooperation and health addressed most aggressively (standardization, youth, and tuberculosis), giving priority to internationalist groups who did not simply happen to be in the mountains but also attached a higher meaning to being there.[64] It gives precedence to institutions that could have been built elsewhere and were not only international in scope but also presented themselves as such, and to the performative practices of people and groups that went through great lengths trying to look "international."

As for mountains, their role increases as the story unfolds. At the outset, they serve as a terrain for international encounters and as a landscape rife with associations used for political purposes. For this reason, the journey begins with an overview of the many people and groups who chose the Alps as their preferred space to instill emotions; a reflection on the big questions of the day—the tensions between modernity and anti-modernity, as well as between nationalism and

---

(January–March 2009), 123. I owe much to their arguments, and I contend that the League influenced the "experience" of transnational associational life also in organizations not primarily or explicitly connected to its own projects, which are usually left out.

[63] League of Nations Archives, R 1549, 39/42978/383, extract from minutes of Directors Meeting, August 26, 1925.

[64] "Functionalism" as an approach emphasized practical cooperation in a variety of fields from health, to finance, to education. A longer explanation of functionalism in the context of the League of Nations is included in Chapter 2.

internationalism—and how these affected large infrastructure works like the one celebrated in *Excelsior*'s famous scene; and the analysis of various cultural productions (e.g., films of diverse genres ranging from *The White Hell of Pitz Palu* to *Heidi*) and products (e.g., cheese fondue), and how these influenced the ways in which contemporaries idealized mountains and the people who inhabited them.

Mountains then become central elements for matters related to visibility, branding, and reputation. As a metaphorical stop in Geneva reveals, the League of Nations and some of its attached bodies constructed its main institutions and sites (most notably, the Palais des Nations) as especially conducive to peace by emphasizing their alpine surroundings and by associating particular emotions with them. They also staged international encounters in the Alps by taking into account every detail to ensure that all participants would feel emotions leading to peace among nations. Associations such as the UIAA followed their model and employed feelings to present their work as effective at improving not only mountaineering but also international relations.

In the following exploration, which takes readers up to an elevation of 1265 meters in the Swiss village of Leysin, mountains fully stimulate the senses and become entrusted to heal at once the human body, the mind, and the international system as a whole. In international sanatoria whose work was connected not only to health and education but also to broader cultural, political, and labor issues, a number of doctors, patients, and visitors engaged in overt emotional expressions; and internationalists used images and words they produced as evidence of success for the internationalist enterprise. Indeed, emotional practices, experiences, and atmospheres in the Alps made individuals *feel* international cooperation; or so many people said, expressed, and later remembered, carrying on the notion that specific settings and encounters foster particular feelings.

By the end, from the vantage point of high mountain peaks, the fundamental role of emotions in shaping political ideas and practices from all sides of the political spectrum appears at its clearest, as do the long-lasting consequences of the interwar story told in this book. A wide-range of present-day questions and phenomena, from globalization to localism, from nostalgia for an imagined more "authentic" past to conflicting visions for the future take on a new light. Also, the fact that the Alps—the view of their landscape from afar or the excavation of tunnels underneath them—are still used to make people feel emotions to promote political agendas become meaningful. But right now all we can hear is a faint sound of pickaxes. More digging is needed. Or, to adopt one more alpine metaphor, what I hope will be a pleasant hike through the following chapters is required to make sense of it all. Time to put our boots on, and go.

1

Associating Emotions and Internationalism with the Alps

Together with deserts, heavens, and seas, mountains have long elicited feelings such as "awe, astonishment, fear, and wonder"; and compared with other "great" sites, "they inspired the most voluminous library" in disparate fields.[1] Scientists such as Horace-Bénédict de Saussure (1740–99) and Alexander von Humboldt (1769–1859) investigated them as a key for understanding the workings and evolution of nature over centuries and millennia. Philosophers such as Jean-Jacques Rousseau (1712–78) and Edmund Burke (1729–97) idealized them as places for experiencing tranquility and beauty, or as ultimate spots for living the strong "pleasures" and "pains" of the "sublime." Poets like William Wordsworth (1770–1850) made them the setting for internal struggles and journeys, or for abandoning worldly concerns. Countless people found refuge on their heights since, in the words of Johann Wolfgang von Goethe (1749–1832), they felt that "Over every mountain-top / Lies peace."[2] As immortalized most vividly by painters such as Caspar David Friedrich (1774–1840), Edwin Church (1826–1900), and J. M. W. Turner (1755–1851), mountains came to embody both the marvel and the horror felt by those who experienced life to the fullest.[3]

As this chapter shows, in the interwar period internationalists gave mountains a different aesthetic from the one that had accompanied them up to that point. Rather than picturing Caspar David Friedrich's "Wanderer above the Sea of Fog" standing still in solitude or silence, they envisioned many people interacting with one another peacefully while surrounded by a serene landscape. As far as time is concerned, they did not think in terms of geological ages nor did they linger on the unpredictability of alpine weather. Instead, they transposed previous notions

---

[1] Richard Bevis, *The Road to Egdon Heath: The Aesthetics of the Great in Nature* (Montreal: McGill-Queen's University Press, 1999), 5; 12; 18–23.

[2] "*Über allen Gipfeln / Ist Ruh*" (Over every mountain top / Lies peace) are the opening lines of Goethe's *Wanderer's Nightsong II* (*Wandrers Nachtlied*), also known as *Ein Gleiches* (Another One), a poem that he famously etched onto the wall of a lodge on top of the Kickelhahn mountain, in the Thuringian Forest, on the evening of September 6, 1780.

[3] Peter Mark, Peter Helman, and Penny Snyder, eds., *The Mountains in Art History* (Middletown, CT: Wesleyan University Press, 2017; Paola Giacomoni, *Il laboratorio della natura. Paesaggio montano e sublime naturale in età moderna* (Milan: FrancoAngeli, 2001). See also Peter H. Hansen, *The Summits of Modern Man: Mountaineering after the Enlightenment* (Cambridge, MA: Harvard University Press, 2013); Sean Moore Ireton and Caroline Schaumann, eds., *Heights of Reflection: Mountains in the German Imagination from the Middle Ages to the Twenty-first Century* (Rochester, NY: Camden House, 2012).

The Emotions of Internationalism: Feeling International Cooperation in the Alps in the Interwar Period. Ilaria Scaglia, Oxford University Press (2020). © Ilaria Scaglia.
DOI: 10.1093/oso/9780198848325.001.0001

of the "sublime" onto the current political situation, using them to express both their abhorrence of war and their longings for peace. They replaced the feelings that had dominated the words and images created by great literary figures from previous centuries with unforgettable encounters, unshakable friendships, and memorable moments of camaraderie among people from all walks of life, thus constructing the Alps as an ideal site for peaceful international cooperation.

This shift derived from fundamental changes taking place in the mountains themselves. After the First World War, the Alps had become indelibly associated with the warfare that had taken place on their terrain, with its memorialization, and with the project of avoiding another conflict. Also, the population that inhabited and visited the Alps was becoming much more diverse. As travel became quicker and more affordable for many, international tourism increased. Socialist, fascist, and especially Catholic groups increased their presence in the mountains, making them a heterogeneous environment in terms of class, ideology, and nationality, and strengthening the notion that they could be employed to create affective bonds among peoples from various countries.

Mountains also served as highly symbolic grounds for both the coexistence and the friction between modernism and anti-modernism, extreme nationalism and internationalism. The construction of infrastructure such as tunnels required a high degree of cooperation, and internationalists connected it with long-term—and emotionally charged—peace-building projects. They presented power lines and railways stretching across borders as a means to unify people and arouse "friendship" among them. Those who opposed this trend also drew upon feelings such as "love" for nature, "fear" of environmental destruction, and "trust" that this could be stopped through international cooperation. In this context, literary and filmic representations of interactions taking place in the mountains, together with the news coverage of major international events hosted there (e.g., from 1924 on, the Winter Olympics) did much to foster the view that the Alps provided the perfect setting for peaceful cooperation.

The construction of "mountain people" (both the *alpinistes* who climbed them and the *montagnards* who inhabited them) as national and a-national, sick and healthy, primitive and modern, most clearly reflects how the negotiation of these extremes played out in both the concrete and the metaphorical settings of the Alps. It also shows the growing influence of various forms of cultural production (ranging from art, to material objects such as "the cup of friendship," to commercial products like cheese fondue) on how people felt about—and on—the mountains, and the importance of health—both physical and metaphorical—for national and international communities.

Novels and films especially (e.g., *Heidi*) affected how contemporaries saw the Alps and their people, and also how they viewed and molded mountains as sites for international cooperation to turn their visions into a reality. This phenomenon was not new. In the words of cultural geographer Ben M. Anderson, in the period between 1885 and 1914 the construction of the alpine landscape had already been driven by the desire to "inculcate a particular affective response" in the growing crowds that consumed them. The paths and the huts built for visitors eager to enjoy mountain sceneries were designed to provide them with a "safe," "comfortable," and "benign" visual experience, one that was concurrently presented and defined by "representations" such as panoramas, exhibitions, and landscape reliefs eliciting and promoting specific ways of enjoying the mountains.[4] In the 1920s and 1930s, this process accelerated and acquired a new internationalist dimension. The Alps became linked with the emotions of internationalism. Their "benign" character became associated with diverse communities, with feeling and expressing "amicability" toward people from other nations, and with the ultimate goal of making and maintaining "peace." The Alps therefore turned into quintessential sites for amicable exchanges, and the adjective "alpine" came to accompany a broad range of emotions deemed indispensable for their success.

1.1 A Diverse Space for "Amicable" Interaction

For the purpose of this study, the history of the Alps began in the nineteenth century, a time when a growing number of people from various nations started to hike them and climb them, and also used them as a site for engendering particular emotions. Alpine towns quickly grew to become "cosmopolitan" resort areas; alpine guides, hotels, and other sport and touristic venues multiplied to meet the demands of international markets, and people of all classes and political orientations chose mountains as their preferred space for vacation and entertainment.[5] This heterogeneity in terms of class and ideology deserves emphasis. To be sure, in the eighteenth and nineteenth centuries many people who practiced alpinism belonged to the cultivated *bourgeoisie*.[6] Other groups too, however, had always been represented, and their presence progressively grew. As Andrea Zannini pointed out, the conventional narrative that portrays local populations as afraid

---

[4] Ben M. Anderson, "The Construction of an Alpine Landscape: Building, Representing and Affecting the Eastern Alps, c. 1885–1914," *Journal of Cultural Geography* 29, no. 2 (June 2012), 155–83.

[5] For an overview of the history of the Alps, see Andrew Beattie, *The Alps: A Cultural History* (New York: Oxford University Press, 2006), 21–102; Jon Mathieu, *The Alps: An Environmental History* (Oxford: Polity Press, 2019), and *History of the Alps, 1500–1900: Environment, Development, and Society* (Morgantown: West Virginia University Press, 2009). On mountain tourism, see Paul P. Bernard, *Rush to the Alps: The Evolution of Vacationing in Switzerland* (Boulder, CO: East European Quarterly, 1978). On the early history of alpine climbing see also Hansen, *The Summits of Modern Man*; Olivier Hoibian, and Jacques Defrance, eds. *Deux siècles d'alpinismes européens. Origines et mutations des activités de grimpe* (Paris: L'Harmattan, 2002).

[6] Olivier Hoibian, ed., *L'invention de l'alpinisme: la montagne et l'affirmation de la bourgeoisie cultivée (1786–1914)* (Paris: Belin, 2008). See also Dagmar Günther, *Alpine Quergänge: Kulturgeschichte des bürgerlichen Alpinismus (1870–1930)* (Frankfurt am Main: Campus Verlag, 1998).

of the mountains and attributes the first set of climbs to outside visitors (most notably from England) was the product of external views and projections rather than a reflection of the actual reality. Local notables—especially doctors and priests, who had a high degree of education and thus occupied prominent positions at the local level—pursued various forms of alpinism well before the first Austrian and British climbers arrived.[7]

Starting from the late nineteenth century, a large number of proletarian associations began going to the Alps, often with the goal of eliciting specific feelings. While some socialists opposed sport altogether because of its competitive nature (which they saw as incompatible with "solidarity"), others considered it a "place for democratic education and political propaganda."[8] In Italy, for instance, the Club Alpino Operaio (CAO) was founded in 1885; and, in 1911, a Unione Operaia Escursionisti Italiani (UOEI) followed. Moved by the desire to curtail "vices" such as drinking and gambling, these groups organized alpine trips to provide workers with a healthier form of leisure. Most notably, they maintained that "in the mountains friendship is consolidated," insisting that the alpine environment could affect people's feelings toward one another.[9] If, after 1919, patriotism and irredentism permeated alpine clubs, socialists nonetheless continued their activities and provided a counterpoint for nationalist rhetoric. With the rise of fascism, these associations were taken over by state bodies such as the *Dopolavoro fascista* (literally, the "fascist after-work," or recreational club), which also organized mountain stays for workers and used mountains to strengthen affective bonds among them. Meanwhile, many alpinists re-cast their endeavors as antifascist and some became anarchists, seeing mountains as the ultimate terrain for sentimentalized forms of freedom.[10] From a political standpoint, by the 1930s the Alps had become a diverse, emotionalized international ground characterized by the coexistence and the exchange of a wide range of people and ideas.

Quite important was the Christian presence in the Alps. Mountains had long been dotted by churches and sanctuaries, and with the rise of alpinism in the nineteenth century numerous members of the clergy climbed and/or wrote guidebooks in which they described the emotions they felt while above the

---

[7] Andrea Zannini, *Tonache e piccozze: il clero e la nascita dell'alpinismo* (Torino: CDA & Vivalda Editori, 2004), 25–6; 47.

[8] Luciano Senatori, *Compagni di cordata: associazionismo proletario, alpini sovversivi, sport popolare in Italia* (Rome: Ediesse, 2010), 53–4.

[9] Senatori, *Compagni di cordata*, 56–63.

[10] For biographies and specific examples of subversive alpinism, see Senatori, *Compagni di cordata*, 69–130. On subversive alpinism, see also Alessandro Pastore, *Alpinismo e storia d'Italia. Dall'Unità alla Resistenza* (Bologna: Il Mulino, 2003), 183–96; Enrico Camanni, *Alpi ribelli. Storie di montagna, resistenza e utopia* (Bari: Laterza, 2016). On similar associations on mountains other than the Alps, see James C. Scott, *The Art of Not Being Governed: An Anarchist History of Upland Southeast Asia* (New Haven: Yale University Press, 2009).

plains.[11] Many of them sought intellectual enrichment as well as leisure while nurturing their interests in nature and while engaging in practices such as collecting minerals.[12] One of the most famous examples from this "enlightened" group is Giovanni Gnifetti (1801–67)—the priest of the small northern Italian town of Alagna to whom the Punta Gnifetti (also known as *Signalkuppe*, at 4563 meters) and the Rifugio Capanna Gnifetti (3647 meters) are dedicated—who strengthened existing associations between mountains, Christianity, and feelings of spiritual elevation.[13]

In the interwar period, the connection between Alps and Christianity—Catholicism in particular—assumed a new internationalist tone with the election of "the Alpinist Pope" Achille Ratti (1857–1939), who reigned as Pius XI from 1922 to 1939. An avid climber in his youth, a year after his election he proclaimed Bernard of Menthon (923–1008) the patron saint of those who inhabited the mountains and of all those who visited and climbed them.[14] As a result, the notion that mountain people constituted a distinct community grew in strength, as did the idea that there was something innocent, sincere, and internationalist about them.[15] Pius XI frequently mentioned mountains in his speeches—most notably in 1929 after signing the Lateran Pacts that normalized relations with the Italian state, which was ruled by Benito Mussolini and the Fascist Party. He often highlighted biblical references to mountains, emphasizing how that these could facilitate peace-making endeavors. In 1934, he welcomed 30,000 Alpini[16] and 200 alpine guides to St. Peter's, and in 1936 he spoke to the lay association Azione Cattolica ("Catholic Action") praising the relationship between people and nature, and mountains in particular.[17]

Achille Ratti's use of the Alps fit into the broader context of "Catholic alpinism," which stressed the mountains' educational value.[18] Figures such as Giovanni Bosco (1815–88), whom Achille Ratti beatified in 1929 and canonized in 1934, saw mountains as a most conducive site for providing disadvantaged youth with a healthy form of leisure, and their work led to people from lower classes visiting the Alps for the first time in excursions and camping trips.[19] Between the 1890s

---

[11] Domenico Flavio Ronzoni, *Achille Ratti. Il prete alpinista che diventò Papa* (Missaglia: Bellavite, 2009), 25–38.

[12] Zannini, *Tonache e piccozze*, 25–6; 53.

[13] Ronzoni, *Achillle Ratti*, 29–30. See also Zannini, *Tonache e piccozze*, 62–71.

[14] Ronzoni, *Achillle Ratti*, 125.

[15] The origins and the complexities of this notion are explained in detail later in this chapter.

[16] The Alpini (literally, the "Alpines") are a specialized mountain warfare infantry corps of the Italian Army, which was established in 1872 to defend the northern border of the newly established Kingdom of Italy.

[17] Ronzoni, *Achillle Ratti*, 126–8.

[18] For an overview of the longer history of "Catholic Alpinism" see Marco Cuaz, "Catholic Alpinism and Social Discipline in 19th and 20th-century Italy," *Mountain Research and Development* 26, no. 4 (November 2006), 358–63.

[19] Ronzoni, *Achillle Ratti*, 135–6. A deeper discussion on mountains and education in this period is entertained in Chapter 2.

and the 1930s, crosses and religious monuments appeared on many peaks. In the words of historian Domenico Flavio Ronzoni, this was a time when "the Italian Catholics are visibly engaged in marking mountains with their own symbols, in celebrating Masses on mountain peaks," and in "making mountains a field to which to transfer the ongoing contrast between State and Church."[20] By "inventing the holiday home and the summer camp," they created venues to pursue their goal of "controlling the youngsters' spare time," as Marco Cuaz put it.[21] And even with the rise of fascist regimes, which placed much importance on regulating people's free time, Catholic alpinism continued to offer an alternative to their lay counterparts, downplaying records and competition and highlighting the educational, moral, spiritual, and emotional aspects that could help connect people across all kinds of borders.[22]

Stories about Ratti's selfless acts while climbing reinforced the belief that mountains represented a preferred site for transcending all sorts of boundaries. Contemporary accounts maintained that he had once bravely rescued a *montanaro* (literally, a "mountain dweller") who had fallen; on another occasion, he had carried for a long distance a boy who had been victim of exhaustion. In the context of the Italian Alpine Club (CAI), of which he was an active member for many years, he also collaborated with overtly non-religious figures such as the atheist philosopher Gaetano Negri.[23]

Emotions played a big part in the pope's alpine experience. Fellow alpinists Giovanni Bobba and Francesco Mauro, who in 1923 curated an edition of Ratti's writings, maintained that the mountain "reawakens and exalts special sentiments in us," at once increasing one's strength while also "changing selfishness of the individual into the holy solidarity that ties bodies in the same roped party (*unica cordata*), in a bundle (*fascio*) for life and death the souls of those who are bound (*avvinti*)."[24] In the aftermath of the "Great War" and a year after the March on Rome, the term *fascio* had a patriotic tinge: a few lines later, he referred to the "Italic square of Alpine feathers" (*quadrato italico of penne montanare*) in an imaginary moment in which they were blessed by the pope. At the same time, he ended his piece with the wish that "all men could be brothers in peace."[25]

---

[20] Ronzoni, *Achillle Ratti*, 139. On placing crosses as a symbolic act to reaffirm the role of the Church and of the clergy see also Zannini, *Tonache e piccozze*, 177–8.

[21] Cuaz, "Catholic Alpinism and Social Discipline in 19th and 20th-century Italy," 361–2.

[22] Victoria De Grazia, *The Culture of Consent: Mass Organization of Leisure in Fascist Italy* (Cambridge: Cambridge University Press, 1981); Julia Timpe, *Nazi-Organized Recreation and Entertainment in the Third Reich* (London: Palgrave Macmillan, 2017).

[23] Ronzoni, *Achillle Ratti*, 62–7.

[24] Giovanni Bobba and Francesco Mauro, eds., *Scritti alpinistici del Sacerdote Dottor Achille Ratti (ora S.S. Pio Papa XI). Raccolti e pubblicati in occasione del cinquantenario della Sezione di Milano del Club Alpino Italiano* (Milan: Bertieri & Vanzetti, 1923).

[25] The text edited by Bobba and Mauro was reprinted in its entirely in Ronzoni, *Achillle Ratti*, 167–263. The page numbers in this section refer to the reprinted version.

The overall message of the 1923 volume was nevertheless more in line with internationalist discourses and emotions than with the fascist rhetoric of the time.[26]

In 1923, Ratti's texts also stood in contrast to contemporary fascist formulations. In recounting his ascensions, he cited a variety of alpine journals from other European countries (including England and Germany), leaving their titles in their original languages. He also acknowledged foreign expeditions and quoted texts written by those who accomplished them in the same fashion in which he—as a scholar and as a librarian—would have read and cited foreign sources. Moreover, in describing Giuseppe Gadin—his friend, guide, and companion during an expedition—he praised his proficiency in both Italian and English while also remarking on how "in serious moments he seems to prefer his own certain French like many in Valle d'Aosta and even more in Courmayeur," his native town. Ratti quoted Gadin in his original French, fully conveying the international character and the linguistic variety of the Alps which, by the time his writings were published in 1923, the Fascist regime condemned and was eager to italianize.

Ratti's account contained details that would have disturbed fascist tastes. For example, he specified that during his mission he ate—and tremendously enjoyed—Swiss and German products such as Liebig broth, Suchard chocolate, and Kirsch. Though he made it a point to note how "Asti Spumante, up there truly priceless, excellently substituted champagne," he nonetheless implied that the latter would have represented the optimal choice.[27] In his account, the Alps were above all a space for travel and exchange, where languages and products circulated freely and people interacted amicably.

In the aforementioned 1923 proclamation that made Bernard of Menthon patron saint of all *montagnards* and *alpinistes*, Ratti also helped to de-nationalize the Alps by including in the same category all mountains and the people who populated them regardless of their geographical location and provenance. The pope was certainly familiar with the implications of adjectives transferred from one mountain range to another in order to highlight particular qualities: his most famous ascent had been on the "Himalayan side" of the Mont Blanc.[28] His references to all mountains as one, and his visions of mountain people as one community— one that spanned across borders—fortified contemporary internationalist rhetoric, and presented emotions as the key for navigating a world that was changing at a rapid pace.

---

[26] Achille Ratti, "Ascensione al Monte Rosa (Punta Dufour)," reprinted in Ronzoni, *Achillle Ratti*, 187–91; 197.

[27] Ronzoni, *Achillle Ratti*, 187–91; 197.

[28] Ronzoni, *Achillle Ratti*, 69; 73. To this day a rifugio and the route he followed on the Mont Blanc during a 1890 ascent he completed with fellow priest Luigi Grasselli are known as via Ratti–Grasselli (or "via del Papa"). A list of his ascensions can be found in Ronzoni, *Achillle Ratti*, 62–94; 130–1. See also 253–5.

1.2 "Modernity" and Anti-modernity

In the words of film historian Christopher Morris, the "experience of the high mountains takes on all of the doubleness of the modern condition." As vividly demonstrated by the music that permeated concert halls, operas, and films in the 1920s and 1930s, the "cult of mountains" expressed both the appealing and the frightening sides of modernity. In Germany, mountains served as *Heimat* (a home for which to long) and also represented a place and a time toward which to feel powerful forms of *Heimweh* (homesickness, or nostalgia for a previous time). At the same time, borrowing Morris' words, they were "haunted by these tensions between traditions and progress."[29]

This emotional tension was exacerbated by the fact that in the mountains change seemed to happen quicker than elsewhere. In the twentieth century, the Alps became important spaces for political, social, and economic development, which, as this section explains, internationalists with different—and at times contradictory—agendas associated with particular emotions.[30] To be sure, this transformation was neither homogeneous nor linear. As a landmark 1989 study by Pier Paolo Viazzo has shown, complex emigration and immigration patterns, the gap between high areas and lowlands, and the great diversity of the populations that inhabited and/or visited the Alpine range make generalizations difficult.[31] Also, the history of the Alps is hard to see in a unified fashion, as it was only with the Alpine Convention of 1991 that for the first time the Alpine region was united under a common political and administrative structure.[32] Despite this fragmentation and the uneven patterns and differentiation that characterized this trend, there is no doubt that in the period from 1500 to 1900, the Alps became progressively more distinct from their surroundings and their economic value grew.[33]

Most notably, starting from the second half of the nineteenth century, the Alps stood at the center of the process of electrification of the European continent, one

[29] Christopher Morris, *Modernism and the Cult of Mountains: Music, Opera, Cinema* (Surrey: Ashgate, 2012), 1; 20–1; 73–7; 95.

[30] A good comparative study on these dynamics is Dylan Jim Esson, "Selling the Alpine Frontier: The Development of Winter Resorts, Sports, and Tourism in Europe and America, 1865–1941," Ph.D. Dissertation, University of California, Berkeley, 2011. On the geo-political and imperialist aspects, see Reuben Ellis, *Vertical Margins: Mountaineering and the Landscapes of Neoimperialism* (Madison: University of Wisconsin Press, 2001). An excellent narrative on global developments in this context can be found in   Maurice Isserman and Stewart Weaver, *Fallen Giants: A History of Himalayan Mountaineering from the Age of Empire to the Age of Extremes* (New Haven: Yale University Press, 2008).

[31] Pier Paolo Viazzo, *Upland Communities: Environment, Population and Social Structure in the Alps since the Sixteenth Century* (Cambridge: Cambridge University Press, 1989).

[32] Mathieu, *History of the Alps*, 5.

[33] On most recent attempts to use mountains as terrains to unite people (from CIPRA to Alpine Convention), see Bernard Debarbieux and Gilles Rudaz, *Les faiseurs de montagne: imaginaires politiques et territorialités: XVIIIe–XXIe siècle* (Paris: CNRS, 2010), chapter 11.

that governments and private actors described and justified in emotional terms. In the words of historian Marc D. Landry II, the Alps in this period turned into "Europe's Battery," "the largest system for storing and exploiting hydraulic power on the planet" with the goal of supporting the continent's military and industrial enterprises. This development profoundly transformed the alpine landscape through the construction of a massive infrastructure made of artificial basins, dams, and a system of diversions to manage growing quantities of water, as well as long-distance wires for transporting electricity. Water—a precious "white coal" now linked to the amount of energy it could produce—rose in value from both an economic and a political standpoint.[34]

The First World War accelerated this process as the demand for power to serve military efforts rose and traditional coal supplies were disrupted. As a consequence, people from all nationalities began to work in this growing sector of the economy. At major internationalist venues—such as the 1924 World Power Conference in London—many experts in the field of electrification emphasized these aspects by arguing that exchanging and interconnecting electrical utilities would lead to deeper emotional links among countries. Most notably, among them were executives of electric companies who put forth plans for unified grids by contending that these could lead to peaceful interactions among nations.[35]

The simultaneous process of internationalizing the railway network furthered this trend and strengthened the opinion that improved transportation could engender "friendship." As Irene Anastasiadou explained, after the First World War a new railway regime was established in Europe. By understanding internationalism as functionalism, or "interoperability across borders," various international organizations (most notably the section on Communication and Transit of the League of Nations, which held its first conference in 1921, and the International Union of Railways, which was founded in 1922) aimed to streamline and standardize international travel—especially across the Alps, since these marked national borders. If national and regional interests led to alternative agreements and the ultimate fragmentation of the European railway system, "a considerable degree of integration had been achieved in the railways of Europe in the interwar years" nonetheless.[36] On the railroad tracks crisscrossing the Alps, peaceful and friendly exchange among nations had become a reality.

---

[34] Marc D. Landry II, "Europe's Battery: The Making of the Alpine Energy Landscape, 1870–1955," Ph.D. Dissertation, Georgetown University, 2013, 6; 25.

[35] Landry, "Europe's Battery," 142–3; 158; 166–7; 176–8. At the same time, nationalist visions emerged—particularly in highly contested places like the South Tyrol—and producing electricity became central to the project of national strengthening and development. Landry, "Europe's Battery," 192–3.

[36] Irene Anastasiadou, *Constructing Iron Europe: Transnationalism and Railways in the Interbellum* (Amsterdam: Amsterdam University Press, 2011), 251. A longer explanation of functionalism as a set of ideas and practices in this period is included in Chapter 2.

The interwar period saw the intensifying of a process that led to mountains resembling more and more the places they were supposed to provide an escape from, especially from an emotional standpoint.[37] The invention of mountain leisure activities, most notably skiing, "refashioned nature in physical and discursive terms." As snow turned into a "white gold" to be managed for economic purposes, invasive infrastructure was built, including artificial slopes and ski lifts, as well as imposing barriers for the protection against avalanches, which "would not be out of place on the beaches of Normandy."[38] As special "mechanics" were devised to facilitate the transportation of people and objects on steep inclines, "the mountain vacation, whose inner dynamic had been transformed into a copy and evocation of urban life even before the First World War, after the Second was taking place in a setting that had come to have an uncanny resemblance to the city."[39] Particularly in the German and Austrian contexts, railroads, cogwheel trains, cable cars, gondolas, and roads dramatically changed the landscape.

At the same time, great energies were devoted to constructing an "alpine atmosphere" to entertain the ever-growing number of visitors.[40] Everywhere on the Alpine range, "typical" products such as "local" mountain cheeses "invented" for economic and political reasons played a big part in creating and transmitting an alpine "feel."[41] Recipes for typical alpine dishes, which with local variations had been documented already in previous centuries, became nationalized in this period. Fondue, for example, was presented as part of the "Swiss Village" at the National Exposition of Geneva in 1896; thereafter, its recipe was "systematically included in home economics manuals"; as a product, it was aggressively promoted by the Swiss Union of Milk Producers; and, in the 1950s, it was finally included in the recipes of military cuisine.[42] Similarly, the quintessential Valle d'Aosta cheese, Fontina, was not defined as such until 1888; previously considered a kind of

---

[37] On the construction of the alpine landscape in this period, see Antonio De Rossi, *La costruzione delle Alpi: il Novecento e il modernismo alpino (1917–2017)* (Rome: Donzelli, 2016); Mauro Varotto, *Montagne del Novecento: il volto della modernità nelle Alpi e Prealpi venete* (Verona: Cierre edizioni, 2017); Giacomo Menini, *Costruire in cielo: l'architettura moderna nelle Alpi italiane* (Milan: Mimesis, 2017). On similar transformations in the mountains in general, see Manfred Perlik, *The Spatial and Economic Transformation of Mountain Regions* (New York: Routledge, 2019).

[38] Andrew Denning, "From Sublime Landscapes to 'White Gold': How Skiing Transformed the Alps after 1930," *Environmental History* 19, no. 1 (January 2014), 97, and *Skiing into Modernity: A Cultural and Environmental History* (Berkeley: University of California Press, 2015). Denning also noted that it was in fact the internationalization of the mountain space that led to its standardization.

[39] Bernard, *Rush to the Alps*, 178. See also Ghazali Musa, James Higham, and Anna Thompson-Carr, eds., *Mountaineering Tourism* (New York: Routledge, 2015).

[40] Tait Keller, *Apostles of the Alps: Mountaineering and Nation Building in Germany and Austria, 1860–1939* (Chapel Hill: University of North Carolina Press, 2016), 32; 160–1.

[41] For instance, on the case of Fontina cheese, see Stefano Allovio, "Strategie e processi di costruzione di un prodotto tipico: il caso della Fontina della Valle d'Aosta," *Annali di San Michele* 19 (2006), 201–34. On the longer history of branding alpine cheeses, the loss of local specificities, the processes of re-invention of taste, and the invention of its "experience," see Cristina Grasseni, *La reinvenzione del cibo. Culture del gusto fra tradizione e globalizzazione ai piedi delle Alpi* (Verona: QuiEdit, 2007).

[42] Fiche "Fondue" in the "Liste des traditions vivantes en Suisse" de l'Office fédéral de la culture (OFC). I thank the librarians of the Swiss reference service *Interroge* for researching this source and

gruyère, it was chosen and made "typical" for commercial reasons. Also, acts such as sharing food from a common pot or drinking from a "cup of friendship" specially designed with multiple spouts became an essential part of the alpine experience in this period. As examined later in this book, internationalists would charge them with political meaning and use them for their own purposes.[43]

A great struggle between those who pushed for these transformations and those who opposed them ensued in the following decades. Alpinists and mountaineers typically stood against "mass tourism" and radical transformations of the alpine landscape, seeing themselves as defenders of a threatened environment. As Chapter 3 of this study explains, alpine clubs were especially active in this respect.[44] An international movement for the protection of the mountain environment arose, together with a transnational push for creating parks, though its internal contradictions were great and its progress far from linear. Most notably, as early as 1913 a Consultative Commission for the International Protection of Nature had been created, with Swiss naturalist Paul Sarasin (1856–1929) at its head.

This form of internationalist environmentalism had profound and long-lasting consequences, as it affected not only how the Alps—and the people who populated them—were perceived but also how they could be used for political purposes. Sarasin blamed the "white man" and the free market for environmental deterioration. He advocated for parks to protect flora and fauna, and also to serve as a safe haven for indigenous people. He envisioned a space where they lived on their own—no Europeans allowed—and where they could stay in contact with nature and be available for scientific studies. As Anna-Katharina Wöbse pointed out, if Sarasin's views were arguably altruistic and gave thrust to the international environmental movement, they also led to the "othering" of indigenous people and normalized the practice of treating them like another kind of fauna.[45]

Moreover, despite multiple setbacks, entities such as "national parks" became crucial and emotionally charged ingredients of both nationalism and internationalism in this period. To be sure, ongoing political tensions stood in the way of achieving concrete results in the field of environmental protection. In the early 1920s, the International Committee on Intellectual Cooperation of the League of Nations debated incorporating the 1913 Consultative Commission but decided against it as Germany, which had been part of it, was not a member of the League.[46] In 1928, the Committee on Arts and Letters of the International

making it available to me by email on January 8, 2016. Allovio, "Strategie e processi di costruzione di un prodotto tipico," 201–34.

---

[43] I thank the librarians of the Swiss reference service *Interroge* for their help in locating relevant information on these "typical" products.
[44] Keller, *Apostles of the Alps*, 67–8. This point is further elaborated upon in Chapter 3.
[45] Anna-Katharina Wöbse, "Separating Spheres: Paul Sarasin and his Global Nature Protection Scheme," *Australian Journal of Politics and History* 61, no. 3 (September 2015), 339–51.
[46] See correspondence in League of Nations Archives R 1007, 13/3514/3514 and related files.

Committee on Intellectual Cooperation took on the matter of protecting natural beauties and sent out questionnaires to all states represented, which now included Germany, asking to explain the laws and actions they had already undertaken in this regard. No particular mention of the Alps was made, although the focus on the creation of parks and the protection of birds would have been of importance in mountain environments.[47] Notwithstanding these complexities, it is safe to say that the history of "national parks" in the interwar period was shaped by its international and transnational aspects.[48] This is not only because of the "world environmental regime" that emerged in the last two centuries but also because "national parks and the safeguarding of the nation's natural beauties became part of the standard repertoire of artificial national paraphernalia, like flags, anthems, and sport teams"; and this in turn signified not only international competition but also openness toward international cooperation.[49]

These developments would prove deep and long-lasting. The model of the "Swiss national park" played a vital part in guiding similar initiatives and in providing means to adapt the blueprint of American national parks to European contexts and beyond.[50] It is relevant to note that the 1991 Alpine Convention originated from CIPRA (The International Commission for the Protection of the Alps), an offshoot of the International Union for the Protection of Nature (created by UNESCO in 1948), which had deepened its roots in the aforementioned committees of the League of Nations.[51] In this case too, the rhetoric that accompanied all of these initiatives was rife with emotions, ranging from "love" for nature, "fear" for its destruction, "anger" at the people who endangered it, and "trust" in both national policies and international cooperation to provide a solution to common problems.

1.3   Nationalism and Internationalism

The Alps' international—and internationalist—history cannot be understood without taking into account the various forms of nationalism with which it was inextricably linked. Starting from the nineteenth century, many mountain ranges, and the Alps in particular, came to mark the borders among newly established nation-states.[52] With the "politic of natural boundaries," the direction

---

[47] A full report is available in League of Nations Archives, R 2237.

[48] Bernhard Gissibl, Sabine Höhler, and Patrick Kupper, eds., *Civilizing Nature: National Parks in Global Historical Perspective* (New York: Berghahn, 2012).

[49] Anna-Katharina Wöbse, "Framing the Heritage of Mankind: National Parks on the International Agenda," in Gissibl, Höhler and Kupper eds., *Civilizing Nature*, 143–6.

[50] Wöbse, "Framing the Heritage of Mankind," 143–6. On this point, see also essay by Patrick Kupper in the same volume.

[51] Mathieu, *History of the Alps*, 5–6.

[52] According to Jon Mathieu, in 1713, "the Peace of Utrecht was the first large-scale treaty in which geographical conditions were mentioned without historical endorsements." See Mathieu, *The Alps: An Environmental History*, 76.

in which rivers and waters flowed increasingly served as a marker to determine frontiers—sometimes in spite of the history, language, or culture of those inhabiting these territories.[53] Religious tenets dictated that natural features represent the most appropriate reference points, as an increasing number of people connected God's will as expressed in creation with proposed political and administrative boundaries. Rationalist thought also supported choosing geographical criteria over cultural ones because of their perceived objectivity and scientific character.[54] "Normative naturalism" and "oropolitics" gave way to arguments about peace, as mountains were selected as the safest limits for emerging nations.[55] The western Alps, previously at the heart of the Savoy kingdom, in 1860 were used as lines to separate the Kingdom of Sardinia from the French provinces of Savoy and Nice.[56] In the following year, this portion of the Alps effectively marked the border between France and newly unified Italy. At the same time, after 1859, the Habsburgs lost their territories south of the Alps, and these later became incorporated in the Italian state. By the end of the First World War, with the demise of the Austro-Hungarian Empire, the entire Alpine range had been divided among independent nations, each claiming possession of a specific section of it.[57] In other regions of the world, too, mountains served as essential reference points for demarcating administrative and political units, and their ranges often determined where boundaries were drawn.[58]

At the same time, the rise of international cooperation as a standard practice in virtually every field led to mountains becoming preferred spaces for international encounters.[59] Numerous Alpine tunnels were built to facilitate travel and trade across the Alps. The first was the Fréjus Rail Tunnel (also called Mont Cenis Tunnel), whose construction lasted from 1857 to 1871.[60] The Gotthard Rail Tunnel opened in 1882, connecting Italy and Switzerland. In the same year, a road tunnel

---

[53] One of the most striking examples in this respect was the South-Tyrol, which was given to Italy regardless of the will or cultural identification of its inhabitants. Debarbieux and Rudaz, *Les faiseurs de montagne*, 71–2.

[54] Debarbieux and Rudaz, *Les faiseurs de montagne*, 57–8.

[55] There were also military arguments in favor of choosing mountains as frontiers. See Debarbieux and Rudaz, *Les faiseurs de montagne*, 64.

[56] This was established in the Treaty of Turin of 1860. The Italian irredentist movement continued to exist until the end of the Second World War; as Davide Rodogno pointed out, during the interwar period it was fueled by the Fascist regime. See Davide Rodogno, *Fascism's European Empire: Italian Occupation during the Second World War*, translated by Adrian Belton (Cambridge: Cambridge University Press, 2004).

[57] Switzerland, however, remained a transalpine state (though its federalist model allowed for linguistic differences and localisms to be expressed in practice without need for separation).

[58] On this point, see for instance the case of Korea, in Debarbieux and Rudaz, *Les faiseurs de montagne*, 75–6; on colonial and post-colonial territorialities see chapter 6, 159–87, in the same volume. For a broader theoretical reflection on borders and frontiers as well as on their implications see Manlio Graziano, *What Is a Border?* (Stanford: Stanford Briefs, 2018).

[59] Francis Lyall, *International Communications: The International Telecommunication Union and the Universal Postal Union* (Burlington, VT: Ashgate, 2011).

[60] In 1854, a system of fourteen tunnels had already been built in Semmering, on the Vienna–Trieste railway line. I thank Jon Mathieu for drawing my attention to this important precedent.

was inaugurated on the Col de Tende separating France and Italy; this was followed by a railway tunnel that opened in 1898. In 1906, the first tube of the Simplon railway tunnel linked Brig, Switzerland, with the Italian city of Domodossola. Work on the second tube of the tunnel began as early as 1912; this second passage was eventually opened in 1921, further increasing communication between the two countries.[61] While serving a wide range of public and private interests, each tunnel expressed and engendered emotions: as most famously immortalized in the scene of the ballet *Excelsior* described in the Introduction to this book, when the Mont Cenis was fully perforated and the people from two nations finally met on December 26, 1870, French and Italian workers expressed friendship towards one another and hugged. On the *Excelsior*'s—as well as on the world—stage, technological and economic expansions served as means to overcome separations imposed by natural barriers.

To be sure, the fact that the Alps served as essential markers of national identity cannot be downplayed, especially since they occupied an important space in what George Mosse has termed "appropriation of nature."[62] Also, the First World War had transformed the Alps, scarring them with trenches and shell holes and turning them into a bloody battleground. Many alpinists participated in the conflict themselves or provided knowledge and equipment to belligerent countries. Moreover, by 1919, the Alps had turned into a site for memory and mourning.[63] Old resentments survived the war. In the case of the German-speaking South Tyrol, which the Treaty of Saint-Germain assigned to Italy, reciprocal feelings worsened, particularly as the Fascist regime proceeded to implement a harsh policy of forced italianization.[64]

In Austria and Germany, many used alpinism as a means to unite all German-speaking areas, and, as historian Tait Keller noted, for them "alpine purity became a metaphor for racial purity."[65] They banned Jewish people and other non-Aryans from Alpine clubs, and, as early as 1930, they completed an *Anschluss* in the Alps by forming a united German and Austrian Alpine Association. As Keller noted, "on March 14, 1938, two days after German troops marched into Vienna," the name was changed into Deutscher Alpenverein (German Alpine Association,

---

[61] On the importance of railways and tunnels, see Beattie, *The Alps*, 174–9. On tunnels and national identity building, see Judith Schueler, *Materialising Identity: The Co-construction of the Gotthard Railway and Swiss National Identity* (Amsterdam: Aksant, 2008).

[62] According to George L. Mosse, "nature" and the Alps in particular became identified with war, and contributed to "mask" its reality, "spiritualize" the nation, and build the "myth of the war experience." George L. Mosse, *Fallen Soldiers: Reshaping the Memory of the World Wars* (Oxford: Oxford University Press, 1990). See in particular 107–26.

[63] Keller, *Apostles of the Alps*, 90; 97; 110–11; 116.

[64] Keller, *Apostles of the Alps*, 124–5. On how the Italian and the German Alpine Club performed their nationalisms in the Tyrol see also Stefano Morosini, *Sulle vette della patria: politica, guerra e nazione nel Club alpino italiano (1863–1922)* (Milan: FrancoAngeli, 2009), 74–5.

[65] Keller, *Apostles of the Alps*, 132; 207. On how the Nazi used the Alps, and on Adolf Hitler's Berghof see also Beattie, *The Alps*, 144–55.

DAV) to reflect the changing political reality.[66] The Nazi party embraced the alpinists' cause of mountain preservation and the fight against consumerism and mass consumption—though, in contradiction with their overt stances, they supported environmentally invasive projects such as the "Alpine Road."[67] Also, if for centuries the Alps had been fortified, this process intensified in the 1930s. The Maginot line included a stretch along the occidental Alps.[68] The Swiss National Redoubt was expanded. And the Italian Vallo Alpino militarized the entire arc surrounding northern Italy.[69] As these developments show, the Alps underwent a progressive process of nationalization and militarization in this period.[70]

This trend, however, does not diminish the importance of internationalist practices that became widespread in the 1920s and 1930s. After the First World War, the contacts made during the conflict led to cooperation and previous military alliances evolved into other forms of collaboration among Alpine clubs during peacetime. For instance, the CAI and the Sierra Club forged their connections during the American military intervention on the side of Italy during the First World War.[71] Also, there was a major gap between rhetoric and implementation: many people did not turn fascist rhetoric into practice at the local level; many alpinists found *Bergfilm* unrealistic and "kitsch," and arguably did not feel the extreme nationalistic emotions most often associated with it.[72]

1.4 "Alpine" Cultural Productions

Cultural productions and film best capture the complexities of the coexistence of nationalism and internationalism in the mountains in this period, especially when it comes to its emotional aspects. Interwar mountain cinema is most often associated with the German *Bergfilm*, a genre focusing on mountaineering and the struggle of humans against nature, and this in turn is often linked to the rise of extreme nationalism. Most famously, in his landmark study *From Caligari to Hitler*, published in 1947, Sigfried Kracauer connected the rise of the *Bergfilm* with the ascendancy of Nazism in Germany. In particular, he saw the characters in Arnold Fanck's movies as performing "the rites of a

---

[66] On resistance and for examples of the partial implementation of some of these measures, particularly the anti-Semitic ones, see Keller, *Apostles of the Alps*, 131–51.

[67] Keller, *Apostles of the Alps*, 201.

[68] William Allcorn, *The Maginot Line, 1928–45* (Oxford: Osprey, 2003).

[69] Alberto Fenoglio, *Il Vallo Alpino: le fortificazioni delle alpi occidentali durante la seconda guerra mondiale* (Sant'Ambrogio di Torino: Susalibri, 1992).

[70] Mathieu, *History of the Alps*, 14.   [71] Morosini, *Sulle vette della patria*, 168–9.

[72] Keller, *Apostles of the Alps*, 191; 155.

cult" permeated by "heroic idealism," and understood them as "rooted in a mentality kindred to Nazi spirit."[73]

However, the *Bergfilm* genre represented only a small part of movie productions dealing with mountains. According to the search engine *Dizionario Cinema delle Montagne* (Dictionary of Mountain Cinema), mountains were the main subject of almost 4000 films. The number of movies featuring mountains grew steadily throughout the interwar period, dipped in the 1940s, and reached its peak in the 1950s. Between 1919 and 1939, 855 movies portrayed mountains prominently. The majority was produced in the United States (48 percent), followed by Germany (20 percent), France (8 percent), Switzerland (6 percent), and Italy (4 percent). In 1936, the year when the highest number of films was made (64), the USA accounted for more than half (52 percent), followed by Germany (16 percent), Switzerland (9 percent), France (6 percent) and Great Britain (6 percent). Albeit iconic, the German *Bergfilm* hardly represented the majority of filmic productions with the Alps as their main subject.[74]

In the collection of posters in the Centro Documentazione of the Museo Nazionale della Montagna (Documentation Center of the National Mountain Museum) of Turin, "love"—void of the deeper meanings attached to it in German *Bergfilm*—figures as one of the main themes.[75] To be sure, numerous posters feature contests of men versus nature and other *Bergfilm* tropes. Yet, many others have as their most significant elements male and female characters engaged in some kind of amorous behavior, most often gazing into each other's eyes against a mountainous background. Moreover, the link between the idyllic aspect of mountain life and conceptions of *Heimat* imbued with racist and exclusionary undertones might not have appeared as explicit to contemporary audiences as it would to later observers.[76] Furthermore, interpretations of German *Bergfilm* as reflective of a nation whose *Heimat* was in the mountains—though useful and valid—might have overshadowed other equally important themes.[77]

---

[73] Siegfried Kracauer, *From Caligari to Hitler: A Psychological History of the German Film* (Princeton: Princeton University Press, 1947), 111–12. For a criticism of Kracauer, and on *Bergfilm* as it related to trauma after WW1, see Wilfried Wilms, "'The Essence of the Alpine World is Struggle': Strategies of *Gesundung* in Arnold Fanck's Early Mountain Films" in Ireton and Schaumann, eds., *Heights of Reflection*, 267–84.

[74] In 2004, the Museo Nazionale della Montagna Duca degli Abruzzi of the Italian Alpine Club (CAI) of Turin completed a multi-year project to collect data of films featuring mountains as a prominent subject. In addition to a printed dictionary, the result of this research was a search engine called *Dizionario Cinema delle Montagne*, which allows to search a database of 4000 films produced all over the world. http://www.museomontagna.org/it/area-documentazione/dizionario.php (accessed on January 16, 2017). I used this database as the main resource for collecting and elaborating the data presented in this section.

[75] Aldo Audisio and Angelica Natta-Soleri, *Film delle montagne: manifesti. Raccolte di documentazione del Museo Nazionale della Montagna* (Scarmagno: Priuli & Verlucca, 2008).

[76] On the idyllic aspects see Gianluigi Bozza, "La gente," in Audisio and Natta-Soleri, *Film delle montagne*, 235–6.

[77] Keller, *Apostles of the Alps*, 152–8.

Indeed, these same movies carried messages that reinforced contemporary internationalist ideas, practices, and emotions. *Der heilige Berg* (*The Holy Mountain*, released in 1926), a classic *Bergfilm* directed by Fanck and starring famous actress—and future director of Nazi propaganda films—Leni Riefenstahl, conveyed a rich set of associations that went beyond those emphasized by Kracauer.[78] The female protagonist, the dancer Diotima (played by Riefenstahl), attracted the love of two male antagonists defined right after the prelude as "two friends from the mountains."[79] The assumption that the Alps led to friendship underlined the entire movie: from the jovial atmosphere of the people hanging out at the Grand Hotel, to the cheerful environment of the skiing competition (one that never turned sour), to the camaraderie among the members of the skiing patrol—portrayed as a gregarious group of men ready to help others.

Even "the friend," who longed for a lonely—and thus deeper—experience of the mountain sought to share "the sublime" with a lover. When Diotima asked him "Why is nature so beautiful to us?," he replied "Because we invest our soul in it," thus confirming the existence of a community who *felt* the Alps in the same way regardless of their nationality. The implication was that many fellow Germans may be excluded, while others from foreign countries might have shared a similar sensibility. As an intertitle emphasized, the people involved in the skiing competition forgot to contemplate their surroundings: "They no longer notice the fairy tale beauty of the snow-concealed firs." Tellingly, there was no mention that such appreciation was the prerogative of one nation; and the protagonists actually carried their own internationalist message, as they raced together and interacted amicably within the same, shared space.

All characters engaged in selfless acts for one another. And if the final words reminded viewers that "above it all looms a holy mountain—a symbol of the greatest values that humanity can embrace—fidelity, truth, loyalty, and faith," the passage right before it explained that "peace lies upon the eternal sea...to spread the world's suffering and strife." While the extreme nationalist undertones of this film cannot be minimized, its associations between mountains and selflessness, friendship, and a universal "world's suffering and strife" were important as well; and the mountains, portrayed as alive and having agency, emerged as a site for extraordinary events and virtue.[80]

Similarly, in another iconic *Bergfilm* entitled *Die weiße Hölle vom Piz Palü* (*The White Hell of Pitz Palu*, released in 1929), also starring Riefenstahl, the mountains served as an arena in which to demonstrate one's worth and as a site for overt

---

[78] *Der heilige Berg*, (*The Holy Mountain*) directed by Arnold Fanck (1926). Restored version, L'immagine Ritrovata, Bologna, 2001.
[79] The name Diotima is symbolic as well, as in Plato's *Symposium* Socrates spoke of Diotima of Mantinea as the priestess who taught him the philosophy and the art of love. I thank Stefania Benini for pointing out this reference to me.
[80] *Der heilige Berg*.

selfless acts, from giving away one's sweater in the midst of a blizzard to the total mobilization of a village for rescuing a group of alpinists lost on the face of the mountain.[81] The celebration of such cooperative spirit echoed internationalist discourses at the time, which presented the project of building and maintaining peace as dependent on people's willingness to work with and for others to solve common problems.

Another useful window onto the emotional aspects of the coexistence of nationalism and internationalism are the many international—and internationalist—events held in the Alps in the interwar period. The most prominent were the Winter Olympics, which were held for the first time in 1924 in the French alpine town of Chamonix. To be sure, the Olympic games often served as grounds for nationalist propaganda and international confrontation.[82] Yet, the establishment of the Winter Olympics as a regular occurrence in international sports also proved that mountains could serve as preferred spaces for international cooperation and amicable exchange among peoples from different countries. When the rhetoric of "olympism" was extended to the mountains, many hoped that alpine sports would help a peaceful cause.[83] Images of representatives from all participating countries gathering their flags during the opening ceremony were widely publicized and amply defined this event. One photograph (see Figure 1.1) captured the moment when the same countries that ten years prior had embarked on a conflict of unprecedented scale and destruction were now coming together peacefully in full respect of their individual identities (symbolized by their respective insignia).[84]

An article published in the newspaper *La Gazette des Alpes* celebrated the "cosmopolitan vibe" that permeated those days in Chamonix, unapologetically referring to the games as the "Olympics" despite the fact that they were yet to be officially named as such.[85] The author noted how "a great number of nationalities are represented, except Germany," but also recounted an episode that made him

---

[81] *Die weiße Hölle vom Piz Palü* (*The White Hell of Pitz Palu*), directed by Arnold Fanck and Georg Wilhelm Pabst (1929). Restored version, Bundesarchiv-Filmarchiv, Berlin, 1997.

[82] Barbara J. Keys, *Globalizing Sport: National Rivalry and International Community in the 1930s* (Cambridge, MA: Harvard University Press, 2006).

[83] This point was made by Gaston Vidal on behalf of the French government during the opening ceremony. Comité olympique français, *Les jeux de la VIIIe Olympiade. Paris 1924. Rapport officiel* (Paris: Libr. de France, 1924), 721.

[84] Participating countries included Austria, Belgium, Canada, Estonia, United States, Finland, France, Great Britain, Hungary, Italy, Latvia, Norway, Poland, Sweden, Switzerland, Czechoslovakia, and Yugoslavia. Germany was excluded from all international competitions until 1925. Comité olympique français, *Les jeux de la VIIIe Olympiade*, 655–6.

[85] Scandinavian countries opposed the idea of the Winter Olympics as they saw them as conflicting with their own international winter games. IOC Archives, CIO JO-1924W-CEREM, "Opening and closing ceremonies of the 1924 Olympic Winter Games in Chamonix: Speeches and timetables" (200170); CIO JO-1924W-FI, "International Federations at the 1924 Olympic Winter Games in Chamonix: Correspondence (200601); and CIO JO-1924W-GENER, "Lunch menu and various documents concerning the 1924 Olympic Winter Games in Chamonix" (206029). Due to their insistence, at the beginning the 1924 "Winter Games" were not called "Olympics"; however, they were renamed as such retroactively.

Fig. 1.1 Opening of the Winter Games in Chamonix, 1924. ©IOC.

hopeful: "I saw by chance at the post office a telegram in German directed to Berlin..." He did not know anything more about it; but in that environment, at that moment, the language and destination alone sufficed to instill hopes for the future.[86]

The idea that the Winter Olympics could serve as a moment of "international solidarity," a force against "consumerism," and therefore as a substantial step toward the achievement of peace was confirmed in St. Moritz in 1928, as the number of participating countries grew from seventeen to twenty-five, with Germany now included.[87] The 1932 Winter Olympics in Lake Placid were also imbued with internationalist rhetoric. In the midst of the Great Depression, funds for building all the necessary facilities were nonetheless obtained with the promise of staging a much-needed moment of international exchange and cooperation. A letter by President Herbert Hoover, which was widely reproduced in an advertising booklet, assured that "The friendly rivalry of the athletes of the nations not only develops sportsmanship but also contributes to the advance of international good-will and fellowship."[88] The same booklet, produced by the Olympic Winter

[86] *Gazette des Alpes*, February 9, 1924, 4.
[87] Such language was used for instance by Schulthess, President of the Swiss Confederation, at the opening ceremony for the Olympic games in St. Moritz 1928. See Comité exécutif des IImes Jeux olympiques d'hiver St-Moritz 1928, *Rapport général du Comité exécutif des IImes Jeux olympiques d'hiver et documents officiels divers* (Lausanne: Comité Olympique Suisse, 1928), 25–7.
[88] This letter by Hoover, dated February 4, 1931, was reproduced in full in a brochure, III Olympic Winter Games Committee, *Setting the Stage for the III Olympic Winter Games* (undated), 2. One copy available at the IOC Library, 710.3 (04).

Games Committee, included a declaration that "the promotion of international good-will through the Olympic Games is an opportunity for far-sighted altruism which all thoughtful Americans will wish to accept."[89] Moreover, in his speech at the opening ceremony, New York Governor and President of the American Olympic Committee, Franklin Delano Roosevelt, who would be inaugurated President of the United States the following year, evoked the ancient custom of interrupting all hostilities during the games, maintaining that the Winter Olympics could serve as an important moment for peaceful international exchange.[90] By the 1930s, the association between Winter Olympics, mountains, and peace—along with the emotions that accompanied them—had been created and buttressed on multiple occasions.

Even at the "Nazi Olympics" of 1936, as they later came to be known, internationalist notions, images, and emotions emerged amidst criticisms of the German hosts and their extreme nationalist policies. In Garmisch-Partenkirchen, swastikas and salutes were accompanied by expressions of international appreciation and goodwill. At the opening on February 6, 1936, the President of the Organizing Committee, Dr. Ritter von Halt, proudly proclaimed: "The youth of the world fights for the victory and prepares every day for new battles. It is a combat of good friendship and contestants will remember the principles of our Life Honorary President Baron Pierre de Coubertin whom we greet today very specially as the renewer of modern Olympic Games."[91] By mentioning the father of olympism, he left no doubt about his interpretation of the spirit of the occasion.

Later that day, at a celebratory dinner, the President of the German National Committee, Hans von Tschammer und Osten, referred to all people present as "ambassadors of peace." He spoke of the Olympic flame in emotional terms, describing it as a reflection of "our hearts"—the place in the body where feelings were harbored.[92] His was also the idea of the Olympic torch relay, a tradition which he had just introduced and which has continued ever since. He then concluded with a toast to the "good camaraderie among all sportsmen and to the universal Olympic ideal."[93] As a major Nazi official openly endorsing internationalist principles, he counterbalanced the many extreme nationalistic messages that accompanied this occasion.

---

[89] III Olympic Winter Games Committee, *Setting the Stage for the III Olympic Winter Games*, 12.

[90] III Olympic Winter Games Committee Lake Placid, NY, USA, *III Olympic Winter Games, Lake Placid 1932: Official Report* (Lake Placid: III Olympic Winter Games Committee, 1932), 179–80.

[91] Speech delivered on February 6, 1936 by Dr. Ritter von Halt (President of Organizing Committee). IOC Archives, Olympic Games of Garmisch-Partenkirchen 1936, "Speeches during the 1936 Olympic Winter Games in Garmisch-Partenkirchen" (200869).

[92] Fay Bound Alberti, *Matters of the Heart: History, Medicine, and Emotion* (Oxford: Oxford University Press, 2010).

[93] Speech delivered on February 6, 1936 by Hans von Tschammer und Osten (President of German National Committee). IOC Archives, Olympic Games of Garmisch-Partenkirchen 1936, "Speeches during the 1936 Olympic Winter Games in Garmisch-Partenkirchen" (200869).

Fig. 1.2 American athletes drinking, playing, and enjoying music with members of the German *Sturmabteilung* (SA). *Olympia Zeitung*, 8 (February 12, 1936), 120. ©IOC. The caption (written in German, English, and French) reads: "Olympic contestants from USA in good comradeship with Garmisch-Partenkirchen SA—A musical reception."

The press coverage of the 1936 Winter Olympics also included images of international cooperation among the many athletes gathered for the event. For instance, a picture published on the magazine *Olympia Zeitung* (see Figure 1.2) showed American athletes drinking, playing, and enjoying music with members of the German *Sturmabteilung* (SA), the paramilitary wing of the Nazi Party most commonly associated with its rise. One of the most prominent figures, a man standing in the center with a swastika on his armband, left little doubt that the host of the 1936 Winter Olympics was not the mountain resort town, nor simply "Germany," but the Nazi regime that ruled it; yet, the smile on his face, his relaxed pose—with the hands casually tucked behind him—and the overall convivial mood of the image conveyed that in the mountains Nazi relations with people from other countries were outwardly gregarious, amicable. And if many articles before the event discussed a possible American boycott due to the discrimination of Jewish athletes in Germany, other newspapers and magazines praised the Olympics for their flawless organization and cheerful atmosphere.

To be sure, many remained skeptical that an international competition that included military ski patrols among its disciplines and was held in the country that most overtly challenged existing agreements could improve international understanding. As this study will later discuss, among them were several members of one of the largest internationalist groups active in the mountains, the International Mountaineering and Climbing Federation (or UIAA). But many people remembered the 1936 Olympics for their unprecedented size, their cosmopolitan feel, and for Sonja Henie's inimitable grace and beauty. The famous Norwegian skater delivered an exceptional performance for which the *Führer* personally congratulated her. To this day, her name is associated with the gentler side of the interwar period, and also with the emotions that permeated these years despite—and arguably even because of—the rise of extreme nationalism at the same time.

The association between the Olympics and the emotions of internationalism would continue for decades to follow, despite the blatant forms of nationalism that have always accompanied these occasions. Much energy was devoted to eliciting these feelings. A report on "Broadcasting during the 1948 Olympic Winter Games in St. Moritz" chronicled the great efforts undertaken to "make all listeners on five continents 'live' the Olympic Games." These included the installation of an extensive network of transmission lines and telephones, the purchase of technical equipment, and the hiring of personnel that had not only technical expertise but also "character, consideration, sense of initiative, and knowledge of languages." 189 circuits had been established to broadcast worldwide in fifteen languages, and the largest radio station in Switzerland had been set up at St. Moritz's Hotel Engadinerhof for this purpose alone.[94]

The Report did not hide the motivations behind this hefty investment: citing the last games—the 1936 Olympics in Germany—as a term of comparison, it emphasized the importance of showing that Switzerland could hold its own when it came to technological advancement. However, there was more to the project of making the Olympics "alive:" R. de Reding, the general director in charge of radiodiffusion who authored the majority of the Report, remarked that reporters had the duty to reflect "the Olympic spirit" of this internationalist event. While providing an assessment of his own work, he was proud of the emotions that the Swiss radio had been able to convey, yet he wondered if technology had begun to overshadow "the atmosphere of peace and entente" it was meant to foster.[95]

[94] IOC Archives, CIO JO-1948W-RADIO, "Broadcasting during the 1948 Olympic Winter Games in St. Moritz: Correspondence and Report."
[95] IOC Archives, CIO JO-1948W-RADIO, "Broadcasting during the 1948 Olympic Winter Games in St. Moritz: Correspondence and Report."

Trying to figure out the interplay of nationalism and internationalism during the event he had been responsible for covering, he pinned his greatest hopes onto the people who had come together for the occasion: all of the communication experts that had entangled "relations, even friendships" that surely would have become "useful in future."[96] R. de Reding, like many others at this time, ultimately saw himself and his colleagues just like the athletes whose performance he chronicled on ever-growing radio waves: heroes and accomplices of international encounters, caught between modernism and anti-modernism, nationalism and internationalism, whose existence and growth seemed inevitable.

1.5 "Mountain People"

The deep transformations of the Alps described so far in this chapter also extended to the people who inhabited them.[97] For centuries, and especially since the Enlightenment, all sorts of images and stereotypes had emerged in relation to the mountains' indigenous population, as dwarfs, giants, and fairies were imagined to inhabit mountainous slopes.[98] Numerous theories circulated on the origins of the indigenous folk (often referred to as *montagnards*), with Huns, Hungarians, Saracens, and Slavs being at one point considered the ancestors of the Alps' native peoples.[99]

It was however in the late nineteenth and early twentieth centuries that "mountain people" gained the spotlight as a subject of study. Numerous proponents of eugenics included them in their taxonomies, although with varying definitions and characterizations. In *The Races of Europe* (1899), William Z. Ripley (1867–1941) referred to "the Alpines" as one of "the three European races" (together with the "Teutonic" and the "Mediterranean"), made of "broad-headed types" who tended to be isolated, "rural," and politically "conservative."[100] In *The Passing of the Great Race* (1916), Madison Grant (1865–1937) wrote about "the Alpine race" as a group of "Eastern and Asiatic origin," with "round face," "round skull," and "stocky build," and singled out "European Alpines" as a subgroup "saturated" with "Nordic blood," who, "because of the warlike and restless nature of the

---

[96] IOC Archives, CIO JO-1948W-RADIO, "Broadcasting during the 1948 Olympic Winter Games in St. Moritz: Correspondence and Report."

[97] A marvelous literary overview of the many imaginaries attached to the Alps by their visitors is in Stephen O'Shea, *The Alps: A Human History from Hannibal to Heidi and Beyond* (New York: W.W. Norton and Company, 2018).

[98] Max Liniger-Goumaz, *De l'éradication du crétinisme et autres phénomènes remarquables tels qu'on peut les observer dans la région des Alpes pennines* (Lausanne: Editions de l'Aire, 1989), 33–41.

[99] Liniger-Goumaz, *De l'éradication du crétinisme*, 147–93. See also René Jantzen, *Montagne et symboles* (Lyon: Presses Universitaires de Lyon, 1988).

[100] William Z. Ripley, *The Races of Europe: A Sociological Study* (New York: D. Appleton and Company, 1899), 128; 142; 544; 550.

Nordics" had been "reasserting" itself and increasingly occupied a larger portion of the continent.[101]

Many "scientists" of this period portrayed "Alpines" as a threat to the "Nordic race," which they considered superior. In Germany, eugenicists such as Eugen Fischer (1874–1967) and Hans Friedrich Karl Günther (1891–1968), whose writings provided the Nazis with a pseudo-scientific justification for their anti-Semitic policies, included "alpines" as one of the six groups who formed the German people, which they qualified as hard-working, narrow-minded, mistrustful of strangers, and overall fit to be led rather than to lead.[102] In the United States, American Klansman and racial theorist Lothrop Stoddard (1883–1950) named "the Alpines" as one the three "white races of Europe," together with the "Nordic" and the "Mediterranean," emphasizing how its rise came at the expenses of the most elevated Nordic element.[103] In *The Rising Tide of Color* (1921), he argued that war had already initiated this trend because, due to his innate predisposition "the Nordic...threw on his shoulders the brunt of battle and exposed him to the greatest losses, whereas the more stolid Alpine and the less robust Mediterranean stayed at home and reproduced their kind." The industrial revolution had then exacerbated the "resurgence of the Alpine, and still more of the Mediterranean, elements" in Europe—as well as in the United States, where many of them had emigrated and now menaced the "natural" Nordic settlers. According to him, since the Nordic "requires healthful living conditions, and quickly pines when deprived of good food, fresh air, and exercise," he suffered in factory and urban environments; in contrast, the other two races were more adaptable and therefore thrived.[104]

Such writings reinforced the notion that there was such a thing as a distinct group of "mountain people," which was defined by biological and environmental factors that influenced their behavior. As Bernard Debarbieux and Gilles Rudaz noted, the "status of the *montagnard*" became caught between two "forms of determination:" a "natural determination," which postulated that nature had imposed special physical and mental characteristics on mountain people, and a "social and historical determination," which assumed that due to their location they could not have access to modernity.[105] Strikingly, by attributing to all *montagnards* common features, scientists were able to apply the term "Alpine"—and

[101] Madison Grant, *The Passing of the Great Race, or The Racial Basis of European History* (New York: Charles Scribner's Sons, 1916), 121–2; 131.

[102] Hans F. K. Günther, *The Racial Elements of European History*, translated by G. C. Wheeler (London: Methuen and Co., 1927), chapter 2.

[103] Lothrop Stoddard, *The Rising Tide of Color: The Threat Against White World-Supremacy* (New York: Charles Scribner's Sons, 1921).

[104] Stoddard, *The Rising Tide of Color*, 162–5.

[105] Debarbieux and Rudaz, *Les faiseurs de montagne*, 34–44.

the Alpine model as a whole—to all mountain ranges.[106] At the same time, they created subcategories of *montagnard* to rationalize local differences and deviations. By doing so, they created a model that fit internationalism well as it accounted for both its localist and its universalist aspects.

Especially in the field of health, conflicting studies and theories emerged, some stressing the higher incidence of conditions such as cretinism and goiter, and others praising the healthy and robust constitution of those who inhabited the Alps. Both placed emotions front and center and shaped how outsiders perceived "mountain people" and how they appropriated them for a wide range of political purposes.

The extensive literature associating mountains with cretinism (a form of mental retardation often accompanied by an enlargement of the thyroid gland, or goiter, caused by iodine deficiency) evoked a wide set of strong feelings, ranging from horror, to compassion, to wonderment, to amusement. Speculation about the causes for cretinism led to its sentimentalization.[107] Philosopher, physician, and occultist Paracelsus (1493–1541) blamed the disease on particular minerals; others faulted water, or the practice of drinking water derived from melted snow; others thought that these were a "peculiar race of people" susceptible to sickness; or they called them "half-men," claiming they lacked even the "natural instinct" to the point they died because "the excrements had accumulated in their intestines." Some observers pointed at the poverty of the diet ("often limited to potatoes, chestnuts, and sometimes boiled corn"), or the excessive consumption of milk and potatoes, or the fact that babies were weaned too late, or the lack of salt in their food. And there were also some who considered cretinism as "absolutely local" and the result of "exhalations" from "swampy waters" (*marais*) coming and going from the mountains themselves. In encountering some Valaisians of "scarily Italian appearance," a traveler was unsure whether to attribute it to their "miserable education in filthiness," or to a "mistake of nature," or to the fact that seeing disfigured bodies might make one exaggerate their number. Yet, nature must have played a part, as even where people lived "very properly" some cases "could still be found."[108]

Theories about homesickness (*Heimweh*) emerged, connecting mountains with longing for a distant place and time, and mountain diseases with feeling. One person even argued that "providence had given them a stupid indifference that prevents them from feeling misery." Numerous visitors did not hide their own

---

[106] A similar development took place in the scholarship related to the physical features of the mountains themselves. See Philippe Frei, *Transferprozesse der Moderne: Die Nachbenennungen «Alpen» und «Schweiz» im 18. bis 20. Jahrhundert* (Bern: Peter Lang, 2017).

[107] The following section is a synthesis of numerous citations collected by Max Liniger-Goumaz. The full texts, references, and citations can be found in Max Liniger-Goumaz, *Nos ancêtres les crétins des Alpes* (Geneva: Les Editions du Temps, 2002), 51–68.

[108] Liniger-Goumaz, *Nos ancêtres les crétins des Alpes*, 52–63.

revulsion as they first encountered people affected by cretinism. For example, poet and traveler Marianne Baillie (1795 *c.*–1831) called them members of a "blighted, blasted, wretched race, hardly deserving the name of human." Even Goethe wrote about how "the goiters have totally altered my mood" and described Sion as a city of "disgusting and black aspect." Humor in all of its shades also entered the vocabulary and the description of the Alps' visitors. In 1850, French author Théophile Gautier (1811–72) spoke of a woman he met in the Valais as his "fantasy" (his "*chimera*"), since "she had three teats, but the third was a goiter and it was the only one hard."[109] From winces to smiles, the experience of meeting "cretins" in the mountains was laden with emotions.

Iconographic representations of people affected with goiter also bolstered its associations with strong feelings such as sensuality, eroticism, ire, and compassion. Since the seventeenth century, when the practice of creating a *sacro monte* (literally a "sacred mountain") with a sanctuary surrounded by chapels intensified, many of the sculpted and painted figures included goiters meant at once to symbolize, express, and elicit emotions in a growing number of visitors. The stereotype of *montagnards* as sick, poor, and unfortunate was perpetuated by in the following decades in films such as *L'enfant du montagnard* (The *montagnard*'s Child, 1908) and *Pauvre aveugle* (The Poor Blind, 1908), which triggered compassion in the viewers by emphasizing their suffering conditions.[110]

Feelings also became part of scientific definitions of peculiarly mountain diseases. In 1911, *Encyclopaedia Britannica* mentioned how the term "cretin" might have derived from "chrétiens, in the sens of 'innocent,'" though it also included the possibility that the term derived from "creta" (*craie*), "a sallow or yellow-earthy complexion being a common mark of cretinism." In *Analyse spectrale de l'Europe* (Spectral Analysis of Europe, 1928), philosopher Hermann von Keyserling (1880–1946) remarked on the "endemic cretinism" that affected Switzerland, which was nonetheless considered a model "of the future Europe"; in his opinion, "It is incontestable that nature, there, has a great part of culpability: not only goiter, but also the noteworthy lack of beauty in people are due certainly in a big measure to its influence."[111] Aesthetic canons and contemporary eugenic language thus entered the study and the perception of people affected with cretinism, shaping the emotional reception of the people who encountered them for the first time in their travels—either real or metaphorical.

The treatment of goiter and cretinism also followed a set of historical trajectories in which superstition, magic, science, and emotions were intertwined. As vividly narrated in a history reconstructed by surgeon Guido Barbieri Hermitte, medical advice over the centuries ranged from drinking from a human skull to

[109] Liniger-Goumaz, *Nos ancêtres les crétins des Alpes*, 52–63.
[110] Roberto Serafin, "Le Storie," in Audisio and Natta-Soleri, *Film delle montagne*, 167.
[111] Cited in Liniger-Goumaz, *Nos ancêtres les crétins des Alpes*, 63.

applying materials as varied as "menstrual blood, mouse excrement, donkey nails, and live frogs."[112] The supposed healing power of the royal touch was also put to work for the cure of this disease, as were all sorts of substances—such as the broths derived from shrimp and viper, as well as from regular and green lizards—chosen because of their resemblance to some aspect of the ailment.[113] Significant progress in the study and treatment of cretinism can be traced back to 1893, when it was first connected to a dysfunction of the thyroid, and then to the studies of Dr. Theodor Kocher (1841–1917), who in 1909 was awarded the Nobel Prize in Medicine for his work on goiter and the thyroid gland.[114]

Scientific discoveries soon ushered health policy changes across borders. As a result of these studies, since 1922, an iodization program of table salt was promoted in Switzerland and numerous scientific articles on cretinism were published. Two international conferences on this disease were held in Bern, in 1927 and in 1933. Similar programs were introduced in other countries, significantly lowering the incidence of cretinism on a worldwide scale;[115] though, to this day, the World Health Organization monitors iodine deficiency and promotes iodization programs in areas that lack this micronutrient (most notably, mountains).[116] And, if as early as 1939 Dr. J. B. Bertrand rejoiced at the disappearance of the disease and declared that we can thus talk "and even smile about the legends and the insanities they inspired," as late as 1985 Dr. Peter Pfannenstiel commented on how "caricatures…as well as a number of crude jokes are the reason why many Germans view in the goiter an aesthetic imperfection or a tribal mark given only to the Bavarians, the people coming from the Allgäu, the Tyrol, and the Swiss."[117] The association between mountains, diseases, and the wide variety of emotions they trigger remains alive and well.

At the same time, a broad spectrum of scientific studies gradually created alternative images of *montagnards* as particularly "healthy" and also connected them with desirable characteristics such as "purity "and "authenticity." This trend deepened its roots in philosophical debates dating back to the mid-nineteenth century. With the rise of autonomous disciplines such as psychology and sociology, an

---

[112] Guido Barbieri Hermitte, *Il gozzo: storia, leggenda, aneddotica* (Venosa: Edizioni Osanna Venosa, 1996), 243.

[113] Hermitte, *Il gozzo*, 245. On the rationale behind this principle of resemblance see also related footnote no. 901.

[114] For details on Kocher's work, see Hermitte, *Il gozzo*, 231–41.

[115] From a cultural standpoint, the first mention of "cretinism" has been traced back to 1220, and countless literary depictions of this disease have been written since. A thorough anthology can be found in Liniger-Goumaz, *Nos ancêtres les crétins des Alpes*. On older references that might be connected to this disease, see Franz Merke, *History and Iconography of Endemic Goitre and Cretinism* (Bern: Hans Huber, 1984). For an overview, see also Antoine De Baecque, *Histoires des crétins des Alpes* (Paris: Vuibert, 2018).

[116] World Health Organization, "Micronutrient Deficiencies" http://www.who.int/nutrition/topics/idd/en/(accessed on January 17, 2017). For an assessment of the current situation (by country) see the *Database on Iodine Deficiency* on the same page.

[117] Liniger-Goumaz, *Nos ancêtres les crétins des Alpes*, 51–68.

increasing number of scholars interrogated the nature of the individual (or the "self") in relation to its surroundings, asking how this changed over time— Ferdinand Tönnies (1855-1936) and his reflections on the shift from tightknit "community" (*Gemeinschaft*) to impersonal "society" (*Gesellschaft*) immediately come to mind.[118] Many criticized the commodification of life and culture in the modern world, and expressed concern over an overall loss of "authenticity" in the human experience—most famously, Walter Benjamin (1892-1940) in his writings on the loss of the "aura" in the modern world.[119] In this context, *montagnards* became constructed as seemingly a timeless type, immune from the "diseases" of modernity and therefore "healthy."[120]

Literary—and increasingly filmic—representations did much to popularize this new type of healthy *montagnard* capable of healing those who came to know him or her. To be sure, the image of alpine peasants as robust people, breathing alpine air and eating nurturing alpine foods had long been propagated by authors such as the Swiss poet Albrecht von Haller (1708-77), together with the presumption that mountain people were democratic (i.e., as in the tale of William Tell) and resistant to control.[121] Yet, the most influential work to add to this tradition was the novel *Heidi*, written by Johanna Spyri (1827-1901) and first published in 1880.[122]

Though prototypically Swiss, the story of the little girl with an infectiously cheery disposition captured audiences around the world and still feeds the association between mountains and the physical—and also moral—hygiene they supposedly engender.[123] As Letizia Bolzani explained, "Heidi is a soul healer": literally, she cures her sick friend, Klara; and, metaphorically, she heals her overly-protective physician, Dr. Classen, as well as her own surly grandpa, by showing them the power of joy in one's life.[124] If the book's less romantic aspects—such as the references to the massive migration from the Alps to the cities—have been lost, the notion that the mountains represented the opposite of the modern city and could treat urban illnesses persisted. The character of Klara, a sick girl from an industrial city—Frankfurt—who in the Alps starts walking again, resonated with the growing number of people who sought physical, mental, and spiritual recovery in the Alps.[125] The belief that people in the mountains resisted formal

---

[118] Ferdinand Tönnies, *Gemeinschaft und Gesellschaft* (Leipzig: Fuess Verlag, 1887).

[119] Walter Benjamin, "The Work of Art in the Age of Mechanical Reproduction," in *Illuminations*, translated by Harry Zohn (New York: Schocken Books, 1969). Orig. *Illuminationen*, 1st (French) edition, 1936.

[120] The scientific and medical discussions are analyzed in detail in Chapters 4 and 5.

[121] Beattie, *The Alps*, 123.

[122] On Heidi and the subsequent creation of "Heidi villages" in the Alps, see Beattie, *The Alps*, 142.

[123] On the commercial aspect, and on the creation of *Heidiland* and of other images of Heidi's Dörfli ("little village") that still dominate people's imagination, see Jean-Michel Wissmer, *Heidi: enquête sur un mythe suisse qui a conquis le monde* (Geneva: Métropolis, 2012), 26-33. A full list of translations can be found in Davide Dellamonica et al., eds., *Heidi: oltre la storia* (Lugano: Biblioteca Cantonale di Lugano, 2013), 75-9.

[124] Letizia Bolzani, "Una piccola sciamana delle Alpi," in Davide Dellamonica et al., eds., *Heidi: oltre la storia* (Lugano: Biblioteca Cantonale di Lugano, 2013), 43.

[125] Wissmer, *Heidi*, 128.

instruction (in the novel, Heidi's caregiver, Uncle Alp, was opposed to her schooling) was also reinforced, as were stereotypes of city education (most famously personified by the strict governess *Fräulein* Rottenmeier) as repressive and ultimately harmful.

A 1937 film featuring Shirley Temple further popularized the story and connected it with the emotions of internationalism.[126] The original brunette in Spyri's novels was replaced with a blond version, played by Temple. The story was changed dramatically from the original, but the same associations between mountains and emotions such as "authenticity," "genuineness," and "trust" in the power of human interaction remained. The quintessential *montagnard*, this time called "grandpa," was rude on the surface but remained, deep down, sweet and caring. The little alpine village (or *Dorfli*, in Swiss German) stood in sharp contrast to the city. Dominated by stunning surroundings, it was poor but overall cozy. The landscape itself exuded joy, unlike the city—a "noisy cage" where "civilized people" engaged in excessive formality and dangerous "gypsies" lingered at night ready to buy little girls from heartless women like Heidi's aunt. The movie's happy-ending capped the work's overall internationalist message and emotions. Tellingly, once with "grandpa" and back to her beloved Alps, Heidi recited a prayer: "make every little boy and girl in the world as happy as I am." Her cheer and kindness now extended well beyond Switzerland to encompass a global community spanning across all types of boundaries.

The archetypal Swiss character of Heidi's story exemplifies how the uniqueness of the Swiss model was attributed to the mountains that surrounded the Swiss people; at the same time, *montagnards* served at once as the symbol of a certain nationality as well as the embodiment of a minority—often unusual and colorful— in charge of its defense. Celebrated when fostering national unity, they were denigrated when they did not. As sciences and politics increasingly influenced one another, *montagnards* were gradually deemed unqualified to be in charge of their own territories. At the same time, outside visitors claimed to know them— and, by extension, to have the authority to make suggestions about which aspects of their "character" should serve as a model for others.[127]

For instance, in 1911, American geographer and first female President of the Association of American Geographers Ellen Churchill Semple (1863–1932) proffered a thorough assessment of the "mental and moral qualities" of the typical "mountaineers":

With this conservatism of the mountaineer is generally coupled suspicion toward strangers, extreme sensitiveness to criticism, superstition, strong religious feeling, and an intense love of home and family. The bitter struggle for existence

---

[126] *Heidi*, directed by Allan Dwan (1937). A lesser known antecedent was a 1920 film by Canadian director Frederick A. Thompson. Wissmer, *Heidi*, 167–70.

[127] Debarbieux and Rudaz, *Les faiseurs de montagne*, 41–3; 82–98; 118–21.

makes him industrious, frugal, provident; and, when the marauding stage has been outgrown, he is peculiarly honest as a rule. Statistics of crime in mountain regions show few crimes against property though many against person. When the mountain-bred man comes down into the plains, he brings with him there-fore certain qualities which make him a formidable competitor in the struggle for existence,—the strong muscles, unjaded nerves, iron purpose, and indifference to luxury bred in him by the hard conditions of his native environment.[128]

If on one hand Semple "othered" all "mountaineers" as if they were part of a separate species, on the other she brought out what she saw as their most desirable features (e.g., strength and frugality), thus presenting them as potentially more successful in a world growing more competitive.

Similarly, in the 1936 book *Mountain Geography*, Roderick Peattie (1891–1955) illustrated the contradictory attitudes associated with interwar *montagnards*, and put forth some suggestions on how their territories should be administered.[129] After describing the physical features of the mountains (which he defined as the result of a "personal evaluation," or a construct "in the minds of the people who daily regard them"), Peattie presented a set of characteristics typical of the moun-tains' native folk: in his opinion, these included "self-reliance," "frugality," and "hard labor," which had originated as a response to living in harsh conditions. Peattie also pinpointed some of the *montagnards'* most common "political" features, which included not only "individualism" but also "conservatism" and a "suggestion of republicanism" derived from having to deal with others in order to solve common problems.[130] Such a blend explained both their longing for freedom and their common identity. For this reason, Peattie decried the use of mountains as borders, denouncing flagrant cases in which alpine communities had been split (most notably in the South Tyrol, where due to the Italian domination it is now "forbidden in the taverns to sing German songs over the convivial glass") and asking for them to be rectified.[131] Overall, though, Peattie's narrative implied that it would be up to outsiders to determine which of the *montagnards'* features were the most desirable, and how to use them at the service of broader agendas.

Many contemporaries agreed with him, and acted accordingly. As historian Alice Travers pointed out in her book on politics and representations of moun-tains by the Vichy regime in France, mountains occupied a prominent role in the cultural and political landscape of the twentieth century. Of particular import-ance was what Travers called the "panoply of the perfect *montagnard*," a set of

[128] Ellen Churchill Semple, *Influences of Geographic Environment: On the Basis of Ratzel's System of Anthropo-Geography* (New York: Henry Holt and Co., 1911), 601.
[129] Roderick Peattie, *Mountain Geography: A Critique and a Field of Study* (Cambridge, MA: Harvard University Press, 1936).
[130] Peattie, *Mountain Geography*, 217.   [131] Peattie, *Mountain Geography*, 213.

"virtues"—and arguably also, of emotions—associated with the mountain that supposedly derived from one's direct contact with them: "energy, will power, self-control, resolve, courage, audaciousness, tenacity, perseverance, discipline, solidarity, sense of hierarchy etc." The Vichy regime devoted considerable energy and resources to creating opportunities for people—the youth especially—to experience mountains and to feel this panoply. Specifically, it built infrastructure to facilitate skiing and alpinism. It actively and deliberately promoted mountains through films that celebrated sports and the individuals who practiced them. It also organized exhibitions of objects and photographs. The result was the creation of the "myth" of the "*montagne éducatrice*" (literally, of the "educational mountain"), which postulated that mountains could teach values such as "disinterested effort" and "team spirit," and that people would be inspired by climbers to pursue ever higher peaks.[132]

"Holistic education" and the glorification of youth, which Travers associated with these developments, were not limited to nationalism. Similarly, the mystic and ascetic aspects of mountaineering were very influential across the political spectrum. The figure of the "*montagnard*-monk"—for whom alpinism was a "religious practice"—confirmed that mountains offered a site for "spiritual experience" and "internal peace and purity." Specific morality and emotions became linked with the physicality and the materiality of mountains (e.g., verticality with catharsis and ascension). Christian morality and its glorification of endurance and suffering was associated with climbing, with the "national revolution," and with the internationalist enterprise as well. To be sure, some of these "virtues" did not transfer as easily. Competition, for example, stood openly at odds with internationalism.[133] Yet, internationalism was not antithetical to nationalism, and the latter's equivalence with patriotism perhaps was not obvious to contemporaries and certainly not absolute.

Notions that the harshness of the mountain terrain required "solidarity" and the symbol of the "rope" (*corde*) as a "*guarante de la communauté*" (warrant of community) fit particularly well with internationalist discourse. Above all, the centrality of "emotions and sentimentalism" in discourse and praxis applied well to internationalism, as did the idea that mountains could serve as the most suitable prism to understand contemporary times.[134]

* * *

Without pretense of being exhaustive, this chapter has identified some of the most important forces that led to mountains becoming associated with "the

---

[132] Alice Travers, *Politique et représentation de la montagne sous Vichy: la montagne éducatrice, 1940–1944* (Paris: L'Harmattan, 2001), 212; 123; 177.

[133] Travers, *Politique et représentation de la montagne sous Vichy*, 179; 186; 198–205.

[134] Travers, *Politique et représentation de la montagne sous Vichy*, 215–17; 254; 263.

emotions of internationalism" in the interwar period. The demographic diversification and the sentimentalization of the Alps made them a preferred site for their politicization. Processes of nationalization and internationalization determined what people thought about mountains, and also what they did while living or spending time on them. Technological innovations also played a big part in changing who could travel, how people used the alpine landscape to fit their needs, and how they engendered emotions in this process. A wide range of cultural productions played a crucial role in making people visualize the Alps in new ways, and also in guiding how they would mold them to fit their visions. Emotions accompanied all of these developments, affecting and legitimizing behaviors, and also giving mountains an appeal they would have not otherwise had.

The "Great War" represented a fundamental turning point in this context: after 1918, the emerging notion that another conflict needed to be avoided at all costs touched all aspects of life in the Alps, particularly since they had served as a bloody battleground and now marked newly-established national borders. After centuries in which they had been idealized and depicted as sites for experiencing strong emotions, mountains came to embody all sorts of hopes and fears related to the ongoing political situation. In an age of anxiety and at a time of obsession over bodies, health, and what these represented for the nation, mountains became the most logical point of reference for all political movements. As for how internationalist individuals and institutions—and the League of Nations especially—appropriated them for their own purposes, this is the subject of the following chapter.

2

Managing Emotions at the League of Nations

Born out of the ashes of World War One as a supranational organization with the explicit goal of ensuring lasting peace, the League of Nations used emotions profusely to promote itself and its own work. Landmark speeches delivered at the 1919 Paris Peace Conference and at the League's first Assembly in 1920 emphasized the emotional toll imposed by the "Great War" and presented the new world order as one that would provide much needed emotional relief. The League's publicity employed feelings to link internationalism with values such as genuineness and integrity. More broadly, the League treated repressing anger and instilling friendship as realist goals, and devoted much energy and resources to their attainment.

The Alps served as an essential tool for the League to achieve its emotional objectives. The League evoked contemporary discourses about mountains as sites for spiritual elevation, solidarity, and friendship, and argued that they could help people form emotional bonds indispensable for a lasting peace. It referred to emotions associated with mountains (e.g., resilience and strength) to display itself as having the qualities required to solve nagging issues. It also drew upon existing tropes about mountains as sites of arduous, noble, yet attainable endeavors to cast its own objectives in the same light. Moreover, it used notions of alpine purity and nobility in order to connect its own ideals—and the people it put in charge of pursuing them—with morality, transparency, and honesty.

From a practical standpoint, the League of Nations fostered the transformation of mountains into concrete grounds for managing people's emotions. Aside from its political sections dealing with the "Implementation of the Peace Treaties" and other "Activities for the Maintenance of International Peace," since the beginning the League also became involved in "Activities in Connection with the Promotion of Functional Cooperation."[1] These included technical committees such as

---

[1] According to Paul Taylor and A. J. R. Groom, "Functionalism stresses the plenitude of relationships of a legitimised character between all manner of diverse actors which form the very fabric of world society: a working peace system exists and functionalism seeks to remove impediments to its further growth. The assumptions of functionalism, as reflected, for instance, in policy advice to governments, are different from those of strategic studies, or crisis management or foreign policy analysis. The billiard ball analogy of international society is rejected; greater significance is attached to the emergence of an increasing range of inter-, cross- and trans-national systems of inter-dependence; the term 'world politics' or 'world society' is preferred to 'international politics'; the role of governments is

The Emotions of Internationalism: Feeling International Cooperation in the Alps in the Interwar Period. Ilaria Scaglia, Oxford University Press (2020). © Ilaria Scaglia. DOI: 10.1093/oso/9780198848325.001.0001

Communication and Transit, Economic and Financial, Health, Intellectual Cooperation, Social Questions, and Legal Work. Many of these "functional" branches, like Communications and Transit, had to conduct work in the mountains in order to establish radiotelegraphic telecommunications as well as railway, hydraulic, and electric lines, and concretely engaged in international cooperation there. Other technical sections deliberately chose to deal with issues that affected mountain regions as a whole. For instance, the League's committee on Arts and Letters became involved in the protection of "beauty spots" and the "beautification of rural life," which also included mountains.[2]

It was the League's work in intellectual cooperation, however, that led to one of the League's longest-lasting intervention on the mountains and on the emotions associated with them.[3] Though not specifically mentioned in the *Covenant*, "culture" soon became one of the League's most important fields of activity.[4] As early as September 1921, both the Council and the Assembly of the League of Nations adopted a proposal for the creation of an international organization for intellectual work with the aim of reinforcing ties among intellectuals and of encouraging the formation of an "international spirit." In January 1922, the International Committee on Intellectual Cooperation was established. Its founding members included prominent personalities: Professor of Political Economy at the University of Calcutta D. N. Banerjee (1895–?); French philosopher Henri Bergson (1859–1941); Norwegian biologist and Norway's first female professor Kristine Bonnevie (1872–1948); physicist Marie Curie-Skłodowska (1867–1934); Brasilian Professor of Medicine Aloysio de Castro (1881–1959); Belgian lawyer, cultural critic and socialist politician, Jules Destrée (1863–1936); German physicist Albert Einstein (1879-1955); American astronomer George E. Hale

---

to be progressively reduced by indirect methods, and integration is to be encouraged by a variety of functionally based, cross-national ties; peace and security are to be guaranteed by the efficient provision of essential services to fulfill commonly-felt needs rather than 'non-war' being induced by fear of threat systems and sanctions." A. J. R. Groom and Paul Taylor, "Introduction: Functionalism and International Relations," in A. J. R. Groom and Paul Taylor, eds., *Functionalism: Theory and Practice in International Relations* (London: University of London Press, 1975), 1–2. On the interchangeability of the terms "technical" and "functional" in this context, see Victor-Yves Ghebali, "The League of Nations and Functionalism," in Groom and Taylor, eds., *Functionalism*, 141. On the meaning and implications of "functional" and "transnational," see Joseph S. Nye and Robert O. Keohane, "Transnational Relations and World Politics: An Introduction," *International Organization* 25, no. 3 (1971), 329–49. See also Martin David Dubin, "Transgovernmental Processes in the League of Nations," *International Organization* 37, no. 3 (Summer 1983), 469–93. On the concept of "practical internationalism" see also Jan Kolasa, *International Intellectual Cooperation: The League Experience and the Beginnings of UNESCO* (Wroclaw: Wroclawskie Towarzistwo Naukowe, 1962).

[2] League of Nations Archives, R 2237, 5B/5189/5189.

[3] The most complete work on this subject is Jean-Jacques Renoliet, *L'Unesco oubliée: la Société des Nations et la coopération intellectuelle, 1919–1946* (Paris: Publications de la Sorbonne, 1999).

[4] "Intellectual Cooperation" was included in the agenda at the meeting of the First Assembly (November 15–December 18, 1920). Henri Bonnet, "La Société des Nations et la Coopération Intellectuelle," *Cahiers d'histoire mondiale* 10, no. 1 (1966), 199. For a debate on the reasons for this omission see Kolasa, *International Intellectual Cooperation*, 18–21.

(1868–1938), substituted later by physicist Robert E. Millikan (1868–1953) from the California Institute of Technology; classical scholar, British politician and chairman of the League of Nations Union Gilbert M. Murray (1866–1957); Swiss historian, Gonzague de Reynold (1880–1970); Italian jurist and minister of public education Francesco Ruffini (1863–1934); and Spanish engineer and mathematician Leonardo Torres y Quevedo (1852–1936).[5] Starting from 1923, and through the late 1930s, "National Committees" were created in different countries with the goal of making "suggestions" to individual governments while respecting their national jurisdiction on cultural matters;[6] in 1926, the International Institute of Intellectual Cooperation opened in Paris;[7] in 1928, the International Educational Cinematographic Institute in Rome followed;[8] and finally, in September 1931, the Intellectual Cooperation Organization was created. After 1945, the latter institution constituted the blueprint for the United Nations Educational Scientific and Cultural Organization (UNESCO).

Many of these organizations deliberately sought to instill emotions and chose mountains as a preferred space for their endeavors. The rationale was that intellectual cooperation had the potential to create a "League of Minds" whose ties would extend from the cultural to the political realm. Through "teaching" and "moral disarmament," intellectuals would win the minds of the peoples of all nations.[9] To this aim, they promoted institutions of learning to facilitate the exchange of objects (such as books, archives, and artifacts) as well as the circulation of people (students and professors). As part of their work, they also supported international open-air schools and vacation colonies (*colonies des vacances*) by endorsing and by collaborating with a wide variety of international groups operating in the mountains (e.g., the League for Open-Air Education) as well as with various youth movements active on the Alps, thus reinforcing the notion that certain landscapes were more suitable for international cooperation than others.

Interestingly, people involved in intellectual cooperation believed that even in the most conducive environment desirable emotions would not develop spontaneously but instead needed to be actively stimulated and carefully managed. As

---

[5] Kolasa, *International Intellectual Cooperation*, 18. On discussions regarding the composition of the committee and on its expansion see Renoliet, *L'Unesco oubliée*, 22–6; 36–8. See also Alvin Leroy Bennett, "The Development of Intellectual Cooperation under the League of Nations and United Nations," Ph.D. dissertation, University of Illinois at Urbana, 1950.

[6] Kolasa, *International Intellectual Cooperation*, 25–30.

[7] Bennett, "The Development of Intellectual Cooperation," 46. The institute remained open until June 1940, when the occupying German authorities forcefully closed it. In 1945 it resumed its activities for a few months before UNESCO formally began its work. See Renoliet, *L'Unesco oubliée*, 44–76.

[8] The International Educational Cinematographic Institute in Rome closed in December 1937, when Italy withdrew from the League of Nations. Its activities were taken over by the International Institute of Intellectual Cooperation in Paris.

[9] Anna-Katharina Wöbse, "'To Cultivate the International Mind': Der Völkerbund und die Förderung der globalen Zivilgesellschaft," *Zeitschrift für Geschichtswissenschaft* 54, no. 10 (2006), 852–64. See also Ken Osborne, "Creating the 'International Mind': The League of Nations Attempts to Reform History Teaching, 1920–1939," *History of Education Quarterly* 56, no. 2 (May 2016), 213–40.

explained at length in this chapter, the International Institute of Intellectual Cooperation in Paris published a set of guidelines in 1933 detailing precise interventions to ensure that participants in international gatherings would feel the "right" things. The project of engendering the emotions of internationalism extended to numerous fields—ranging from leisure, to education, to health—and shaped how the League engaged internationalist ideas and practices. In this context, the alpine landscape provided both a concrete and a metaphorical ground for international exchange and served as a means to further the League's internationalist message.

Emotions represented one of the League's utmost concerns, and also became one of its great challenges. As exemplified by the process of creating its largest artifact, the Palais des Nations in Geneva, the League went out of its way to use pictures and descriptions of the alpine landscape in order to gain "trust" and to "brand" itself as the embodiment of quintessentially "alpine" qualities and emotions.[10] At the same time, wary of triggering fears of one-worldism, the League hesitated to engage in forthright propaganda and to adopt emotionally charged symbols such an international flag. This apprehensiveness toward skeptics and political opponents—and the avoidance of "strong" emotions such as pride in the internationalist enterprise—frustrated supporters, leading many to associate internationalism with weakness. In contrast, many nation-states—those who according to the *Covenant* should have given strength to the international community—increasingly embraced passionate feelings and used them for their own purpose. Most notably, the fascist regime in Italy and the Nazi in Germany used the Alps as their preferred symbol of strength (*Kehlsteinhaus*, Hitler's Eagle's Nest, immediately comes to mind); and across the political spectrum, many came to mock the image of Geneva—with its serene alpine landscape and lake—as a visible expression of the League's aloofness and ineptitude in a world growing more frightful by the day.

2.1 Emotions in Rhetoric

The speeches given during the 1919 Paris Peace Conference and at the League of Nations Assemblies of the early 1920s played an important part in associating internationalism with specific emotions in this period. Carefully prepared, emphatically delivered, and widely reproduced in specialized publications and

---

[10] On internationalism and nation-branding, see Ilaria Scaglia, "Branding Internationalism: Displaying Art and International Cooperation in the Interwar Period," in Carolin Viktorin, Jessica C. E. Gienow-Hecht, Annika Estner, and Marcel K. Will, eds., *Nation Branding in Modern History* (New York: Berghahn Books, 2018), 79–100. On nation-branding, see also Jessica C. E. Gienow-Hecht, "Nation Branding," in Frank Costigliola and Michael J. Hogan eds., *Explaining the History of American Foreign Relations*, 3rd edition (New York, Cambridge University Press, 2016), 232–44.

newspapers, these texts emphasized how the League was aware of the emotional toll imposed by the First World War. Contending that the League had been especially designed as a body capable to ease this toll, internationalists promised to handle conflicts by building an unbreakable bond among nations, turning the international community into a family. Moreover, from a moral standpoint, the League assured that it would act as the custodian of a shared patrimony of emotions that all nations cherished and considered under threat.

As early as January 25, 1919, in an address to the Peace Conference, US President Woodrow Wilson (1856–1924) introduced his project for a League of Nations as a means to lift the emotional burdens imposed by the "Great War."[11] Arguing that "the real strain of the war has come where the eye of government could not reach, but where the heart of humanity beats," he framed conflict as a plague that affected a metaphorical space ("the heart of humanity") imbued with feeling.[12] He spoke of his project as a work of emotional relief, contending that once completed "we shall by that single thing have lifted a great part of the load of anxiety from the hearts of men everywhere."[13] The new postwar order would heal people by bringing them calm and by helping them to mature the right attitude toward each other.

In the following months, Wilson continued to frame the postwar situation as an emotional crisis. In July 1919, while arguing for the ratification of the Versailles Treaty before the US Senate, he referred to the League as "the only hope for mankind." He famously asked: "Dare we reject it and break the heart of the world?," thereby presenting the decision to join the League of Nations as one attuned to what people of other nations felt. He also cast the ratification of the treaty as an act of emotional expression: "The fact that America is the friend of the nations, whether they be rivals or associates, is no new fact; it is only the discovery of it by the rest of the world that is new."[14] Acts such as ratifying the treaty therefore represented not only a meaningful gesture but also an overt expression of "friendship." His words implied that a nation ("America") could feel and could move other nations to reciprocate, and that the League of Nations as a supranational body would later have the power to influence what people felt at this time.

---

[11] J. Michael Hogan, *Woodrow Wilson's Western Tour: Rhetoric, Public Opinion, and the League of Nations* (College Station: Texas A&M University Press, 2006). On Woodrow Wilson and his apparent disconnect with the effects that his rhetoric would have worldwide see Lloyd E. Ambrosius, *Woodrow Wilson and American Internationalism* (New York: Cambridge University Press, 2017). See also Erez Manela, *The Wilsonian Moment: Self-Determination and the International Origins of Anticolonial Nationalism* (Oxford: Oxford University Press, 2007).

[12] On the heart as a site for emotions, see Fay Bound Alberti, *Matters of the Heart: History, Medicine, and Emotion* (Oxford: Oxford University Press, 2010).

[13] Woodrow Wilson, "Address to the Peace Conference in Paris, France, January 25, 1919," http://www.presidency.ucsb.edu/ws/index.php?pid=117770 (accessed on November 29, 2016).

[14] Woodrow Wilson, "Address to the Senate on the Versailles Peace Treaty, July 10, 1919," http://www.presidency.ucsb.edu/ws/index.php?pid=110490 (accessed on March 1, 2018).

The underlining assumption of Wilson's arguments was that nations and international organizations could feel and react just like humans do—a notion that was shared by fascists as well in this period.[15] In his famous "Pueblo speech," the last of many addresses he gave in September 1919 while travelling around the United States trying to muster domestic support for the League, he likened nations to individuals who are subject to "passions" and sometimes need "cooling off." He told the story of "a couple of friends," "who were in the habit of losing their tempers, and when they lost their tempers they were in the habit of using very unparliamentary language." When others convinced them to hold off their swearing until they reached the town limits, their relationship improved; by the time they got there, they no longer wanted to swear, and "they came back convinced that they were just what they were, a couple of unspeakable fools, and the habit of getting angry and of swearing suffered great inroads upon it by that experience." Wilson then explained the moral of the story: "Now, illustrating the great by the small, that is true of the passions of nations. It is true of the passions of men however you combine them. Give them space to cool off."[16] He humanized countries by describing them as people, in fact "friends" capable of experiencing feelings toward themselves and others. Most strikingly, he described the League as a wise companion, adept at imposing a "cooling off" period on unruly nations while bringing them back to reason.

Familialism frequently appeared as a rhetorical device to emphasize how relations among nations were already close and could be further improved. For example, in his welcoming address at the opening of the conference in Paris, French President Raymond Poincaré (1860–1934) commented on how "America, the daughter of Europe, crossed the ocean to wrest her mother from the humiliation of thraldom and to save civilization." The terms "humiliation" and "thraldom" conveyed scorn of subjugation; in turn, references to the filial relationship between "America" and "Europe" put their bond front and center and made it natural and unbreakable, as well as capable of balancing strong emotions like shame. Poincaré argued that the "free people" represented in Paris "want their intimacy of yesterday to assure the peace of tomorrow," trusting that the memory and the lasting quality of a feeling ("intimacy") would unite them. Calling the conference a "grand work in faith and brotherhood," he framed its activities as an intervention in emotional matters, downplaying conflict as part and parcel of an otherwise united family of nations whose bond remained sturdy.[17]

---

[15] On this point, see Alessandro Pes, "Parola di Mussolini: Discorsi propagandistici ed emozioni collettive nell'Italia fascista," in Penelope Morris, Francesco Ricatti, and Mark Seymour, eds., *Politica ed emozioni nella storia d'Italia dal 1848 ad oggi* (Rome: Viella, 2012), 136–41.

[16] Woodrow Wilson, "Address at the City Hall Auditorium in Pueblo, Colorado, September 25, 1919," http://www.presidency.ucsb.edu/ws/index.php?pid=117400 (accessed March 1, 2018).

[17] "Raymond Poincaré's Welcoming Address, 18 January 1919," http://www.firstworldwar.com/source/parispeaceconf_poincare.htm (accessed on February 21, 2017).

One of the most recurring themes was that the success of any treaty ultimately depended on the mutual feelings of those who signed it. In accepting the role of President of the conference, French Prime Minister Georges Clemenceau (1841–1929) insisted that "success is possible only if we remain firmly united." He then reinforced his point by declaring: "We have come here as friends. We must pass through that door as brothers." The term "friends" portrayed all who participated as willing and well disposed. In turn, Clemenceau's aspiration to make their link a familial one exemplifies the centrality of feeling in internationalist rhetoric as well as the assumptions that underlined it. In his speech, Clemenceau implied that through personal commitment and exchange people could turn "friends" into "brothers," making their links a natural and constitutive part of international relations.[18] The fact that Clemenceau did not mention the feelings of those who did not have a seat at the table—most notably, Germany—was a conspicuous omission. The precarious status of colonies that the League would eventually place under Mandates—rather than granting them independence—also made it evident that brotherhood did not extend equally to all people. Yet, Clemenceau's call on individuals to work on their own feelings shifted the conversation to intangible—yet essential—emotional elements that people would value no matter what their nationality.

The idea that the negotiation process could serve as an opportunity to form meaningful emotional bonds among international leaders emerged beyond official speeches. To be sure, as Margaret MacMillan vividly described in *Paris 1919*, the conference took place amidst skepticisms and resentments of all sorts. Differing views on fundamental questions—such as reparations, border disputes, and racial equality—made it hard for delegates to even dine with another, let alone to dabble in the personal relations implied by the term "friendship."[19] That Clemenceau was quick to admit that he was "always a bit afraid" every time he heard Wilson starting a sentence with "my dear friend…" serves as a reminder that emotion words cannot be taken literally.[20] Yet, undeniably, the Paris Conference represented the longest international gathering to date; for months, an international crowd of leaders of unprecedented size and power shared time in the French capital; and the length and hardship of the negotiations create bonds that are hard to dismiss. There was neither irony nor sarcasm when Clemenceau commented "I feel as though I were losing one of the best friends I ever had" as he bid Wilson goodbye.[21] At a time when feelings had emerged as an element of crucial importance, many took emotions seriously.

---

[18] "Georges Clemenceau's Opening Address as Conference President, 18 January 1919," http://www.firstworldwar.com/source/parispeaceconf_clemenceau.htm (accessed on February 21, 2017).

[19] Margaret MacMillan, *Paris 1919: Six Months that Changed the World* (New York: Random House, 2003), 32.

[20] Quoted in MacMillan, *Paris 1919*, 275.   [21] Quoted in MacMillan, *Paris 1919*, 477.

In this period, emotions were often presented as humanity's most precious treasure, as the League's ultimate objective, and also as the main factor that would ultimately determine the outcome of its work. At the opening of the first League of Nations Assembly in Geneva, on November 15, 1920, the President of the Swiss Confederation Giuseppe Motta (1871–1940) recalled how during the war "there have been moments when we asked ourselves if the greatest achievements (*conquêtes supérieures*) of civilization—the law (*loi*) of love, the virtue of piety, the sense of law (*droit*), the links of solidarity, art and beauty—were going to sink and disappear forever in the catastrophe." His words implied that feelings such as "love" or "piety," sentiments of "solidarity," and the emotions that accompanied aesthetic experiences had been the result of a positive evolution of "civilization"; at one point, they had been conquered; war had imperiled them; and now, more than anything else, they needed to be restored. For this reason, he wished that the League would be "a work of solidarity and love." Finally, he gave a blessing meant to reach people of all faiths by quoting the last verse of Dante Alighieri's *Paradiso*: "*L'amor che move il sole e l'altre stelle*" ("Love that moves the sun and other stars"). In doing so, he made a feeling (the "love" from a higher being) the ultimate factor that would determine how events would unfold.[22] From his depiction, the League emerged as a secular custodian of a set of emotions that was widely shared and cherished, and also as a body capable of engendering them in other people.

The League's emotional approach to building peace was also articulated in pragmatic terms. Belgian representative Paul Hymans (1865–1941), who at the League's first Assembly was named the League's President, explained in detail how good feelings and relations could be spun in a concrete setting. He maintained that "our goal is to establish among independent states frequent and amicable contacts, rapprochements that will gush forth (*jailliront*) currents (*courants*) of affinity and sympathy." He used natural metaphors in order to express a notion of internationalism filled with vitality and dynamism: once the proper conditions had been set, feelings would spontaneously "gush forth" in "currents" as water or blood would in the physical world. Hymans postulated the existence of an element of necessity: once people met in a cordial environment, emotions would inevitably happen as a result.[23]

Hymans countered the criticisms by those who looked at his approach with skepticism or cynicism by employing emotions to drive home his point. Recalling the horrors of war, he explained that the League responded to "a need (*besoin*), a sentiment (*sentiment*)…of justice, harmony, and peace." It was therefore the League's emotional value that constituted its most valuable contribution, as it addressed people's needs in terms of feelings. Moreover, by successfully managing emotions, the League would induce a broader "international morality" (*morale*

[22] *Journal de Genève*, November 16, 1920, 1.   [23] *Journal de Genève*, November 16, 1920, 2–3.

internationale) that would determine how peoples and nations would live and behave in the international arena.[24]

Hymans placed great faith in the power of rhetoric to engender emotions, especially during face-to-face international encounters. At the closing of the first Assembly of the League of Nations on December 18, 1920, he marveled at what he perceived to be a great success: if at the beginning people had been "in a sort of inorganic state," by the end of the Assembly they had established meaningful personal relations. The very fact that they had met served as a rebuttal to the skepticism that accompanied all "great works" at the outset. The League's first solemn gathering had galvanized people, and now he encouraged them to persist in their endeavors with a "heart filled with hope and the conscience filled by a sentiment of high duty."[25] The resilience of the League of Nations ultimately rested on the emotional support of individuals. Making people feel that the League of Nations could and would work therefore represented the organization's most important goal, and words, images, and symbols would play an essential role in this context.

2.2 Feelings in Practice

Despite its emphasis on the power of words, it was in concrete settings that the League of Nations devoted most of its efforts at emotional management. The League's work on intellectual cooperation in the field of international open-air schools, camps, and vacation colonies illustrates well the pervasive and tangible ways in which internationalists sought to make others feel the "right" emotions. As they fostered the physical process of internationalization of the mountains, internationalists assessed each step mindful of the effect that it would have on people's feelings. When dealing with the youth in particular, they treated each matter as a work of social and emotional engineering and shaped their activities accordingly.

The significance of the League's engagement with the youth cannot be overstated. As Daniel Laqua pointed out, the fact that this group was still relatively limited made it even more influential, as its members "could fashion themselves as political and intellectual leaders in the making."[26] As a consequence, students increasingly had a bearing on matters of foreign policy and empire.[27] At the same

---

[24] *Journal de Genève*, November 16, 1920, 2–3.

[25] *Journal de Genève*, December 19, 1920, 3–4.

[26] Daniel Laqua, "Activism in the 'Students' League of Nations': International Student Politics and the Confédération Internationale des Étudiants, 1919–1939," *English Historical Review* 132, no. 556 (June 2017), 605–7.

[27] Tamson Pietsch, "Many Rhodes: Travelling Scholarships and Imperial Citizenship in the British Academic World, 1880–1940," *History of Education* 40, no. 6 (2011), 723–39, and *Empire of Scholars: Universities, Networks and the British Academic World, 1850–1939* (New York: Manchester University

time, they traveled more than ever, fueling—and fueled by—assumptions and feelings about the inherent virtue of international exchanges, and contributing to the formation of what Daniel Gorman identified as a new "international society."[28] As a growing social entity, they had the power to affect large portions of the population.

Central to the emergence of the youth as a social and a political force was its growing attachment to nature. From the German *Wandervogel* (literally, "wandering birds" longing for nature and freedom) and *Bündische Jugend* ("associated youth"), to scouting groups sprouting up virtually everywhere in the 1920s and 1930s, young people increasingly engaged with the natural environment and used it as a means to express and realize larger aspirations.[29] Their ideas circulated widely and had a deep influence on a broad range of questions, from religion, to pedagogy, to gender and sexuality, to ability and disability. Figures such as Gustav Wyneken (1875–1964) and Adolf Brand (1874–1945)—the initiator of the *Gemeinschaft der Eigenen* (literally, the "community of uniques") celebrating ancient Greek-style *paideia*, homosexuality, and nature, while also "outing" political opponents—laid the foundation for activism across the political spectrum. The vitality of these movements was promptly exploited by nationalist regimes seeking to shape the "New Man";[30] at the same time, it was also incorporated by groups committed to crafting "good citizens."[31] Every societal and political project in this period traversed the intersection of youth and nature.

Well aware of this fact, the League publicized—and sometimes even supported—numerous international organizations that connected nature—and mountains especially—with international cooperation and the emotions associated with it. The 1936 League's *Handbook of International Organizations* (*Repertoire des organizations internationales*) listed the Boy Scouts (founded in London, in 1920), the International Ski Association (Chamonix, 1924), the International Committee of Open-Air Schools and Preventoria (Paris, 1928), the World Association of Girl Guides and Girl Scouts (London, 1928), the International Office for the Protection of Nature (Brussels, 1928), and the International Federation of Camping Clubs

Press, 2013). See also Paul A. Kramer, "Is the World Our Campus? International Students and U.S. Global Power in the Long Twentieth Century," *Diplomatic History* 33, no. 5 (November 2009), 775–806.

[28] Daniel Gorman, *The Emergence of International Society in the 1920s* (New York: Cambridge University Press, 2012).
[29] Walter Laqueur, *Young Germany: A History of the German Youth Movement* (London: Transaction Books, 1984). On different notions of *"Bund"* as a unifying element, see Robbert-Jan Adriaansen, *The Rhythm of Eternity: The German Youth Movement and the Experience of the Past, 1900–1933* (New York: Berghahn Books, 2015), 128.
[30] Alessio Ponzio, *Shaping the New Man: Youth Training Regimes in Fascist Italy and Nazi Germany* (Madison: University of Wisconsin Press, 2015).
[31] Siân Edwards, *Youth Movements, Citizenship and the English Countryside: Creating Good Citizens, 1930–1960* (Cham: Palgrave Macmillan, 2018).

(London, 1932).[32] As a result, the links that tied mountains to internationalism grew stronger in the 1920s and 1930s and led to an increasing number of people from various countries travelling to the mountains to entertain and edify themselves as well as to heal their body, the environment, and the international system as a whole.

Along similar lines, the League soon became involved in youth and international education. In the 1920s, it sponsored a full report entitled *Instruction of Children and Youth in the Existence and Aims of the League of Nations*, which was submitted to the sixth Assembly in 1925 and was later followed by several supplements and recommendations.[33] The report described "encouraging contact between the younger generations of different nationalities," particularly through international travel, as a matter of great importance. In an annex, a long list of countries followed by the measures they had taken (ranging from tariff reductions to collective passports for youth groups) suggested that the program had already proved successful at creating new relationships among young people from various nations.[34]

A section on school textbook and curricula reforms made it clear that emotions should become a subject of learning in themselves. A draft syllabus—presented in multiple formats to meet the needs of various school levels—listed "friendly agreement" and "a spirit of cooperation and solidarity" as the answers to the question "How is it hoped to guarantee Peace?."[35] Individual countries even committed to the teaching of specific feelings: Czechoslovakia, for instance, in 1922 introduced a class on "Civic Instruction and Education," which included a section on "Humanity." Among the subjects treated (and explicitly related to the League of Nations and to the international relations it coordinated) were "fraternity" and "amity between nations."[36]

Major "non-official organizations," as the aforementioned report called them, expanded the League's efforts well beyond its institutional boundaries. Despite the fact that the United States did not belong to the League, the American School Citizenship League had followed Geneva's lead by organizing an essay-context on the promotion of "world friendship and world solidarity" and also by facilitating international correspondence among American pupils and children from other countries. The scout movement had also become involved. Since "a Scout is a friend to all and a brother to every other Scout," the Boy Scouts International Bureau had strengthened its commitment to international relationships by

---

[32] *Répertoire des organizations internationales* (Genève: Série des publications de la Société des Nations, XII, 1936).

[33] *Instruction of Children and Youth in the Existence and Aims of the League of Nations*. Report submitted by the Secretariat to the sixth Assembly. League of Nations publications, A.10.1925.XII.

[34] *Instruction of Children and Youth*, Annex part II, 26–33.

[35] *Instruction of Children and Youth*, Annex part I, 10–11.

[36] *Instruction of Children and Youth*, Annex part I, 15.

organizing correspondences and exchanges among members from various nations. The report detailed that in 1923 more than 3000 British scouts had visited other countries; in 1924 the same number had been maintained while numerous parties from other countries had visited Great Britain. In addition, international "jamborees" and conferences had been organized to bring about international amity and cooperation.[37]

Women's groups were on board too, as were some of the largest professional and religious organizations active in this period. The International Council of the Girl Guides Association and the International Council of Women organized events to which they invited members from all over the world, convinced that "a first-hand knowledge of, and an insight into, the life and outlook of other nations is of vital importance in the interests of the peace of the world." The International Federation of League of Nations Unions, the International Federation of Secondary School Teachers, and the International Moral Education Congress all promised the full weight and support of their well-established organizations. Religious groups such as the International Secretariat of the Catholic Youth, the Universal Union of Jewish Youth, and the YMCA also participated in efforts to teach and inspire feelings conducive to peace.[38]

The rationale by which internationalists thought these initiatives could be effective in instilling emotions was based on two main assumptions. The first was that feelings could be propagated by talking about them. As articulated effectively by Polish activist, neurologist, and psychiatrist Witold Chodźko (1875–1954) in a speech delivered in 1928 at the 6th Commission of the League, international schools exchanges would play a pivotal role in promoting the goal of fostering peace among nations as they represented a means for a "propaganda of rapprochement." In presenting the work of a Polish association (the Universal Organization of the Exchange of School Children during the summer break), Chodźko contended that ignorance of the other was the enemy. Programs like these openly discussed emotional practices such as rapprochement and were essential to further mutual knowledge and, more broadly, a "spirit of peace."[39]

As explained in a memorandum about this organization preserved in the same file, the second assumption was that moments of international encounter would elicit a "sentiment of tolerance and solidarity" because students would be given ample time to develop friendships.[40] Similar ideas were expressed in a report by the League of Nations dealing with school exchanges, which also

---

[37] *Instruction of Children and Youth,* Annex part III, 33–5.
[38] *Instruction of Children and Youth,* Annex part III, 34–44.
[39] League of Nations Archives, R 2273, 5C/12600/12600, Discours fait par M.W. Chodzko le 13.9.1928 dans la sixième commission de la Société des Nations.
[40] League of Nations Archives, R 2273, 5C/12600/12600, Memorandum dated May 23, 1929.

stressed the "spirit of camaraderie" that these initiatives could nourish.[41] In the minds of the proponents of such programs, negative emotions represented one of the greatest challenges to peace and security. Feeling international cooperation thus went hand in hand with implementing it and represented the core of the internationalist project.

Open-air schools were deemed especially suited for the purpose of triggering amicable feelings among youth of different nations. In fact, the movement for open-air schools itself was international and outwardly internationalist. It deepened its roots in the Enlightenment, and particularly in the writings of Jean-Jacques Rousseau (1712–78). In *Émile* (1762), the French philosopher had made engagement with the world the cornerstone of education and he had also emphasized the centrality of sentiments such as friendship.[42] A large number of thinkers followed: most notably, Swiss educational pedagogue John Heinrich Pestalozzi (1746–1827), whose book *Wie Gertrud ihre Kinder lehrt* (*How Gertrude Teaches Her Children*) published in 1801, and the educational institute he opened in Yverdon in 1804 garnered international attention; and Friedrich Fröbel (1782–1852) whose work on early childhood education—embodied by the "kindergarten"—stressed the importance of outdoor holistic education.[43]

By the 1920s and 1930s, a revolution in the field of education was emerging, with figures such as Jane Addams (1860–1935) arguing for the need to expand access to education to all social classes; John Dewey (1859–1952) emphasizing experiential learning; and Maria Montessori (1870–1952), centering on children actively interacting with their environment.[44] Theories elaborated in this period proved very influential across multiple disciplines: their impact can be seen in the "ecological theory" developed by Urie Bronfenbrenner (1917–2005), in the work by Carl Rogers (1902–87) on self-actualization and self-esteem, in the notions of "flow" and "happiness" by Mihaly Csikszentmihalyi (b. 1934), or in the reading of emotional expressions in order to measure "well being and involvement" by Ferre Laevers (b. 1950), to name just a few. Moreover, starting from 1907, a series of international congresses on school hygiene (which also dealt with outdoor education) facilitated the exchange and dissemination of these ideas and practices across borders.[45]

---

[41] League of Nations Archives, R 2273, 5C/20615/12600, Rapport sur l'échange de la jeunesse des écoles secondaires (C.E.66).

[42] Michel Soëtard, *Méthode et philosophie: la descendance éducative de l'Émile* (Paris: L'Harmattan, 2012).

[43] On the development of the "Pestalozzi cult" see Daniel Tröhler, *Pestalozzi and the Educationalization of the World* (New York: Palgrave Macmillan, 2013).

[44] On the dissemination of Montessori's ideas, see Gerald L. Gutek and Patricia A. Gutek, *Bringing Montessori to America: S. S. McClure, Maria Montessori, and the Campaign to Publicize Montessori Education* (Tuscaloosa: The University of Alabama Press, 2016).

[45] Anne-Marie Châtelet, Dominique Lerch, and Jean-Noël Luc, eds., *L'école de plein air. Une expérience pédagogique et architecturale dans l'Europe du XXe siècle* (Paris: Éditions Recherches, 2003), 337–9. See also Anne-Marie Châtelet, *Le souffle du plein air* (Geneva: MétisPress, 2011).

Though deeply embedded in this tradition and trajectory, the 1920s and the 1930s represented a unique moment in which this movement turned from "cosmopolitan" ("worldly," from an academic and a cultural standpoint) to "internationalist" (explicitly aligned with the political goal of maintaining peace). For instance, it was at this time that Maria Montessori became directly involved in the International Montessori Association and in the peace movement.[46] And it was then that the movement for open-air schools presented itself in international— and internationalist—terms. After the first *Waldschulen* (literally, "forest schools") opened in Germany at the beginning of the twentieth century, open-air schools had appeared in virtually every European country.[47] In 1922, the first International Congress on open-air schools was held in Paris; a second one took place in Brussels in 1931; and a third in Bielefeld in 1936, each defining the open-air school movement as an international phenomenon characterized by standardization and exchanges among experts in different countries.[48]

To be sure, as Anne-Marie Châtelet pointed out, fascist regimes appropriated open-air education in the 1930s. And the Bielefeld Congress, which took place a week prior to the 1936 Summer Olympics in Berlin, served as the opportunity to expose all attendees to the propaganda celebrating a "New Germany." Yet, "at no point were the institutions or the ideas of the Nazi Party ever mentioned," and internationalist rhetoric seemed to offer a counterpoint to ongoing political discourses.[49] If on one hand the choice of Rome as the site for the following congress cannot be downplayed as a sign that nationalist sympathies had come to weigh heavily in the group's decisions, on the other it would be simplistic to construe the International Congress—or the international open-air school movement it represented—as fascism in disguise.

In an age when visual culture and performances played an increasingly important role, overtly communicated messages cannot be discounted. Indeed, as early as 1931, the committee in charge of these congresses sought patronage from the Health organization of the League of Nations.[50] In the same year, it also adopted a resolution to provide a "precious contribution to universal brotherhood through the rapprochement and the collaboration among educators."[51] Similar wording also appeared in the general introduction of the proceedings of the Second

[46]   Nick Lewer, *Physicians and the Peace Movement* (London: Frank Cass, 1992), 58–60.

[47]   Châtelet, *Le souffle du plein air*, 19–70.

[48]   Châtelet pointed out that the 1922 Congress was mostly a French endeavor, as only Belgium, Luxembourg, the Netherlands and Poland sent delegates. The second congress instead was much more inclusive. More than twice as many participants attended, and all major countries were represented. Châtelet, *Le souffle du plein air*, 105–6; 156–60.

[49]   Châtelet, *Le souffle du plein air*, 275–80.

[50]   See letter, dated April 11, 1931, from A. Mola and G. Lemonier to Dr. Rajchman, Head of the Health Section of the League of Nations, published in *Second congrès international des écoles de plein air, Bruxelles, 6–11 avril 1931: rapports et comptes rendus* (Brussels: Librairie Castaigne, 1931), 17–18.

[51]   See resolution n. 6, *Second congrès international des écoles de plein air*, 11–12.

Congress, as a comment on the unanimous decision of holding the subsequent gathering in Germany.[52]

Language about "international cooperation" made it into speeches and proceedings, confirming that the health and education of children were realms in which all people could peacefully cooperate and often agree. Similarly, in 1929, the first international congress of vacation colonies and open-air activities took place in Pau, on the French Pyrenees; a second meeting in Geneva followed in 1931, and a third one in Paris in 1937. The publications related to these events touted their international—and internationalist—aspects. The report of the 1929 Conference in Pau (a bound volume of 216 pages) was largely a collection of speeches celebrating the connection between health, education, and peace. Much emphasis was placed on the fact that experts from different countries had met in person to discuss their work and patients from all nationalities had been able to interact in a peaceful setting. The report of the 1937 Conference in Paris, an even more comprehensive review whose size (339 pages) reflected the growing success of the organization, also devoted much attention to the internationalist purpose of these initiatives and stressed the good feelings among experts from various countries that had been engendered there.[53]

In turn, the League of Nations gave strength and legitimacy to these attempts at building emotional bonds across borders. As early as March 1922, F. Marié-Davy of the League for Open-Air Education wrote to the General Secretary of the League of Nations asking for patronage for an International Congress on Open-Air Schools to be held in Paris later that year. This request was denied because the "question of open-air education is not yet … in the realm of activity of the League of Nations."[54] Yet, despite this lukewarm start, in 1931 the League served as official patron and sent a delegate to the international congress that was held in Geneva.[55] And, in 1937, the Committee on Intellectual Cooperation, the International Labor Office, and the League's General Secretary agreed to act as patrons, an honor displayed prominently in the Congress' program under the sub-heading "Committee of International Patronage."[56] The League at once nurtured and was nurtured by these organizations. It legitimized and was also legitimized by them, effectively including them in an internationalist movement with itself at the center.

---

[52] See "Introduction" by Dr. René Sand, in *Second congrès international des écoles de plein air*, 17–18.

[53] Copies of these reports are available at the League of Nations Archives, Box R 3094, (1929–1931), folder 11C/27516/9518.

[54] League of Nations Archives, Box R 1011, 13/19803/19803: Organization d'un Congrès international des écoles de plein air. Letter, dated March 29, 1922, from F. Marié-Davy (Ligue pour l'éducation en plein air) to the Secretary General, asking for patronage for an international congress that will take place in Paris (June 24–9, 1922). See also in the same folder: letter, dated April 17, 1922, from Secretary General to President of the Ligue pour l'éducation en plein air.

[55] League of Nations Archives, R 6141, 8A/21741/21741, letter dated January 19, 1937 from Dr. Dequidt to Secretary General Avenol.

[56] This is true for both editions of the official program, which can be found in League of Nations Archives R 6141, 8A/21741/21741.

Emotions occupied a central place in determining these associations' vision and work. At the aforementioned 1929 conference in Pau, Joel Gradel articulated the value of emotional factors and spoke of eliciting desirable emotions as a realist and feasible goal.[57] Not only would young participants observe directly the customs of others but they would also have the unique opportunity to strengthen their feelings of fraternity toward fellow human beings. According to Gradel, "while it is difficult to love someone who has never been seen, it is much easier and fruitful (*fécond*) to love the fellow man (*le prochain*) whom one sees, touches, and with whom he can communicate sorrows and joys." "Love" was therefore aspired to and believed to be a reachable goal, one that could be attained through specific sensorial experiences. Strengthened by its physicality, this emotional approach would yield to a new kind of authentic, concrete, effective, and long-lasting internationalism.[58] The achievement of this emotional outcome thus represented a central objective for these programs and, as such, attracted much attention from proponents.

And much attention it needed, since many believed that these programs had to be carefully managed if they were to be successful from an emotional point of view.[59] In an essay entitled "*Le rôle éducatif des colonies des vacances*" (The Educational Role of Vacation Colonies), Jacques Guerin-Desjardins argued that "four dangers" menaced the international effort on open-air schools: "bad methods," "commercialization," the "penetration of politics," and "the ineptitude of leaders." Nefarious interests and negative emotions could all too easily take over, and only through wisely-staged international cooperation could these perils be averted.[60] Moreover, the "right" emotions would not develop spontaneously, and much energy had to be devoted to monitoring and, when needed, to molding the feelings produced by bringing together people from different nations.

The strongest model for the systematic management of emotions came from the International Institute of Intellectual Cooperation in Paris. In 1933, the Institute published a dossier entitled *L'entente des peuples par la jeunesse* (The Entente among Peoples by the Youth), which made explicit the principles behind its support for international exchanges among students.[61] It also provided a survey of existing initiatives, as well as a vision for the Institute—and the

---

[57] M. Gradel, "Les Colonies d'Echange Internationales." League of Nations Archives, Box R 3094, folder 11C/9518/9518.

[58] Gradel, "Les Colonies d'Echange Internationales," 7–8.

[59] League of Nations Archives, R 2273, 5C/20615/12600, Rapport sur l'échange de la jeunesse des écoles secondaires (C.E.66).

[60] M. J. Guerin-Desjardins, "Le rôle éducatif des colonies des vacances," in *Compte Rendu et Rapports* of the 1937 Conference in Paris, 23–34. A copy is at the League of Nations Archives, Box R 6141, folder 8A/27463/21741.

[61] *L'entente des peuples par la jeunesse: études sur les voyages et les échanges scolaires internationaux* (collection des dossiers de la coopération intellectuelle). Société des Nations, Institut International de Coopération Intellectuelle, 1933. One copy is available at the UNOG library in Geneva, Switzerland, UNOG 004 I61d.

League's—larger role in coordinating them in the future. The report clearly stated that the goal of these exchanges was to "develop sentiments of benevolence." According to the study, each country the students visited would retain a special place "in their heart." For this reason, the League of Nations was eager to back opportunities for international exchange and also to generate new ones.[62]

The dossier was conceived as a substantial step in that direction, as it surveyed existing programs with particular attention to their emotional aspects. First was the careful assessment of existing initiatives, taking care in evaluating their success in instilling the proper feelings among participants. According to this report, as of 1933 there were already numerous forms of international exchange in place, which included individual exchanges among families, collective exchanges among groups, international colonies and camps, group travels and excursions, and open-air schools. All of these, in one way or another, facilitated international cooperation and mutual understanding by nurturing the core sentiments that would make them possible. Each child taking part in individual exchanges would spend weeks with another family, chosen with the utmost care, where he would be treated "like a son." Collective exchanges took different forms: sometimes, two schools would agree to host each other's students while also sharing books and other resources; in other cases, international camps would be set up with equal percentages of foreign and domestic students. From an emotional standpoint, either model had proven successful. International colonies were also set up for pupils from various countries to practice foreign languages "in an atmosphere of good camaraderie" for a period from four to six weeks. In this case, too, what participants *felt* seem to constitute both the main concern and the proudest achievement.[63]

These successes, the report emphasized, rested upon the careful management of emotions. Accommodations, courses, and excursions had been specifically designed "to foster in the students a camaraderie that leads to live in common without distinction of nationality." The goal was not only for pupils to study foreign languages and to strengthen their bodies with open-air activities but also to "incline their spirits in the way of peace among peoples." Numerous challenges hindered the desired emotional outcomes. In setting up individual exchanges, it was sometimes difficult to find an equal number of families ready to receive students on both sides. Standards of morality and comfort were at times hard to meet, and not every student was ready to cherish this experience. In group-travel, too, all sorts of problems could arise. Moreover, the international spirit raised during these programs might quickly dissipate upon returning home. Organizers should therefore work intensely to overcome these obstacles. Also, families ought to collaborate with them and ensure that the links created during these

---

[62] *L'entente des peuples par la jeunesse*, 11–18.   [63] *L'entente des peuples par la jeunesse*, 11–18.

international experiences continue for years to come. With adequate intervention, all of these initiatives had the potential to "prepare the terrain for more lasting forms of international relations."[64]

Because "nothing can be left to chance" when making moral, intellectual, and material arrangements, the dossier dedicated a specific section on the ideal method to be followed. Without it, people would "turn their critiques toward the hosting countries," thus obtaining a less than desirable outcome. Preparations ideally would start long before departure by having students exchanging letters with the peers they would eventually meet. These preliminary contacts would "form among them links of amicable sympathy" and ensure that their "spirit" would be "disposed to understand" foreign life and civilization. Also, organizers would explain any custom that might be different in order to reduce the chances of a negative experience. Studying their destinations' history and geography in advance would also help to whet their appetite, thereby enhancing their experience.[65]

Contemporary concerns about potential resentments deriving from class differences made their way into this report. Like many of their US counterparts (e.g., corporate foundations) active in the same field in this period, the people responsible for setting up these programs "detached peace from justice" and did not question "vertical political-economic and racial-colonial ordering."[66] They often advocated for progressive and inclusive policies to mitigate class differences and often took a pragmatic approach to avoid the conflicts that they believed would have inevitably arisen unless they intervened. When organizing collective programs, students had to be selected sensibly and groups had to be formed carefully. The minimum age should be fourteen, as younger pupils would not be prepared. It was recommended that different ages and social classes be mixed. Otherwise, a "spirit of caste" could form and lead to antagonisms. The group-size should not be too large, twenty-five people at most. When organizing international encounters, it was better to have only two nationalities meeting at one time. Participants should also be matched in terms of age and social condition (although each group, the dossier reiterated, should be mixed in this respect). Camp leaders played a crucial role in designing and monitoring activities and in making sure that every moment of the day would serve the higher purpose of nurturing "international friendship"—an emotion which in their mind served as a remedy for social ills and as an antidote against revolution.[67]

In times of recreation and especially while playing sports, anger and resentment would be prevented from the start. In contrast to the contemporary Olympic movement, which presented competition among nations a means to obtaining

[64] *L'entente des peuples par la jeunesse*, 19–21; 31; 34–5.
[65] *L'entente des peuples par la jeunesse*, 37–9.
[66] Paul A. Kramer, "Embedding Capital: Political-Economic History, the United States, and the World," *The Journal of the Gilded Age and Progressive Era* 15, no. 3 (July 2016), 350–1.
[67] *L'entente des peuples par la jeunesse*, 37–47.

peace, the report recommended avoiding one team comprised of one nationality playing against one comprised of another. The leaders should also encourage political discussions and allow each side to present its view in an atmosphere of "perfect courtesy." Such moments, however, ought to be somewhat subdued, as political engagement should not be the defining character of these initiatives.[68]

In general, the proponents of these programs advocated for somber choices and lifestyles. The persistent economic crisis had placed much strain on many people, and reducing cost was therefore of paramount importance not only from a financial but also from an emotional point of view. The report recommended that organizers encourage students to save money, instilling at once solidarity and virtue in frugality. When organizing travel, they should look for reductions (the dossier itself included an appendix detailing cost-saving opportunities available to help them in this endeavor). When looking for accommodations, they should consider using schools—especially for stays taking place during the summer. Youth hostels—already quite common in Germany—provided a viable alternative, with the added benefit of giving students the opportunities to meet factory, office, and rural workers. This experience, too, could open their horizons, thus fostering the larger goals of these programs.[69] More broadly, thriftiness and measure would facilitate the achievement of the desired emotional outcomes.

Despite this detailed set of rules and regulations, the report made it clear that the League of Nations did not seek to control or take responsibility for all initiatives of international exchange. On the contrary, it opposed the idea of one central agency. Instead, the League offered "material and moral coordination" to existing programs, whether by encouraging or by documenting their efforts. For this purpose, the dossier provided individual reports by country, including Germany, Austria, Denmark, Spain, the United States, Finland, France, Great Britain, Hungary, Italy, Norway, The Netherlands, and Sweden. A separate entry detailed programs endeavored by the "Northern Countries" of Denmark, Finland, Norway, and Sweden. Finally, the full text of a declaration by the Comité d'entente des grandes associations internationales and a bibliography was included for reference.[70] The message was that the League was there to facilitate national initiatives; in turn, participants from various nations would reinforce the League's overarching rhetoric and do their part to achieve its goals.

Emotions lay at the core of this plan. Like a wise camp-leader (or "scout-master"), the League of Nations would manage the feelings of all participant-nations as they interacted with one another in a controlled environment. In this vision, the international arena would resemble a well-run summer colony, one constructed as benign, safe, and accommodating like the mountain landscape that surrounded it. A carefully designed structure and a clear set of rules would prevent most

[68] *L'entente des peuples par la jeunesse*, 37–47.   [69] *L'entente des peuples par la jeunesse*, 51–5.
[70] *L'entente des peuples par la jeunesse*, 58; 61.

problems. Direct interventions, if at all needed, would be benevolent and always mindful of how they would be perceived, since what nations felt—more than any other factor—would determine their behavior.

2.3 Images, Symbols, and Emotional (Mis)management

"Trust," "reputation," and other people's feelings represented a major concern for the League as they did for other organizations in this period. If, as Ute Frevert pointed out, the rise of the modern state led to the creation of institutions (like the legal system, for instance) which were able to kindle emotions such as "trust," and if this trust had a moral value (allowing the people who held it to present themselves as "honest, sincere, and trustworthy"), a similar process took place within the international system.[71] With the rise of a plethora of international organizations—ranging from international courts to field-specific international bodies—in the nineteenth century, individuals became entrusted with furthering internationalist ideas and practices; in turn, internationalist people and institutions gained the trust of an ever-growing crowd in the process of turning from "strangers" to fellow world citizens.[72]

To be sure, as Geoffrey Hosking noted, internationalism chronically suffered from lack of trust; yet, moments of "crisis" should not overshadow the importance of internationalist institutional and symbolic systems built in the twentieth century that continue to be relevant in the twenty-first.[73] Furthermore, for internationalists, trust represented a vital element, a defining character, and a driving principle for their choices. If in fascist movements "boundless trust" among members was accompanied by "deep mistrust" for those who would or could not join, and if for communist regimes "confidence" in common ideals entailed "mistrust" and the monitoring of individuals within society, trust played a central role for internationalism as well.[74]

The League of Nations took concrete steps to build trust in internationalist ideas, practices, and institutions by prioritizing various forms of "moral disarmament,"[75] whose goal, in the words of Kaarle Nordenstreng and Tarja

---

[71] Ute Frevert, *The Moral Economy of Trust: Modern Trajectories* (London: German Historical Institute, 2014), 33–5. The literature on trust is extensive. A useful overview of various theorizations of trust and a lucid analysis on how these can inform historical inquiry can be found in Geoffrey Hosking, *Trust: A History* (Oxford: Oxford University Press, 2014), 22–49.

[72] Frevert, *The Moral Economy of Trust*, 28–34.   [73] Hosking, *Trust*, 171–94.

[74] Frevert, *The Moral Economy of Trust*, 25–6.

[75] On moral disarmament, see Heidi J. S. Tworek, "Peace through Truth? The Press and Moral Disarmament through the League of Nations," *Medien & Zeit* 25, no. 4 (2010), 16–28. On the League's programs to ensure that education would foster moral disarmament see also Renoliet, *L'Unesco oubliée*. On "moral disarmament" outside of the League of Nations, see Mona L. Siegel, *The Moral Disarmament of France: Education, Pacifism, and Patriotism, 1914–1940* (Cambridge: Cambridge University Press, 2011); Gearóid Barry, *The Disarmament of Hatred: Marc Sangnier, French Catholicism and the Legacy of the First World War, 1914–45* (Basingstoke: Palgrave Macmillan, 2012).

Seppä, "was not merely to disarm men's minds but to transform them with a view to establishing a firm psychological basis for the future development of the international community."[76] The League also devoted much energy to crafting its public image. Since it highly valued public opinion and deemed it crucial to manage carefully the messages disseminated to broader audiences, the League created a specific "information" section to advertise itself; and, as part of this effort, it published pamphlets reminding the media of their responsibilities.[77] It also took substantial steps to handle its relationship with the press, most notably by gathering foreign journalists and by holding specialized conferences of experts.[78] Moreover, the League set up a network of informal bureaux in London, Paris, Tokyo, Bombay, New Delhi, Rome, and Berlin to gather news for the Secretariat by collecting clippings and by monitoring radio coverage of international events.[79]

In practice, the League tried to combat "hatred" by controlling fake and/or inflammatory news about its work and by preventing propaganda wars among nations—this ran parallel to initiatives ranging from educational programs to the revisions of school textbooks that were organized by branches dealing with intellectual cooperation. Furthermore, the "information" section of the League encouraged the use of "modern means," including cinematography and radio, to disseminate internationalist messages. Most notably, in 1936 it sponsored the "International Convention on the Use of Broadcasting in the Cause of Peace," which provided a framework to do so. The League's battle against "hate" and "mistrust" revolved around emotions, since popular trust and sentiment were ultimately at stake.

Against this backdrop, it is significant that the League placed much emphasis on the fact that its main site, Geneva, was surrounded by the Alps. Such a connection was neither obvious nor easy. Viewed from afar, Geneva appears as a city on a lake. Its contours blend with the sky-blue, half-moon shaped waters of Lake Geneva and are framed by the round green heights of the Jura. From the center,

[76] Kaarle Nordenstreng and Tarja Seppä, "The League of Nations and the Mass Media," in Kaarle Nordenstreng, Ulf Jonas Björk, Frank Beyersdorf, Svennik Høyer, and Epp Lauk, eds., *A History of the International Movement of Journalists: Professionalism versus Politics* (Basingstoke: Palgrave Macmillan, 2016), 13.

[77] See for instance Thomas Cox Meech, Esq., *The Press and the League of Nations* (London: C. F. Roworth, undated).

[78] This section changed name: it was called "Public Information" (1919–27), "Information" (1928–32), and then again "Public Information" (1933–46). On the League of Nations' relationship with the press, see Tworek, "Peace through Truth?," 16–28. See also Conference for the Reduction and Limitation of Armaments, *Co-operation of the Press in the Organisation of Peace* (Geneva: League of Nations, 1932); International Institute of Intellectual Co-operation, *Le rôle intellectuel de la presse* (Paris: Société des Nations, Institut international de coopération intellectuelle, 1933).

[79] See also Kaarle Nordenstreng and Tarja Seppä, "The League of Nations and the Mass Media: A Forgotten Story," XV Conference of the International Association for Mass Communication Research (IAMCR/AIERI), Section of International Communication session on "Communication and Peace; The Role of the Media in International Relations," New Delhi, 27 August 1986. http://www.uta.fi/cmt/en/contact/staff/kaarlenordenstreng/publications/The_League_of_Nations_and_the_Mass_Media.pdf_1 (accessed on February 23, 2017).

the Alps are present merely in the city's toponymy, and it is only on a clear day that the Mont Blanc emerges from a distance.[80] Nonetheless, the League of Nations often connected its internationalist ideas and practices with the city's "alpine" aesthetics. The League's publicity argued that Geneva's mountain landscape would instill in people involved in international cooperation the emotions (e.g., calm, composure, and steadfastness in tackling difficult problems) necessary to make decisions on important matters. In turn, the alpine landscape symbolized the League's strength and commitment to the internationalist cause.

This argument built upon contemporary internationalist rhetoric, which often contained metaphors connecting emotions with nature. For example, Woodrow Wilson concluded his last speech by promising that internationalism "is going to lead us, and through us the world, out into pastures of quietness and peace such as the world never dreamed of before."[81] Along similar lines, Paul Hymans at the first League Assembly praised Swiss nature, its "haughty peaks" (*cime altières*), valleys, clear lakes, that are like eternal images of beauty, greatness, grandeur, and peace."[82] Such references were not coincidental; instead, they belonged to a widely shared set of associations that connected nature—and mountains—with the emotions deemed conducive to internationalism. "Pastures" evoked spiritual nourishment, cleanliness, and tranquility; and, as explained in the first chapter of this book, the Alps embodied a wide constellation of emotions ranging from resilience in the face of uncertainty to purity in opposition to the corrupting influences of the modern world. The League of Nations drew heavily upon these associations and used them to promote itself and its work.

The deeper implications and consequences of this choice become apparent when looking at the process of making Geneva the League's main site. The selection of the city itself had been the result of a heated debate, particularly since Switzerland was not a founding member of the League and other "peace cities" (e.g., Brussels, The Hague, Constantinople) had been put forth as preferable options.[83] Perhaps because of this rough start, the Alps provided a useful endorsement of the League's final choice. Soon after the League moved there, the argument emerged that the alpine landscape would engender the emotional

---

[80] According to the *Dictionnaire des rues de Genève*, the list of streets and bridges named after mountains include Rue et place des Alpes, Rue du Beulet, Avenue de la Croisette, Rue de la Dôle, Rue et sentier des Falaises, Rue de la Faucille, Rue du Grütli, Avenue Joli-Mont, Rue du Jura, Rue du Môle, Rue du Moléson, Rue pont et quai du Mont-Blanc, Rue du Mont-de-Sion, Rue du Petit Salève, Rue des Pitons, Chemin des Pléiades, Rue du Reculet, Rue du Simplon, and Rue du Vuache. *Dictionnaire des rues de Genève* edited by Jean-Paul Galland with d'Armande Berger, 3rd edition (Geneva: Promoédition, 1988). I thank the librarians of La Bibliothèque de Genève and the *Interroge* service in Geneva for preparing this list for me.

[81] Woodrow Wilson, "Address at the City Hall Auditorium in Pueblo, Colorado," September 25, 1919 http://www.presidency.ucsb.edu/ws/index.php?pid=117400 (accessed on March 1, 2018).

[82] *Journal de Genève*, November 16, 1920, 2.

[83] Glenda Sluga, *Internationalism in the Age of Nationalism* (Philadelphia: University of Pennsylvania Press, 2013), 57.

qualities needed in order to deliberate wisely on weighty issues. A first mention of this line of reasoning can be traced back to 1920, when the League of Nations moved its headquarters from London to the Hotel National (renamed Palais Wilson in 1924) on Lake Geneva.[84] An early pamphlet accented how the site of the League Secretariat sat on the *quai du Mont Blanc*—Geneva's fashionable lakeside promenade—and was surrounded by the Jura.[85] The aesthetic experience of this landscape, with its peaceful lake and mountains all around, would inspire feelings and actions of mutual understanding and peace. In this place where "noble and representative sentiments come free," peace would thus be easier to build.[86]

A different—yet, related—argument was put forth in the late 1920s, when plans for the construction of a new and permanent site for the League of Nations headquarters began and the mountains' strength and nobility were evoked to reinforce the institution's credibility. In 1927, a major competition was launched to display the League's willingness to conduct an open and inclusive process for all of its endeavors. Hundreds of projects were submitted by architects from around the world. Strikingly, many included a prominent view of the mountains and incorporated them as an integral part of the architectural plan.[87]

In some cases, the size and shape of the mountains were exaggerated, subordinating the palace and the institution it hosted to the surrounding landscape (see Figures 2.1 and 2.2).[88] The boldest submission, #345 by Joseph Rings from Essen, Germany, even contemplated a building in the middle of the lake with mountains all around it (see Figure 2.3). A caption explained that a "white mountain giant" would protect the building shining in the calm lake, associating the Alps with the "sublime."[89]

---

[84] For the location on the first period in London, then in Geneva, see Jean-Claude Pallas, *Histoire et architecture du Palais des Nations (1924–2001): l'art déco au service des relations internationales* (Geneva: Nations Unies, 2001), 16–19. Pallas also mentions a 1920 proposal by architect Jean-Jacques Dériaz who proposed a new city at the Petit-Saconnex. Pallas, *Histoire et architecture du Palais des Nations (1924–2001)*, 17.

[85] League of Nations Archives, pamphlet #159, "La Societé des Nations: son activitée par l'image." Deuxième Assemblée—Genève—1921 (Edition Atar, Genève, 1921), 59.

[86] P. Devanthéry and I. Lamunière, "SdN: un palais moderne?" In AAVV, *Le Corbusier à Genève, Exhibition Catalog* (Geneva, 1987), quoted in Ilia Delizia and Fabio Mangone, *Architettura e politica: Ginevra e la Società delle Nazioni, 1925–1929* (Rome: Officina Edizioni, 1992), 28.

[87] On this competition, see Delizia and Mangone, *Architettura e Politica*, and Jörg Martin Merz, "Pushing Corb: Campaigning for Le Corbusier's Project for the Palace of Nations in Geneva (1926–33)," in Shai-shu Tzeng, ed., *Agents of Modernity*, Shida Studies in Art History 1 (Taipei: SMC, 2011), 227–84.

[88] See League of Nations Archives, 341.251 L429pr, League of Nations, Designs Submitted in the Architectural Competition, 1927. Project #229, submitted by Clemens Holzmeister, Vienne and Ernest Egli, Vienne; and project #330 by Johannes Petrus Leonardus & Jean Maria de Ligne, Bruxelles, Belgium.

[89] League of Nations Archives, 341.251 L429pr. League of Nations, Designs Submitted in the Architectural Competition, 1927. Project #345 by Joseph Rings, Essen, Germany.

Fig. 2.1 League of Nations, designs submitted in the architectural competition, 1927. Project #229, submitted by Clemens Holzmeister and Ernest Egli, Vienna, Austria. The bird-eye view emphasizes how the building would maximize the view from the mountains, which appear oversized from this angle. ©United Nations Archives at Geneva, 341.251 L429pr.

Like the League's goals, mountain peaks represented high and noble objectives that through perseverance could eventually be reached. At the same time, the sheer size of the Alps symbolized the strength of the League and its commitment to world peace. As a 1928 League report made explicit, mountains constituted a central feature of the project, and "the Council would shortly have the great satisfaction of seeing in the midst of the Swiss mountains, and framed in the majesty of those lofty heights, an edifice worthy of the League of Nations and worthy to be the future Temple of Peace and Concord."[90] The aesthetic quality of the League's chosen site thus moved the spotlight away from Switzerland—from its national environment and from its financial and political status—onto an alternative set of positive alpine qualities and associations.

[90] League of Nations, *Official Journal* 9, no. 4 (April 1928), 386.

Fig. 2.2 League of Nations, designs submitted in the architectural competition, 1927. Project #330 by Johannes Petrus Leonardus and Jean Maria de Ligne, Brussels, Belgium. Note the oversized shape of the mountains. ©United Nations Archives at Geneva, 341.251 L429pr.

Fig. 2.3 League of Nations, designs submitted in the architectural competition, 1927. Project #345 by Joseph Rings, Essen, Germany. ©United Nations Archives at Geneva, 341.251 L429pr. The caption reads: "In the direction of the east in the light of the rising sun / standing in the shelter of the white mountain giant in symbolic purity / the imposing Palace of the Nations / as an impression of the biggest word / "humanity / design" / coming from the sky / real cut crystal / timeless / bright shimmering in the calm lake." I thank Wilma Iggers and Verena Specht for their help with this translation.

Fig. 2.4 The Palais des Nations in its mountain surroundings. Photograph by Romano1246. https://commons.wikimedia.org/wiki/File:Geneve_Palais_Nations_2011-08-05_08_10_35_PICT0047.JPG (accessed on April 2, 2019).

As the largest artifact built by the League, the Palais des Nations still conveys the symbolic importance of the alpine landscape—and of the emotions associated with it—for those who created it (see Figure 2.4). The construction did not follow any of the projects submitted in 1927 but was designed instead by a team of five architects from different countries. Not coincidentally, the building was the product of international cooperation and has a 400 meter-long facade facing the Alps.[91] As noted by one of the architects, Carlo Broggi, the court of honor was purposefully "closed on three sides and open toward the lake facing the magnificent sight of the Mont Blanc," so that delegates walking out of the main Assembly Hall would enjoy its full view through the tall glass windows lining the gallery wall.[92] As the *Journal de Genève* commented at the laying of the first stone on September 7, 1929, the new home of the League of Nations would be equal (*digne*) "of the eternal lake in its frame of mountains" (*du lac éternel dans son cadre de*

---

[91] The team was composed by Henri Paul Nénot (Paris), Carlo Broggi (Rome), Julien Flegenheimer (Geneva), Camille Lefèvre (Paris), and József Vágó (Budapest). On the history of the building and its features, see Pallas, *Histoire et architecture du Palais des Nations (1924–2001)*.

[92] Carlo Broggi, "Il Palazzo della Societa' delle Nazioni a Ginevra," 71. Clipping conserved at the League of Nations Archives 341.251:720 P 155.

montagnes).[93] The message was that the mountains' size and strength would reflect the League's resilience, their apparent timelessness would somehow add to the institution's endurance, and the sublime long associated with their heights would now be applied to its elevated objectives and to the people put in charge of fulfilling them.

Many forms of the League's publicity included mountains as symbols of internationalist dignity and purpose. For instance, stamps and medals issued by the organization portrayed mountains as a prominent element (see Figure 2.5).[94] A painting still hanging on the walls of the Palais des Nations represents the League's delegates debating a serious issue against an oversized mountainous backdrop (see Figure 2.6). The copy of a 1931 creation by artist F. Rackwitz, it was given to the United Nations by the Parliament of Åland—an autonomous Swedish speaking territory of Finland in recognition of the League of Nations' 1921 ruling that sanctioned their status.[95] The landscape occupies most of the picture and is

Fig. 2.5 Stamps issued by the League of Nations, 1938. ©United Nations Archives at Geneva, Historical Collection & Museum Items.

---

[93] *Journal de Genève*, September 8, 1929, 1.

[94] League of Nations Archives, Historical Collection & Museum Items, Printed Materials and Stamps, Boxes 1 and 2, Timbres-postes spéciaux, May 1938. See also reproduction of UN stamps from 1960 and 1990 in Pallas, *Histoire et architecture du Palais des Nations (1924–2001)*, 352–5; and M. McMenamin, "A medal depicting the Palace of Nations and the Jura Mountains," *Numismatics International Bulletin* 46, nos. 3–4 (2011), 55.

[95] I thank Riitta Puukka of the Permanent Mission of Finland in Geneva for her help in identifying this painting.

Fig. 2.6 F. Rackwitz, Nationernas förbund beslutar om Åland, 1931 (The League of Nations decides on Åland). A copy was given as a present to the United Nations by the Parliament of Åland, an autonomous Swedish speaking territory of Finland in recognition of the League of Nations's 1921 ruling that sanctioned their status. ©United Nations Archives at Geneva.

emphasized by the artist's use of color and light, diverting attention from the people and the institution it was meant to celebrate. More than the figures of the delegates at the bottom, the Alps portrayed them and their endeavors as legitimate and noble. The mountain landscape therefore elicited trust in the internationalist cause by evoking a set of emotions that could be transferred from the aesthetic, to the personal, to the political realms.

Ironically, by the time the Palais des Nations had been completed, the League had lost much of its power and moral authority. The Secretariat officially moved to the League's new location on February 17, 1936. Three weeks later, on March 7, Germany flagrantly breached the terms of the Treaty of Versailles by reoccupying the Rhineland. Two months thereafter, on May 5, Italian troops entered the Ethiopian capital of Addis Ababa without any opposition on the part of the international community. On June 30, the Palais' grand Assembly Hall echoed the impassionate plea delivered by Emperor Haile Selassie I (1892–1975), who travelled to Geneva to denounce the atrocities committed by the Italian fascist army while it was illegally invading the Ethiopian territory and butchering its people. The screams of Italian journalists heckling him as he approached the podium—the lights turned on and off in the attempt of bringing back order—reduced the grandiose stage to an auditorium of ridicule. The applause of delegates who initially expressed sympathy but in the end voted to lift sanctions against Italy—thus leaving Ethiopia to its destiny—only amplified dissonances and revealed the void left at the core of the Geneva-based institution. The new Palais had already lost its solemnity and seemed out of touch with reality: its majestic white stone looked distant from the gritty world of politics, and the serene alpine view a delusion of bygone idealistic dreams.

Many League supporters expressed frustration at this situation and lamented that the League worried too much about other people's feelings. Most notably, in 1934, British pacifist Lord Allen of Hurtwood (1889–1939) denounced the "complete lack of skill on the part of us all in presenting to the public the idea of international government."[96] In his opinion, statesmen treated public opinion as "a drag upon the wheel" and often limited their otherwise progressive policies to what they believed they could sell to their domestic audiences. Instead, they should have the courage of putting forth a bold statement to the public. Following the example of the American President Franklin Delano Roosevelt, whose strong leadership and "politics of conscience of opinion" had proven successful, the League of Nations ought to bravely take ownership of its role as defender of world peace.[97] In an age when broadcasting had brought people back "to the condition of the Greek city state," where politicians can speak directly to them, its leaders and supporters should use new technologies to deliver a strong message. Allen insisted that countering the "fear and emotion" mustered by nationalist movements with the "fear and emotion" of their victory could not possibly yield a positive result; nor could the Labour strategy of "resistance" (one that he saw as "a technique of peace which contemplates failure") lead to anything else but failure.[98] Fighting the urge of joining extreme nationalists in dwelling on the League's flaws, internationalists needed to embrace their responsibilities as representatives of a legitimate world government. Widespread defeatism represented the main culprit in Allen's opinion, and emotions such as courage, confidence, and enthusiasm thus provided the only viable way forward.

Along the same lines, a 1944 piece published on *The Public Opinion Quarterly* concluded that the League's "failure" in "public relations" was connected to its undue management of emotions. The author, political scientists Dell G. Hitchner, warned that, "If league publicity in the future is to be tied to sensitive national sentiment in each of its states-members, and if it is always to choose the role of arbiter instead of champion, it can hardly expect to play a forceful part in the

---

[96] Lord Allen of Hurtwood, "Public Opinion and the Idea of International Government," *International Affairs* 13, no. 2 (March–April 1934), 186.
[97] Hurtwood, "Public Opinion," 187–90.   [98] Hurtwood, "Public Opinion," 191–5.

reconciliation of international controversies."[99] Conflict resolution ultimately would come down to reconciliation (an emotionally-charged term in itself), and an effective international body needed to stand above individual "sensitivities" while "championing" a stronger set of unifying feelings and values without fear of being accused of self-aggrandizement.

A similar argument underscored the debate over symbols such as hymns and flags, which the League of Nations always shied away from adopting in the inter-war period.[100] Numerous internationalists kept clamoring for them. Piles of proposals and designs for the League's flag, replete with hand-colored models and cloth samples, are still preserved at the League of Nations Archives in Geneva.[101] In the same files are also stacks of letters making an argument for the League's need for its own insignia. In these documents, too, emotions appeared as the most prominent element. To provide only a few examples, as early as 1921 Herbert Stead of the League to Abolish War contacted the Secretary General to recommend that the Geneva organization "should at the earliest moment proceed to the adoption of a distinctive FLAG [sic], as of the utmost importance in impressing the popular imagination and especially the minds of young people with such an outward and visible sign of the inward unity of mankind which the League stands for."[102] In 1923, a private citizen, C. F. Fryer, argued that "some appeal to the emotions of the various peoples, as well as to their intellects is needed, and a flag round which to centre these emotions seems to me a desirable object."[103]

Some people went even further in their quest for something to feel, and endeavored to give the League a jump-start: in the same folder are sample materials of all kinds, including a set of pins, stamps, a booklet, and indeed a flag, which Reverend J. W. Van Kirk of Youngstown, OH, designed, produced, and mailed in 1925.[104] In 1929–30, the International Federation of League of Nations Societies—a body separate and independent from the League—even launched a contest for the best design; and in 1935, the *Tribune des Nations* published an article decrying the

[99] Dell G. Hitchner, "The Failure of the League: Lesson in Public Relations," *The Public Opinion Quarterly* 8, no. 1 (Spring 1944), 68.

[100] The only exception was the temporary adoption of a flag in the village of Leticia, which was disputed between Columbia and Peru. See Yannick Wehrli, "Du pavillon de Leticia au 'non drapeau' de la Société des Nations. Échec de représentation symbolique d'une organisation internationale," in F. Briegel and S. Farré, eds., *Rites, hiérarchies* (Chêne-Bourg: Georg, 2010), 102–16. On the proposed League of Nations' hymns, see Carl Bouchard, "'Formons un chœur aux innombrables voix…': hymnes et chants pour la paix soumis à la Société des Nations," *Relations Internationales* 155, no. 3 (Fall 2013), 103–20. I thank Pierre-Etienne Bourneuf for these useful references. On the history and political debates surrounding flags, see Tim Marshall, *A Flag Worth Dying For: The Power and Politics of National Symbols* (New York: Scribner, 2017); Thomas Hylland Eriksen and Richard Jenkins eds., *Flag, Nation and Symbolism in Europe and America* (London: Routledge, 2007).

[101] See League of Nations Archives, R 1549, R3568, and R 5645.

[102] League of Nations Archives, R 1549/383/383, letter dated July 25, 1921, from Herbert Stead of the League to Abolish War [based in England] to Sir Eric Drummond.

[103] League of Nations Archives, R 1549/383/383, letter dated June 11, 1923, from C.F. Fryer, Esq. to the League of Nations Secretary.

[104] League of Nations Archives, R 1549/383/383.

absence of a League's flag precisely because of the sentimental value it would have.[105] From all directions, the argument came that eliciting the right emotions would have been vital for the League. At a time when extreme nationalist movements preyed on people's anger, resentment, and pride, many urged the League to adopt symbols that would engender equally powerful feelings.

Throughout the time of its existence, the League gave only a tepid response to these impassionate pleas for stronger feelings. In the case of the flag issue, each unsolicited piece of correspondence was replied to with a generic line stating that the League had never adopted an official flag, but never addressing the question of whether or not it should. In 1925, the information section held a meeting on the matter. The surviving summary reveals that only one person, Robert Haas, suggested that a flag be adopted for practical reasons; Van Hamel and Erik Colban found it unnecessary; and Professor Bernardo Attolico expressed his opposition to the idea contending that as soon as a flag would be adopted, "it would be said 'here is the Super State.'" In the end, the subject was dropped.[106] Another document shows that the same argument resurfaced ten years later, in 1935, when the Director of the Information Section replied to yet another proposal for a League flag by pointing out that "The League of Nations, of course, is not a superstate nor a super-government, and has never adopted the principle of a special flag." Once again, no more than a perfunctory response came out of Geneva.[107]

The debate, in the end, was about feelings. At a time when fascist insignia and Nazi flags covered a good part of the European continent and an increasing number of people begged for the League to arouse "pride" in the internationalist project and "trust" that cooperation would be effective, the League reacted— perhaps defensively—by reiterating its promise of not infringing on national rights. What Yannick Wehrli called a "failure of symbolic representation" was ultimately a failed attempt at managing emotions, one from which the League would never recover.[108]

* * *

Emotions constituted a fundamental part of the work of the League of Nations throughout the time of its existence. The League employed emotional rhetoric and images, often embodied and symbolized by the Alps, in order to legitimize

---

[105] A clipping is preserved in League of Nations Archives, R 5645, 50/223/223 (jacket 1).
[106] League of Nations Archives, R 1549, 39/42978/383, extract from minutes of Directors Meeting, August 26, 1925.
[107] League of Nations Archives, R 5645/50/223/223 (jacket 2), letter dated April 9, 1935 from Director of Information Section to Mr. Lewis Carl Seelbach.
[108] Wehrli, "Du pavillon de Leticia au 'non drapeau' de la Société des Nations," 113. Wehrli also pointed out the differences between the League of Nations and the United Nations, which acquired a flag fairly quickly, attributing them to the "more pragmatic" Anglo-Saxon (and especially American) intervention.

itself and its policies. It used feelings to brand itself as capable and noble, to draw associations with positive values such as resilience, purity, and honesty, and to argue for its own viability in the post-1919 world. It also took emotions into account while staging international encounters, devoting much energy and resources trying to shape what people felt during the meetings and long-term stays in the Alps organized in this period.

The League's carefully-managed emotional style—which was deliberately based on "nobility," "dignity," and "friendship" rather than "force" and "pride"—frustrated many of its supporters while fueling its opponents' argument that it was inherently weak; at the same time, it led to a set of ideas and practices (e.g., school exchanges to foster "mutual understanding") that—for better or for worse—still influence many forms of international cooperation to this day.[109] One reason is that already in the 1920s and 1930s the impact of the League's work extended to the countless internationalist groups outside of its official boundaries (e.g., the international open-air schools examined in this chapter).

In order to dig deeper into the functions that emotions performed in this imaginary space around the League, we shall now turn to one of the largest and most sentimentalized groups active in the Alps in this period: the International Mountaineering and Climbing Federation, or UIAA. After all, who better than alpinists can offer us a bird's-eye view of how the emotions of internationalism came to permeate what people thought, did, and felt while surrounded by mountain peaks and by the troubled countries that claimed them.

---

[109] See for instance Eduard Vallory, *World Scouting: Educating for Global Citizenship* (New York: Palgrave Macmillan, 2012).

3

International Mountaineering while Talking about Emotions

In September 1945, Swiss journalist Charles Egmond d'Arcis (1887–1971) wrote a letter to all members of the Union Internationale des Associations d'Alpinisme (UIAA, or International Mountaineering and Climbing Federation), an international organization created in 1932 "to promote mountaineering and climbing worldwide."[1] It read:

> The cannons are silent. After almost six years of unspeakable sufferings, the world glimpses at an age of peace and tranquility, and people resume their impetus to start again and pursue their eternal ascension. They need not only to recuperate their forces, but also to find again the cohesion and the spirit of cooperation that alone will allow them to achieve their goals. Alpinists can and must help nations to restart contacts, to unite, and to act. It is necessary that the solidarity that binds them on the glaciers and among the rocks resurrects, affirms itself, and develops for everybody's greater good.[2]

After suspending activities for the duration of the war, in his capacity as President d'Arcis contended that "without going outside of the realm of alpinism...the UIAA can play a major role in the moral reconstruction of the world." "Certain that no member of the great alpine family will shy away from his responsibility," he asked for full support for what he saw as the association's most important goal of uniting people across national borders.[3]

According to fellow-journalist and mountaineer Guido Tonella, d'Arcis' letter was met with such a warm response that he set aside any hesitation and resumed his work after the war.[4] A few months later, the UIAA met again in Zermatt.[5] In a

---

[1] UIAA, "Mission Statement," http://www.theuiaa.org/our-mission.html (accessed on July 27, 2016).

[2] UIAA Archives, Correspondance Président, 1933–1979, draft of letter dated September 1945.

[3] UIAA Archives, Correspondance Président, 1933–1979, draft of letter dated September 1945.

[4] See Guido Tonella, *50 anni di alpinismo senza frontiere. La storia dell'UIAA. Unione Internazionale delle Associazioni d'Alpinismo* (Milan: Club Alpino Italiano, 1983), 24–5. One copy is available at the UIAA Archives.

[5] The meeting took place on September 5–6, 1946, with alpine clubs from Belgium, Czechoslovakia, France, Great Britain, Italy, the Netherlands, and Switzerland sending a representative, and with associations from Greece, Norway, Poland, Spain, Sweden and Yugoslavia asking to be represented by "friend-nations." Tonella, *50 anni di alpinismo senza frontiere,* 24.

The Emotions of Internationalism: Feeling International Cooperation in the Alps in the Interwar Period. Ilaria Scaglia, Oxford University Press (2020). © Ilaria Scaglia.
DOI: 10.1093/oso/9780198848325.001.0001

poignant, defining moment, the minutes from the 1939 session were read and approved. The loss of many friends was mourned, and the enduring friendship among others celebrated. To be sure, some could not—or would not—participate in this gathering due to travel difficulties or reluctance to engage former enemies; yet, those present would later recall an atmosphere full of promise. In 1949, at a meeting in the French resort town of Chamonix, Egmond d'Arcis remarked that "there was a more than satisfactory recovery of activities, life, and cordiality in the relationships among the mountain associations from different countries, one that let us hope that it will be possible to re-establish the ancient links that before the war had made alpinists a true family."[6] Further invigorated by the congress in Chamonix, he committed to lead the UIAA for the foreseeable future.[7]

D'Arcis' use of emotional rhetoric—and the familialism and fraternalism that imbued it—serves as a useful vehicle to explore the "moral economy"[8] of internationalism, or the dynamics through which internationalist groups used feelings to attribute moral values to specific beliefs and behaviors.[9] Such rhetoric gave the UIAA a higher purpose, and provided it with a stronger argument to retain and attract its members: their commitment to the UIAA would benefit not only them and their passion for mountains but also the higher cause of promoting world peace. Religious references to "spirit" and "eternal ascension" added a transcendent and a teleological quality to their endeavors.

Evoking emotions such as "brotherhood" framed the bond among UIAA members as a strong, indissoluble kinship. "Friendship" allowed all actors to justify their choices of belonging to or withdrawing from the organization—and also to rationalize the presence of people and countries that openly contradicted the UIAA's internationalist mission—without losing any moral capital in the process.[10]

---

[6] Cited in Tonella, *50 anni di alpinismo senza frontiere*, 25.

[7] D'Arcis would maintain his post until 1964. On Egmond d'Arcis' role in fostering "the spirit of brotherhood and of alpinism without frontiers," see also the "Preface" by the President of the Italian Alpine Club, Giacomo Priotto, in Tonella, *50 anni di alpinismo senza frontiere*, 5.

[8] The term "moral economy" was first introduced by E. P. Thompson in a landmark study on the formation of a "popular consensus" over "legitimate" and "illegitimate" economic practices among eighteenth-century English peasants. E. P. Thompson, "The Moral Economy of the English Crowd in the Eighteenth Century," *Past & Present* 50, no. 1 (February 1971), 76–136. On transcending the limits of the definition of "moral economy" imposed by Thompson, see Didier Fassin, "Les économies morales revisitées," *Annales HSS* 64, no. 6 (2009), 1237–66; Norbert Götz, "'Moral Economy': Its Conceptual History and Analytical Prospects," *Journal of Global Ethics* 11, no. 2 (May 2015), 147–62; Lorraine Daston, "The Moral Economy of Science," *Osiris* 10 (1995), 2–24. On the concept of "moral economy" and "moral economies" see also the research statement of the International Max Planck Research School for Moral Economies of Modern Societies, https://www.mpib-berlin.mpg.de/en/research/research-schools/imprs-mems/research/research-statement (accessed on July 17, 2018); Ute Frevert, *The Moral Economy of Trust: Modern Trajectories* (London: German Historical Institute, 2014), 28–34.

[9] On the "moral economy" of internationalism, and the idea that it presented itself as "balanced" and therefore morally superior to other contemporary ideologies, see Ilaria Scaglia, "The 'Hydrologist's Weapons': Emotions and the 'Moral Economy' of Internationalism, 1921–1952," in Sara Graça Da Silva, ed., *New Interdisciplinary Landscapes in Morality and Emotion* (London: Routledge, 2018), 140–52.

[10] On the use of "friendship" in political causes, see Eliah Matthew Bures, "Fantasies of Friendship: Ernst Jünger and the German Right's Search for Community in Modernity," Ph.D. Dissertation, University of California, Berkeley, 2014; Luisa Passerini, *Love and the Idea of Europe*, translated by Juliet Haydock and Allan Cameron (New York: Berghahn Books, 2009).

Indeed, by referring to feelings in their rhetoric, UIAA officers and members were able to present themselves as neither appeasers nor opponents of other competing ideologies (e.g., fascism), but as moderate and conciliatory members of the international community.

Furthermore, by staging a wide set of aesthetic and sensorial experiences and by describing them as moments when emotional bonds among people from various nations were built, the UIAA displayed itself and the mountains as especially conducive to international cooperation. Through published commentaries of these events, the UIAA framed its mission in terms of emotional objectives. It then argued that the shared enjoyment of the mountains' beauty had led to lasting ties among its members, employing written descriptions of emotions as evidence that its own internationalist agenda had been fulfilled. In this context, the emotions of internationalism—constructed as authentic, enduring, and transferrable to the political realm—embodied a modern approach to international cooperation in the twentieth century, one that promised to be effective at reaching people's hearts.

Mountains inspired a set of associations readily applicable to the political landscape of the 1930s and 1940s. Contemporary notions about *alpinistes* and *montagnards* forming a separate and morally elevated community that spanned across national borders fit well within the universalist vocabulary adopted by many internationalists at this time. Also, the broad set of extreme sensorial experiences available in the mountains (from the gusts of their wind to the warmth of their huts) made them an apt laboratory for testing a wide variety of feelings.[11] Finally, competing visions of mountains (i.e., modernization vs. preservation of what many construed as "authentic" natural beauty) at once contradicted and overlapped with the League of Nations' agenda in this period. Mountains thus worked as an important space for the negotiation of competing aspirations, and emotions served as an essential ingredient for managing and communicating what internationalism was—or should have been—in this period.

3.1 Envisioning a League of Nations in the Alps

The UIAA originated from a set of internationalist ideas and practices that had developed in the mid-nineteenth century. As mountain climbing became more popular, almost immediately the idea arose for an international association to unite people interested in mountains.[12] Twenty years after the establishment of the first Alpine Club in England in 1857, international gatherings of alpinists were

---

[11] The very experience of climbing was emotionalized and connected to the body in new ways in this period. Alan McNee, *The New Mountaineer in Late Victorian Britain: Materiality, Modernity, and the Haptic Sublime* (Cham, CH: Palgrave Macmillan, 2016).

[12] For a general overview of this history, see Andrew Beattie, *The Alps: A Cultural History* (Oxford: Oxford University Press, 2006).

organized in various places in the Alps. International congresses were held in Annecy and Aix-les-Bains in 1876, and in Grenoble-Uriage and Ivrea in 1877. In 1879, an International Conference of Alpine Clubs took place in Geneva under the chairmanship of A. Freundler, President of the Swiss Alpine Club. Participants came from Austria, England, France, Germany, Spain, the United States, and of course, Switzerland.

Although plans for an international organization were discussed at these gatherings, no international body was established in this period. It was only in 1930 that the Polish Tatra Society organized the First International Alpine Congress in Zakopane, Poland. This was followed in 1931 by the Second International Alpine Congress in Budapest, and by the Third Alpine Congress in Chamonix in 1932. It was in Chamonix that the Union International des Associations d'Alpinisme (UIAA) was established, following the initiative of the President of the French Alpine Club, Jean Escarra. Shortly thereafter, Charles Egmond d'Arcis was nominated as its President.[13]

Since its inception, the UIAA associated itself with the League of Nations both in terms of structure and emotional rhetoric. Though none of its officers were formally active in the League, it overtly adopted "*formule e strutture esdeniane*" ("League formulas and structures," to borrow Guido Tonella's clever acronym based on the initials *es-de-en* of the French name of the League, Société des Nations).[14] Like the League, the UIAA presented itself as an association that would unite people across borders with the overall goal of avoiding another "Great War." It had an assembly that included representatives of all member associations, a permanent bureau with executive functions similar to the secretariat, and an executive committee with functions similar to the League's council, comprising the President—a representative of the Swiss Alpine Club—and seven members elected at the third congress in Chamonix. In 1932, the seven were the President of the French Alpine Club, Jean Escarra; the President of the English Alpine Club, Sir John Withers; Giovanni Bobba of the Italian Alpine Club; Walery Goetel of the Polish Tatra Society, also representing the Union of Slavic Societies of Tourism; János Vigyazo, President of the Hungarian Tourist Association; Otto Sjögren of the Swedish Alpine Club; and a representative of the German Alpine Club to be designated at a later time.[15] As time went on, the names of individual representatives changed but the general structure did not, and the UIAA effectively served as a league of nations in the field of mountaineering.

Akin to the League, the UIAA placed great emphasis on tangible, concrete "functional cooperation."[16] It included six "sections" whose focus mirrored—and

---

[13] UIAA Archives, Anciennes Circulaires, Circulaire n. I, January 5, 1933.

[14] Tonella, *50 anni di alpinismo senza frontiere*, 12.

[15] UIAA Archives, Assemblée Générale, 1932–1935, IIIème Congrès International d'Alpinisme, voeux adoptés & décisions prises par le Congrès dans la dernière séance plénière du 27 août 1932, 1–3.

[16] On "functionalism" as an approach emphasizing international cooperation in a wide variety of fields from health, to education, to finance, see also Chapter 2.

sometimes even overlapped with—the League's technical work in communication and transit, health, and intellectual cooperation. The first, "Alpinism and Mountain Organization," was the largest, and included subcommittees for the protection of mountain huts from vandalism; the standardization of signs, paths, and maps; issues related to what they called the "democratization" of alpinism (i.e., the over-crowding of mountain regions by an ever-increasing number of people from all social classes) and youth education; the creation of a standard climbing rating system; the use of artificial means for climbing (to discourage the installation of permanent cables and bolts); the monitoring of the condition of alpinism in selected mountain ranges; the study of the history of alpine associations; the study of camping at high quotas; the protection and insurance of guides and porters; and ski and winter alpinism, to mark areas at danger of avalanches and to educate the public in this regard. There was also a sub-section on publications and one on preventative measures against accidents, which handled rescue procedures by promoting the use of the international code of distress and by training all alpinists—and guides in particular—in emergency medical care.[17]

The second section, "Mountain and Science," encouraged alpinists to provide information for scientific studies in the fields of geology and meteorology. The third on "Forestal and Pastoral Management" dealt with the protection of flora and fauna and hunting regulations. It also had a sub-section that tried to mitigate the environmental impact of hydro-electrical plants, schools, and facilities to accommodate tourists, and another promoting the establishment of parks and reserves. "Mountain Transportation" pushed for the improvement of access to mountains through the construction of airports and roads. "Health" sought to educate the masses on both the benefits and the dangers of mountains (especially of heliotherapy when practiced improperly); it oversaw the creation of a perimeter around sanatoria to avoid the propagation of diseases and supervised the mandatory teaching of skiing in schools. Finally, the sixth section on "Art and Mountains" organized concerts of alpine music, exhibitions of alpine photographs, and the exchange of publications on any and all topics connected to mountains at large.[18]

Like the League, the UIAA promoted standardization and the exchange of people, objects, and ideas with the explicit goal of fostering peaceful relations among nations.[19] As the association grew its work steadily expanded, especially in the sectors closest to the League's Committee on Intellectual Cooperation. The UIAA devoted considerable energy to the compilation of indexes and bibliographies of alpine literature, to youth education, to practical issues such as rescue, and to sta-ging a wide variety of exhibitions displaying art and literature inspired by "the

---

[17] UIAA Archives, Assemblée Générale, 1932–1935, IIIème Congrès International d'Alpinisme, voeux adoptés & décisions prises par le Congrès dans la dernière séance plénière du 27 août 1932, 3–16.
[18] UIAA Archives, Assemblée Générale, 1932–1935, IIIème Congrès International d'Alpinisme, voeux adoptés & décisions prises par le Congrès dans la dernière séance plénière du 27 août 1932, 3–16.
[19] *Bulletin du Club Alpin Suisse, Section Genevoise*, July 1932, 110.

Alps."[20] Furthermore, the UIAA opposed the construction of cable cars in areas such as the Meije, the Salève, and the Matterhorn (Cervin).[21] Most notably, the UIAA campaigned against building a cable car on the Matterhorn and scored a resounding victory for the League's policy of protecting mountain beauty.[22] In all of these realms, the UIAA indirectly met the League's goals while also fulfilling its overall internationalist mission.

Like the League, the UIAA was deeply rooted in Geneva and its "spirit," a notion fueled by contemporary authors such as Robert de Traz and also deliberately promoted by the Swiss government.[23] Its President, Egmond d'Arcis, was an "international being," so to speak: born in Florence from an English father and a Swiss mother, he was fluent in four languages (Italian, English, German, and French). In Geneva, he worked as a correspondent for English papers (including *The Economist* and *The Times* of London) covering the League's activities in the interwar period. He thus operated in a crucial place and time when the League devoted much energy to controlling its own image, to managing its reputation, and to negotiating its relationship with the press.[24]

D'Arcis played a leading role in the internationalization of the press community and in the promotion of Geneva as an international city.[25] His career as a journalist continued to thrive after the Second World War: in 1955–6 he would serve as President of the Foreign Press Association in Switzerland (Association de la Presse Etrangère en Suisse, or APES), one of the first to "facilitate contact and communication for its members with Swiss government bodies, national organizations, institutions, and private sector companies."[26] And, if during the interwar period he had yet to achieve such high status, he was already part of the Circle of International Friendships (Le Cercle des Amitiés Internationales), an association established in 1920 to bring together the Geneva press community with foreign correspondents from all over the world, and even served as its President in 1934.[27] He thus combined his local identity with an international outlook, and, as

---

[20] On each of these items, see the aforementioned work by Guido Tonella. See also Pierre Bossus, *Les cinquante premières années de l'Union internationale des associations d'alpinisme* (Geneva: UIAA, 1982).

[21] A thorough summary of the UIAA's activities was presented by the President at the 1939 general assembly in Zermatt. A copy can be found in UIAA Archives, Assemblée Générale, Zermatt, 1939.

[22] See for instance newspaper coverage on *Journal de Genève*, November 4, 1950.

[23] Robert de Traz, *L'esprit de Genève* (Paris: Grasset, 1929).

[24] On the relation between the League of Nations and the press, and on the overall issue of "reputation," see also Chapter 2.

[25] *Journal de Genève*, December 8, 1971, 13. On the progressive internationalization of the press in the twentieth century, see Kaarle Nordenstreng, Ulf Jonas Björk, Frank Beyersdorf, Svennik Høyer, and Epp Lauk, eds., *A History of the International Movement of Journalists: Professionalism versus Politics* (Basingstoke: Palgrave Macmillan, 2016). See also Chapter 2.

[26] APES, http://www.apes-presse.org/en/(accessed on July 17, 2018). I thank APES President Emilia Nazarenko for making available all materials at the APES Archives at the Palais des Nations in Geneva, which are normally closed to the public.

[27] Le Cercle des Amitiés Internationales, http://www.cai-geneve.org/historique/(accessed on October 25, 2016).

explained later in this chapter, he popularized the idea that the Alps represented a "Geneva" on the mountains and an emotional meeting ground that transcended all kinds of boundaries.

Other UIAA officers also helped to reinforce the notion that Geneva had a unique internationalist "*Geist*." For instance, Maurice Trottet, who in 1936 substituted Louis J. Fatio, was also the President of Sonor SA, the publishing house of the newspaper *La Suisse* and of d'Arcis' first book.[28] The delegates of the National Alpine clubs who joined the UIAA and became members of its executive varied greatly in terms of background, experiences, interests, and political affiliations. Some were prominent figures in their own communities and also prolific writers on mountains and other issues. Of others, little is known besides their name as listed in the official minutes of the association's meetings. As a whole, they formed a very heterogeneous group, a fact that in itself contributed to Geneva's reputation as an international meeting ground.

Jean Escarra (1885–1955) of the French Alpine Club (CAF) deserves special attention as the principal mind behind the UIAA and as one of the most influential people in shaping its complex—if at times contradictory—brand of internationalism. A jurist and an expert on China, in the 1920s he served as a consultant for the Chinese Nationalist government, providing advice in reforming the Chinese legal system.[29] Proficient in the Chinese language, though always reluctant to call himself a "sinologist," he wrote extensively on Chinese law celebrating its richness and long history.[30] He supported, and later defended, the work of the League of Nations, particularly after the 1931 Manchurian crisis and the subsequent rising tensions with Japan.[31]

As the Sino-Japanese conflict worsened in the late 1930s, however, Escarra denounced the overall inaction of the international community, calling fears of a communist takeover "illusive" and referring to Japan's "unrestrained ambitions" as "one of the greatest dangers that had ever menaced international peace."[32] In a 1938 publication provocatively entitled *L'honorable paix japonaise* (The honorable Japanese peace), he suggested that China should stop trusting the League as "it would be a dangerous illusion for her to believe in the effectiveness of an organism that nowadays is no more than a cadaver." Yet, if it was now time to stop "the pursuit of the magnificent chimeras of international mutual assistance and collective security," the moral superiority of these "magnificent chimeras" still stood.[33]

---

[28] *La Suisse*, February 26, 1963. *Journal de Genève*, August 9, 1967, 9.
[29] See obituary by Miriam Underhill published on the *American Alpine Journal* 10, no. 2 (1957), 143. See also Jean Escarra (1885–1955), *T'oung Pao* 44 (1956), 304–10.
[30] See obituary by A. F. P. Hulsewé, *T'oung Pao* 44 (1956), 307.
[31] Jean Escarra, *Le conflit sino-japonais et la Société des Nations* (Paris: Publications de la Conciliation internationale, 1933).
[32] Jean Escarra, *Réflexions sur la politique du Japon à l'égard de la Chine et sur quelques aspects juridiques du conflit actuel* (Perpignan: Imprimerie de l'Indépendant, 1937), 26–7.
[33] Jean Escarra, *L'honorable paix japonaise* (Paris: Grasset, 1938), 224–31.

Escarra's complex internationalism might be best understood through his alpinistic endeavors, and vice versa. To quote one of his obituaries, "No picture of this big and sturdy man with his indefatigable appetite for work and his love of music would be complete without at least a mention of his great love for the mountains," one which also carried a political meaning.[34] In 1936, Escarra participated in a famous—though failed—French Himalayan expedition, whose journey he detailed in a book written together with fellow alpinists Henry de Ségogne, Louis Neltner, and Jean Charignon.[35] In recounting his experience, he provided two seemingly contradictory suggestions: the first, that French expeditions achieve the rank of those conducted by Great Britain, Germany, or Italy; the second, that mountaineering on the Himalayas become governed by "an amicable synchronization of the efforts by various countries" in the name of a common humanity.[36] Such tension between national celebration and universalism informed the guiding principles of the UIAA for years to come, and deeply influenced its interpretation of internationalism as a balance between national and international interests.

A similar universalist, environmentalist position—always rooted in the assumption that progress would come through amicable cooperation among distinct nations—was put forth by Polish Tatra Society representative Walery Goetel (1889–1972). A Polish professor of geology and paleontology, he was deeply involved in the environmental protection of mountains and played a seminal role in the creation of the Tatra National Park.[37] As one of the founders and longest-lasting members of the UIAA, he spearheaded the organization's efforts to oppose the indiscriminate construction of cable cars and the defacing of the mountain landscape. Together with historian Otto Sjögren of the Swedish Alpine Club, he served continuously on its executive committee, from its inception until well after the Second World War.

As explained later in this chapter, this continuous trust in international cooperation would not come without frictions and contradictions, especially at a time when the League progressively lost credibility. Crucially, emotions provided an essential ingredient to balance these extremes. In order to appreciate how these worked at the UIAA during a troubled period of time, to such feelings we shall now turn.

3.2 Writing about Mountaineering Feelings

Egmond d'Arcis wrote several works detailing his emotional experiences in the mountains. One of them, *En montagne: récits et souvenirs* (In the Mountains:

---

[34] See obituary by A. F. P. Hulsewé, *T'oung Pao* 44 (1956), 306.

[35] Jean Escarra, Henry de Sègogne, Louis Neltner, and Jean Charignon, *Karakoram. Expédition française de l'Himalaya, 1936* (Paris: Flammarion, 1938).

[36] Escarra, *Karakoram*, 36–8.   [37] See obituary *Tribune de Genève*, January 17, 1973.

Tales and Memories), which was published in 1936, offered a deeper understanding of the feelings he associated with alpine endeavors while also explaining their wider implications for the UIAA and its internationalist mission. *En montagne* recounted episodes illustrating the unique character of the Alps and their people. Written for fellow *alpinistes* who might find "known sites, impressions, and emotions felt by them as well," the book was intended to "celebrate in all simplicity alpine nature (*la nature alpestre*) and to resurrect the type of men—guides, *montagnards, alpinistes*—that one meets in the Alps."[38] The book thus constituted a useful companion for investigating the rhetoric d'Arcis employed in the UIAA's public and private communications, and also to explore the multiple functions that emotions performed in the context of this internationalist organization.

D'Arcis described emotions as making people transcend not only their national distinctions but also their differences in terms of economic and social status. In d'Arcis' account, emotions had the power to restore a "spirituality" that he believed had been lost with the rise of modernity, or elements such as aesthetic appreciation for beauty, sobriety, and authenticity in human relations, the lack of which had led to international conflict and overall societal decay. For d'Arcis, emotions gave internationalism a special power that would allow it to win over competing ideologies. In his tales, even soldiers—the quintessential symbol and embodiment of nationalism—would ultimately succumb to them. D'Arcis emphasized emotional expressions in few, defining moments, implying that these mattered more than ordinary behavior. As the most authentic manifestation of people's true nature, emotional expressions in these moments represented a person's feelings more accurately than other, more overt displays.

In d'Arcis' rendition, all "men"—and he mostly talked about males—were equal in the mountains. The formality that often regulated their relationships did not apply there. In one of his tales he recounted how as a young student, during an excursion on the Balfrin, he once met a person who later turned out to be King Albert I of Belgium. Skirting the question of each other's identity, they chatted casually about those subjects "which impassion all *alpinistes*." To him, the episode demonstrated the equalizing effect of the mountain landscape as well as the unifying force of mountaineering as a passion and a worldview. When, many years later, he had the pleasure of meeting the king again and reminding him of that encounter, the monarch recalled it without hesitation. Seemingly oblivious to what one might consider unsurpassable differences, he enthusiastically praised the true "democratic" character of Swiss alpinism and the fact that people from all paths of life shared the same passion for climbing.[39]

D'Arcis also learned from one of the king's companions that he liked to hike *incognito* under the fake name Lefebure. One time, an old man from Chamonix

---

[38] C. Egmond d'Arcis, *En montagne: récits et souvenirs* (Geneva: Sonor, 1936).
[39] D'Arcis, *En montagne*, 11–15.

found out his real identity and teased the king by referring to a peak named Albert I as "the tip Lefebure." The king was known to recall "the clever jab of the good old Chamoniard," praising his discrete, subtle humor as well as the fact that on alpine peaks the two of them could banter while forgetting their differences in class.[40] In d'Arcis narrative, *alpinistes* like the king and the old man from Chamonix exemplified the whole of humanity, and the mountains provided a protected, enchanted space for them to interact in a relaxed and amicable manner.

A unique spirituality characterized the Alps, one that only true *alpinistes* could fully appreciate. D'Arcis' casual encounter with legendary climber Edward Whymper, the first man to reach the top of the Matterhorn in 1865, reminded him—and his readers—that "in the Alps one must walk not only with his legs but also with his head." D'Arcis was unsure whether to interpret this advice by Whymper as a fatherly warning, aimed at preserving his safety, or to attach to it a more profound meaning. He nonetheless ventured that Whymper might have alerted him to the danger of "eating space like a locomotive" without appreciating "the poetry and science of nature." He thus re-paraphrased Whymper's words by stating that one should climb "with his brain and his heart," recasting the Alps as a space that required a special predisposition, exceptional concentration, and an openness to its aesthetic and emotional gifts.[41]

Such sensibility was not peculiar to any specific nationality. Instead, it marked the members of a community that spanned across national borders, a "chosen society made of people who were simple, good-willed, and attracted by the incomparable beauty of alpine sites that the absence of a drivable road protects from snobs better than anything else." This group defined itself against the "cosmopolitan society of the *viveurs*, of mundane braggarts who disdain the *alpinistes* and scorn the locals" that had taken over destinations such as Zermatt and Chamonix. In contrast to these people, "when facing a chosen public, the *alpiniste* likes to narrate his exploits" not because he wants to brag but because "he feels the need to share with those who can understand them the emotions he felt, his enthusiasm, sometimes his disappointments." D'Arcis argued that such tales are moving "because they breathe sincerity, because they emanate a beneficent impression of physical vigor, of moral balance" while celebrating "the tenacious fight of man against brutal nature." On the mountains, now turned into a welcoming hearth, this masculine, primitivist community could transcend national differences while drawing a line to keep out those who, according to them, could not fathom its *Geist*.[42] As such, the Alps represented a quintessential ground for internationalism, and the *alpinistes*, regardless of their national origin, their ideal citizens.

---

[40] D'Arcis, *En montagne*, 11–15.   [41] D'Arcis, *En montagne*, 74–9.
[42] D'Arcis, *En montagne*, 98–142.

D'Arcis insisted that in the Alps even soldiers fraternized across national lines, as the hospitability and amicability that imbued the mountain landscape beat all other factors that might set people apart. One of d'Arcis' stories chronicled the adventure of a group of Swiss soldiers who accidently crossed the border with Italy high up in the Alps late one New Year's Eve. When they knocked at the door of a remote stone chalet, a group of Italian Alpine guards opened. In broken Italian, the stranded men explained they were "*Svizzeri...perduti*" (Swiss...lost). "The rifles immediately lowered," d'Arcis described, and hot wine, sweets, and cigars were passed around. Mention of the "White War" had no place in d'Arcis' account—though readers might have immediately thought of contemporary tales of troops singing in unison at Christmas-time during the war.[43] Yet its memory would have made readers appreciate even more how after toasting to the "sons of the storm, to the friends who had come from the other side of the Alps," the men continued to fraternize late into the night. Enjoying the warmth of the fire, they sang songs from Switzerland and from the Italian Valle d'Aosta. The next day, the two units went their separate ways, keeping their encounter secret while recalling the pleasures of the best New Year's Eve they had ever had. As the most concrete and symbolic representatives of their nations, these men conveyed the significance of this moment of international friendship in a territory marred by conflict, while demonstrating the exceptional character of the Alps and of the emotions they engendered.

Local people who were born and lived in the mountains also carried specific emotional traits, which d'Arcis praised highly in his tales. Affable, simple, honest, and sincere, they represented a model for all other men to follow. In a chapter entitled "Il Signore della Montagna" (the Lord of the Mountain), d'Arcis provided a vivid description of one of them. Raised on alpine peaks, during the summer he moved from place to place. Come autumn, he returned to his wife and nine children (a family which, d'Arcis remarked, kept growing every year). Sleeping in stables and surviving on a diet of black bread and dry chestnuts, this man lived "a hard life, ungrateful, all made of arduous work, of deprivations, without a pleasure, without sweetness." Yet he remained "optimist, gay, sensible to the beauties of nature that in a clumsy way he tried to depict for us." Unapologetically a misanthrope, "he spent months in the company of his dog, his sheep, talking to them like human beings." But when d'Arcis and his group gave him whatever was left of their white bread, "a royal gift" for a man like him, he almost cried as he held their hands and said goodbye.[44]

Il "*signore della montagna*" embodied what d'Arcis considered the ideal alpine and world citizen. He was not distracted by modern conveniences but instead

---

[43] Mark Thompson, *The White War: Life and Death on the Italian Front, 1915–1919* (London: Faber and Faber, 2008).

[44] D'Arcis, *En montagne*, 200–3.

maintained a physical and a spiritual connection with nature. He did not waste time with empty words and gestures but focused his energies instead on a few defining moments in which he established meaningful and unshakable bonds with select individuals. His poverty and the family that had to do without him most of the year did not matter (if anything, the fact that he sought solitude and time away from his wife and children added to his persona). Even his harsh words could be forgiven: if he called fellow men "cruel" and proudly declared his preference for hanging out with "beasts" rather than humans, he redeemed himself by being there when it counted. In d'Arcis' account, his handshake meant more than anything else he had said or done.

These conceptions of alpine "character" and "friendship" emerged throughout d'Arcis' writings and deeply affected people's relationships within and beyond the UIAA. Overt gestures and explicit affiliations could be easily downplayed, as an unspoken bond was assumed to unite officers and members. Moreover, mountains—their aesthetics and their emotions—overpowered ongoing political tensions, as a person's appreciation for them inevitably formed a connection with fellow *alpinistes*. This bond epitomized both the expediency and the promise of tying friendships across borders, as well as the complex, contradictory reality of internationalism during this period. This imagined *ethos* and d'Arcis' aim to "resurrect" this kind of "man" and make him an actor in moments of international encounter cannot be underestimated, as it provided a moral backbone and a justification to the UIAA and also allowed for effectively negotiating the failures and successes of the internationalist movement in this period.

3.3 Negotiating Emotions and International Cooperation

Central to the UIAA was its aspiration to encourage emotional bonds among mountaineers from all over the world. Like the League, the UIAA attached not only a pragmatic but also a moral value to being as wide-reaching as possible. Tellingly, invitations to the third Congress in Chamonix (1932) were sent to all the known alpine clubs.[45] As a result, in addition to France (the host), representatives from eighteen countries attended: Germany, Austria, Belgium, Canada, Spain, Great Britain, Greece, the Netherlands, Hungary, Italy, Poland, Romania, Sweden, Switzerland, Czechoslovakia, Yugoslavia, New Zealand, and the United States.[46] Out of these, only seven agreed to become founding members with a representative

---

[45] A complete list of invitations is in UIAA Archives, Assemblée Générale, Chamonix, 1932. Each club was asked to recommend any other association dealing with mountaineering around the world.

[46] UIAA Archives, Assemblée Générale, Chamonix, 1932, liste des associations & groupements ayant des représentants officiels adhérant au Congrès d'alpinisme.

in the executive committee—Austria, France, Germany, Great Britain, Italy, Poland, and Yugoslavia—which was presided by a member of the Swiss Alpine Club.[47]

This is not because the UIAA did not try to live up to its promise of being a truly global organization. In fact, as early as 1933, d'Arcis expressed that "one of the main concerns has been to establish relations with the alpine associations of all countries" and included a list of participating nations from all continents which he hoped to expand even further.[48] The association continued to encourage the inclusion of new countries, actively seeking the involvement of non-European partners such as Japan;[49] but it was only in 1947 that substantial progress was made in this respect.[50] In the ensuing decades, both membership and geographical reach continued to expand and to be presented as positive qualities: as showcased on its website, in 2019 the UIAA "has a global presence on six continents representing over 90 member associations and federations in 68 countries."[51] But this trend was far from linear, both from a political and an emotional standpoint. The UIAA suffered many setbacks when some of its members withdrew and others remained even while their nations openly challenged the League of Nations and its values. In this context, feelings and the rhetoric that described them served as important tools for the negotiation of each member's position within the organization, and protected the UIAA's reputation by avoiding it being associated with either appeasement or idealism.

According to the minutes of a UIAA executive committee meeting held in Pontresina, Switzerland, on September 6, 1934, the UIAA had twenty-five members, ten "effective" and fifteen affiliates, for a total of fifteen countries represented: Austria, Belgium, Bulgaria, Czechoslovakia, France, Germany, Hungary, Italy, the Netherlands, Poland, Romania, Spain, Sweden, Switzerland, and Yugoslavia.[52]

---

[47] UIAA Archives, Assemblée Générale, Chamonix, 1932, III Congrès internationale d'alpinisme, voeux adoptés et décisions prises par le Congrès dans sa dernière séance plénière, August 27, 1932, 3.

[48] UIAA Archives, Comité Exécutif, rapport du President du Comité Exécutif, pour l'exercise 1933, 3.

[49] UIAA Archives, Comité Exécutif, procès-verbal de la séance du Comité Exécutif de l'Union International des Associations d'Alpinisme, Pontresina, September 6, 1934, 2.

[50] UIAA Archives, Comité Exécutif, procès-verbal de la séance du Comité Exécutif de l'Union International des Associations d'Alpinisme, Geneva, July 4, 1947, 5.

[51] UIAA, https://www.theuiaa.org/about/(accessed on March 18, 2019).

[52] Listed as they appear in the original source, the ten effective members were: 1. Centro Excursionista de Catalunya (Spain); 2. Club Alpin français (France); 3. Magyar Turista Szövetség (Hungary); 4. Club Alpino Italiano (Italy); 5. Nederlandsche Alpen-Vereeniging (Netherlands); 6. Polish Tatra Society—Polskie Towarzystwo Tatrzańskie (Poland); 7. Svenska Fjällklubben (Sweden); 8. Club Alpin Suisse (Switzerland); 9. Klub Alpistu Ceskoslovenskych (Czechoslovakia); and 10. the Confederation of Yugoslav Alpine Societies (Yugoslavia). The fifteen affiliates were: 1. Deutscher Alpenverein (Germany); 2. Oesterreichische Bergsteiger Vereinigung (Austria); 3. Donauland Alpenverein (Austria); 4. Club Alpin Belge (Belgium); 5. Union of Bulgarian Tourists (Bulgaria); 6. Sociedad Española de Alpinismo Peñalara (Spain); 7. Spanish Alpine Club (Spain); 8. Union of Polish Tourist Societies (Poland); 9. Polish Skiing Federation (Poland); 10. Club Suisse des Femmes Alpinistes (Switzerland); 11. Fédération suisse de ski (Switzerland); 12. Societatea Carpatina Ardaleana (Romania); 13. Klub Ceskoslovenskych Turistu (Czechoslovakia); "James" Spolok Tatrzanskych

A few sobering announcements, however, accompanied the presentation of this list. Most notably, one of the founding members, the Alpine Club (AC) of Great Britain, had withdrawn, and the German and the Austrian clubs, which had recently been merged into a new entity called German and Austrian Alpine Club (D. u. Oe. Alpenverein), had stopped replying to all correspondence.[53] In this context, evoking emotions served as an essential means to negotiate relationships within the organization and also as a tool to manage the moral economy of the UIAA and of the internationalism it embodied.

Specifically, UIAA officers downplayed the withdrawal of groups such as the AC and the D. u. Oe. Alpenverein by blaming these choices on personal feelings and emotions. Moreover, individual delegates from various Alpine clubs accompanied their membership to or their withdrawal from the organization with emotional expressions effectively mitigating the consequences of their choices. Also, emotions such as "alpine friendship" justified seeking or maintaining relationships with people or nations who stood overtly at odds with the UIAA's internationalist positions. Emotions reduced the impact of failures, evened out contradictions, and provided the UIAA with a flexibility in managing its own setbacks, successes, and its overall moral economy.

The case of the Alpine Club (AC) of Great Britain illustrates how, by referring to particular emotions, Egmond d'Arcis minimized the effects of losing one of the UIAA's greatest assets. The AC was the oldest of all alpine clubs and one of the founding members of the organization. It was therefore quite surprising that it left, effective October 3, 1933, soon after its first formal meeting. The stated reason was that "unlike the great Foreign Societies, the Alpine Club possesses no territorial rights or Club huts in the Alps. It considers that the privileges of its members are guaranteed sufficiently by their membership in several or all of the great said Alpine Societies. Consequently...participation as a club...would be both assertive and redundant."[54] Such line of reasoning would not have sounded very convincing, as the AC had eagerly attended all of the international gatherings that had preceded the founding of the UIAA. Although the actual reasons for the AC leaving are not clear, it is relevant that d'Arcis made it a point to reassure the UIAA that there was "no bad intention in this withdrawal." He pointed out how "the pain that the English feel to engage new enterprises and new ways is well known" and expressed the hope that their involvement could soon be resumed.[55]

[53] UIAA Archives, Comité Exécutif, procès-verbal de la séance du Comité Exécutif de l'Union International des Associations d'Alpinisme, Pontresina, September 6, 1934, 1–2.
[54] *Alpine Journal* 44, no. 245 (November 1932), 340; *Alpine Journal* 45, no. 247 (November 1933), 403. The Archives of the English Alpine Club do not provide any further explanation in this regard.
[55] UIAA Archives, Comité Exécutif, procès-verbal de la séance du Comité Exécutif de l'Union International des Associations d'Alpinisme, Pontresina, September 6, 1934, 2.

Explaining the AC's withdrawal in terms of individual feelings—rather than as institutional policies and deliberate decisions—effectively mitigated the setback to the UIAA as a fledgling organization. The lack of English representation was conspicuous, and throughout the interwar period the UIAA continued to seek it.[56] At one point, a proposal was considered that would have invited the Ski Club of Great Britain instead, but it was rejected.[57] In 1939, in Zermatt, d'Arcis was happy to communicate that the English Alpine Club "was no longer as categorical in its attitude toward the UIAA" and sought to form an alternative association that could take the seat on the committee that the Alpine Club itself could not take for "known personal reasons."[58] In 1947, at the first assembly held after the war in Geneva, the question was solved when d'Arcis announced that a newly formed British Mountaineering Club would thereafter represent Great Britain in the UIAA (the Alpine Club would not join until 2003).[59]

In the case of the German and Austrian Alpine clubs, references to emotions enabled all sides to at least try to maintain relations while in the midst of a tense international situation. In 1934, when it was announced that a new German and Austrian Alpine Club (D. u. Oe. Alpenverein) might have been established and had not returned communications, a long debate ensued, after which "it was decided to ignore this association until it will have resumed its contacts with the UIAA." The minutes also noted that "the committee made this decision with much regret," and efforts to resume Austrian and German representation continued throughout the 1930s.[60] In July 1935, Austria was still listed as a participating country, and there was mention of inviting the Österreichischer Alpenklub to join the UIAA, as "this would be an excellent recruit for our union." With regard to the joint German and Austrian Alpine Club (the D. u. Oe. Alpenverein), the committee accepted the proposal of the Swedish representative, Dr. Otto Sjögren, to await the best opportunity for an intervention, or a "step" (démarche), as he called it.[61] As late as 1938, in Prague, upon news that even the Austrian Donauland Alpenverein had been absorbed by the "Deutscher Alpenverein," d'Arcis made it a point to express that since the founding of the UIAA a space had been reserved for the German Alpine Club. He hoped "that this great association will not refuse us their collaboration which would be one of the most precious in our union

---

[56] See UIAA Archives, Grand Bretagne, which contains the bulk of the correspondence between d'Arcis and the British Alpine Club in this regard.

[57] UIAA Archives, Comité Exécutif, procès-verbal de la séance du Comité Exécutif de l'Union International des Associations d'Alpinisme, Pontresina, September 6, 1934, 2.

[58] UIAA Archives, Comité Exécutif, procès-verbal de la séance du Comité Exécutif de l'Union International des Associations d'Alpinisme, Zermatt, August 20, 1939, 2.

[59] UIAA Archives, Comité Exécutif, procès-verbal de la séance du Comité Exécutif de l'Union International des Associations d'Alpinisme, Geneva, July 4, 1947, 2.

[60] UIAA Archives, Comité Exécutif, procès-verbal de la séance du Comité Exécutif de l'Union International des Associations d'Alpinisme, Pontresina, September 6, 1934, 2–3.

[61] On the attached list of affiliated members Germany is crossed out, while the two Austrian clubs are still included. UIAA Archives, Comité Exécutif, procès-verbal de la séance du Comité Exécutif de l'Union International des Associations d'Alpinisme, Barcelona, July 3, 1935, 1–2.

given the experience it has acquired in the field of alpinism." At the same meeting, Otto Sjögren shared his intention to make a further attempt at involving them in the UIAA.[62]

This friendly opening towards Germany at a time of rising political tensions did not come without opposition. In a 1939 letter, Sjögren complained to Egmond d'Arcis that "Hitlerophobes" on all sides stood in the way of what he saw as rapprochement. The previous year, they had denied him "a half an hour" with Hermann Göring, and now they forced him to resign as President of the Swedish club. He nonetheless asked to maintain his place at the UIAA and to attend the following meeting of the executive committee at Zermatt (he ended up not going, but his absence was excused).[63] He used emotions to counter accusations of appeasement and philo-Nazism, presenting his doings as a set of symbolic acts devised to reassert the value of personal connections that he believed transcended the political mood of the day. If the escalating conflict and the subsequent German defeat ended up dictating how the story would unfold, emotional rhetoric continued to play an important role in legitimizing international cooperation.

The Austrian and German clubs would not rejoin the UIAA until 1951, when the Verband alpiner Vereine Osterreich (VAVÖ) and a new Deutscher Alpenverein (D.A.V.) were readmitted at the general assembly held in the Slovenian town of Bled. On this occasion, the German representative, Dr. F. Hiess, expressed the many reasons why both associations "wanted to be part of the UIAA" as well as their gratitude to the UIAA for accepting their candidature.[64] The minutes signalled that this was a momentous decision: a new era had been inaugurated. The Austrian and German involvement in the UIAA represented their joining the international system at large, and showed that the tensions left by the Second World War were gradually being eased through the development of institutional and emotional bonds among individuals and institutions.[65] Such a development was framed against the backdrop of old alpine friendship left unshaken, which now buttressed the promise of a peaceful future.

The case of Italy, which followed a different trajectory and set of dynamics, illustrates well how emotions served to rationalize relations with countries and people openly at odds with the UIAA's internationalist mission while allowing the UIAA's reputation to remain untarnished. The Italian Alpine Club (CAI), which was one of the UIAA founding members, remained active throughout the 1930s

---

[62] UIAA Archives, Comité Exécutif, procès-verbal de la séance du Comité Exécutif de l'Union International des Associations d'Alpinisme, Prague, August 29, 1938, 1; 3.

[63] UIAA Archives, Correspondance Président, 1933–1979, letter (undated; spring 1939?) from Otto Sjögren to Egmond d'Arcis.

[64] UIAA Archives, Assemblée Générale, Bled, 1951, procès-verbal de l'Assemblée Générale.

[65] On the 1951 Congress in Bled as a turning-point in this context see also Tonella, *50 anni di alpinismo senza frontiere*, 25–7.

even after Italy withdrew from the League of Nations in December 1937.[66] No less than two Italian representatives, Eugenio Ferreri and Vittorio Frisinghelli, attended the general assembly in Zermatt on August 20, 1939, only a few days before the beginning of the Second World War.[67]

This was not because the CAI had resisted the influence of Mussolini's fascist regime.[68] In fact, as historian Alessandro Pastore pointed out, "the moral atmosphere" in the alpinist organization was "impregnated of a patriotic vision constant and pervasive, a vision still marked by the idea of the sacred union between mountain and war, cementified by the sacrifice of fallen soldiers and of the blood shed by combatants."[69] Moreover, its head, Angelo Manaresi, was a fervent member of the party and wore his fascist uniform even when performing his functions as President of the Centro Alpinistico Italiano (as the CAI had been renamed in 1938, as part of the fascist policy of Italianization and language purity).[70] Writing on letterhead adorned with Mussolini quotes (and ostentatiously stamped across with red ink to highlight the new, fully Italian name of the organization), Manaresi had never hesitated to play hardball with the UIAA. As early as 1933, he had taken exception to the UIAA's rejection of medals and competitions, and, starting from 1934, he had suspended the CAI's reciprocity agreements for the use of alpine huts that allowed foreigners to use many Italian shelters (*rifugi*).[71] Such an attitude, however, did not prevent the Italian delegation from showing itself open to international cooperation throughout the 1930s. In August 1939, Ferreri and Frisinghelli asked for "the honor of hosting the UIAA in 1942 in Rome," when an international exposition was scheduled to take place.[72] Due to the war this gathering never took place, but the CAI was one of the first to resume contact with d'Arcis at the end of hostilities.[73]

Many of the actors involved in this relationship justified its continuation by arguing that personal bonds were stronger than national or political distinctions.

[66] On the contradictory relationship between Italy and the League of Nations, see Elisabetta Tollardo, *Fascist Italy and the League of Nations, 1922–1935* (Basingstoke: Palgrave Macmillan, 2016).
[67] UIAA Archives, Comité Exécutif, procès-verbal de la séance du Comité Exécutif de l'Union International des Associations d'Alpinisme, Zermatt, August 20, 1939, 1.
[68] The Italian representatives at the UIAA changed several times throughout the 1930s: Giovanni Bobba served on the first executive committee, followed by Angelo Manaresi (1933), Dr. V. Frisinghelli (1934–5; 1939), Ardito Desio (1936), and Eugenio Ferreri (1937; 1939).
[69] Alessandro Pastore, *Alpinismo e storia d'Italia: dall'Unità alla Resistenza* (Bologna: Il Mulino, 2003), 106.
[70] This detail is cited in the history section of the webpage of the Turin section of the CAI. CAI, http://www.caitorino.it/centro-alpinistico/ (accessed on July 25, 2016). For a thorough examination of Manaresi's role in the "fascistizzazione dell'alpinismo" see Pastore, *Alpinismo e storia d'Italia: dall'Unità alla Resistenza*, 145–81.
[71] See correspondence on this topic in UIAA Archives, binder Club Alpino Italiano, AVST, FISI.
[72] UIAA Archives, Comité Exécutif, procès-verbal de la séance du Comité Exécutif de l'Union International des Associations d'Alpinisme, Zermatt, August 20, 1939, 8.
[73] Alessandro Pastore noted how Manaresi used the UIAA for his own internal propaganda purposes, describing its meetings—and the 1933 annual congress in particular—as celebratory of the fascist regime. Pastore, *Alpinismo e storia d'Italia: dall'Unità alla Resistenza*, 179–80.

In September 1945, Eugenio Ferreri—now General Secretary of the CAI—wrote to d'Arcis. He vividly recalled their last meeting at Zermatt in 1939, and also gave him an update on Manaresi, who was safe despite undergoing many "misadventures" (*disavventure*) following July 25, 1943, when "with the first fall of Fascism everything had changed." Ferreri expressed how "the tragedy of war has hit many of our friends, we all have felt the most lively emotions (*emozioni vivissime*) and witnessed tragedies and pains." He also confided how he had read "with *emozione*" the news contained in a bulletin d'Arcis had sent him, and closed his letter by affirming his "unchanged sense of sincere alpinistic friendship" (*immutato senso di sincera amicizia alpinistica*). He enclosed a summary of the CAI's activities during the war, expressing much optimism for the future of what had been named again the Italian Alpine Club (the stationary had now been stamped across again to highlight the significance of this change).[74]

In his reply, d'Arcis rejoiced in learning that his friend Manaresi had survived: having read in Swiss papers that the neo-fascist government had arrested him, he had feared for his fate.[75] D'Arcis' words implied that despite his allegiance to the Italian Fascist Party and the obstacles that he had placed in the UIAA's path, Manaresi remained an *alpiniste*. To be sure, the war was still very much present in d'Arcis' mind. In the same letter, he made reference to how he was still working without the UIAA Archives, "which had been placed in safety since the Germans wanted to put their hands on them" and had yet to be returned.[76] But, in his rhetoric, these stark political differences strengthened rather than weakened the argument that the UIAA could connect people across boundaries, and the alpinistic friendship that united UIAA members was, in the end, stronger than all other feelings. A few months after this exchange, d'Arcis and Ferreri met near the Swiss-Italian border. Shortly afterward, the relationship between the CAI and the UIAA returned to its pre-war normalcy.

A new urgency and a heightened symbolic value attached to technical matters gave the UIAA a strength it previously did not have and increased the role of emotional rhetoric making it an indispensable tool for international communication. In 1949, the CAI asked the UIAA to intervene in assigning huts that were being disputed by the Italian and the French Alpine clubs. Count Ugo di Vallepiana of the CAI—an old-timer, expert alpinist who had been set aside by the fascist

---

[74] UIAA Archives, Club Alpino Italiano, AVST, FISI, letter dated September 1, [1945], from Eugenio Ferreri to Egmond d'Arcis.

[75] UIAA Archives, Club Alpino Italiano, AVST, FISI, letter dated November 14, 1945, from Egmond d'Arcis to Eugenio Ferreri. After the collapse of Mussolini's rule, Manaresi swore allegiance to Marshal Pietro Badoglio. He was later arrested by fascist supporters of the Repubblica di Salò and remained imprisoned until the end of 1943, when Mussolini himself intervened to ensure his liberation. Pastore, *Alpinismo e storia d'Italia: dall'Unità alla Resistenza*, 209–10.

[76] UIAA Archives, Club Alpino Italiano, AVST, FISI, letter dated November 14, 1945, from Egmond d'Arcis to Eugenio Ferreri.

regime because he was Jewish—[77] asked d'Arcis for help: "in front of the European federal ideal," which represented "the only possibility of salvation for European civilization," he argued that "it is not a bad idea…to eliminate those causes of friction whose effect and damage are disproportionate, especially when compared to the immensity of the forces that someday could be in combat."[78] D'Arcis replied by promising to do his best to solve this "very delicate question," reassuring Ugo di Vallepiana that "it did not seem impossible [to him] to find a satisfying solution."[79]

Never had the UIAA's role as a potential mediator assumed such critical value. On March 23, 1950, Ugo di Vallepiana contacted d'Arcis again on behalf of the CAI President, Bartolomeo Figari. When discussing candidates for non-permanent membership in the UIAA executive committee, he expressed the CAI's wish to nominate the Slovenian Alpine Society, and to "make public" (*rendere noto*) that "it is really us [the CAI] that wishes for its nomination." He explained that "even if today for political reasons the contacts between this Society and the CAI are limited, we still hope that this special situation evolves so as to allow more collaboration in the field of alpinism with our neighbors and colleagues on the oriental frontier."[80] Two months later, in preparation for the Annual UIAA Congress that would take place in Milan in 1950, d'Arcis contacted the CAI asking for documentation to allow the Slovenian delegation to enter Italian territory.[81]

The CAI promptly responded by soliciting the Italian foreign ministry to ensure a smooth passage for their friends. To be sure, skepticism remained. A handwritten note from Ugo di Vallepiana quipped: "*entre nous*, I am convinced that the difficulties for their entry in Italy do not come from Rome but from Belgrade."[82] However, notwithstanding the anti-communist tinge of this remark, the CAI, the Alpine Association of Slovenia, and the UIAA interacted across one of the most contested borders of Europe.[83] Due to the Second World War, the UIAA had grown stronger in its role as a mediator. Issues such as participation in international congresses had become representative of larger political questions, and so expressions of alpine courtesy and friendship represented essential ingredients of high symbolic value.

[77] Pastore, *Alpinismo e storia d'Italia: dall'Unità alla Resistenza*, 199–204.
[78] UIAA Archives, Club Alpino Italiano, AVST, FISI, letter dated March 5, 1949, from Ugo di Vallepiana to Egmond d'Arcis.
[79] UIAA Archives, Club Alpino Italiano, AVST, FISI, letter dated March 20, 1949, from Egmond d'Arcis to Ugo di Vallepiana.
[80] UIAA Archives, Club Alpino Italiano, AVST, FISI, letter dated March 23, 1950, from Ugo di Vallepiana to Egmond d'Arcis.
[81] UIAA Archives, Club Alpino Italiano, AVST, FISI, letter dated May 7, 1950, from Egmond d'Arcis to the CAI President.
[82] UIAA Archives, Club Alpino Italiano, AVST, FISI, letter dated May 11, 1950, from Bartolomeo Figari to Egmond d'Arcis.
[83] This area in particular witnessed first fascist violence and later anti-Italian retaliations, most famously with the mass killing of civilians who were thrown alive into deep sinkholes, known as *foibe*.

The case of Guido Tonella (1903–86) clearly illustrates how emotions—and the way they were used, expressed, and felt—allowed for the coexistence of contradictory ideas within the UIAA, leaving unscathed both its reputation and its status as an international organization. An open supporter of the fascist regime and its policies, Tonella became an active UIAA member in the 1930s, served as the CAI representative at the UIAA General Assembly held in Geneva in 1948, and remained involved in the UIAA until his death. In 1983, he authored one of the few available accounts of the history of this organization, one in which he celebrated its internationalist scope. He dedicated his work, "50 Years of Alpinism with No Boundaries" to Egmond d'Arcis—"A life consecrated to the ideal of fraternity among the alpinists of all countries"—emphasizing his spiritual connection to Geneva and its quintessential institution, the League of Nations.[84]

Such enthusiastic endorsement of internationalism is puzzling, since Tonella had never hidden his fervent fascist views. In fact, as a journalist for the Italian newspapers *Il Corriere della Sera* and *Il Tempo* in the 1930s, Tonella had written extensively in support of Mussolini and his attacks against the League. And when the information section of the League of Nations revoked the license of a group of Italian journalists who had infamously heckled the Emperor Haile Selassie when he gave his famous address at the League of Nations on June 30, 1936, to protest the illegal and violent Italian invasion of Ethiopia, Tonella returned his own license in a symbolic act of protest and solidarity with his fellow countrymen.[85] In fact, it was while these events unfolded that he became increasingly involved in the UIAA. Tonella's case illustrates how the inclusion of people from the most disparate political positions buttressed the notion that the UIAA could serve as a ground for peaceful exchange. Tonella represented the quintessential "Signore della Montagna:" unapologetic, harsh, and ultimately redeemed—at least in the eyes of his fellow *alpinistes*—of his fascist past.

3.4 Describing Emotional International Experiences

The UIAA devoted much energy and significant resources to organizing a series of annual congresses each year in a different country. These were held in the Italian resort town of Cortina d'Ampezzo (1933); Pontresina, Switzerland (1934); Barcelona, Spain (1935); Geneva, Switzerland (1936); Paris, France (1937); Prague, Czechoslovakia (1938); and Zermatt, Switzerland (1939).[86] After the end of the

---

[84] Tonella, *50 anni di alpinismo senza frontiere*, 11–12.

[85] League of Nations Archives, R 5175, 13/24624/1750 (1936), letter dated July 8, 1936, from Guido Tonella and Ugo Sacerdote to A. Pelt, Director of the Information Section of the League of Nations. On this episode, see also Chapter 2.

[86] In Zermatt on August 22, 1939, a few days before the beginning of the Second World War, representatives of only ten countries were present (Belgium, Czechoslovakia, France, Greece, Hungary Italy, the Netherlands, Poland, Switzerland, and Yugoslavia. Tonella, *50 anni di alpinismo senza frontiere*, 20.

Second World War, on September 5–6, 1946, the UIAA organized a "friendly reunion" (*reunion amicale*) in Zermatt, which was followed by a formal congress in Geneva in 1947. After that, yearly congresses resumed in Geneva (1948); Chamonix, France (1949); Milan (1950); and Bled, Slovenia (1951).[87]

The UIAA staged these international gatherings with the explicit purpose of instilling a wide range of emotions in all participants, as well as in members of the broader public who would later read about these events either in UIAA publications or in the general press. By trying to affect what people felt about each other—and also about internationalism as a whole—in this period, the UIAA presented itself as a proactive agent of internationalist experimentation and change. UIAA officers often engaged feelings, either by overtly expressing emotions or by describing physical sensations associated with them. Most importantly, they accompanied this rhetoric with realist arguments that connected these emotions with the effects they would have on the relationships among peoples and nations. The bond that connected all *alpinistes* would be stronger than the factors that might divide them; the alpine landscape—and the unique sensorial and emotional experiences it engendered—would have a unifying effect on people enjoying it as a group; moreover, the collaborative aspect of mountaineering and the mutual dependency it entailed made *alpinistes* predisposed to international cooperation. For such dynamics to kick in, people needed to appreciate alpine aesthetics, taking in the mountains' sights and sounds. Also, international outings required the right settings to fulfill their internationalist purpose. For these reasons, every detail had to be taken into account to ensure that all participants would accumulate a set of unforgettable internationalist experiences of the Alps. Finally, newspaper articles, magazines, and written memoires would guide people's interpretation of these moments, making explicit their internationalist character and arguing for their potential to positively affect international relations.

An overall trust in the bond among *alpinistes* underlined many of these arguments. As early as 1931, the President of the French Alpine Club, Jean Escarra, argued that "the common sentiment that unites us must balance the political and economic contrasts that can divide people." He then added that it was in light of "this work of rapprochement" that he was inviting all national representatives to join in the third International Alpine Congress in Chamonix.[88] The establishment of the UIAA only reinforced his contention that such bonds could take an institutional form and become an active player affecting relations among people and groups from various countries.

---

[87] I ended this list in 1951 as it was in this year that Germany and Austria were readmitted, the association's priorities somewhat changed, and an important chapter closed for the UIAA and its members. Details about congresses in the following periods can be found in the aforementioned works by Tonella and Bossus. At the UIAA Archives, I could not find any source to illuminate why the German clubs did not re-join until 1951.

[88] Cited in Tonella, *50 anni di alpinismo senza frontiere*, 14.

The UIAA's message was that for *alpinistes* the mountain landscape possessed a unifying power, which derived not only from its aesthetic qualities but also from feelings spontaneously instilled in those who found themselves within it. In 1933, at the congress in Cortina d'Ampezzo, Egmond d'Arcis duly remarked that "if the sun frowns at the time of welcoming us in the kingdom of the Dolomites, we find [the sun] in the warmth of the friendship demonstrated by our Italian colleagues." For this reason, in the mountains "we feel…like in our own home, the alpinists' home." If bad weather had diminished the aesthetic and the overall sensorial experience of being together on the Dolomites, the set of emotions associated with sharing time in the mountains remained nonetheless strong. Moreover, *alpinistes* knew from experience that collaboration was necessary in the mountains. As d'Arcis explained by evoking the image of climbing partners tied to one another by a rope, "international cooperation, which is at the foundation of the UIAA, is not an empty word among alpinists because the spirit of mutual help is a form of devotion that knows neither frontiers nor obstacles."[89] He argued that these emotional expressions and these shared emotional experiences were not simply courteous or maudlin talk but instead stood at the center of the internationalist project of uniting peoples and nations.

At a time when the League of Nations' management of emotions disappointed many of its supporters, the UIAA responded by staging events with the specific goal of exposing peoples from various countries to a broad range of aesthetic and sensorial experiences. At each congress, participants took part in joint excursions and expeditions; they admired alpine photographs and art, and they enjoyed picnics, dinners, and banquets together.

The case of the seventh International Alpine Congress, held jointly with the UIAA third general assembly in Geneva from August 27 to September 6, 1936, provides the ideal case study in this respect since it included the broadest range of UIAA activities geared towards making people feel emotions deemed conducive to international cooperation and peace. Representatives from twenty associations from fourteen different countries gathered in Geneva for the occasion. Working from its strongest—and from an internationalist point of view, its most symbolic—location, the UIAA had the opportunity to fully implement its vision for this gathering, organizing numerous events not only to entertain its guests but also to meet the association's goal of creating opportunities for international exchange and mutual understanding. In this context, emotions—both as a set of feelings that were expressed through multiple means and as the sensorial experiences that fed them—represented arguably the most important part of this occasion.

From August 22 to September 2, 1936, the UIAA organized two exhibitions that employed images and language to elicit shared emotions in their audience:

---

[89] Cited in Tonella, *50 anni di alpinismo senza frontiere*, 17.

one of materials for mountain rescue and one of alpine photographs, both held in the Salles du Conservatoire de Musique facing the elegant Place de Neuve in central Geneva.[90] Spurred on by the rise in the number of accidents that had stemmed from the growing interest in mountains, the "Exposition of materials for mountain rescue" (Exposition de matériel de sauvetage en montagne) showcased the tools that people in various countries had devised in order to save as many lives as possible. It gathered the latest innovations in the field of mountain rescue, from pharmaceutical products, to lamps, to different kinds of stretchers (some professionally crafted and some made on the spot, with sticks and other fortuitous objects). This event described much of the effort by the UIAA to standardize alpine maps, as well as security and rescue procedures. It also brought out the human aspect of this work. By showing the concrete objects involved in such endeavors, the exhibition allowed audiences to visualize the people who benefitted from them, thereby triggering strong feelings of empathy.[91] As an article in the *Journal de Genève* observed, this exhibition was a "manifestation of human solidarity" that made people not just learn but also *feel* international cooperation in the mountains.[92]

Through aesthetic and sensorial experiences, visitors could capture at once the universalism and the national peculiarities of the mountain experience. The "First International Exhibition of Alpine Photographs" featured 518 pictures of the Alps and mountains all over the world, from the Spanish Guadarrama to the Himalayas, from the Swedish Lappland to the Caucasus, and from the gorges on the Yangzi river to the Mexican Popocatepetl. By stretching the meaning of the adjective "alpine" to its fullest, the exhibition depicted all mountains as one, and all of the dedication, the efforts, and the passions that led people all over the world to admire them as a shared set of feelings—it is relevant to note that contemporaries used of the term "the Alps" to refer to ranges from various parts of the world (e.g., the "Japanese Alps"). At the same time, the pictures were classified and displayed according to the nationality of the person who took them, regardless of the location of the subject. As a result, the venue was divided into eleven sections, each dedicated to one country (Belgium, Spain, France, Hungary, Italy, the Netherlands, Poland, Sweden, Czechoslovakia, Yugoslavia, and Switzerland), making the exhibition the first international event of its kind.[93] By balancing the

---

[90] The first was curated by Dr. E. A. Robert; the second by Albert Roussy. Both were members of the UIAA Permanent Bureau.

[91] Photographs of this show were published on the front page of *La Suisse* on August 24, 1936, and also on the magazines *L'illustré*, August 27, 1936, 1103, and *La Patrie Suisse*, August 29, 1936, 824.

[92] *Journal de Genève*, August 25, 1936, 4.

[93] For a full list of the work on display, see the catalogue of the exhibition, *Première exposition internationale de photographies alpines* (Geneva, 1936). One copy is conserved at the Bibliothèque de Genève (Br 1544). Although other photographic exhibitions previously organized by various alpine clubs had included works from authors from different countries, this was the first exhibition to call itself "international" because of this feature.

universal with the national aspects, the exhibition represented an example of internationalism at work and allowed all visitors to experience it.

Numerous newspaper articles pointed out that the exhibition's photographs provided the audience with a shared emotional experience. Only a few pictures conveyed a realistic impression of the mountains; the majority instead embraced modern artistic trends, playing with light and color to communicate feelings to the audience. Ice, fog, and mist often appeared as central features in these pieces, providing the same effect as an impressionist work. Like painters, these photographers created art whose "power of suggestion is extraordinary" (*puissance de suggestion est extraordinaire*), to cite one description published in *La Suisse*. One "would be moved" (*on est ému*), to cite another passage from the same article, as much by nature as by a work of art, not only in the viewing of it also by experiencing mountains on a deeper level.[94]

The Swiss Exhibition of Alpine Art, organized by the Geneva section of the Swiss Alpine Club during the same period, was also conceived and described as an emotional event.[95] Held at the Rath Museum, one of the largest venues in the city located a few steps away from the Music Conservatory where the other exhibitions were held, this show featured more than 200 works, mostly paintings of mountain scenes in tempera, oil, and watercolor.[96] Mountains other than the Alps were included, and emphasis was placed on artistic expression over realistic representation. As art critic L. Florentin noted in a review published in the newspaper *La Suisse*, realism had given way to "an impressionism romantic or decorative…and an architectonical vision of shapes in their relationship with space." The result was an exhibition whose works "proposed to our whole sensibility and to our imagination fuller pleasures."[97] To be sure, doing justice to the mountains required "exceptional acuity of vision and a power of touch" (*une acuité de vision et une vigueur de touche exceptionelles*) which few works demonstrated; yet the

[94] *La Suisse*, August 25, 1936, 5. The fact that both exhibitions were very successful was reported by *La Tribune de Genève* in a note informing the public that the shows could not be prolonged. See *La Tribune de Genève*, September 2, 1936, 3.

[95] The Exhibition of Swiss Alpine Art opened on August 19 and closed on September 19, 1936. The organizing committee was presided by Paul Naville. For details on the rest of the committee, see Archives de la Ville de Genève, Section genevoise du Club alpin suisse, CASG.B.13.4/1 C.A.S. Section genevoise/Exposition d'art alpin 1936/Procès-verbaux/December 20, 1935. An undated entry in the minutes of the organizing committee provided the figure of 6,018 spectators, accompanied by the comments that the exhibition had been "well attended." Archives de la Ville de Genève, Section genevoise du Club alpin suisse, CASG.B.13.4/1 C.A.S. Section genevoise/Exposition d'art alpin 1936/Procès-verbaux/undated comments at the end.

[96] The first exhibition was held at the Museum of Arts and Crafts (*Kunstgewerbemuseum*) in Zürich in 1933. See *Erste Ausstellung Schweizerischer alpiner Kunst, im Kunstgewerbemuseum bei Hauptbanhof Zürich, 26. März bis 17. April [1933]* (Zürich, 1933). For a full list of the works exhibited in Geneva see the exhibition catalogue, *La deuxième exposition Suisse d'art alpin, Genève 1936* (Geneva, 1936). One copy is conserved at the Bibliothèque d'art et d'archéologie (Ex 103/1936/5278). The President of the Organizing Committee was André de Rivaz of the Swiss Alpine Club of Sion.

[97] *La Suisse*, September 1, 1936, 5.

show still offered many powerful moments for all visitors, regardless of their provenance, to appreciate.[98]

Another article on the same page, written by Egmond d'Arcis and entitled "The Musical Compositions whose themes are inspired by the Alps," articulated further how "the Alps" provided a universal, shared, emotional experience. In this piece, the UIAA President argued that although there is no such thing as natural alpine music, the Alps had often served as the pretext for wonderful music and poetry. Robert Schumann's *Manfred* and Jaques Dalcroze's *Poème alpestre* had been inspired by them; d'Arcis himself had written an overture for a rendition of *William Tell* by Guilbert de Pixérécourt and also a symphonic poem, both set on the alpine peaks. If these mountains did not have their own music per se, he insisted, they still served an essential role for artistic and emotional expression.[99]

Even outside of the formal exhibition space, the UIAA made full use of the aesthetic and emotional power of the mountains to achieve its internationalist goals. In addition to the aforementioned exhibitions, the association provided opportunities for participants to live and feel their passion for mountains. On August 30, all who had convened in Geneva for the UIAA Congress took a scenic boat tour on Lake Geneva to admire the view of the Alps in all of their grandeur. The chorale of the Geneva section of the Swiss Alpine Club provided a suggestive soundtrack, and a banquet at the exclusive Hotel des Bergues followed. The lavish venue, situated on the Geneva lakefront, was decorated with the colors of all the countries represented at the international gathering. Participants addressed the others in both French and their native tongues, showing how the UIAA, like the League of Nations, fostered international exchange while also respecting national individualities. According to those who were there, cordiality and good cheer characterized the occasion.[100]

The following week, three excursions to the mountains were organized for people of all levels of alpine skill in order for them to experience the strongest emotions that the Alps could offer.[101] "Tourists" went on a three-day tour of the region by car, crossing at the Petit St. Bernard, reaching first the Italian resort town of Courmayeur and then Aosta. The next day, they crossed at the Grand St. Bernard to follow the road all the way to Bulle, at the foot of the Fribourg pre-Alps. They then spent the last day visiting the quaint town of Gruyères and the medieval Castle of Chillon. *Bon marcheurs* (literally, "good walkers") undertook instead a seven-day tour to Interlaken, Reichenbach, Sion, and Zermatt, with

---

[98]   See review by W. Matthey-Claudet, *La Tribune de Genève*, August 29, 1936, 5.
[99]   *La Tribune de Genève*, August 29, 1936, 5.   [100]   *La Suisse*, August 30, 1936, 9.
[101]   Archives de la Ville de Genève, Section genevoise du Club alpin suisse, CASG.B.13.4/2: Expositions d'Art alpin/Documents administratifs (1933–1936), folder 1936. Brochure advertising events held in conjunction with the UIAA Congress. See also *Bulletin du Club Alpin Suisse, Section Genevoise* (June 1936), 88–9. A detailed description of these trips was published on *Die Alpen/Les Alps/Le Alpi* (1936), 311–13.

guided hikes and an easy climb of the Mettelhorn (3410 meters above sea level). Expert *alpinistes* were based in Zermatt, from which they climbed some of the most famous alpine peaks, including the Matterhorn/Cervin (4482 m).[102] For this occasion, the Alps had been opened to all who desired to appreciate them. According to those who attended, the atmosphere was one of inclusion, relaxation, and communal enjoyment. As Roussy described in a report published on *Les Alpes*, in the evening the *alpinistes* met with the people in the second group, "drank the cup of friendship and danced."[103]

A set of shared sensorial experiences sealed the event in the memory of those who were present and were later described in their accounts. Nearby hotels welcomed all guests, and comfortable alpine huts (or *cabanes*, as they were called) awaited those who attempted to venture among alpine peaks. The *bon marcheurs* stayed at the *Cabane Hohtürli* (2781 m); the *alpinistes* slept instead at the *Cabane Britannia* (3031 m), which had been built in 1912 thanks to the support of a few English members and represented the crown jewel of the huts managed by the Swiss Alpine Club. Writing in *La Tribune de Genève* at the time of the UIAA Congress in Geneva, John Michel (President of the Swiss Association of Ski Clubs and also a member of the UIAA permanent bureau) explained how, in terms of comfort, it "left nothing to be desired." Even in the middle of winter, up to eighty people could find "a welcoming home, well-heated," complete with metal-frame beds, gas lamps, and stewards to ensure the perfect maintenance of the dwelling. "What joyous gatherings up there with our English colleagues, and what genuine international intermingling," Michel commented in his piece, thus evoking the friendly atmosphere of the place.[104]

Descriptions of the sight of the mountains and their artistic representations, the sounds of the Alps and their musical renditions, the cold of the mountains' glaciers and the warmth of their huts all conveyed a deep feeling of camaraderie among the people who enjoyed them. These sensorial experiences became associated with a set of emotions that came to define internationalism in this period and reverberated in the years that followed.

* * *

Like the League of Nations, the UIAA used emotions to promote its own image and mission. As the Second World War began, the pages of the *Bulletin* of the Swiss Alpine Club became dotted with articles remembering the old days, speaking of "the Alps"—no matter the national sovereignty—as the quintessential site of peace. In 1940, L. Gianoli, who collaborated in the staging of the 1936 Exhibition

---

[102] The first group (tourists) had six participants (four men and two women). The second group (*bon marcheurs*) had fourteen people, six of which were women. The third group comprised eight men of five different nationalities. *Die Alpen/Les Alps/Le Alpi* (1936), 311–13.
[103] *Die Alpen/Les Alps/Le Alpi* (1936), 313.   [104] *La Tribune de Genève*, August 30–1, 1936, 7.

of Alpine Art, wrote a short piece entitled "Notre Paix, là-haut!" ("Our Peace, Up High") in which he explained how "in the anguish (*angoisse*) of current times we find on the peaks the necessary remedy that calms our nervous system and allows us to endure the dreadful calamity to which Europe had fallen victim."[105] In 1941, Swiss author Eugène Rambert celebrated the Alps as the powerful barrier that had protected Switzerland from the war that surrounded it, allowing for a space where "a German majority respects the French-speaking minority, a Protestant majority respects the Catholic minority, and a number of states relatively populous and strong, launched at full speed in the current of modern life, respect the slow pace of those old pastoral democracies for which centuries could be years."[106]

Both concretely and metaphorically, the UIAA had turned the Alps into a symbol against war, cynicism, and destruction. In February 1942, the President of the Geneva section of the Swiss Alpine Club, C. Vernet, explained how alpinists remained a much-needed resource for a world now thrown into chaos: "The harder the journey becomes, the narrower the path shrinks and perhaps soon turns into the fine edge that only the alpinist crosses with a steady foot, the more our people will need steady men to guide its steps and give an example."[107] Two years later, Egmond d'Arcis would make a similar argument in his appeal to his fellow *montagnards* as he invited them to participate in rebuilding a world finally at peace.

Taken out of context, his and other messages of this kind read like caricatures of interwar idealism. Indeed, they have been interpreted as such by historians for some time. Yet, set against the background of the emotions that had created them and accompanied them throughout their history, they become the meaningful expression of a complex set of ideas and practices that defined internationalism during and following the Second World War. After 1945, the practices promoted by the UIAA would become normative in foreign and international policy (e.g., staging in-person encounters became essential tools for peace building and soft power), and also in "non-political" realms (e.g., in corporate team building). To one such realm—health—we shall now turn.

---

[105] *Bulletin du Club Alpin Suisse, Section Genevoise*, September 1940, 133.
[106] *Bulletin du Club Alpin Suisse, Section Genevoise*, August 1941, 124.
[107] *Bulletin du Club Alpin Suisse, Section Genevoise*, February 1942, 28–30.

4

Seeing Emotions while Healing
the Body and the World as a Whole

The final stop of a narrow-gauge railway, nestled at an elevation of 1265 meters, the Swiss village of Leysin offers a breath-taking view of the Mont Blanc and the Dents du Midi. Enhanced by modern facilities for various sports and excursions, today it thrives as an alpine resort and as the main site for prestigious institutions for international education, such as the Leysin American School (or LAS, an international boarding school established in 1961), the Swiss Hotel Management School (founded in 1992 and moved to the Leysin campus in 2004), and the Kumon Leysin Academy of Switzerland (a private high school bringing students from Japan since 1990). Thousands of people from all over the world go there every year, eager to enjoy its landscape as well as its atmosphere. As emphasized by the website of the Leysin Tourist Office, together with its spectacular scenery, Leysin's "international and cosmopolitan character" represents one of its main attractions and sets it apart from other destinations on the Swiss Alps.[1]

This chapter undertakes a metaphorical journey to this remarkable village, which in the 1920s and 1930s stood out as a major center for the treatment of tuberculosis and also as an international and internationalist destination. It demonstrates that so much energy was devoted to the staging, production, reproduction, and distribution of particular images that the content and the form of internationalist practices could hardly be distinguished from one another. Especially-designed aesthetics strengthened the assumption that feelings mattered to both medical and political health. Internationalists used visible emotional expressions—as immortalized in the numerous photographs they produced—as evidence of their success. Accompanied by other overt displays of internationalism (e.g., rosters of names, programs of international conferences, and writings in various languages and alphabets), pictures of people involved in international exchanges came to represent the values attached to the internationalist movement. Bodies served as "mass ornaments" for the internationalist cause, while expressions of shared enthusiasm symbolized open support for "modern" internationalist enterprises and trust in their viability.

---

[1] Leysin Tourist Office, "Leysin Tourist Office—Presentation." http://www.leysin.ch/en/resort/presentation-leysin (accessed on September 12, 2016).

The Emotions of Internationalism: Feeling International Cooperation in the Alps in the Interwar Period. Ilaria Scaglia, Oxford University Press (2020). © Ilaria Scaglia.
DOI: 10.1093/oso/9780198848325.001.0001

Images helped to reconcile contradictory elements within internationalism (e.g., its modernist and anti-modernist aspects) and emphasized its balanced, and therefore morally-elevated aspects.[2] Doctors, patients, and visitors became at once subjects and commentators for photographs employed in publicity materials, giving credibility and authenticity to internationalist arguments. In this context, the mountain landscape provided a highly symbolic background, gave meaning to these pictures, and associated them with internationalist emotions. The dynamics and the images internationalists created there in the 1920s and 1930s persist to this day and still shape international cooperation (what it looks like, what it feels like, and therefore what it is) in the twenty-first century.

Until recently, Leysin's fascinating history as an international center has been seldom acknowledged in the town's public image. Yet, this can be traced back to 1888, when the village of 397 inhabitants working mostly as farmers, shepherds, and lumberjacks underwent a sudden change. In that year, a series of meteorological studies concluded that Leysin's unique position (south-facing and surrounded by forests) and exceptional microclimate (with dry air and no wind) would benefit people with tuberculosis and other pulmonary diseases.[3] Soon afterward, a Société Climatérique was established to build a sanatorium in an open pasture known as Le Feydey, which was located at 1450 meters, well above the fog that would cover the valley during the winter. On August 26, 1892, the "Grand Hotel" opened; with 120 beds and a name that triggered more positive associations than the word "sanatorium," it quickly filled up. Encouraged by this success, the Société Climatérique soon added more structures of the same kind; and, as local historian Maurice André later remarked, in a short period of time Le Feydey became "a true center, with its own post office, its own bank, its own businesses, and its own train station!"[4] Leysin's history as a worldwide destination—albeit not for tourists or students but for people affected by tuberculosis—had officially begun.

In 1903, down in the village, Dr. Auguste Rollier expanded on the work of the Société Climatérique by opening the first center for heliotherapy, a treatment for

---

[2] On bodies in the modernist imagination, see Siegfried Kracauer, *Das Ornament der Masse: Essays* (Frankfurt am Main: Suhrkamp Verlag, 1963). On the "moral economy" of internationalism, and on the idea that it was "balanced" and therefore morally superior to other contemporary ideologies see Ilaria Scaglia, "The 'Hydrologist's Weapons': Emotions and the 'Moral Economy' of Internationalism, 1921–1952," in Sara Graça Da Silva, ed., *New Interdisciplinary Landscapes in Morality and Emotion* (London: Routledge, 2018), 140–52. See also Chapter 3.

[3] On the various "legends" surrounding the origins of Leysin as a climatic and medical station, see Dave Lüthi, *Le compas & le bistouri: architectures de la médecine et du tourisme curatif. L'exemple vaudois (1760–1940)* (Lausanne: BHMS, 2012), 149–57. The literature on the history of tuberculosis is very extensive. A useful overview can be found in Thomas Dormandy, *The White Death: A History of Tuberculosis* (London: Hambledon Press, 1999). For a summary of its main historiographical debates, see Flurin Condrau and Michael Worboys, eds., *Tuberculosis Then and Now: Perspectives on the History of an Infectious Disease* (Montreal: McGill-Queen's University Press, 2010).

[4] Maurice André, *Leysin, station médicale* (Pully: Les Iles futures, 2002), 17–23.

non-pulmonary forms of tuberculosis based on the principle that controlled exposure to the sun could benefit the patients' condition.[5] By 1930, he ran thirty-seven such clinics housing a total of 1100 patients, and Leysin as a whole became home to eighty treatment centers, hosting 3000 patients, fifty doctors, and 300 nurses. Multiple societies administered them, attracting a wide range of guests from all over the world. Luxurious accommodations were built for the wealthiest, who expected maximum comfort while undergoing long periods of treatment. Simpler dwellings accommodated hundreds of people of limited means. Clinics for children opened, together with establishments for workers, students, single women, and members of religious organizations of all faiths. Sanatoria thus came to define Leysin's history and architecture: to this day, many of the buildings that dominate its landscape are former clinics.[6]

Acknowledgments of Leysin's medical past, however, remain rare. In a 1990 article, Geneviève Heller poignantly described how for a long time in Leysin, tuberculosis was "a shame, an anguish, a spectrum they wanted to forget"; it was "a past nobody wanted to talk about."[7] This tendency deepened its roots in the late nineteenth and early twentieth centuries, when tuberculosis was surrounded by a stigma that made it an uncomfortable topic of discussion for both the patients and those who treated them. As Susan Sontag pointed out in a landmark study, *Illness as Metaphor* (1978), tuberculosis was mystified more than other diseases. Frequently associated with melancholy, it was long imagined as a spiritual illness that attacked sensitive people, poet-types, and creative artists whose internal struggles materialized in physical forms.[8] Moreover, as Erving Goffman theorized, tuberculosis long held a "social stigma": it was an affliction that discredited and "spoiled" the existence of both those who had it and those who came into contact with them, and one that defined their identity for the rest of their lives.[9] As an aesthetic object, it was first romanticized (most notably, with artistic depictions of the pale, "consumptive look" and the spiritual and sentimental stirrings it reflected) and later shamed as a mark of financial indigence and as a threat to social, public, and national health.[10]

Because of their romanticization and stigmatization, sanatoria became powerful symbols of broader societal issues. As reflected by the many literary works set in

[5] On the history of heliotherapy, see Simon Carter, *Rise and Shine: Sunlight, Technology, and Health* (Oxford: Berg, 2007); Daniel Freund, *American Sunshine: Diseases of Darkness and the Quest for Natural Light* (Chicago: University of Chicago Press, 2012). The literature pertaining to Dr. Auguste Rollier is examined later in this chapter.

[6] A complete list with extensive data on all of these establishments can be found in André, *Leysin, station médicale*, 17–23.

[7] Geneviève Heller, "Leysin et son passé médical," *Gesnerus* 47, nos. 3–4 (1990), 330–1.

[8] Susan Sontag, *Illness as Metaphor* (New York: Farrar, Straus and Giroux, 1978).

[9] Erving Goffman, *Stigma: Notes on the Management of Spoiled Identity* (New York: Simon & Schuster, 1963).

[10] On the history of tuberculosis as an aesthetic object see Clark Lawlor, *Consumption and Literature: The Making of the Romantic Disease* (New York: Palgrave Macmillan, 2006).

them (Thomas Mann's *The Magic Mountain* constituting the most famous example), tuberculosis and the establishments where it was treated carried a complex meaning for those who interacted in or fantasized about them.[11] Four notions were associated with sanatoria's aesthetics and emotions: first, sanatoria were deemed to be dangerous places that could easily contaminate the world that surrounded them. In Sheila Rothman's words, they carried a "shadow of death" that defined them in cultural terms.[12] Second, as secluded and remote spaces, they were often imagined to affect people's behavior in fundamental ways. In particular, they were believed to exacerbate passions and licentiousness, inevitably turning into sites of sin and excess.[13] Third, because various countries devised extensive social policies to deal with tuberculosis in this period (and the opening of sanatoria—particularly the ones reserved for lower classes—represented the cornerstone of these policies), these institutions came to represent the larger political movements that had led to their establishment.[14] Fourth, and especially important for the purpose of this chapter, sanatoria in the Alps were "cosmopolitan" both in imagination (e.g., in Thomas Mann's aforementioned fictional account) and in reality.[15]

In Leysin, most clinics attracted foreign patients, and two were overtly international: the Clinique Manufacture Internationale, which was inaugurated by Dr. Auguste Rollier in 1930 and remained active as an international institution until 1944, and Dr. Louis Vauthier's University Sanatorium, which opened its doors in 1922 and continued its activities through the 1960s. Though the continuity between older and newer institutions is seldom acknowledged, it is nonetheless there, as is the sentimentalization of international spaces: to quote only one case, the website of the Leysin American School promises a "campus community with a global perspective and a family atmosphere."[16] Indeed, this notion deepens its roots in the League of Nations' activities in the field of tuberculosis and in the scientific communities that connected their work to them. To these we shall therefore now turn as we officially embark on our journey.

---

[11] Thomas Mann, *Der Zauberberg* (Berlin: S. Fischer Verlag, 1924). After publication, the book soon appeared in English, French, and Italian. See *The Magic Mountain* (New York: Alfred A. Knopf, 1927); *La montagne magique* (Paris: Fayard, 1931); *La montagna incantata* (Milan: Modernissima, 1932).

[12] Sheila M. Rothman, *Living in the Shadow of Death: Tuberculosis and the Social Experience of Illness in American History* (Baltimore, MD: Johns Hopkins University Press, 1995), 238.

[13] This idea was reinforced and disseminated by novels such as Michel Corday, *Les embrasés* (Paris: Flammarion, 1902), Joseph Kessel, *Les captifs* (Paris: Gallimard, 1926), as well as the aforementioned classic work by Thomas Mann, *Der Zauberberg* (1924).

[14] On social aspects, see Barbara Bates, *Bargaining for Life: A Social History of Tuberculosis, 1876–1938* (Philadelphia: University of Pennsylvania Press, 2015).

[15] This is in contrast to the United States, where patients in sanatoria were often divided by ethnicity. See Rothman, *Living in the Shadow of Death*, 218.

[16] Leysin American School, https://www.las.ch/about/welcome/(accessed on June 29, 2017).

4.1 Tuberculosis, Internationalism, and Their Emotions

Health represented a major concern for the League of Nations since the beginning of its existence. Article 23 paragraph (*f*) of the *Covenant of the League of Nations* mandated that all members "will endeavour to take steps in matters of international concern for the prevention and control of disease."[17] In February 1920, the Council decided to summon an "International Conference of health experts to prepare the constitution of the Health Organisation."[18] To respond to the heightened spread of infectious diseases after the First World War, the committee immediately set up an "epidemic commission." They also organized a Provisional Health Committee to address what they saw as the most urgent matters by establishing a set of commissions. These included Public Health Training; Far East Commission; Malaria Commission; Cancer Commission; Tuberculosis Commission; Opium Commission; Temporary Mixed Anthrax Commission; Commission on Standardization of Sera, Serological Reactions, and Biological Products; Commission of Experts for the Study of Sleeping-Sickness and Tuberculosis in Equatorial Africa; International Sleeping-Sickness Commission; and a Smallpox and Vaccination Commission.[19]

Starting from 1932, a *Quarterly Bulletin of the Health Organization* was produced to share news on the work of the organization. The main themes treated were the standardization of medicines, sera, and vitamins; initiatives to curtail infectious diseases (especially tuberculosis, syphilis, rabies, malaria, and tropical diseases); and efforts to improve public health and hygiene (many pieces dealt with the proper ways to ensure the safety of milk and other food products). As a result, the Health Organization of the League of Nations quickly became a reference point for the many groups that corresponded with it and reported on their work. In all of these areas, much energy was devoted to studies and statistics to evaluate the situation, identify needs, and provide national governments with guidance on how to meet them. In this case, too, the rhetoric echoed the internationalist speeches given in Geneva and elsewhere in this period, and mentions of amicability, solidarity, and peaceful cooperation appeared in virtually every document.

The emotions associated with mountains concretely affected how the League either framed its work on the ground. For instance, the League sponsored a report on rural hygiene and was also abreast of initiatives for battling quintessentially mountain diseases, such as goiter.[20] And, if as late as 1939 the Health Section of the League of Nations had not directly dealt with this disease, many international conferences were nevertheless held on the subject. The League of Nations had

---

[17] *The Covenant of the League of Nations*, http://avalon.law.yale.edu/20th_century/leagcov.asp (accessed on July 30, 2018).

[18] *Annual Report of the Health Organisation for 1925–1930*, 2. C.H. 442. (A.17.1926. III)

[19] *Annual Report of the Health Organisation for 1925–1930*, 3–6.

[20] League of Nations Archives, R 998.

received notice of two of these, which took place in Bern in 1927 and in 1933.[21] Experts from various countries, including Germany and the United States, assessed the incidence of goiter and cretinism and debated the benefits of adding iodine to the salt and water supplies to reduce the number of cases. They deliberated that "tacit" approaches (i.e., proceeding with such interventions rather than simply encouraging mountain populations to take iodine supplements) should be ventured, since these could circumvent the supposed reluctance and stubbornness of the mountains' indigenous inhabitants.[22] In this case, the grumpiness associated with Heidi's grandpa and the pity *montagnards* elicited in many visitors during this period allowed for taking action without consulting local authorities, and their double association with both health and disease affected how these were treated by internationalist bodies.[23]

It is however the case of tuberculosis that best illustrate the dynamics through which the League's technical work (via the Health Section and the groups it either supported or collaborated with in the 1920s and 1930s) affected the process of internationalization of the Alps as well as its emotional aspects. In 1925, the League completed an extensive study on the reasons for the decline of death by tuberculosis occurring in different countries.[24] General improvements in food and housing, the segregation of known cases in hospitals and sanatoria, and increased knowledge of prophylactic measures proved to be the main factors that influenced this trend.[25] The League informed national representatives of these results and invited them to implement changes in their countries accordingly to reduce the spread of the disease. It also distributed information on the use of tuberculin for early detection and on current studies on the Bacillus Calmette–Guérin (aka BCG) vaccine, which had just begun to be administered to humans.

Moreover, the League promoted the standardization of units of measurement and medical products, the exchange of experts from various countries, and the creation of rosters of existing and new organizations—both national and international—that were already conducting work in these areas. The Health section encouraged governments to increase their interventions—namely by building sanatoria—and to exploit the healing effect of mountains on those affected by the disease. As Iris Borowy noted, much of this work remained incomplete; yet the League's blueprint was important.[26] The emotions engendered through

---

[21] League of Nations Archives, R 6090, 8A/4255/4255. Letter, dated from Yves M. Biraud (Service des renseignments epidémiologiques et des statistiques sanitaires) to the Director [of the League's Health Section].

[22] League of Nations Archives, R 991, 12B/56702/56702 and R 6090, 8A/4255/4255.

[23] On these stereotypes and associations see Chapter 1.

[24] On the League of Nations Health Organization, on other Health sections and committees, and also on the interaction with the Public Health Office, see Iris Borowy, *Coming to Terms with World Health: The League of Nations Health Organisation, 1921-1946* (Frankfurt am Main: Peter Lang, 2009).

[25] *Annual Report of the Health Organisation for 1925-1930*, 30-1.

[26] Borowy, *Coming to Terms with World Health*, 13.

these efforts proved especially influential on many individuals and associations that mirrored the League's activities while emulating its rhetoric.

In 1920, a group of experts founded the International Union against Tuberculosis (*Union Internationale contre la Tuberculose*) in Paris. Uniting governments and national associations from forty-two different countries, the association published a *Bulletin of the International Union Against Tuberculosis*, a quarterly written in the two official languages of the League of Nations, English and French.[27] The association soon asked for the formal support from the Health Organization of the League of Nations, and regularly published reports on its activities.[28]

This organization explicitly connected its own work with the overall goal of fostering peace. In an article published in July 1938, for example, Dr. J. B. McDougall argued that "once a discovery is made it becomes the property of all the world and is free to be used by those who have the will to use it." Just as "the achievements of Wagner, Elgar, and the others on the same plane" did not belong to a single nation but instead were "medicine for the emotions of the people of the entire world," so could progresses in the medical field, now quickly shared through medical presses in various languages, enrich humanity as a whole.[29]

McDougall explicitly referred to contemporary discourses on the role of "universal languages" in fostering peace, equating medicine to Esperanto, art, or music. On one hand, McDougall's argument is not surprising: as Carolyn Biltoft pointed out, in the 1920s "reversing the curse of Babel" became an essential step for the establishment of permanent peace after the tragedy of the First World War.[30] The search for "international" or "universal" forms of communication extended to disparate disciplines including law, medicine, and finance. Starting from the second half of the nineteenth century, resources were devoted to "the cause of 'universal jurisprudence'" and the codification of a unified body of international law.[31] In the fields of biology, medicine, and epidemiology, the keyword "standardization" began to appear in the title of countless speeches, publications, and conferences aimed at promoting cooperation among experts in different countries.[32] Yet the aesthetic and emotional aspects of scientific standardization

[27] *Répertoire des organizations internationales* (Geneva: Série des publications de la Société des Nations, XII, 1936), 209.

[28] *Bulletin of the International Union Against Tuberculosis*, 1924, III, 62.

[29] J. B. McDougall, "Nos campaignes antituberculeuses—et ensuite?," *Bulletin of the International Union Against Tuberculosis*, 1938, III, 296–7.

[30] Carolyn N. Biltoft, "Reversing the Curse of Babel? International Language Movements and Inter-war Chasms," in Patrick Manning, ed., *World History: Global and Local Interactions* (Princeton: Markus Wiener Publishers, 2005), 179–94.

[31] Philip Marshall Brown, "The Codification of International Law," *American Journal of International Law* 29, no. 1 (January 1935), 25–39.

[32] A few examples: "International Conference on Biological Standardization" (December 1921, London and October 1935, Geneva); "Conference on the Standardization of Biological Remedies" (July 1923, Edinburgh); "Second International Conference on the Standardization of Medical Statistics" (September 1925, Geneva); "International Conference for Vitamin Standardization" (June 1931, London); "Conference of Experts for the Standardization of Dietary Studies Methods" (September 1932, Rome); "International Conference on the Standardization of Penicillin" (1944, London).

deserve to be underlined: McDougall chose two renowned composers—a German, Richard Wagner, and an Englishman, Edward Elgar—to express and emphasize the depth of the bond uniting doctors and scientists across borders.

Although McDougall acknowledged that sometimes "the desire to make profits obscured the major criteria," his conclusion was still positive because of the emotions that permeated his colleagues' endeavors regardless of their provenance:

> In a world in which nations compete for priority in such things as armaments there is much satisfaction in knowing that there are still problems of international importance which can be dealt with by doctors and which have as their object the saving of human life.

By creating a stark dichotomy between the political and the functional aspects of international cooperation, J. B. McDougall reinforced the League's rhetoric in these areas, forwarding the notion that experts and intellectuals had the power—and inherently the duty—to put their talents at the service of international interest. It was the universal, intangible, yet powerful ingredient of emotions that ultimately allowed him to derive "much satisfaction" from an otherwise dire political moment.[33]

Countless institutions built up such feelings by opening sanatoria in the mountains with the explicit goals of treating tuberculosis and instilling the emotions of internationalism. As illustrated later in this book, these also emulated the work of the League in ways so far unexplored by historians. For now, what is relevant is that the League at once supported and was supported by groups such as The International Union against Tuberculosis, and together these turned mountains into a concrete and metaphorical ground for international cooperation in the field of health. It is against this backdrop that the history of Leysin unfolded, and that the therapies offered there acquired a holistic character spanning across the medical and the political realms.

4.2 Dr. Rollier's Holistic Project

Dr. Auguste Rollier (1874–1954) played a fundamental role in connecting Leysin's sunlight with the emotional health of the body, of society, and of the international system. To be sure, concerns about the lack of sunlight had been widespread for decades, since industrialization and urbanization had drastically reduced the amount of time people spent in the sun. Light therapies involving exposure to both natural and artificial lamps had become popular, and theories about the best

[33] McDougall, "Nos campaignes antituberculeuses—et ensuite?," 297; 310–11.

way to administer light proliferated in this period.[34] Most notably, Faroese doctor Niels Ryberg Finsen (1860–1904) earned a Nobel Prize in 1903 for pioneering the field of phototherapy. Cultural shifts toward nudism and naturalism, and rising criticisms against older, aristocratic—and pale—models led to the ascendancy of what sociologist Simon Carter called the "helio-human," a type who associated darkness and paleness with poverty, and tanned skin with health, beauty, and a new "social morality."[35]

Medical theories praising the benefit of sun exposure for the treatment of rickets and tuberculosis and for the overall strengthening of the body advanced the practice of sunbaths.[36] These cultural changes affected architectural trends and touristic flows and also created new markets for a wide range of products (e.g., sun-creams). Especially after the end of the First World War, people began to develop a "photophilic relationship" that would affect every discipline and realm of life for decades to follow.[37] Nonetheless, Auguste Rollier quickly became the most prominent and influential figure within the heliotherapy movement.

Rollier stood out because of his extensive writings and research in Leysin, which quickly earned him the nickname of "sun doctor." His interest in mountains did not originate from direct experience: he was born and raised in Saint-Aubin-Sauges, on the flat banks of Lake Neuchâtel, and obtained his medical degrees in Neuchâtel, Zürich, and Bern. He nonetheless became interested in the health benefits of high altitudes through his studies. He served for four years as assistant to the renowned surgeon Emil Theodor Kocher (1841–1917), winner of the 1909 Nobel Prize in Physiology or Medicine "for his work on the physiology, pathology and surgery of the thyroid gland."[38] He then collaborated with Dr. Oskar Bernhard (1861–1939), who conducted research on the effect of the sun on skin ulcers, applying the same principles to non-pulmonary forms of tuberculosis and other diseases.[39]

Inspired by these mentors, in 1903, Rollier opened his first heliotherapeutic clinic in Leysin. He then quickly established a reputation for himself within the international scholarly community. As early as 1907, he spoke at the International

[34] Freund, American Sunshine, 18; 25; 66–96. The sun was also the subject of many studies for both scientific and military purposes. On Nazi studies in this context, see Michael P. Seiler, Kommandosache "Sonnengott": Geschichte der deutschen Sonnenforschung im Dritten Reich und unter alliierter Besatzung (Frankfurt am Main: Deutsch, 2007).

[35] Carter, Rise and Shine, 106; 89; 72. On nudism, heliotherapy, and modernism, see also Sarah Schrank, "Naked Houses: The Architecture of Nudism and the Rethinking of the American Suburbs," in Sarah Schrank and Didem Ekici, eds., Healing Spaces, Modern Architecture, and the Body (New York: Taylor and Francis, 2016), 7–31.

[36] On the rising fashion of air-baths, light-baths, and sun-baths, see also Simone Tavenrath, So wundervoll sonnengebräunt: kleine Kulturgeschichte des Sonnenbadens (Marburg: Jonas, 2000).

[37] Carter, Rise and Shine, 89; 3; 5.

[38] "The Nobel Prize in Physiology or Medicine 1909." http://www.nobelprize.org/nobel_prizes/medicine/laureates/1909/(accessed on April 8, 2016).

[39] Numerous clippings of Rollier's obituaries are available in the Biographic Catalogue of newspaper articles at the Swiss National Library.

Congress of Physiotherapy presenting heliotherapy in the mountains as the ideal method for strenghtening the body and the person as a whole: "Stimulated by the mountain air appetite resuscitates, intestinal functions become regular, and weight increases," he pointed out; and by arguing that "the climate of a high mountain, the alpine climate, is undoubtedly one of the most favorable for heliotherapy," he advocated taking full advantage of it in order to improve human health.[40] In 1915, he published *La cure de soleil* (The Sun Cure), a full-length study of the medical uses of sun exposure that spelled out the rationale behind this treatment.[41] In this landmark study, and in the many other publications that followed, Rollier described in detail the positive effects of sunlight on the body and the techniques to administer sunbaths (*bains de soleil*) for therapeutic purposes as well as the deeper meaning and implications that these would have for society and for the world. Years later, the tenets he put forth would still be considered the foundations of occupational therapy and other related disciplines.[42]

Rollier's ultimate objective was the improvement of the patient's emotional state through a holistic approach.[43] Like many experts at the time, he was concerned about the psychological and the mental health of the general population.[44] In his studies, he postulated that exposure to the sun—if managed properly— could have a positive effect on one's mood and overall outlook.[45]

Strict discipline and expert supervision were indispensable for the treatment to be effective.[46] In *Le pansement solaire* (The Solar Bandage), published in 1916, Rollier argued that the sun could heal a wide variety of lesions, from traumatic scars to syphilitic ulcers, to all kinds of burns and fractures.[47] In order to work, though, heliotherapy needed to be administered in the proper conditions. Architecture, for instance, constituted an essential part of the treatment: Rollier advised hospitals to build galleries to expose patients to the sun, stressed the

---

[40] Auguste Rollier, *La cure d'altitude et la cure solaire de la tuberculose chirurgicale: communication faite au Congrès International de Physiothérapie (octobre 1907)* (Neuchâtel: Delachaux & Niestlé, S. A. Geneva, 1908), 10; 18.

[41] Auguste Rollier, *La cure de soleil* (Paris: Baillière & Fils, 1915).

[42] See for instance A. L. Towe, "Arbeitstherapie in Leysin," *Der Tuberkulosearzt* 8, no. 4 (April 1954), 245–50.

[43] On holism, the tendency to see diseases as psychosomatic, and the connections with emotions, see Bettina Hitzer and Pilar León Sanz, "The Feeling Body and Its Diseases: How Cancer Went Psychosomatic in Twentieth-century Germany," *OSIRIS* 31, no. 1 (2016), 67–93. For an overview of the many intersections between medicine and emotions see Fay Bound Alberti, ed., *Medicine, Emotion, and Disease, 1700–1950* (New York: Palgrave Macmillan, 2006).

[44] Gregory M. Thomas, *Treating the Trauma of the Great War: Soldiers, Civilians, and Psychiatry in France, 1914–1940* (Baton Rouge: Louisiana State University Press, 2009).

[45] On contemporary notions of "heliotherapeutic euphoria" see Tania Woloshyn, "Le Pays du Soleil: The Art of Heliotherapy on the Côte d'Azur," *Social History of Medicine* 26, no. 1 (February 2013), 84–6.

[46] Such emphasis on discipline was mainstream in Europe, while it was much criticized in the United States. See Rothman, *Living in the Shadow of Death*, 197.

[47] Auguste Rollier, *Le pansement solaire: héliothérapie de certaines affections chirurgicales et des blessures de guerre* (Lausanne: Payot & Cie, 1916), 72.

importance of proper aeration, and suggested the use of gardens as a space for sun and air exposure during fair weather.[48] In a 1936 booklet entitled *Le bain de soleil: Pourquoi? Où? Comment?* (The Sun Bath: Why? Where? How?), he conceded that one could sunbathe anywhere and obtain some benefit. However, picking the proper climate was essential. If too hot, the sun "depresses and congests"; if too cold, it can be dangerous. To be sure, if on the plains one needed to be careful about choosing the right season and time of the day, and if some sea shores were appropriate at some times of the year and not others, in the mountains sun therapy "can be practiced for the entire year with the same profit." Yet, the proper technique needed to be followed. For this reason, he harshly criticized those who attempted sun-therapy or sunbathing without supervision. He decried their "snobbism," as they deemed it unnecessary to seek expert advice; he scorned their goal of "acquiring in record time a tan darker than their neighbor's"; and he emphatically listed possible medical consequences, from erythema and sunburns, to vertigo and palpitations, to lung and brain congestion.[49]

The proper "solar technique," he explained, was "direct" and "progressive": while it eliminated all barriers between sun radiation and the body, it managed exposure in carefully-timed increments. A specific chart indicated the precise number of minutes each body part required (see Figure 4.1). Sunbathing had to begin and end at the lower extremities, and all reactions (i.e., headaches or lack of appetite) had to be carefully monitored to be able to adjust the therapy without delay. Hats and sunglasses were recommended, as was moderate exercise.[50] Even if booklets such as the ones he authored could offer some guidelines, supervision by a doctor was essential to ensure that the patient would not only be but also *feel* better.

A strict diet and schedule were also of paramount importance for both the physical and the emotional health of the patient.[51] Rollier's therapy "condemn[ed] categorically (*sans appel*) game and aged meats." While white meat—preferably cold—was allowed in moderation, the bulk of the patient's nutrition derived from

---

[48] Rollier, *Le pansement solaire*, 75–86. The idea that hospital gardens constituted an important part of the therapeutic space was not new. See Clare Hickman, *Therapeutic Landscapes: A History of English Hospital Gardens since 1800* (Manchester: Manchester University Press, 2013). On hospital architecture see Lüthi, *Le compas & le bistouri*; and Annmarie Adams, *Medicine by Design: The Architect and the Modern Hospital, 1893–1943* (Minneapolis: University of Minnesota Press, 2008).

[49] Auguste Rollier, *Le bain de soleil: Pourquoi? Où? Comment?* (Montreux: Nouvelle Ch. Corbaz S.A., 1936), 3–9.

[50] Rollier, *Le bain de soleil*, 10–14.

[51] This concern about nutrition was particularly strong in Switzerland at this time. Most notably, in 1903, the same year in which Dr. Rollier opened his first sanatorium, Dr. Maximilian Bircher-Benner (1867–1939), who is most often associated with popularizing muesli, opened his first clinic in Zurich. Materials describing Bircher-Benner's approach appear among the Rollier papers, confirming that they belonged to the same cultural environment that connected food with nature and healing. Archives cantonales vaudoises, PP 1028/150.

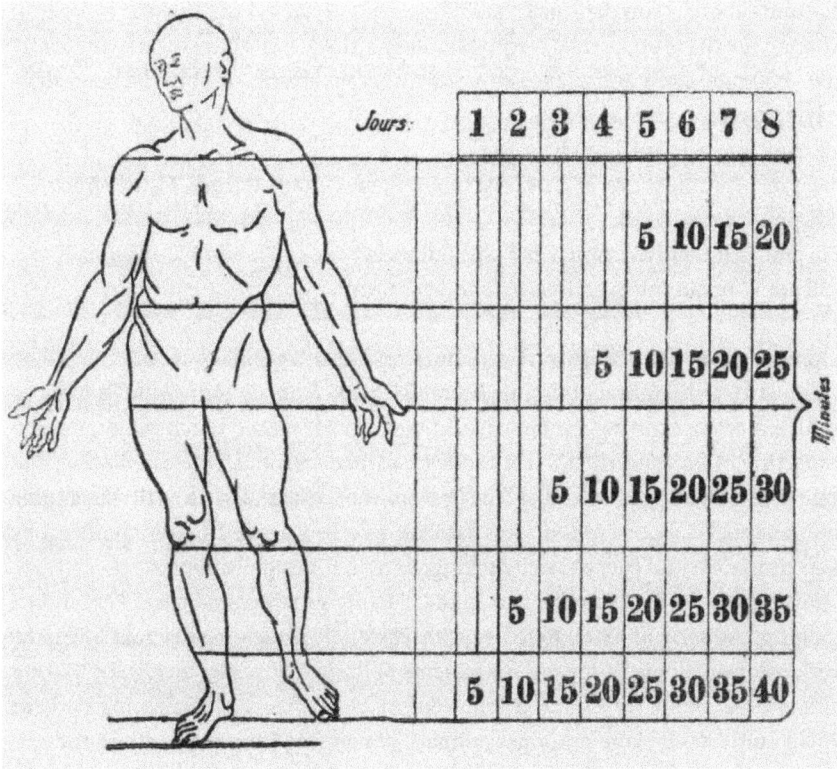

Fig. 4.1 Chart illustrating the exact time increments for the proper administration of heliotherapy. Auguste Rollier, *Le bain de soleil: Pourquoi? Où? Comment?* (Nouvelle Ch. Corbaz S.A., 1936), 11. I thank Martine Gagnebin for granting me permission to publish this image.

cereals, fruits, vegetables, and dairy products.[52] In a booklet entitled *L'école au soleil* (The Sun School) he described in detail the typical day of a patient:[53]

7:00 am: wake-up, bath, and toilette (grooming)
7:30 am: breakfast (dairy or cocoa, bread, butter, and fruit)
8:00–10:00 am: "sun school" (in stationary and mobile classes) and breathing exercises (in case of bad weather, classes would be held in the covered terraces adjacent to the building or in the study room)
10:00 am: milk
10:00–11:00 am: physical exercises, games, summer or winter sports

---

[52] Rollier, *Le pansement solaire*, 74–5.
[53] Rollier, *L'école au soleil* (Paris: Baillière, 1915), 12. League of Nations Archives, R 3094, 11C/27516/9518.

11:00 am–noon: sun cure and rest

Noon: lunch (soup, cereals, vegetables, side dishes—very little meat—and fruit)

1:00–3:00 pm: rest and silence cure (*cure de repos et de silence*) in the open air in lying position, dorsal or ventral

3:00 pm: snack (milk or chocolate)

3:30 pm: promenades, excursions, sport. Games on the terrace. Calisthenics

5:00 pm: schoolwork

6:15 pm: dinner (like lunch, but without meat)

7:30 pm: breathing exercises, *toilette*, lay down[54]

A precise division of time gave structure and also legitimacy to the treatment, with regimen and moral discipline becoming part of the therapy itself. Influenced by his experience during the First World War, Rollier placed much importance on respecting orders and rules.[55] He explicitly forbade alcohol, coffee, smoking, and gambling, and also dictated that "the best spirit of camaraderie must reign among the patients."[56] Since "mood" was crucial, this too needed to be regulated by managing each and every activity taking place in his establishments.

Work played a fundamental part in the patients' recovery and overall emotional uplifting. As early as 1909, together with Pastor E. Hoffet, Rollier had opened a work colony (*colonie de travail*) for patients of limited financial means. In 1910, an agricultural colony for children followed. At both clinics, convalescing patients would cultivate the land and raise animals, benefitting from the exercise and sun exposure that their work demanded while also helping to defray the cost of their own treatment.[57] The "joy" of being in the open air, together with the pride and satisfaction of supporting oneself, would do much for the overall improvement of the patients.

Rollier spoke to concerns about people's lack of "joy," which were widespread at this time. Particularly in Germany, the idea that work could—or should—give "joy" (*Arbeitsfreude*) was widely debated across the political spectrum; if some argued that in the industrial age fulfillment would have to come at the end of one's shift, others insisted that all work implied an inherent "joy in creating" (*Schaffensfreude*). Rollier belonged to this second group, arguing that work—executed both in

---

[54] Rollier, *L'école au soleil*, 12. League of Nations Archives, R 3094, 11C/27516/9518.

[55] Rollier, *La cure de soleil et de travail à la clinique militaire suisse de Leysin* (Lausanne: Impr. Réunies S.A., 1916).

[56] Rollier, *La cure de soleil et de travail à la clinique militaire suisse de Leysin*, 5. An elaboration of such activities in sanatoria at this time can be found in Chapter 5.

[57] On the rise of "open care" as an important model in psychiatric treatments, see Thomas Mueller, "Re-opening a Closed File of the History of Psychiatry: Open Care and Its Historiography in Belgium, France and Germany, c. 1880–1980," in Waltraud Ernst and Thomas Mueller, eds., *Transnational Psychiatries: Social and Cultural Histories of Psychiatry in Comparative Perspective, c. 1800–2000* (Newcastle upon Tyne: Cambridge Scholars Publishing, 2010), 172.

groups, and individually—would make people feel healthy and thus turn them into productive national and world citizens.[58]

Rollier agreed with many of his contemporaries who believed that tuberculosis was not only a physical but also a social disease. As historian Flurin Condrau noted while discussing the British context, it was for this reason that "the Sanatorium was strategically placed within a complex system of social insurance, Poor Law, and public health campaigns."[59] Many countries enacted measures to offer sanatoria to the poor in this period, and Rollier's work certainly fits this trend.[60] Also, Rollier was convinced that curing tuberculosis was tied to the well-being of the nation. "The return to the earth, which is so ardently recommended from a social point of view, is not less desirable for the safeguard of national health," he argued; properly supported, healed patients "will form stronger generations, the most resistant and the healthiest race."[61]

From the celebration of land and agricultural life, to the emphasis on physical health, to the assumptions about how this was connected to the health of society and the "race" of its people, Rollier's rhetoric echoed contemporary arguments in the field of public health. His views on women as nurturers of the health of the nation also fit into the mainstream during his time: according to him, "we are never going to remind women enough that maternity is the crown of their destiny" and of the obligations to do anything and everything to ensure the health of the child.[62] More generally, he lamented "excessive civilization," which made people forget that sun and air are necessary. He spoke of the importance of prophylaxis and prevention (for this reason he recommended sending feeble people—children especially—to *preventoria* where they would be preemptively exposed to the sun as well as to healthy habits).

Rollier also urged "legislators, educators, doctors, architects, families, etc." to do everything possible to make sure that children would spend time in the sun. Such practices, he insisted, would improve their "souls" and "fortify the blood."[63] These measures were imperative for poor people who most often inhabited

---

[58] On the issue of joy in the workplace (*Arbeitsfreude*) and related debates see Joan Campbell, *Joy in Work, German Work* (Princeton: Princeton University Press, 1989).

[59] Flurin Condrau, "Urban Tuberculosis and Sanatorium Treatment in the Early Twentieth Century," in Anne Borsay and Peter Shapely, eds., *Medicine, Charity and Mutual Aid: The Consumption of Health and Welfare in Britain, c. 1550–1950* (London: Routledge, 2016), 203–4.

[60] For instance, extending sanatorial treatments to the poor became a cornerstone of health policy in Italy and in the United States. See Silvano Franco, *Legislazione e politica sanitaria del fascismo* (Rome: APES, 2001). See also Bates, *Bargaining for Life*. On return to nature vs. modernism as the driving forces behind these initiatives, see Stephanie Pilat, "Shaping Fascist Bodies: Children's Summer Camps in Fascist Italy," in Schrank and Ekici eds., *Healing Spaces*, 139–49. For an overview of sanatoria in Europe and Italy in particular, see Davide Del Curto, *Il sanatorio alpino: architetture per la cura della tubercolosi dall'Europa alla Valtellina* (Rome: Aracne editrice, 2010).

[61] Ligue Vaudoise contre la Tuberculose, *Un projet de colonie agricole maraîchère pour tuberculeux guéris* (Lausanne: La Concorde, 1919), 25.

[62] Auguste Rollier, *La santé par le travail au soleil* (Montreux: Nouvelle Ch. Corbaz S. A., 1928), 1.

[63] Rollier, *La santé par le travail au soleil*, 3.

overcrowded, insalubrious living quarters and could afford only a limited diet. Indeed, he was very proud of the enfranchisement that his program yielded to this underprivileged population. "The indigent patients will be promoted to the rank of privileged!" he concluded, framing his work as essential not only for the individual but for society and the nation as a whole.[64]

Moreover, heliotherapy contributed to a much deeper, holistic movement of spiritual healing. In 1933, Rollier wrote the introduction for Jean Poucel's *Le natu-ralisme et la vie: la joie d'être sains* (Naturalism and Life: The Joy of Being Healthy), backing the book's principles and arguments.[65] Poucel was a big supporter of heliotherapy.[66] He spoke of mountains as ideal places for both air bathing and sunbathing. He also insisted on the moralizing action of nudism, especially in coed settings.[67] By endorsing his work, Rollier solidly placed himself in the nud-ist/naturalist tradition and, by association, within its broader philosophical stream.[68] Also, in 1949, Rollier wrote the introduction to Louis-Marcel Sandoz's *Hormones: Leur rôle dans la vie du corps et de l'esprit* (Hormones: Their Role in the Life of Body and Spirit), which stressed the importance of the mental and spirit-ual elements of one's treatment.[69]

Rollier traced the "problem of psycho-physical correlations" back to the Greek philosopher Heraclitus. After giving credit to two eminent physiologists—Ivan Pavlov for his studies on conditioned reflexes and Claude Bernard for his work on "international secretions"—he touted the discipline of endocrinology for its study of human moods.: Rollier argued that "science must have the effect of bringing back man to his authentic humility, one that allows him to become conscious of the narrow limits of his knowledge, of his power, and of the existence of a super-ior will (*volonté superiore*)."[70] Rollier's work thus had a transcendent element and an international scope, one that placed feeling at the center of the modern world.

Rollier's all-encompassing notion of emotional well-being and its centrality in its overall system of thought was best articulated in a 1953 publication entitled *Une thérapeutique qui vise l'homme tout entier* (A Therapeutic that Looks at Man

---

[64] Rollier, *La santé par le travail au soleil*, 11.

[65] J. Poucel, *Le naturalisme et la vie: la joie d'être sains* (Paris: Baillère & Fils, 1933).

[66] Poucel, *Le naturalisme et la vie*, 102–26.   [67] Poucel, *Le naturalisme et la vie*, 163.

[68] The movement toward naturalism and naturopathy was heterogeneous, and included a diverse group of people ranging from philosophers to agrarian experts who were often "radical visionaries" and who blended methods from domestic medicine (e.g., homeopathy) in protest against the profes-sionalization of science. See Susan E. Cayleff, *Nature's Path: A History of Naturopathic Healing in America* (Baltimore, MD: Johns Hopkins University Press, 2016). On naturism in various countries, see Sylvain Villaret, *Histoire du naturisme en France depuis le siècle des Lumières* (Paris: Vuibert, 2005). On the political undertones of naturism, see Carmen Cubero Izquierdo, *La pérdida del pudor: el naturismo libertario español (1900–1936)* (Madrid: LaMalatesta editorial, 2015). On commercial aspects, see Stephen L. Harp, *Au naturel: Naturism, Nudism, and Tourism in Twentieth-century France* (Baton Rouge: Louisiana State University Press, 2013).

[69] Louis-Marcel Sandoz, *Hormones: leur rôle dans la vie du corps et de l'esprit* (Neuchâtel: Attinger, 1949).

[70] Auguste Rollier, "Préface," Sandoz, *Hormones*, 7–9.

as a Whole).[71] Published on the fiftieth anniversary of the founding of his first clinic, this celebratory volume sought to convey the broader implications of Rollier's vision. The book was formally dedicated to the doctor's "medical and humanitarian" work, since, as the *avant-propos* explained in detail, Rollier's practice was not only medical but also "truly and totally human." Rollier treated "the whole patient" (*malade tout entier*), paying attention to both physical and emotional health, as the afflicted typically arrived with "a heart heavy with pains (*peines*), preoccupations, and inquietudes." On the topic of disease, "though it immobilized the being (*l'être*), it did not interrupt the normal flux of its vitality"— and the "need of creating—a man in his profession, a woman in her foyer—gives to the entire existence a rush/burst (*élan*) and a balance (*équilibre*)." Rollier's approach did much more than treat a disease: by regulating particular emotions it restored the integrity of the human being. Despite the absence of formal transcendent elements, his emotional cures had quasi-religious qualities that would give life meaning, purpose, and a vision to guide both present and future. The assumption was that no improvement could be attained while neglecting "these moral elements" (*éléments moraux*), and all aspects of life needed to follow the rules imposed by his system of thought. It was essential to create around each patient a "framework of life" (*cadre de vie*) to make him or her feel like a person, and not simply a patient. This framework must contain "all of the usual elements necessary for the mental equilibrium of the human being: a cerebral as well as a manual occupation, gaiety (*gaîté*), beauty (*beauté*), human relationships, the culture of an ideal (*culture d'un idéal*), and preparation for the future (*avenir*)."[72]

As exemplified by a "Club" that had been created in 1950 to unite all patients recovering at Leysin, the ultimate goal was to create an "atmosphere" and to enrich patients with "new perspectives" that would help them when the time came for them to "re-descend on the plains." The club was also a "spirit" and a "faith" matured through a wide variety of activities ranging from conversations in foreign languages, to playing bridge, to watching cinema.[73] Such "spirit" and "faith" needed to be felt, and emotional expressions were of the essence as they provided both the substance and the proof of the success of Rollier's holistic cures.

4.3 Visible Emotional Expressions as Evidence of Success

Tania Woloshyn has pointed out the importance of aesthetics in Rollier's medical practice by arguing that his photographs of patients taken before and after a

---

[71] *Une thérapeutique qui vise l'homme tout entier ou Les adjuvants de l'héliothérapie pratiquée dans les cliniques du prof. Rollier à Leysin, 1903–1953*: Au prof. Auguste Rollier, hommage de ses collab. à l'occasion du jubilé cinquantenaire de son activité méd. et humanitaire (Leysin: Soc. des établissements héliothérapiques, 1953).

[72] *Une thérapeutique qui vise l'homme tout entier*, 4–5.

[73] *Une thérapeutique qui vise l'homme tout entier*, 21–5.

treatment served as proof of physical and moral healing and often overshadowed other, less visible, forms of recovery.[74] I contend that images also played a major role in supporting Rollier's social and political arguments because they provided evidence that he had successfully infused the desired emotions.[75]

Many of his publications included numerous photographs. Carefully staged, meticulously captioned, and widely disseminated, these images showed patients working and exercising while expressing desirable emotions, thus making the success of his methods visible to readers. Experts appeared in groups, with texts emphasizing the emotional links between them or the aesthetic and emotional experiences they shared. Also, images helped to balance the modern and the anti-modern aspects of Leysin as a location for holistic healing: if the buildings and the treatments available were the newest, pictures of bodies with nature in the background suggested that a successful harmony between old and new had been found. Furthermore, photographs of patients manifesting particular emotions added to the moral capital of Rollier's enterprise. Their concentration represented his dedication to his patients, their joyous expressions reflected the overall "mood" of his establishments, and the mountains that surrounded them further enriched these pictures by adding associations to contemporary internationalist discourses.[76]

Photographs of fit bodies proved that Dr. Rollier had succeeded in creating healthy, international citizens. Many publicity shots displayed the patients' naked torso and legs (kept bare to maximize sun exposure) and accentuated their athletic features. A photograph in a pamphlet sponsored by the Ligue Vaudoise contre la Tuberculose, for instance, portrayed soldiers at Rollier's military clinic while emphasizing their physical might. The cluster of men did not follow any martial or rigid pattern, implying that theirs was not a systematic approach to the task at hand. Instead, they assembled in proximity to one another, in a pose that suggested they could enjoy the landscape or talk while completing their job

---

[74] Tania Woloshyn, "Le Pays du Soleil," 83. See also Tania Anne Woloshyn, "Patients Rebuilt: Dr Auguste Rollier's Heliotherapeutic Portraits, c.1903–1944," *Medical Humanities* 39, no. 1 (June 2013), 44. See also Kirsten Ostherr, *Medical Visions: Producing the Patient through Film, Television and Imaging Technologies* (New York: Oxford University Press, 2013), 3–27; Tanya Sheehan, *Doctored: The Medicine of Photography in Nineteenth-century America* (University Park: Pennsylvania State University Press, 2011). On the particular relationship between photography and psychiatry, not only to document both disease and treatment but also to trigger emotional performances in subjects who posed and performed for the camera see Georges Didi-Huberman, *Invention of Hysteria: Charcot and the Photographic Iconography of the Salpetrière*, translated by Alisa Hartz (Cambridge, MA: MIT Press, 2003).

[75] On photographs and the debate over their scientific/objective versus their artistic character, see Lorraine Daston and Peter Galison, *Objectivity* (New York: Zone Books, 2010), 125–38.

[76] On how historians have used photography as a source to explore emotions see Gian Marco Vidor, "Fotografia e approcci storiografici alle emozioni," *Rivista Storica Italiana* 128, no. 2, (2016), 669–85. On theoretical approaches, see Elspeth H. Brown and Thy Phu, eds., *Feeling Photography* (Durham, NC: Duke University Press, 2014). Particularly useful is also Heide Fehrenbach and Davide Rodogno, eds., *Humanitarian Photography: A History* (New York: Cambridge University Press, 2015).

Cliniques militaires : la fenaison.

Fig. 4.2 Soldiers haying at Auguste Rollier's military clinic in Leysin. Ligue Vaudoise contre la Tuberculose, *Un projet de colonie agricole maraîchère pour tuberculeux guéris: Avec une conférence du Dr. A[uguste] Rollier et plusieurs illustrations* (Lausanne: La Concorde, 1919), 19. I thank Martine Gagnebin for granting me permission to publish this image.

(see Figure 4.2).[77] The alpine lawn occupied the most prominent place in this image, celebrating it as a source of income and health, as well as a communal space for encounter and healing. While recovering on the Swiss Alps, these soldiers strengthened the health of a newly-built international system.

Numerous images portrayed children in groups, with their bodies demonstrating the effectiveness of the doctor's treatments and the nurturing of new generations of healthy world citizens.[78] In many of these photographs, they held the same pose, suggesting that Rollier's therapy instilled some discipline in them. One picture in *L'école au soleil* presented them carrying their foldable desks through the snow (see Figure 4.3). As a caption specified, despite their disease they had become "robust and expert skiers."[79] The trees in the background, the alpine view

[77] Ligue Vaudoise contre la Tuberculose, *Un projet de colonie agricole maraîchère*, 13; 19. On the correlation between "healthy" and "beautiful" see Sander L. Gilman, *Picturing Health and Illness: Images of Identity and Difference* (Baltimore, MD: Johns Hopkins University Press, 1995).

[78] On the peculiarities of children's emotional experience see Stephanie Olsen, ed., *Childhood, Youth and Emotions in Modern History: National, Colonial and Global Perspectives* (New York: Palgrave Macmillan, 2015).

[79] Rollier, *L'école au soleil*, 11. See also League of Nations Archives, R 3094, 11C/27516/9518.

Une classe mobile dont les élèves sont devenus, à « l'Ecole au Soleil », de robustes et experts skieurs.

Fig. 4.3 Children on skis. Auguste Rollier, *L'école au soleil* (Paris: Baillière & Fils, 1915), 11. I thank Martine Gagnebin for granting me permission to publish this image.

at a distance, and the incline at the foreground solidly placed their figures within a mountainous landscape, which simultaneously served both a therapeutic and a pedagogical purpose.

Another photograph highlighted the material objects that had been specially created to aid them in their healing, conveying the idea that science had been put to work to help them in their physical recovery and in their education (see Figure 4.4). Children wore a hat and an undergarment (the *"culotte Rollier"*) expressly designed to ensure maximum sun exposure while protecting the most vulnerable areas of their bodies as well as their modesty. Their writing desks, which the picture deliberately showed in both the folded and unfolded positions, allowed them to move from place to place and to write comfortably once settled.

These material objects demonstrated that every detail had been taken into account to facilitate the healing process. Scientific knowledge had been applied to each case and need, creating an environment impossible to replicate in a non-medical setting. If only to get access to these objects, patients needed to undergo their treatments in one of Rollier's clinics. The mountain peak and the large trees in the background offered a counterpoint, allowing nature (together with its

Au premier plan : La leçon pendant le bain de soleil, pupitres dépliés.
Au second plan : Le départ d'une classe mobile, pupitres au dos.

Fig. 4.4 Open-air classroom. Auguste Rollier, *L'école au soleil*, 7. I thank Martine Gagnebin for granting me permission to publish this image.

aesthetics and emotions) to balance an otherwise artificial scene. If each child sat straight up, immobile and aligned in a rigid pose, the alpine landscape all around gave the impression that pupils could nonetheless enjoy their open-air learning experience.[80]

Many pictures were accompanied by detailed explanations to guide readers in their interpretation and to ensure that they would appreciate the full implications of the treatments offered in Leysin. For example, in the aforementioned *Le bain de soleil*, Rollier noted how pigmented skin gave strength to the body and tanned patients were less sensitive to cold temperatures in the winter. The sun also had a positive effect on developing muscles "in a harmonious and often athletic fashion." Reinforcing contemporary aesthetic canons that associated athleticism with overall health, Rollier contended that sun exposure would endow abdominal muscles with a "natural ventral strap," which in turn would enhance the viscera's functioning and well-being.[81]

---

[80] On open-air schools, see Chapter 2.   [81] Auguste Rollier, *Le bain de soleil*, 10–14.

This kind of celebration of athleticism is commonly associated with fascist movements. As J. A. Mangan pointed out, there was an inextricable relationship between fascism and the human body, whereby the "projection of the martial state body as a symbol of state power" was one of its constitutive elements.[82] Yet, this was a time of much broader "preoccupation with physicality," as confirmed by a variety of trends, from the rise of the pantomime to the retreat from speech in drama, to the rise in popularity of dance movements, to the emergence of sports and physical activities as literary objects.[83] As the publications by Dr. Rollier illustrate, such preoccupation affected not only nationalism but also internationalism as well.

Numerous images featured people experiencing "joy" in work, another essential emotion in Rollier's overall vision. For instance, an illustrated page in *La santé par le travail au soleil* (Health by Working in the Sun) contained two photographs (see Figure 4.5). The one at the top captured the moment right before the sale of the objects that the patients had produced. A caption invited the reader to notice the patients' expression and the "gravity of their soul" (*sérieux de l'âme*) brought out by work; theirs was not a mere "whim" (*caprice*) but a sincere dedication toward Dr. Rollier's healing project. The alpine landscape appeared merely from a distance; only some foliage seemed to peek in from the side. The spotlight instead was on the sanatorium's gallery, especially designed to maximize sun exposure in a shared healing space, while alpine nature set off modern medical architecture.[84]

The patients seemed intent in their work. Their pose—facing away from one another to avoid distractions—and the expression on their faces stood as evidence of a full emotional experience. The internationalist emotion of joy in work was not connected with sociability but was at once individual and shared in a meaningful space.

The image at the bottom, captioned "*silhouettes alpestres*," showed a female patient alone in the act of embroidering. Sitting up in bed with her legs stretched, the mountains in the background, she too personified the strength and moral character of Dr. Rollier's enterprise.[85] Straight, muscular, and active, she represented the opposite of the idleness associated with disease. As suggested by the plural noun in the title and the adjective "*alpestre*"—shared by both her and the mountains—she had become one with the landscape that surrounded her.

In contrast to the image above, the Alps played a dominant role as they exuded their qualities of purity and strength to the person in the foreground; in turn, the

[82] J. A. Mangan, "Global Fascism and the Male Body: Ambitions, Similarities, and Dissimilarities," in J. A. Mangan, ed., *Superman Supreme: Fascist Body as Political Icon—Aryan Fascism* (London: Frank Cass, 2000), 5.

[83] Harold B. Segel, *Body Ascendant: Modernism and the Physical Imperative* (Baltimore, MD: Johns Hopkins University Press, 1998).

[84] This kind of gallery stood in contrast to others that featured dividers to ensure the patient's privacy and rest.

[85] Rollier, *La santé par le travail au soleil*, 6–7.

V. Avant la vente. Galerie de cure en plein travail où l'on voit que le dernier répond aussi au sérieux de l'âme et non pas à un simple caprice.

VI. Silhouettes alpestres.

Fig. 4.5 Dr. Rollier's patients working in the sun. Auguste Rollier, *La santé par le travail au soleil* (Montreux: Nouvelle Ch. Corbaz S.A., 1928), 7. I thank Martine Gagnebin for granting me permission to publish this image.

woman's resolve reflected back onto the place that hosted her, as her presence made the Alps the home of those who had not surrendered to disease. The fact that she sat there alone did not expose loneliness but introspection, and the picture above connected her experience with those of many others. The Alps stood there for all to enjoy as a universal—and also an internationalist—asset.

Photographs of working patients revealed the mental intensity and the sense of duty that permeated Dr. Rollier's clinics, as well as the pragmatic benefits that these emotions could deliver. In *Une thérapeutique qui vise l'homme tout entier*, the photograph of a young man making springs on a machine while lying in bed fully conveyed these feelings (see Figure 4.6). His modern *lit Rollier* (literally, "Rollier bed"), movable and adaptable to various machineries, allowed the subject to learn a trade. The pieces already completed, prominently displayed in a box in the foreground, demonstrated his concrete contribution to the economic life of the clinic. His machine looked like one from a newly-opened workshop; as a material object, it embodied not only a form of Fordist modernism widely appreciated at this time but also a message of social enfranchisement. Once done with his treatment, this man would be prepared for a job in any factory. No longer an apprentice, he would be ready to work and be a productive member of society. His sleeves rolled up in a working-class outfit, he already dressed the part. Despite his disease, at the sanatorium he had learned and practiced the necessary discipline and ethics. Though out of focus and only in the background, the alpine landscape supplied a meaningful backdrop. It formed the bearing wall of an open-air factory, a smithy of economic wealth, social enfranchisement, and emotions of internationalism.

The image of a recovering little girl in the same publication added authenticity to Dr. Rollier's display (see Figure 4.7). The picture had been carefully choreographed. Almost completely naked, her hair well-coiffed, she held a copy of *Pollyanna* while looking at the camera. Her Heidi-like story would have evoked contemporary notions about the power of joy to heal every ill. On the next page was a written explanation of the message this picture: playing with the words of the subtitle of the book, the "glad game," the author posed a rhetorical question: "Doesn't she want to live that game like all the other children in the world?" The sanatorium afforded her a healthy life, and "the light of joy (*lumière de joie*) that radiated from her face" was evidence of its success.[86] The young age of the subject suggested that her emotions were unmediated. The reference to "all the other children in the world" separated her from a specific place and time, and sublimated her experience to that of all children, regardless of their nationalities. Similarly, on the cover of the same book, the image of a young girl stretching her arms to mimic the outline of the mountains in the background communicated

---

[86] *Une thérapeutique qui vise l'homme tout entier*, 6–7.

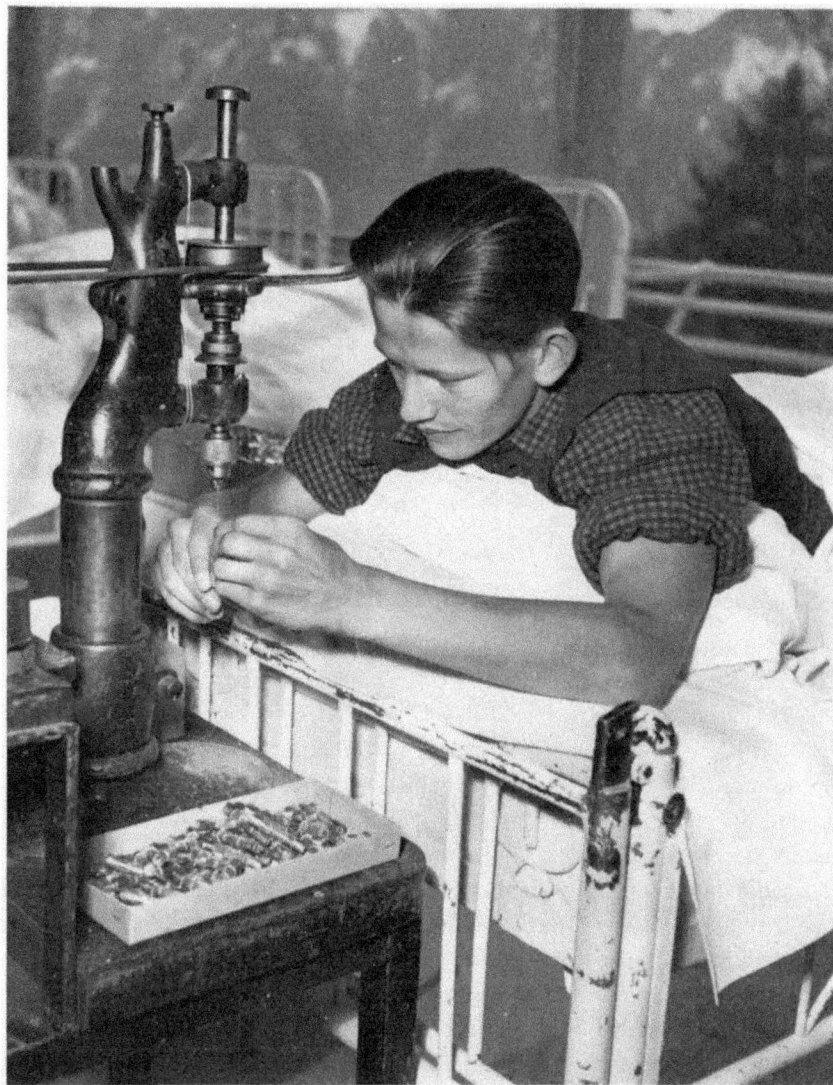

Fig. 4.6 Patient lying on a "Rollier bed" especially designed to accommodate work during heliotherapy. *Une thérapeutique qui vise l'homme tout entier ou Les adjuvants de l'héliothérapie pratiquée dans les cliniques du prof. Rollier à Leysin, 1903-1953*:
Au prof. Auguste Rollier, hommage de ses collab. à l'occasion du jubilé cinquantenaire de son activité méd. et humanitaire (Leysin: Soc. des établissements héliothérapiques, 1953), 35. I thank Martine Gagnebin for granting me permission to publish this image.

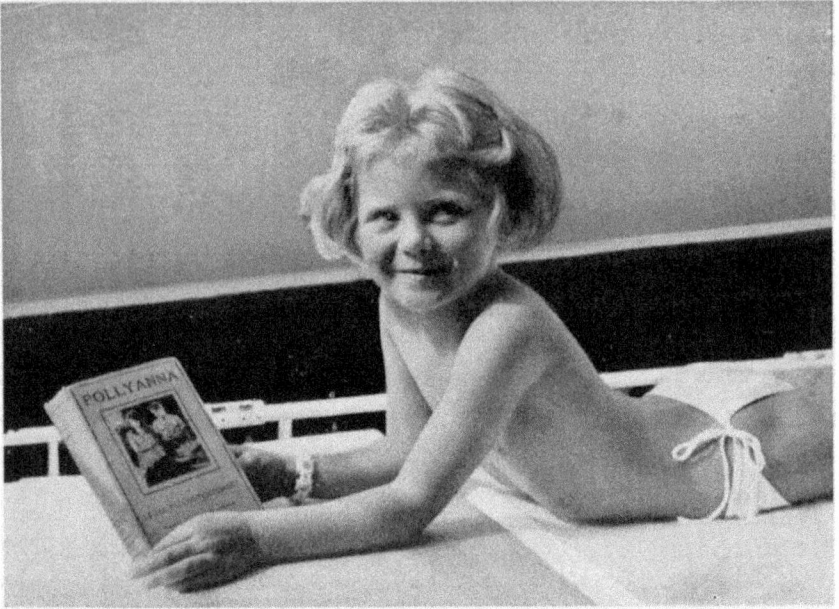

Fig. 4.7 Little girl-patient posing with Pollyanna. *Une thérapeutique qui vise l'homme tout entier*, 6. I thank Martine Gagnebin for granting me permission to publish this image.

the essence of Rollier's work, as it aptly illustrated how internationalism revolved around the enthusiasm of its members. Bodies in the mountain landscape had become an effective vehicle to make internationalism elevated and noble.

Images portraying the emotions of internationalism also dominated the publicity for the many international events that Dr. Auguste Rollier hosted at his clinics, showing how people felt the internationalism that permeated these occasions. One example was the First International Conference on Light, which was held in Lausanne and Leysin on September 10–13, 1928. This scientific gathering attracted experts from a wide variety of medical fields, from radiation therapy to gynecology to nutrition. Seventeen countries were represented, including France, Great Britain, Germany, Denmark, Austria, the United States, Belgium, Italy, and of course Switzerland. As demonstrated by a group picture published on *Le Siècle Médical*, on this occasion men—and also a few women— had engaged in a "fecund *(féconde)* collaboration." And if the leadership of one man, Dr. Auguste Rollier, deserved to be celebrated in an individual portrait, his largest achievement was best symbolized by the international crowd that had gathered in his honor and actively participated in international cooperation (see Figure 4.8).

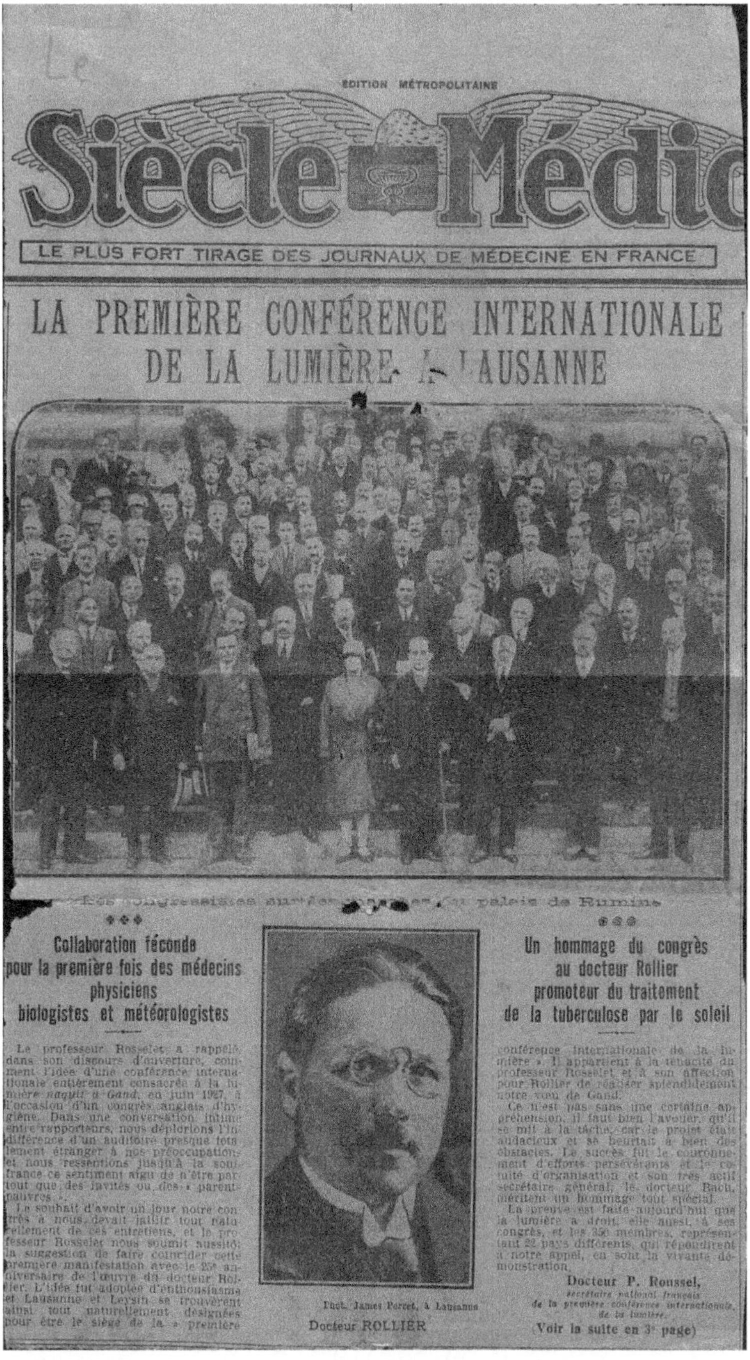

ÉDITION MÉTROPOLITAINE

Siècle Médic

LE PLUS FORT TIRAGE DES JOURNAUX DE MÉDECINE EN FRANCE

LA PREMIÈRE CONFÉRENCE INTERNATIONALE DE LA LUMIÈRE À LAUSANNE

Les congressistes sur les marches du palais de Rumine

Collaboration féconde pour la première fois des médecins physiciens biologistes et météorologistes

Le professeur Rosselet a rappelé dans son discours d'ouverture, comment l'idée d'une conférence internationale entièrement consacrée à la lumière naquit à Gand, en juin 1927, à l'occasion d'un congrès anglais d'hygiène. Dans une conversation intime entre rapporteurs, nous déplorions l'indifférence d'un auditoire presque totalement étranger à nos préoccupations et nous ressentions jusqu'à la souffrance ce sentiment aigu de n'être partout que des invités ou des « parents pauvres ».

Le souhait d'avoir un jour notre congrès à nous, devait jaillir tout naturellement de ces entretiens, et le professeur Rosselet nous soumit aussitôt la suggestion de faire coïncider cette première manifestation avec le 25e anniversaire de l'œuvre du docteur Rollier. L'idée fut adoptée d'enthousiasme et Lausanne et Leysin se trouvèrent ainsi tout naturellement désignées pour être le siège de la « première

Phot. James Perret, à Lausanne

Docteur ROLLIER

Un hommage du congrès au docteur Rollier promoteur du traitement de la tuberculose par le soleil

conférence internationale de la lumière ». Il appartient à la ténacité du professeur Rosselet et à son affection pour Rollier de réaliser splendidement notre vœu de Gand.

Ce n'est pas sans une certaine appréhension, il faut bien l'avouer, qu'il se mit à la tâche, car le projet était audacieux et se heurtait à bien des obstacles. Le succès fut le couronnement d'efforts persévérants et le comité d'organisation et son très actif secrétaire général, le docteur Bach, méritent un hommage tout spécial.

La preuve est faite aujourd'hui que la lumière a droit, elle aussi, à ses congrès, et les 350 membres, représentant 22 pays différents, qui répondirent à notre appel, en sont la vivante démonstration.

Docteur P. Roussel,
secrétaire national français de la première conférence internationale de la lumière.

(Voir la suite en 3e page)

Fig. 4.8 Group photo of the First International Conference on Light, 1928. Newspaper clipping. ©Archives Cantonales Vaudoises, PP 1028/80, Ière Conférence internationale de la lumière, 1928.

The article elaborated on how the idea had originated during an "intimate conversation" among experts who had reunited for a congress on hygiene the previous year, emphasizing the boldness of this plan and the importance of its success.[87] Papers were delivered in various languages (French, German, and English). On the program, a long list of names celebrated the Swiss Committee of Honors. A five-page roll of the members of the Committee of Patronage, each identified by their nationality (in descending order, the countries represented included Switzerland, France, Germany, Italy, Belgium, England, and the United States), demonstrated the wide reach of the event. If the organization committee was all Swiss, the roster of "foreign national secretaries" placed right underneath reminded readers of the international character of this occasion.[88]

For the first three days, all sessions were held in the elegant Palais de Rumine at the University of Lausanne, while participants also joined in excursions to the city's Cathedral and to the nearby town of Gruyères. On the evening of the third day, a formal banquet was held in Ouchy—Lausanne's most scenic spot on the lake. The next morning, all attendees embarked on a train journey to Leysin, where they visited Dr. Rollier's clinics. From there, they had the choice of either returning to Lausanne or taking part in a "special program" featuring a trip to Zermatt and a visit to the meteorological station at Gornergrat ridge, located at more than 3000 meters up on the Pennine Alps.[89] The conference report with papers in German, French, English, and Italian, each followed by a commentary by a peer often from a different country, provided tangible evidence of what international cooperation and exchange looked like. This scientific gathering reinforced the idea that the Alps, their landscape, and their light had the power to heal bodies and minds, and also to create lasting emotional ties among people from different nations.

A similar aesthetic appeared again at the end of the same month during "Dr. Rollier's Jubilee," held on the twenty-fifth anniversary of the opening of the first heliotherapeutic clinic in 1903. The official invitations to the event included many quotations. First was an Italian proverb: *dove va il sole no va il medico*, literally "where the sun goes, the doctor does not." This was followed by a quote from Michelet: "*la fleur humaine est, de toutes les fleures, celle qui a le plus besoin de soleil*" (the human flower, among all flowers, is the one that needs sun the most). The list ended with Goethe's famous deathbed cry (*Mehr Licht!*—"More light!"). This compilation of quips, adages, and quotes, communicated that both literary

---

[87] See clipping (undated, but certainly related to the Ière Conférence internationale de la lumière, 1928) in Archives Cantonales Vaudoises, PP 1028/80.

[88] See conference program and other related documents in Archives Cantonales Vaudoises, PP 1028/80.

[89] See conference program and other related documents in Archives Cantonales Vaudoises, PP 1028/80. According to the official conference report, seventy people participated in this excursion. *Première Conférence internationale de la Lumière: physique, biologie, thérapeutique; Lausanne et Leysin, 10–13 septembre 1928* (Paris: L'expansion scientifique française, 1928), 538.

and folk culture agreed on the value of the sun and celebrated it for both its concrete and metaphorical effects. All left in their original languages, these phrases reinforced the universality of light and its self-evident power to unite people across idioms and boundaries. Well-read individuals would have recalled that aside from his famous *History of France* and *History of the French Revolution*, Jules Michelet had also written *La montagne* (*The Mountain*, published in 1868), and surely they would have known about Goethe's extensive climbs, or would have been familiar with *Faust*'s mountain scenes.[90] Such quotes represented a set of references widely recognized at this time.

Against this symbolic backdrop, images of healing bodies served not merely as ornaments but as meaningful imagery to further the event's internationalist message. For instance, a menu for a banquet held on the occasion of Rollier's Jubilee in 1928 featured not only a golden consommé, trout, and poultry grilled with lard but also the picture of the naked body of a patient undergoing therapy (see Figure 4.9).[91] This carefully-staged photograph captured a healing man deeply engaged in his artistic endeavors. A caption connected his concentration to Dr. Rollier's labors in the field of medicine. "Solid as a tree," the doctor had "preached everywhere the virtues of the sun." The patient's body thus epitomized his physician's devotion to scientific knowledge across borders, while paintings of Leysin's view of the Dents du Midi embodied his commitment to the internationalist cause. The sum of these associations fostered the idea that mountains represented sites of particular aesthetic and emotional value, legitimized Dr. Rollier and his enterprises, and supplied visible tokens of their moral weight.

In presenting his work to the public, Rollier employed images to argue that at Leysin nature and modernity coexisted without clashing. An undated pamphlet stressed how well-connected Leysin was with Aigle (25 minutes by train, 35 minutes by car, by "a good road"), dispelling doubts that patients would be forced to stay in a remote location. At the same time, natural elements such as the "alpine climate whose quality is well known" guaranteed the effectiveness of the treatment in an environment left untouched by industrialization. The latest science would maximize the disinfectant and re-calcifying effects of the sunlight; a diet of cereals, fruits and vegetables, all foods rich in vitamins and themselves "irradiated by the sun," would foster the heliotherapeutic benefit of the place. If the sun and the products that grew under it held a higher value because of the mountainous terrains from which they had spontaneously grown, the rigid and modern diet in which they were administered guaranteed maximum benefits for all who consumed them. Human intervention had assured that many clinics "with varying degrees of comfort" would have something for people of every means, age, and need; yet the alpine landscape remained the central feature. A set of large

---

[90] See leaflets in Archives Cantonales Vaudoises, PP 1028/80.
[91] Archives Cantonales Vaudoises, PP 1028/80 and PP 1028/59.

La cure de soleil et de travail dans une clinique du Dr Rollier

1903 - 1928

Pendant ces vingt-cinq ans d'études et de peine,
Mais aussi vingt-cinq ans de succès sans pareil
Sans faiblir un instant, solide comme un chêne,
Il a prêché partout les vertus du soleil.

Nous fêtons aujourd'hui ses œuvres magnifiques,
Son talent médical, son labeur journalier
Et nous venons ensemble, au nom de ses cliniques,
Présenter notre hommage au bon docteur Rollier!

S. R.

Fig. 4.9 Photo and poem on menu for Rollier's Jubilee, 1928. ©Archives Cantonales Vaudoises, PP 1028/80.

photographs occupied a prominent space in the booklet. Some depicted the beautiful panorama on a snowy day while offering a breath-taking view of the Mont Blanc's most famous peak. Many pictures showed patients lying in the sun or in the act of exercising. Mass ornaments for an internationalist scope, their bodies conveyed the idea that Leysin combined the most modern conveniences with holistic, natural approaches to healing.[92]

A 1944 newsreel entitled *Kampf gegen die Tuberkulose* (The Struggle Against Tuberculosis) portrayed Leysin as a site where the modern and the anti-modern had found a successful balance.[93] The film alternated shots of the mountain landscape, state-of-the-art buildings, and new equipment, with patients lying in the sun, or sitting at long tables while working at their craft, or performing academic research with typewriters and microscopes artfully tied to special boards connected to their beds. The final segment—the climax of this promotional piece—featured children and women doing calisthenics, moving rhythmically and harmoniously in a natural setting.

One of the sources of Rollier's interest in the aesthetic and emotional aspects of the treatment in a modern—yet natural—environment was the Margaret Morris Movement. Since 1914, British dancer and teacher Margaret Morris (1891–1980) opened a Club, later enlarged into a school, teaching moving techniques based on the notion that spontaneous movements for personal expression could have a beneficial effect. She devoted much attention to breathing and posture, emphasizing the importance of movement for freeing body and mind. Margaret Morris also gave lectures at many venues including the Heritage Craft school in Chailey, where Dr. Rollier first saw her in 1926 and became interested in her work.[94] Soon afterward, Margaret Morris stayed in Leysin for three weeks, and from then on students from her school often came to visit.[95]

Rollier adopted Margaret Morris' techniques and made them the backbone of physical activity at his clinics. He also expanded on Morris' work on the aesthetic aspects of movement by delving deeper into emotional aspects and connecting them to his larger medical and political goals. In this context, photographs

---

[92] *La cure de soleil dans les cliniques héliothérapiques du Dr. Rollier à Leysin*, undated. One copy is available at the Archives Cantonales Vaudoises PP 1028/59. See also the leaflets in the same folder.

[93] Schweizer Filmwochenschau 03.03.1944, *Kampf gegen die Tuberkulose*. A copy is preserved at the Swiss Federal Archives in Bern, J2.143#1996/386#180#3*.

[94] In the 1930s, Margaret Morris opened numerous training headquarters in Europe (specifically in Paris, Edinburgh, Glasgow, Manchester, and Aberdeen) and taught her techniques in "USA, Australia, Belgium, Cuba, Canada, France, India, New Zealand, South Africa, Switzerland, and the West Indies." An explanation of the fundamental principles behind these techniques, some historical notes and numerous images illustrating their practical implementation can be found on the official website of the Margaret Morris Movement, http://www.margaretmorrismovement.com/welcome (accessed on July 17, 2018).

[95] *Une thérapeutique qui vise l'homme tout entier*, 13. Like Rollier, Morris also valued diet, exercise, and "mental attitude." Margaret Morris, *My Life in Movement* (London: Peter Owen, 1969), 68; 151–2; 160.

Fig. 4.10 Cover of *Une thérapeutique qui vise l'homme tout entier*. I thank Martine Gagnebin for granting me permission to publish this image.

transmitted the meaning and success of his life's work. In *Une thérapeutique qui vise l'homme tout entier*, the picture of three children exercising outdoors, their arms imitating the shape of the nature that enveloped them, shows how much the aesthetic aspects of movement in nature had become part of life at Leysin (see Figure 4.10). More than any book or pamphlet, this image connected the physical and metaphorical landscape of the Alps with the aspirations and the emotions of those who temporarily inhabited them while yearning to be healed.

4.4 Crafting Images and Emotions at the Clinique Manufacture Internationale

The act of crafting images expressing specific emotions did much to advertise Rollier's clinics as a preferred site for feeling them. At the Clinique Manufacture Internationale in particular, patients and visitors posed as subjects and played an active role in producing images and infusing them with meaning. They also offered vivid testimonies of their experiences, thereby presenting their emotions as "sincere" and "authentic." Moreover, they vouched for the success of Dr. Rollier's approach, and confirmed that his therapies furthered not only medical but also social and political goals.

Since 1929, when an *Appel* was put forth to collect funds for its realization, the Manufacture vowed to heal the person as a whole by combining the "sun cure" (*cure de soleil*) with the "work cure" (*cure de travail*), thus ensuring that people could tend to an occupation while undergoing lengthy heliotherapeutic therapies (see Figure 4.11). As Rollier explained in his inauguration speech, which he delivered on July 1, 1930, the Clinique Manufacture Internationale was meant to realize his most ambitious medical and political objectives. Rollier reaffirmed the principles that guided this initiative and his holistic approach to medicine. He referred to the biblical recommendation "six days shalt thou labour" to argue that work would serve at once a "muscular" and a "moral" purpose: "manual work, rightly dosed, represents physiological exercise *par excellence*." He contended that labor would improve circulation, "and circulation is life." Work, he continued, "regularizes thermogenesis, re-establishes the equilibrium of the nervous system, and improves the general condition" (*l'état général*).

Most importantly, work helped patients to fight depression and boredom (*ennui*), an invisible illness that destroyed people's will to recover. Rollier spoke of the "miraculous transformation" that work would bring to the new sanatorium's guests, as it would provide financial relief to a population forced to choose between therapies and livelihood (as patients could subtract what they earned from what they owed), and help society to defeat endemic poverty and disease. Furthermore, the Clinique Manufacture Internationale would become a "true center of moral education" for people of all nations and religions, a place where the commandment "You shall love your neighbor as yourself" would emerge as "the only and true solution of the great social problems of all times" which lay at the core of contemporary ills.[96]

At the Clinique Manufacture Internationale, work was presented as a means to promote productivity and financial gain, economic and social enfranchisement, and overall emotional uplifting.[97] The effect that work would have on the patients' feelings constituted a key aspect of the treatment. Rollier explained that after pondering which kind of manual labor to promote at the Sanatorium, artisanal or industrial, he chose the latter. To be sure, there were economic and financial reasons for this choice: handmade products would be hard to sell at a feasible price, and artisanal work would fail to prepare patients to re-enter a workforce that was increasingly mechanized. Yet, considerations about emotions played a big part in influencing his decision.

---

[96] A reprint of Dr. Rollier's inaugural speech is preserved at the Archives Cantonales Vaudoises, PP 1028/80.
[97] A thoughtful reflection on debates linking work, emotions, and disease is in Daphne Rozenblatt, "Work: Disease, Cure, and National Ethos in Modern Italy," *Social History of Medicine* 31, no. 2 (May 2018), 348–72.

LA SANTE PAR LE TRAVAIL AU SOLEIL

APPEL

EN FAVEUR DE

LA FONDATION DE LA

CLINIQUE-MANUFACTURE

INTERNATIONALE

DU

Dr A. ROLLIER A LEYSIN

Fig. 4.11 *Appel en faveur de la fondation de la Clinique-Manufacture Internationale du Dr. A. Rollier à Leysin* (Neuchâtel: Paul Attinger S. A., 1929). ©Manufacture Archives, Leysin.

The homogeneity and the regularity of industrial work would prevent differences and resentments among patients with various physical conditions. It would also protect them from potential abuses and from the dangers of overwork.[98] At the Sanatorium's ateliers, which at one point mass-produced items as diverse as

---

[98] *Une thérapeutique qui vise l'homme tout entier, 27–8.*

jigsaw puzzles, springs, and slippers, patients were allowed to work only three to six hours per day for a maximum of 120 hours per month. The pay was good, 1 franc per hour minimum, which was twice the typical amount earned by healthy employees performing the same job or by women working at home on the putting-out system (*travail à domicile*).[99] In detailed descriptions of the rationale that had guided the complex organization of this establishment, Rollier insisted that the patients' joy and satisfaction were of the utmost importance. He used pictures to convey these points most effectively: numerous photographs depicted patients working on machines or performing crafts while continuing their treatment in the sun. The expression on their faces, which showed concentration and passion for work, was proof of success.

The Clinique Manufacture Internationale's *Annual Reports*, which were printed for broader distribution, helped to disseminate the idea that the establishment excelled both in terms of the number of people it attracted and the outcome of their stay.[100] These publications stressed that the roster of patients continued to grow longer, approaching 250 during the Second World War when many soldiers were sent there to convalesce.[101] They also included detailed figures that testified to the heterogeneous nature of the patient population. Though the majority were men, the number of women never dipped below 30 percent of the total.[102] In terms of age, the only data available pertains to the people who were able to return home after being healed. In 1935 (the first year when this information was collected and included in the Annual Report), 55 percent of the people who had been cured were between 21–30 years of age; 20 percent were between 31–40; 13 percent between 41–50; 9 percent between 17–20; and 3 percent over 50. As for the overall success of the treatment, in the same year—before streptomycin had been discovered—the majority of patients had been healed (70 percent) and many (30 percent) had improved.[103]

To be sure, Dr. Rollier often complained about the fact that many patients had been sent there at too late of a stage to fully benefit from the opportunities offered by the Manufacture; yet, the overall message remained positive. In every report from 1934 on, Rollier called attention to the problems created by admitting patients too sick to work, and in 1942 he decried how "all too often it is forgotten that the Clinique Manufacture is not a hospice (*asile d'incurables*)."[104] Nonetheless,

---

[99] *Une thérapeutique qui vise l'homme tout entier*, 30–9.

[100] The exact distribution figures are not available, but numerous copies of each issue still survive at the Manufacture Archives.

[101] The data is derived from the Annual Reports 1930–1944, Manufacture Archives, Leysin.

[102] For the years 1931, 1932, and 1943, however, the data is not available.

[103] Manufacture Archives, Leysin, Fondation de la Clinique-Manufacture Internationale du Dr. A. Rollier, à Leysin, *Rapport de 1935*, 6.

[104] Manufacture Archives, Leysin, Fondation de la Clinique-Manufacture Internationale du Dr. A. Rollier à Leysin, *Rapport de 1942*, 3.

as confirmed by encouraging before/after photographs, the sun-cure worked.[105] Similarly, if "technical reports" frequently mentioned the difficulties arising from patient turnover (with healthy, well-trained workers constantly leaving, and untrained, sicker patients replacing them), they also stressed how salaries went from adequate to good and the production continued to increase (especially during the war, when the Manufacture's workforce was not mobilized due to health conditions and demand for their products remained high). In 1944, the goods made by the Manufacture included puzzles (57 percent of the production, with sales figures of CHF 70,000) and springs (22 percent, for CHF 27,318.36), as well as slippers, a wide variety of small mechanical parts, and other works such as frames and embroideries.[106] At the center of it all, as the annual reports often highlighted, were the patients, who were never forced to work but instead eagerly demanded to do so. Of paramount importance were the "good mood" and the "atmosphere" that permeated the place, which formed an integral part of the establishment's internationalist mission. Images of patients at work, carefully staged against an alpine background, drove home this point (see Figure 4.12).

In its public profile, the Clinique Manufacture Internationale maintained a strong international—and internationalist—image, despite the fact that its international population continued to decline (see Chart 4.1). Already when the Clinique Manufacture Internationale opened in 1930, less than half (44.22 percent) of its patients came from abroad. Of these, the largest number originated from European countries: England (26 percent), followed by Germany and France (14 percent each). In 1931 (the year with the highest number of foreign patients, 79), the majority came from Germany (19 percent), followed by France (15 percent), England (14 percent), Poland (10 percent), and Italy (8 percent). To be sure, between 1930 and 1944, no less than twenty-three countries were represented in the foreign patients' roster of the Manufacture.[107] Yet, the majority of people still came from Europe, specifically from France (25 percent), Germany (22 percent), England and Poland (7 percent each), and the Netherlands and Lithuania (6 percent each). Moreover, with the rising international tensions, the number of foreign patients declined and eventually bottomed out during the Second World War. In 1943, the Manufacture stopped calling itself "international"; and in 1944 it adopted the new

---

[105] In the early 1940s, the Clinique began experimenting with sulfonamides, although these did not seem to be very successful. Better results seemed to be achieved with the "Liqueur de Villate," a solution of sub-acetate of lead, sulfate of zinc, sulfate of copper and vinegar. Manufacture Archives, Leysin, Fondation de la Clinique-Manufacture Internationale du Dr. A. Rollier à Leysin, *Rapport de 1942*, 7.

[106] Manufacture Archives, Leysin, Clinique Manufacture Bernoise, Fondation du Dr. A. Rollier à Leysin, *Rapport de 1944*, 9–10.

[107] According to the Manufacture's publicity materials preserved at its archives, the list of countries represented included Albania, Austria, Belgium, Bulgaria, Czechoslovakia, Denmark, England, Estonia, France, Germany, Hungary, India, Ireland, Italy, Lithuania, Luxemburg, the Netherlands, Palestine, Poland, Romania, Russia [*sic*], the United States, and Yugoslavia.

Fig. 4.12 Patient at the Clinique Manufacture Internationale against the backdrop of the Alps. The caption reads: "A sick person: happy worker among his beautiful crafts in an admirable nature." Auguste Rollier, *La Clinique Manufacture Internationale pour la cure de soleil et de travail des tuberculeaux, "chirurgicaux", indigents* (Paris: Payot, 1929), figure 92. I thank Martine Gagnebin for granting me permission to publish this image.

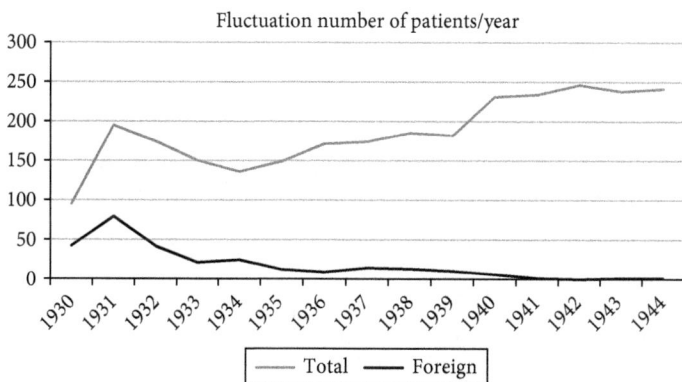

Chart 4.1 Clinique Manufacture Internationale. Fluctuation of the number of patients by year, 1930–44. The data is derived from the Annual Reports held at the Manufacture Archives.

title of Clinique Manufacture Bernoise, reflecting the Swiss—rather than the international—aspect of the establishment.

However, this downward trajectory was not reflected in the Manufacture's international profile throughout the time of its existence. If all of Rollier's clinics were open to international patients, the adjective "international," which the Clinique Manufacture used from 1929 to 1943, defined its purpose regardless of the actual number of foreign patients it housed. As early as 1929, an *Appel* to raise funds for the establishment presented it as a work of international cooperation. A large "International Committee of Patronage" was chaired by Albert Thomas (1878–1932), the first Director of the International Labor Office, bestowing a clear endorsement by one of the best-known internationalists and also associating the "Manu" with one of the most progressive international bodies in this period.[108] This connection was further reinforced by the fact that the Manufacture building had been designed by George Epitaux (1873–1957), the same architect who had worked on the headquarters of the International Labor Organization (ILO) in Geneva.[109] As in other examples described earlier in this chapter, the roster of Committee members extended several pages, with dozens of people listed under their countries of origin. These included Germany, England, Austria, Belgium, Bulgaria, Denmark, Spain, the United States and Canada, France, Greece, the Netherlands, Hungary, Italy, Latvia, Norway, Poland, Portugal, Russia, Sweden, Czechoslovakia, and Switzerland.[110] The same roll was also reproduced at the beginning of all annual reports from 1930 to 1933, further accentuating the international character and support for the organization.[111]

The *Annual Reports* also emphasized the international reputation of the Manufacture by noting how it attracted much attention from experts worldwide. Much weight was placed on the fact that numerous foreign doctors routinely came to visit and that groups such as the International Hospital Association in 1934 sent more than one hundred of its members to tour the Manufacture's facilities.[112] In 1937, more than 150 doctors came, most of them from Germany, France, and the United States. As a Report proudly hailed, others travelled from "Japan,

[108] Carlos A. Fernández Pardo pointed out how Albert Thomas, the International Labor Organization, and the International Labor Office presented themselves as a viable alternative for constituencies attracted by communist internationals, while also coexisting with interwar unionism and corporatism. Carlos A. Fernández Pardo, *Régimen internacional del trabajo: la OIT en la política mundial* (Buenos Aires: AD-HOC, 2001), 75–6. See also Isabelle Lespinet-Moret, and Vincent Viet, eds., *L'Organisation internationale du travail: origine, développement, avenir* (Rennes: Presses universitaires de Rennes, 2011). On various notions of internationalism in the field of labor see Thomas Cayet, *Rationaliser le travail, organiser la production: le Bureau International du Travail et la modernisation économique durant l'entre-deux-guerres* (Rennes: Presses universitaires de Rennes, 2010).

[109] Del Curto, *Il sanatorio alpino*, 100.

[110] *Appel en faveur de la fondation de la Clinique-Manufacture Internationale du Dr. A. Rollier à Leysin.* (Neuchâtel: Attinger S. A., 1929). A copy is held at the Manufacture Archives, Leysin.

[111] A full set of these reports is available at the Manufacture Archives, Leysin.

[112] Manufacture Archives, Leysin, "Fondation de la Clinique-Manufacture Internationale du Dr. A. Rollier, à Leysin," in Manufacture Archives, *Rapport de 1933*, 10; *Rapport de 1934*, 4.

Poland, Italy, Holland, Switzerland and British India, Belgium, China, Lebanon, Brazil, Algeria, Chile, Austria, Hungary, Czechoslovakia, Turkey, Yugoslavia, Egypt, Lithuania, Cyprus, Siam, South Africa, Argentina, Indochina, Australia, Palestine, East Africa, Greece, and Tanganyika," spreading the reputation of the Manufacture in all continents.[113]

Furthermore, Dr. Rollier was invited to speak about the Manufacture at numerous international congresses, and the Manufacture was routinely represented at the International Congress of Medicine and at the International Union against Tuberculosis.[114] Most notably, in 1932, Albert Thomas of the ILO invited Rollier to address the XVI session of the International Labor Conference, which was attended by forty-seven countries.[115] Regardless of the declining number of foreign patients, Dr. Rollier was able to make a strong case for the Clinique Manufacture's international character by highlighting the many ways in which it was associated with the international medical establishment and to the international—and internationalist—institutions active in the field of health during this period.

The patients themselves played an active role in reinforcing Dr. Rollier's message by producing a broad range of images, providing texts to guide their interpretations, and disseminating them to a wider public. Most notably, they crafted a magazine entitled *Manu-Revue* to connect all who experienced life in this establishment.[116] Written in both French and German, *Manu-Revue* circulated among patients (both old and new), members of the staff, and their families, uniting them in the common cause of physical, spiritual, social, and political healing. This publication did not supply figures on the composition of the Clinique's population. Instead, it adopted universalistic terms to highlight commonalities and build a sense of shared values among readers. Creating a link (*lien*) between old and new patients, *Manu-Revue* spoke of the bond they shared. The "intimate journal of our clinic" was meant to give voice to the deepest values of the people who inhabited it and made it their own.[117]

The fact that the patients themselves provided most of the content gave authenticity to the magazine's internationalist tone. Each issue reminded readers that contributors were paid fairly, a detail that confirmed the integrity of the establishment whose life it chronicled. Moreover, the magazine's artisan quality conveyed the great care with which each page had been produced and also reinforced the idea that patients were involved in it. From articles to poems, to hand-drawn

---

[113] Manufacture Archives, *Rapport de 1933*, 10; *Rapport de 1937*, 4.
[114] Manufacture Archives, *Rapport de 1931*, 12.
[115] Manufacture Archives, *Rapport de 1932*, 7.
[116] A full set of thirteen issues, from 1933 to 1935, is preserved at the Manufacture Archives, Leysin. Other sanatoria had similar magazines. For instance, Jean Houriet in a later account mentioned that at the sanatorium Beau Site they had an internal publication called "La Gazette de [sic] Beau-Site (G.B.S.). Jean H. Houriet, *Années perdues, années retrouvées: sous un toit sanatorial* (Neuchâtel: Messeiller, 1974), 51.
[117] *Manu-Revue*, 12; 3.

images, to crossword puzzles, everything in *Manu-Revue* looked like a work of craft. Full-size drawings and vignettes decorated every page, giving it vitality, humor, and an aesthetic quality rare in mass-produced periodicals. Leysin's distinctive landscape found its way into each issue, making the journal unique for its special community (see Figures 4.13 and 4.14).[118]

As *Manu-Revue* described in detail, a series of internal contests engaged all who inhabited the Clinique Manufacture Internationale. The December 1933 issue challenged all readers to submit their best try at tangram (*combinn*), an assemblage game meant to trigger creativity and occupy idle time. In February 1934, the results of small sports competitions between patients appeared on the first page, together with the growing sense of camaraderie among them. In May 1934, a photography competition was launched. Subjects could include work scenes, life at the Manufacture, or views of Leysin. By October, prizes were announced to those who best captured the place's aesthetic qualities.

Moreover, a rich selection of book excerpts, novels, and poems afforded readers the chance to express or take in the emotions that imbued the days spent at Leysin. Some of these pieces came from well-known authors, such as France Pastorelli (1880–1958) and Robert de Traz (1884–1951), whose reflections on "suffering" or on the sanatorium's "hours of silence" resonated with patients forced to experience both for months and years at the time. Others came from the patients themselves, who shared what they felt with each other in profound ways while realizing the depth of their common experience.[119]

Overt emotional expressions represented a central part of their stay, as being and showing oneself disposed to interacting with others was deemed essential at the Clinique. After arrival, one was expected to come out of his or her shell. "A pale spot in a bed well-made, calm and immobile in the middle of other patients loud and tanned, this is what you look like to us when we enter a room," read an open letter entitled "To the new patients!" published on the first page of *Manu-Revue*'s March 1934 issue.[120] Associating paleness not only with disease but also with isolation, the piece celebrated its opposite—a tan—as the embodiment of health and openness to others. While wishing the newly arrived a prompt recovery, the article invited them to join in the joyous community to which they now belonged.

Along similar lines, a piece published in the last issue of *Manu-Revue* (May 1935) by the Director of the Technical Section, Engineer Théo Chevalley, remarked on the difference between the patients who had just arrived and the ones who were about to leave. If the first could notice only "the severe entrance porch," the others would forever remember the moment of their departure, and the

---

[118] See image of crossword puzzle in Figure 4.14. Notice the distinctive shape of the mountain view from Leysin.

[119] Robert de Traz, *Les heures de silence* (Paris: Grasset, 1934).   [120] *Manu-Revue*, 6; 1.

Fig. 4.13 *Manu-Revue*, 10, July 1934, cover. A full set of thirteen issues, from 1933 to 1935, is preserved at the Manufacture Archives, Leysin. ©Manufacture Archives.

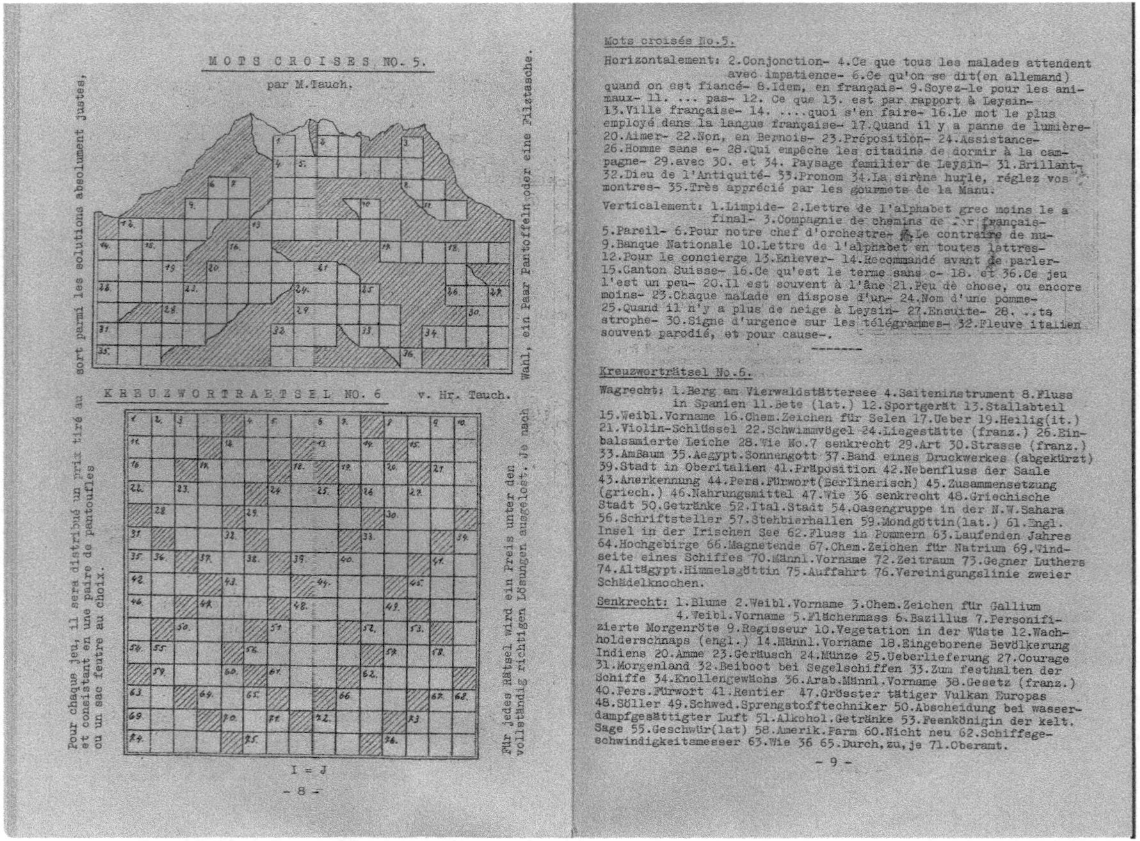

MOTS CROISES NO. 5.

par M.Tauch.

Pour chaque jeu, il sera distribué un prix tiré au sort parmi les solutions absolument justes, et consistant en une paire de pantoufles ou un sac feutre au choix.

KREUZWORTRAETSEL NO. 6 v. Hr. Tauch.

I = J

Für jedes Rätsel wird ein Preis unter den vollständig richtigen Lösungen ausgelost. Je nach Wahl, ein Paar Pantoffeln oder eine Filztasche.

- 8 -

Mots croisés No.5.

Horizontalement: 2.Conjonction- 4.Ce que tous les malades attendent avec impatience- 6.Ce qu'on se dit(en allemand) quand on est fiancé- 8.Idem, en français- 9.Soyez-le pour les animaux- 11. ... pas- 12. Ce que 13. est par rapport à Leysin- 13.Ville française- 14. ....quoi s'en faire- 16.Le mot le plus employé dans la langue française- 17.Quand il y a panne de lumière- 20.Aimer- 22.Non, en Bernois- 23.Préposition- 24.Assistance- 26.Homme sans e- 28.Qui empêche les citadins de dormir à la campagne- 29.avec 30. et 34. Paysage familier de Leysin- 31.Brillant- 32.Dieu de l'Antiquité- 33.Pronom 34.La sirène hurle, réglez vos montres- 35.Très apprécié par les gourmets de la Manu.

Verticalement: 1.Limpide- 2.Lettre de l'alphabet grec moins le a final- 3.Compagnie de chemins de fer français- 5.Pareil- 6.Pour notre chef d'orchestre- 8.Le contraire de nu- 9.Banque Nationale 10.Lettre de l'alphabet en toutes lettres- 12.Pour le concierge 13.Enlever- 14.Recommandé avant de parler- 15.Canton Suisse- 16.Ce qu'est le terme sans c- 18. et 36.Ce jeu l'est un peu- 20.Il est souvent à l'âne 21.Peu de chose, ou encore moins- 23.Chaque malade en dispose d'un- 24.Nom d'une pomme- 25.Quand il n'y a plus de neige à Leysin- 27.Ensuite- 28. ..tastrophe- 30.Signe d'urgence sur les télégrammes- 32.Fleuve italien souvent parodié, et pour cause-.

Kreuzworträtsel No.6.

Wagrecht: 1.Berg am Vierwaldstättersee 4.Saiteninstrument 8.Fluss in Spanien 11.Bete (lat.) 12.Sportgerät 13.Stallabteil 15.Weibl.Vorname 16.Chem.Zeichen für Selen 17.Ueber 19.Heilig(it.) 21.Violin-Schlüssel 22.Schwimmvögel 24.Liegestätte (franz.) 26.Einbalsamierte Leiche 28.Wie No.7 senkrecht 29.Art 30.Strasse (franz.) 33.AmBaum 35.Aegypt.Sonnengott 37.Band eines Druckwerkes (abgekürzt) 39.Stadt in Oberitalien 41.Präposition 42.Nebenfluss der Saale 43.Anerkennung 44.Pers.Fürwort(Berlinerisch) 45.Zusammensetzung (griech.) 46.Nahrungsmittel 47.Wie 36 senkrecht 48.Griechische Stadt 50.Getränke 52.Ital.Stadt 54.Oasengruppe in der N.W.Sahara 56.Schriftsteller 57.Stehbierhallen 59.Mondgöttin(lat.) 61.Engl. Insel in der Irischen See 62.Fluss in Pommern 63.Laufenden Jahres 64.Hochgebirge 66.Magnetende 67.Chem.Zeichen für Natrium 69.Windseite eines Schiffes 70.Männl.Vorname 72.Zeitraum 73.Gegner Luthers 74.Altägypt.Himmelsgöttin 75.Auffahrt 76.Vereinigungslinie zweier Schädelknochen.

Senkrecht: 1.Blume 2.Weibl.Vorname 3.Chem.Zeichen für Gallium 4.Weibl.Vorname 5.Flächenmass 6.Bazillus 7.Personifizierte Morgenröte 9.Regisseur 10.Vegetation in der Wüste 12.Wacholderschnaps (engl.) 14.Männl.Vorname 18.Eingeborene Bevölkerung Indiens 20.Amme 23.Geräusch 24.Münze 25.Ueberlieferung 27.Courage 31.Morgenland 32.Beiboot bei Segelschiffen 33.Zum festhalten der Schiffe 34.Knollengewächs 36.Arab.Männl.Vorname 38.Gesetz (franz.) 40.Pers.Fürwort 41.Rentier 47.Grösster tätiger Vulkan Europas 48.Söller 49.Schwed.Sprengstofftechniker 50.Abscheidung bei wasserdampfgesättigter Luft 51.Alkohol.Getränke 53.Feenkönigin der kelt. Sage 55.Geschwür(lat) 58.Amerik.Farm 60.Nicht neu 62.Schiffsgeschwindigkeitsmesser 63.Wie 36 65.Durch,zu,je 71.Oberamt.

- 9 -

Fig. 4.14 "Alpine" Crossword puzzle in *Manu-Revue*, 13 (1935), 8–9. ©Manufacture Archives.

"vibrant hive (*ruche toute frémissante*) of flags, cloths, and handkerchiefs waved frenetically, and the shouts (*cris*) from fifty chests (*poitrines*) overpowering the sound of the rack-and-pinion train and making tears shine in the eyes of the most hardened (*endurcis*)."[121] The image of people waving goodbye, accompanied by an intense, shared, sensorial experience, was evidence that a strong emotional bond had been built, one that would accompany them home, wherever this may be, and remain with them for decades to follow. Most importantly, these visible emotional expressions served as a testament to the success of the "Manu" as an internationalist establishment and of the promise of internationalism as a viable set of ideas and practices in the post-1919 world.

*   *   *

The images of the emotions produced in Leysin proved to be long lasting. Despite the change in name, la Clinique Manufacture Bernoise maintained the entire structure and staff of the old establishment. In 1971, in contrast to the ongoing trend of leaving the memories of sanatoria behind, it published a booklet entitled "Clinique Manufacture Bernoise, Leysin, Service Technique, 1930 à 1970," high-lighting its interwar roots.[122] In 1978, the Clinic was closed but the manufacture remained open, continuing to produce springs and jigsaw puzzles while employ-ing people with various forms of disability. In 1980, it produced a booklet com-memorating its fiftieth anniversary, and in 1990 it published another one for the sixtieth; both reproduced images from the old publicity materials described in this chapter.[123] In 2004, Daniel Seydoux published *La Manu: histoire d'espoirs, 1903–2004* (The Manu: History of Hopes, 1903–2004), which traced the Manufacture's origins back to Dr. Rollier's first heliotherapy center.[124] The book celebrated its "international vocation" by quoting a passage from Rollier's first Annual Report: "The diversity of nationalities has never been an obstacle to good harmony (*bonne harmonie*)."[125]

To be sure, sweeping changes have taken place in Leysin since antibiotics made sojourns in sanatoria no longer necessary for treatment; yet, the Manufacture and the emotions that accompanied its existence still exist.[126] In 2004 it moved to a new building, while its old edifice now houses a Hotel Management School, "hosted in former traditional Swiss Palace hotels" located in the "birthplace of hospitality." On their website, a picture of one of the old sanatorium's most lavish

[121] *Manu-Revue*, 13; 1.   [122] A copy is available at the Manufacture Archives, Leysin.
[123] Copies of both are available at the Manufacture Archives, Leysin.
[124] Daniel Seydoux, *La Manu: histoire d'espoirs, 1903–2004* (La Manufacture bernoise, Fondation du Dr Rollier, 2004).
[125] Seydoux, *La Manu*, 28.
[126] La manufacture, "La Manufacture: accueil," http://www.lamanufacture.ch/wq_pages/fr/manu-facture/accueil.php (accessed on July 18, 2016).

rooms drives the point home.[127] While there is no caption to make this continuity explicit, the aesthetics and emotions that had constituted such an important part of Rollier's work in the twentieth century still defines the ideas and the products made and sold there and elsewhere in the twentieth-first. The fifth and final chapter suggests additional dimensions that need to be integrated in this history, particularly as feelings, experiences, and atmospheres emerge as central features of international encounters to this day.

---

[127] Swiss Hotel Management School, http://www.shms.com/en/page/about/(accessed on June 29, 2017). See also SHMS brochure http://www.shms.com.hk/pdf/SHMS_Brochure.pdf (accessed on June 29, 2017).

5

A University for Feeling the Emotions of Internationalism

On October 2, 1922, the first patient of the University Sanatorium arrived in Leysin on a stretcher. Years later, the doctors and nurses who received him at the station still remembered the emotions of that moment. As chronicled in a surviving report, they recounted "his joy and gratitude" for a "happy day awaited for more than two years."[1]

This final chapter examines the experiences of the many people who made his same journey, bringing readers inside the University Sanatorium to explore the emotions they experienced in this establishment and in its alpine surroundings.[2] Drawing upon literature that tried to transcend the "nature vs. nurture" debate (or the discussion over emotions being either constructed or universal), this study emphasizes the role of spaces (especially their aesthetics and their "materialities," or the "*doing* things" that shaped the experience of the bodies existing and operating with and within them).[3] It also reflects on how previous experiences and memories of similar environments might have made some emotions expected and therefore more likely—albeit, as Margrit Pernau noted, "by no means certain." Finally, it takes into account the "temporalization of emotions," or how certain moments (e.g., meals, excursions, or Christmas-time) bore associations with particular feelings.[4] The material reproduction of domestic spaces in a clinical environment, the performance of certain poses, and the acting out of familial and fraternal gestures suggest that many people yearned for the feelings associated with these settings; and if emotional practices, expressions, and displays make emotions serve as "emotives," leading to them being sensed while in the

---

[1] UNESCO Archives, FR PUNES AG 1-IICI-C-VII-7, "Le sanatorium universitaire depuis son ouverture, le 1 octobre 1922, au 31 décembre 1923," 1.

[2] The University Sanatorium of Leysin has never been the subject of a published academic work. The only study available to date is Annick Vancampenhout, "La tuberculose et le sanatorium universitaire de Leysin, 1922–1961," Mémoire de licence, Université de Fribourg, 1990. University sanatoria including the one in Leysin, however, have been mentioned in the literature on the history of tuberculosis. For an overview, see Barbara Bates, *Bargaining for Life: A Social History of Tuberculosis, 1876–1938* (Philadelphia: University of Pennsylvania Press, 2015); Flurin Condrau and Michael Worboys, eds., *Tuberculosis Then and Now: Perspectives on the History of an Infectious Disease* (Montreal: McGill-Queen's University Press, 2010).

[3] Jo Labanyi, "Doing Things: Emotion, Affect, and Materiality," *Journal of Spanish Cultural Studies* 11, nos. 3–4 (September 2010), 223–33.

[4] Margrit Pernau, "Space and Emotion: Building to Feel," *History Compass* 12, no. 7 (July 2014), 544.

The Emotions of Internationalism: Feeling International Cooperation in the Alps in the Interwar Period. Ilaria Scaglia, Oxford University Press (2020). © Ilaria Scaglia.
DOI: 10.1093/oso/9780198848325.001.0001

process of being uttered or performed, then these can serve as evidence of what people felt.[5]

As a "total institution," the University Sanatorium deeply influenced the emotional experiences of those who inhabited it.[6] At the same time, individual doctors, patients, and visitors all contributed in shaping the feelings lived and expressed there.[7] Moreover, emotional experiences represented a central part of making the argument for a new, enlarged International University Sanatorium in Leysin. Although it never became a reality, the assumptions and the aesthetics on which this project was based continued to be influential in the subsequent decades. Indeed, the centrality of "atmospheres" and the notion that international encounters inherently entail emotional experiences continue to shape international cooperation—what it is, as well as what it looks and what it feels like—into the present.

5.1   A Place for Intellectuals to Feel

The University Sanatorium of Leysin sought to affect the emotional state of university students and faculty ill with tuberculosis by providing them with a cosmopolitan academic environment. It was the brainchild of Swiss physician Dr. Louis Vauthier (1887–1963), who first proposed its establishment in 1918 and then acted as its Director from 1922 to 1953. According to Vauthier, one of the main obstacles to recovery was the psychological toll imposed by tuberculosis and by the long periods of convalescence its treatment required. He was especially concerned about the mental health of intellectuals, who seemed to be more prone to "depression" and "nerve diseases." Strikingly, Dr. Vauthier did not follow any of the approaches his contemporaries adopted to fight the depression and the neurasthenia that afflicted his patients. Rejecting both the old Darwinian "biological psychiatry," which attributed mental disease to inherited flaws and degeneration, and the emerging Freudian trends in neurology and psychotherapy, he contended that the mental diseases that often accompanied life at the sanatorium could be

---

[5] On the concept of "emotives," see William M. Reddy, *The Navigation of Feeling: A Framework for the History of Emotions* (New York: Cambridge University Press, 2001).

[6] Erving Goffman mentioned sanatoria as the quintessential examples of a "total institution," or a "place of residence and work where a large number of like-situated individuals, cut off from the wider society for an appreciable period of time, together lead an enclosed, formally administered round of life." Erving Goffman, *Asylums: Essays on the Social Situation of Mental Patients and Other Inmates* (New York: Anchor Books, 1961), xiii; 4. On institutions of confinement see also Michel Foucault, *The Birth of the Clinic: An Archaeology of Medical Perception*, translated by Alan Sheridan (New York: Pantheon Books, 1973), and *Discipline and Punish: The Birth of the Prison*, translated by Alan Sheridan (New York: Random House, 1975).

[7] For an overview of the critiques of the works by Erving Goffman and Michel Foucault and on the mechanics of bargaining and negotiation that characterized life at the sanatorium see the aforementioned edited collection by Flurin Condrau and Michael Worboys.

healed by allowing patients to conduct intellectual work in an inclusive, amicable, international atmosphere.[8] He therefore conceived an institution where students and faculty could receive the treatments and the intellectual stimulation they needed in order to heal, one which included not only a vibrant university life but also a lively international environment enhanced by a suggestive alpine setting.

To turn his project into a reality, Dr. Vauthier drew on his own academic network as well as on the broad range of connections and experiences he had accumulated in his youth. After completing his studies in native Neuchâtel and in Geneva, he served first as an assistant and then as a replacement for Dr. René Burnand at the Sanatorium Populaire in Leysin, maturing a social consciousness that would be reflected in the University Sanatorium's inclusive character. He also collaborated with Dr. Auguste Rollier and with other members of the local medical establishment, and he was heavily influenced by their studies on helio-therapy and on its effect on the emotional well-being of the patients. When called for his military service, he worked in one of the medical units of the Swiss army, an experience that shaped his handling of discipline and morality at his institu-tion. He also attended as an intern at the canton hospital in Lausanne under Professor Louis Michaud (1880–1956), who would later become involved in the administration of the University Sanatorium.[9]

After falling sick, he himself experienced a long convalescence while complet-ing his thesis. In 1920, he married Madeleine Piaget (1899–1976), the daughter of the professor of medieval literature Arthur Piaget (1865–1952) and the sister of the famous clinical psychologist and expert in child development Jean Piaget (1896–1980), who throughout his life would act as his closest collaborator and partner. As early as 1918, he contacted his old professors at the universities of Geneva, Lausanne, and Neuchâtel to propose the idea of a University Sanatorium— an international institution where university students and professors affected by tuberculosis could recover while pursuing their intellectual interests in a cosmo-politan environment and while maturing amicable feelings toward fellow-patients from other countries.[10]

---

[8] Vauthier followed what would later be called an "interactional model" of emotions, which postu-lates that feelings originate from social interactions rather than from biological processes internal to the body exclusively. Among the followers of this model were John Dewey (1859–1952), Hans Heinrich Gerth (1908–78), and C. Wright Mills (1916–62). For an overview of "organicist" vs. "interactional" approaches, see Appendix A in Arlie Russell Hochschild, *The Managed Heart: Commercialization of the Human Feeling* (Berkeley: University of California Press, 1983), 201–22. On various approaches to psychiatry in this period, see Greg Eghigian, ed., *From Madness to Mental Health: Psychiatric Disorder and Its Treatment in Western Civilization* (New Brunswick, NJ: Rutgers University Press, 2010); Edward Shorter, *A History of Psychiatry: From the Era of the Asylum to the Age of Prozac* (New York: John Wiley & Sons, 1997).
[9] A copy of Dr. Vauthier's *curriculum vitae* is preserved at the UNESCO Archives, IICI CVII7. A set of clippings of articles and obituaries is available through the Biographic Catalogue of Newspaper Articles (BioKat) at the Swiss National Library.
[10] Vancampenhout, *La tuberculose et le sanatorium universitaire de Leysin*, 51.

Building upon his experience at the Sanatorium Populaire, Dr. Vauthier insisted that this new institution make its services available to all.[11] He succeeded: after it opened in 1922, the University Sanatorium accepted both males and females.[12] A system of annual dues (10 francs for students and private-docents and 20 for professors) kept prices affordable for people of limited means.[13] Most strikingly, from a medical standpoint, the University Sanatorium treated patients who also suffered from a wide range of concurrent pathologies, ranging from heart conditions to fevers to scoliosis to nervous diseases classified under categories such as "nervosism," "neurasthenia," "anguish neurosis," "hysteria," and "neuropathic tremors."[14] As detailed in yearly reports, which included scientific analyses of the medical conditions of all guests as well as precise descriptions of the therapies administered to them, treatment was characterized by "careful and thorough medical observation of each case" and "attention to detail." Patients needed to undergo "a complete re-education" which involved physiotherapy, traditional medicine (such as the administration of tincture of garlic or injections of camphor oil), pneumothorax, and heliotherapy.[15] Like at the nearby clinics managed by Dr. Rollier, the latter was dispensed in carefully dosed intervals, with gradual increments and much attention devoted to the individual parts of the body and their position during exposure. The sun and the air of the mountains combined with the latest therapies available were employed to improve the health of all patients. In addition, in a regime of strict discipline, university students and faculty would receive treatments especially tailored for their physical and mental condition.[16]

The University Sanatorium synthesized Dr. Vauthier's medical, social, and personal experiences while centering all of its efforts on healing not only individuals but also society and the world as a whole. Although Dr. Vauthier envisioned an international sanatorium, not all of the people and institutions he collaborated with agreed with his plan. Negotiations on who could be admitted (only Swiss citizens; only people from countries who belonged to the International League of the Red Cross, which did not include Germany, Turkey, Russia, or Albania; or students from all nationalities) dragged on for a long time. Some preferred the idea of an institution that "benefitted Switzerland first." In the end, it was decided that students from all nationalities could be admitted provided that they had been enrolled in one of the Swiss founding institutions for at least two semesters

---

[11] A more extensive discussion on the social aspects of sanatoria in this period can be found in Chapter 4.

[12] Archives Cantonales Vaudoises, PP 911/5, Règlement général et conditions d'admission.

[13] UNESCO Archives, FR PUNES AG 1-IICI-C-VII-7, "Sanatorium Universitaire, IIIe rapport annuel du médicin directeur," 1925.

[14] See chart from Archives Cantonales Vaudoises PP 911/197, enclosed with the first annual report of the Director and Chief Doctor, years 1922–3.

[15] Archives Cantonales Vaudoises PP 911/197, first annual report of the Director and Chief Doctor, years 1922–3, 2–5.

[16] Detailed yearly medical reports can be found in Archives Cantonales Vaudoises PP 911/197.

(though for Swiss students, one semester sufficed).[17] If since the beginning the Medical Commission of the League of Red Cross Societies and the International Confederation of Students endorsed it as an initiative of international character, "it was in Switzerland of course that the idea spread the quickest,"[18] and it was there that by 1922 the Sanatorium had obtained sponsorship from a group of Swiss universities including those from Basel, Bern, Geneva, Lausanne, Neuchâtel and Zurich and the École polytechnique fédérale and thus was able to open its doors in Leysin.[19]

Despite its exclusively Swiss management, the University Sanatorium remained strongly international. Between 1922 and 1945, it hosted hundreds of patients from forty-two countries all over the world. Throughout the first decade, the number of guests continued to grow. The peak was reached in 1930, when 102 people (including seventy-five male students, seventeen female students, six assistants and four professors) convalesced there. If the total number declined significantly in the 1930s (dipping as low as sixty-two in 1938), enrollment picked up again shortly afterwards (see Chart 5.1). At the end of the Second World War, ninety-four

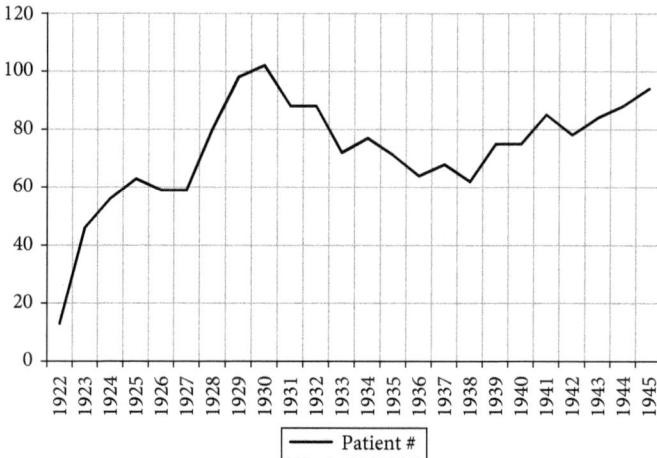

Chart 5.1 University Sanatorium of Leysin. Fluctuation of the total number of patients by year. Data derived from Archives cantonales vaudoises, PP 911/197-235, Rapports annuels du Directeur et du Médecin-Chef 1922–61.

---

[17] Vancampenhout, *La tuberculose et le sanatorium universitaire de Leysin*, 50–5; 64.

[18] Louis C. Vauthier, "Du Sanatorium Universitaire Suisse au Sanatorium Universitaire International," in Charles Bernard, *Un projet magnifique: le sanatorium Universitaire International de Leysin et son initiateur* (Geneva: Jent, 1930), 8. One copy is preserved at the UNESCO Archives, IICI CVII 7.

[19] According to the act of foundation, the institution was to be funded by an initial patrimony of 100.000 Swiss Francs gathered through participating universities, gifts, and individual contributions by students and professors housed at the Sanatorium itself. Archives Cantonales Vaudoises, PP 911/3, *Acte de Fondation* (1924).

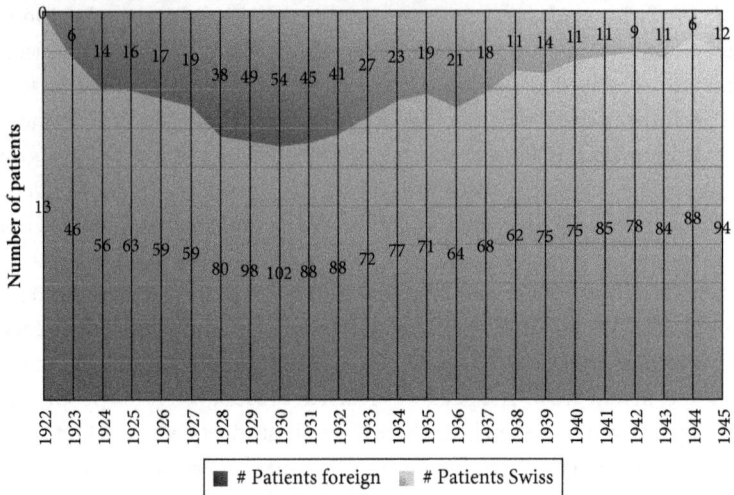

Chart 5.2 University Sanatorium of Leysin. Number and proportion of Swiss vs. foreign patients by year. Data derived from Archives cantonales vaudoises, PP 911/197–235, Rapports annuels du Directeur et du Médecin-Chef 1922–61.

people recovered at Leysin while also pursuing their studies, although in terms of foreign representation after 1930—perhaps as a result of the Great Depression—the percentage of international patients continued to decline (see Chart 5.2).[20] In terms of nationality, in the period 1922–45, the largest group of foreigners came from France (19 percent), followed by patients from Germany (13 percent), Poland (7 percent), Hungary (6 percent), and Belgium (5 percent) (see Chart 5.3). Among the non-European countries, the United States comprised the largest group (11,28 percent), followed by China (7,1 percent), Egypt (6,15 percent), and India (4,10 percent). In terms of continents, the majority of the students came from Asia (16,40 percent), followed by North America (11,28 percent, all from the United States), Latin America (7,17 percent), and Africa (6,15 percent, all from Egypt).

If seen year by year, however, the composition of the international body appears quite different, with students from Egypt clustered in the 1920s and those from the United States in the 1930s. As far as Europe is concerned, the number of French patients, who represented the great majority in the 1920s, began to decline sharply in the early 1930s (by 1936, there were none). In contrast, the number of German patients grew in the 1930s, peaked in 1936, and then decreased with the beginning of the Second World War (see Chart 5.4). As seen later in this chapter, such changes deeply affected the life and mood of the Sanatorium, posing

---

[20] See Chart 5.1. In his report for the year 1933, Vauthier attributed this decline to the economic crisis and to the restrictions on the import of foreign currency. Archives Cantonales Vaudoises PP 911/197, eleventh annual report of the Director and Chief Doctor, year 1933, 1.

France | 81
Germany | 53
Poland | 31
Hungary | 25
Belgium | 21
Latvia | 18
England | 16
Greece | 16
Romania | 16
Bulgaria | 15
Italy | 13
Turkey | 13
United States | 11
Serbia (since 1926 Yugoslavia) | 11
Lithuania | 9
Austria | 7
China | 7
Egypt | 6
Cyprus | 4
India | 4
Luxembourg | 4
Colombia | 3
Estonia | 3
Netherlands | 3
Portugal | 3
Scotland | 3
Spain | 3
Russia | 3
Bolivia | 2
Denmark | 2
Finland | 2
Iran | 2
Japan | 2
Norway | 2
Sweden | 2

0 10 20 30 40 50 60 70 80 90

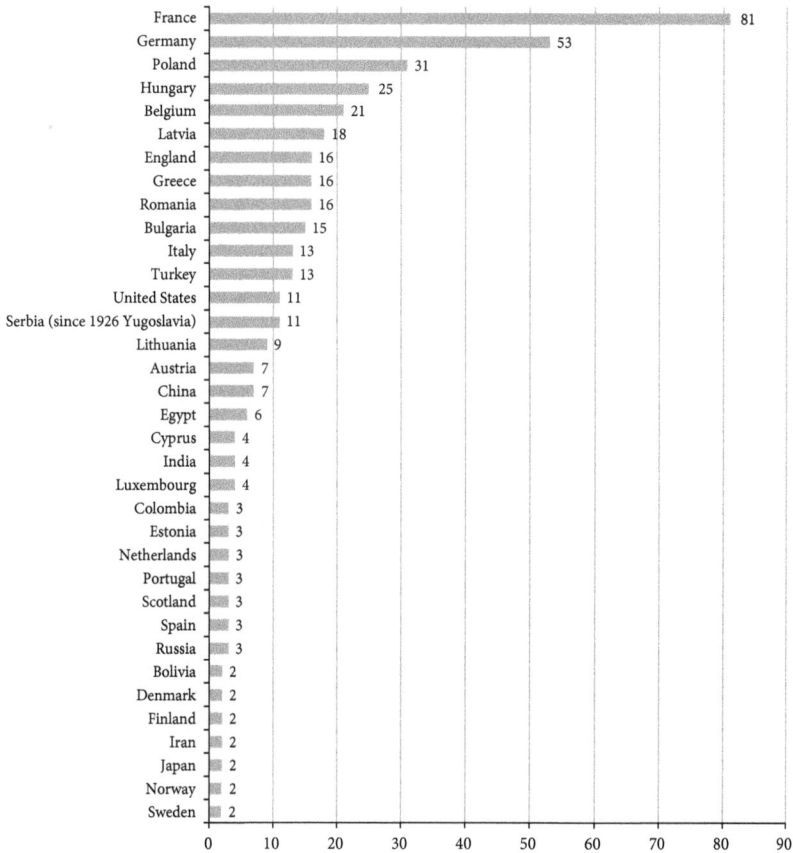

Chart 5.3 University Sanatorium. Percentage of foreign patients by nationality, 1922–45 (sum, countries with 1 percent or more only). Data derived from Archives cantonales vaudoises, PP 911/197–235, Rapports annuels du Directeur et du Médecin-Chef 1922–61.

increasing challenges as time went on. Regardless of these fluctuations, the clinic continued to be international and as such it appealed to patients and visitors from all over the world.

The combination of emotional, intellectual, and internationalist elements made the University Sanatorium stand apart from other institutions. Its first printed document (a 1920 leaflet jointly produced by the universities of Geneva, Lausanne, and Neuchâtel to advertise the establishment of an institute to be led by Dr. Vauthier), opened with a description of the "state of depression" that afflicted university students and professors with tuberculosis: "pulled out from a milieu necessary to them, kept away from all intellectual life, these wretched (*malheureux*) become discouraged and fall into a state of depression (*dépression*) from which all too often they cannot recover." In Leysin, these patients would find not only the

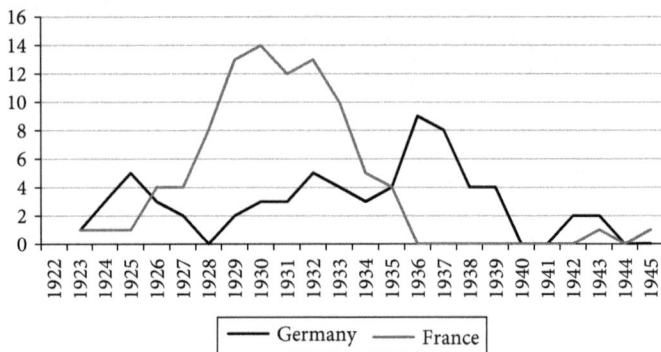

Chart 5.4 University Sanatorium of Leysin. Fluctuation of German vs. French patients, 1922–45. Data derived from Archives cantonales vaudoises, PP 911/197–235, Rapports annuels du Directeur et du Médecin-Chef 1922–61.

most modern therapies but also "a moral and intellectual milieu whose benefic influence will be immense."[21]

As Director of the University Sanatorium, Vauthier reiterated this point in his annual reports. In the first, he emphasized that the "originality" of the new establishment resided "in the influence of regular intellectual work on the course of the patients' disease." Far from being harmful, carefully-dosed work would be at once "sedative and tonic" (*sédatif et tonic*) and protect patients from "demoralization and neurasthenia."[22] In his report for the year 1930, Vauthier confirmed the success of his methods, pointing out how it had become increasingly apparent that "intellectual work is indispensable for our guests to maintain their psychic equilibrium (*équilibre psychique*) and their good mood (*bonne humeur*) so necessary for the re-establishment of their health."[23]

Because of its centrality in the institution's goals and approach, academic life received a great deal of attention. Despite the relatively small size of the establishment, students and professors had the possibility of pursuing their studies no matter what their specialties. The majority of the students were enrolled in some form of science or pharmacy (31 percent), medicine (27.1 percent), letters (15.1 percent), law (14.4 percent), economics (6.1 percent), and theology (5 percent), while 1.3 percent did not belong to any specific discipline.[24] The teaching was

[21] UNESCO Archives, FR PUNES AG 1-IICI-C-VII-7, loose sheet entitled "Sanatorium Universitaire." An anonymous handwritten note on the header indicates that this is the oldest printed document about the Sanatorium.

[22] Archives Cantonales Vaudoises PP 911/197, first annual report of the Director and Chief Doctor, years 1922–3, 5.

[23] Archives Cantonales Vaudoises PP 911/197, eighth annual report of the Director and Chief Doctor, year 1930, 1.

[24] These numbers refer to the first ten years and were collected in 1932 on the occasion of the tenth anniversary of the opening of the Sanatorium. Archives Cantonales Vaudoises PP 911/197, tenth annual report of the Director and Chief Doctor, year 1932, 1.

performed by numerous visiting professors who travelled to Leysin to give lectures or to hold conferences. The inevitable constraints imposed by the limited number of faculty were largely overcome by a sizeable contingent of external speakers. These included professors from Swiss and French universities, some of them quite prominent.[25]

A fully stocked library, with thousands of volumes and subscriptions to more than 150 journals—most of them donated—supported the work of students and faculty who used its resources to prepare for exams, write theses, and complete academic work. In the 1930s, when the cost of such endeavors became too high and the administration asked Vauthier to reduce the number of lectures, he insisted on the "biological" and "somatic" effects of intellectual work, which he regarded as an integral part of the therapy. Similarly, entertainment (usually offered in the form of lectures, concerts, and excursions to Leysin's magnificent mountain surroundings) had a positive effect on the "mood" of the house and on the overall well-being of its inhabitants and as such represented an essential ingredient for its success.[26]

Even the institution's internationalist objectives were presented as crucial and framed in terms of the emotions patients there would feel. An *Appeal* directed to all of the countries which had adhered to the International League of Red Cross Societies explained:

> This warm atmosphere of life and friendship is not going to be only a source of spiritual and physical forces extremely beneficial (*favorable*) for the healing of the sick: by offering over long months, sometimes even years to hundreds of students and professors from all disciplines and from different countries the occasion to grow closer (*se rapprocher*) and understand one another (*se comprendre*), it will create among them links of affection and solidarity (*liens d'affection et de solidarité*) whose benefits will not cease to be felt. Our project thus represents a movement of mutual aid among universities (*entr'aide universitaire*) and of international fraternity (*fraternité internationale*).[27]

Therapeutic, economic, social, moral, and political issues were thus presented as emotional objectives (e.g., "growing closer"). Feelings such as "affection" and

---

[25] A few of these visitors, such as philosopher Frank Abauzit and author Georges Duhamel, would later write some of the publicity materials for the sanatorium and advocate for its expansion. Also, Albert Roussy, who would later play an important role in the UIAA (see Chapter 3), gave a public lecture in at the University Sanatorium in Leysin in June 1923. UNESCO Archives, FR PUNES AG 1-IICI-C-VII-7, "Le Sanatorium Universitaire du 1er octobre 1922 au 1er mars 1924," Liste des professeurs visitants, des causeries données au Sanatorium, et des conférences publiques organisées dans la station, 3.

[26] Archives Cantonales Vaudoises PP 911/197, thirteenth annual report of the Director and Chief Doctor, year 1935, 2.

[27] UNESCO Archives, FR PUNES AG 1-IICI-C-VII-7, loose sheet titled "Sanatorium Universitaire."

"solidarity" became connected with their expressions and implementation for political purposes. And since peace was conceived in fraternalist terms, each aspect of the institution's life was organized as to ensure that patients would feel the necessary emotions.

5.2 Managing "Atmosphere" through Time and Aesthetics

Dr. Vauthier did not have full control over the University Sanatorium. The institution was governed by a complex administrative structure comprised of a *Conseil de Fondation*, a *Comité de Direction*, plus several other bureaucratic positions. Some worried that Vauthier actually did not have enough power to effectively implement his will as Medical Director; and at one point, a group of students felt compelled to write to the administration in his defense, confirming that Dr. Vauthier's say was far from absolute.[28] Nonetheless, together with his family of wife and three children, Dr. Vauthier lived at the Sanatorium 24/7 and held the greatest influence over the institution's emotional life.

Dr. Vauthier devoted much energy to the creation and the maintenance of what he considered a positive "atmosphere."[29] He carefully monitored the institution's internal rhythms and schedules as he deemed them to be of importance in determining the overall tone, morality, and feel. Since the beginning, he saw the University Sanatorium as a site of physical and moral propriety. For this reason, he spelled out a set of precise rules in an austere, disciplinary tone. Article 1 of the institution's *Réglement* recited that, "sentiment of honor and fraternal help is the fundamental law of the university sanatorium" [underlined in the original], setting the tone for all items to follow.[30] Participation in the 4 o'clock tea was "indispensable"; only the Director could designate rooms or determine seat assignments in the refectory at mealtime. Guests were expected to keep their rooms "in perfect order." Between 2:30 and 3:30 in the afternoon, they had to be in absolute rest: no noise, and not even silent reading would be allowed (in fact, an ordinance imposed silence on the entire town of Leysin, restricting the circulation of vehicles and all noisy activities, and also imposing a fine of 300 francs on those who spit anywhere but in the proper *crachoirs*).[31] In the evening, all patients had to lie down at 9 o'clock on the dot. After thirty minutes, lights would be off to

[28] Vancampenhout, *La tuberculose et le sanatorium universitaire de Leysin*, 72; 139; 142.

[29] For a theoretical framing of "atmospheres" and their particular place between affect and emotion, see Ben Anderson, "Affective Atmospheres," *Emotion, Space and Society* 2, no. 2 (December 2009), 77–81; Mikkel Bille, Peter Bjerregaard, and Tim Flohr Sørensen, "Staging Atmospheres: Materiality, Culture, and the Texture of the In-Between," *Emotion, Space and Society* 15 (May 2015), 31–8.

[30] UNESCO Archives, FR PUNES AG 1-IICI-C-VII-7, *Réglement* included in the 1922–3 set of documents submitted by Dr. Vauthier in his application for funds for a new International University Sanatorium.

[31] Geneviève Heller, "Leysin et son passé médical," *Gesnerus* 47, nos. 3–4 (1990), 340–1.

guarantee appropriate rest. Alcohol, smoking, and gambling were strictly forbidden, as were "visits from room to room between men and women."[32] Dr. Vauthier carefully devised a schedule to ensure that patients would remain active, staging times for "healthy" and morally upright interaction.

Many of these measures derived from the fact that in this period sanatoria were associated with the dissolution of their guests. Descriptions of patients' heightened sexual tension and of reckless behavior (especially in gambling) often found their way into romances and novels set there. As early as 1902, in *Les embrasés* (literally, "The Inflamed"), Michel Corday described a doctor trying to catch in flagrante an illicit encounter in an international sanatorium's dark room, and a world where people were more "sentimental" and "passionate" than they would have otherwise been.[33] Joseph Kessel's *Les captifs* ("The Captives"), published in 1926, portrayed the sanatorium as a "prison" where protagonists battled love and poker, attempted suicide, and wrestled with inner demons.[34] Most notably, Thomas Mann's *The Magic Mountain* would irreversibly associate sanatoria with sensual temptations and the Dionysian aspect of life, as well as with selfishness, futility, and isolation; its ending, with the protagonist joining the war effort, openly challenged internationalist discourses and aims.[35] Even before the book was first published in German in 1924, Vauthier was concerned about the corruptive effects of sanatorium life (real or imagined) and proposed an alternative model based instead on rigid discipline and on the careful management of emotions.[36]

While deliberately intervening to avoid the effects of excessive fraternization, Vauthier worked incessantly to ensure that patients would "develop a sense of cooperation." As detailed in his reports, he assigned each patient "a small social function," such as sending thank you notes to donors or distributing papers, or completing small tasks for their peers (e.g., a pharmacy major ran a small apothecary, while an advanced student in dentistry took care of his peers' teeth). Some students helped others with their exams, or tutored them for a fee. For a time, he encouraged "family gatherings" (*réunions des famille*) to discuss matters of common interest and to provide suggestions for improving communal life (although these were soon discontinued as they had evolved into real "councils" with pre-set agendas, a President and a Secretary, and—at least in Vauthier's opinion—had

---

[32] UNESCO Archives, FR PUNES AG 1-IICI-C-VII-7, *Réglement*.

[33] Michel Corday, *Les embrasés* (Paris: Flammarion, 1902), 124–5.

[34] Joseph Kessel, *Les captifs* (Paris: Gallimard, 1926).

[35] Thomas Mann, *Der Zauberberg* (Berlin: S. Fischer Verlag, 1924). After publication, the book soon appeared in English, French, and Italian. See *The Magic Mountain* (New York: Alfred A. Knopf, 1927); *La montagne magique* (Paris: Fayard, 1931); *La montagna incantata* (Milan: Modernissima, 1932).

[36] Increased sexual practices in sanatoria were in fact well documented. On "cousining" and relationships among patients, and on both the accuracy and deception of Thomas Mann's depiction of life in a sanatorium, see Sheila M. Rothman, *Living in the Shadow of Death: Tuberculosis and the Social Experience of Illness in American History* (Baltimore, MD: Johns Hopkins University Press, 1995), 236–7; 226.

begun to deal with matters outside of their purview).[37] Moreover, he decided that the library would be open for only one hour a day to encourage "a less selfish atmosphere" among students.[38]

Dr. Vauthier especially minded aesthetic and material aspects, as he believed that more than others these would influence the general feel of the place. In 1938, when the administration unilaterally ordered a rearrangement of the refectory and substituted "two large family tables" with many smaller ones, Vauthier expressed his frustration at the mindlessness of such act and at the negative effect this would have on the sanatorium's atmosphere. "Such arrangement makes more like a 'restaurant,' but the general communion (*communion générale*) had suffered," he decried. "For those who are not aware of the multiple means that need to be employed to create ceaselessly an atmosphere a bit communal, this detail might seem minimal. But its impact is real nonetheless."[39] Creating and maintaining a sense of community was central to Vauthier's project, and in his view every effort needed to be made to help in this respect.

Dr. Vauthier effectively shaped what the Sanatorium looked and felt like, particularly during staged moments of communal life. To mitigate the constraining effect of the many restrictions he imposed on the University Sanatorium, he coordinated a wide range of acceptable forms of entertainment such as cinema, concerts, excursions, and picnics. Not only did these social activities break up the monotony of the many days, months, and sometimes even years of convalescence but they also represented forms of cultural enrichment that would complement the patients' intellectual work. Most importantly, in his mind, they helped students to overcome national differences by making them share common interests and by fostering the development of relationships among them. Vauthier elaborated on this point in a 1934 report: while coming to terms with the fact that the new university youth wanted only to talk about politics and could not agree on common interests in any other discipline, he praised how "beautiful music" was able to

[37] Archives Cantonales Vaudoises PP 911/197, first annual report of the Director and Chief Doctor, years 1922–3, 7–8. Once such gatherings spontaneously stopped, Vauthier did nothing to revive them. In his view, due to his regular presence at the sanatorium, he had plenty of opportunities to hear about his patients' needs anyway and he was always ready to meet them whenever possible.

[38] Archives Cantonales Vaudoises PP 911/197, ninth annual report of the Director and Chief Doctor, year 1931, 3. The notion that medical libraries represented a preferred space for emotional management proved long lasting. In 1958, Regina Frank completed a project at the medical library of Leysin (which was reserved for the patients of Dr. Rollier's clinics) for the attainment of her library science degree. She eliminated some of the books that she deemed to be too gloomy, excessively focused on disease, or immoral, and marked others with a black dot to signal that they should be kept from general circulation. Frank also noted that she avoided dressing in white "to show that she represents the world outside and does not belong to the world of disease." This too was an attempt to influence the patients' emotional experience. Regina Frank, "Intégration d'une donation de livre français et allemands dans la bibliothèque 'Le Livre du Malade' à Leysin," Thesis, École de bibliothécaires de Genève, 1961, 2.

[39] Archives Cantonales Vaudoises PP 911/197, sixteenth annual report of the Director and Chief Doctor, year 1938, 3. Meals were important times in sanatorium's life. In his account, René Burnand described them as a moment when patients dressed with regular clothes and displayed themselves in a social environment. René Burnand, *Une ville sur la montagne* (Paris: Attinger, 1936), 66–70.

"rally all suffrages and always give pleasure."[40] Perhaps for this reason, references to friendship, fraternity, and sociability during times of entertainment peppered the sanatorium's activity reports, suggesting that such exchanges were universally valued.

The pictures taken on these occasions, depicting scenes of cheerful and amicable interactions during lectures and picnics, concerts and fondue dinners, reveal that Dr. Vauthier had effectively given to the University Sanatorium the looks, shape, and feel of a home.[41] Indoor shots show the decor one would find in a house, with couches, pillows, and carpets (see Figure 5.1). Many photographs portray people gathered in groups, often in the act of enjoying a shared experience (a lecture, or some form of art, or food they all seemed to appreciate). Patients wore regular clothes and seemed to be at ease. Sitting or laying in relaxed, informal poses, they interacted as they would in any non-clinical environment. The moments captured in these images included some intense sensorial experiences—listening, or tasting something—associated with feelings. Fondue-dinners appeared frequently in the Sanatorium's photographs and descriptions (see Figure 5.2). And if having

Fig. 5.1 University Sanatorium in Leysin. Social occasion. ©Archives cantonales vaudoises, PP 911/16, photograph 12.

---

[40] Archives Cantonales Vaudoises PP 911/197, twelfth annual report of the Director and Chief Doctor, year 1934, 3.
[41] Archives Cantonales Vaudoises, PP 911/15, photographs 25, 28; PP 911/16, photographs 2, 3, 12, 23, 28.

Fig. 5.2 University Sanatorium. La fondue. ©Archives cantonales vaudoises, PP 911/16, photograph 28.

sick people dipping food in a communal pot might have been questionable from a hygienical point of view, sharing a quintessential alpine food associated with a gregarious atmosphere held great meaning from an emotional standpoint.[42]

Outdoor poses during picnics and excursions, scenic strolls, and *déjeuners sur l'herbe* reinforced the notion that the mountain landscape provided the ideal setting for lifting people's spirits and establishing harmony among them (see Figure 5.3). The impression was that these events allowed all participants to come together despite their differences in gender, race, class, and nationality. The mountainous landscape offered an aesthetically pleasing setting for their encounters, alpine lawns to lay on, mountain paths to stroll, and majestic views to admire. Annual reports included detailed descriptions of these moments of shared enjoyment, emphasizing their positive effect on the overall "mood" of the place.

The annual Christmas party represented the climax of these shared moments of amicable exchange and also the most poignant example of how Vauthier effectively orchestrated the Sanatorium's rhythms and environment to engender desirable emotions in his patients.[43] "Our Christmas celebrations—the most beautiful

---

[42] On the invention of "alpine" aesthetics and products in this period, see Chapter 1.

[43] Christmas was celebrated with particular fervor in other sanatoria as well. In his account of his life at the sanatorium Bienvenue in Riondaz, René Burnand called it a "masterpiece Christmas" filled with emotions and dedicated several pages to its description. Burnand, *Une ville sur la montagne*, 200–5.

Fig. 5.3 University Sanatorium. Picnic scene. ©Archives cantonales vaudoises, PP 911/16, photograph 3.

and intimate—have a largely religious character to which the most disparate spirits can associate themselves wholeheartedly around the traditional tree," he pointed out in one of his reports.[44] Although from a religious standpoint the institute was not affiliated with any specific denomination, the Christian holiday of Christmas served as a means to mark the year with a special occasion of heightened significance and emotions. Measures were taken to ensure that nobody would feel alienated, providing religious services in French and German to accommodate as many guests as possible. As the population of the sanatorium grew more diverse, the Christmas celebration maintained an atmosphere "intimate and familial, of a tonality largely religious, where Catholics, Protestants, Orthodox, Israelites, agnostic, etc. can feel perfectly at ease."[45]

French writer Claude Aveline later published the text of an address he gave during one of these parties, one which vividly communicated its special atmosphere and unifying effect. In his impassioned speech, Aveline expressed how he understood the sadness that must have filled the patients' hearts as they spent Christmas away from their families. Yet, he called on his dear "friends" and

---

[44] Archives Cantonales Vaudoises PP 911/197, third annual report of the Director and Chief Doctor, year 1925, 4.
[45] Archives Cantonales Vaudoises PP 911/197, eleventh annual report of the Director and Chief Doctor, year 1933, 5.

"comrades" to appreciate the fact that in the misfortune of their disease, they had encountered a "tribe" that someday—once healed and at home—they will surely miss. He knew of people who had actually returned just for the sake of living "an hour of such quality." He emphasized how patients were spending Christmas in a famous home (*maison célèbre*), a "collection of memories, an album of images, a museum in miniature," which elicit "a respect and often an emotion [that is] commendable [*louable*]." He was aware that "Christmas night puts in the mouth of all humans, believers or not, a drought [*sécheresse*] for hope, the foretaste of miracle." While enjoying the scents, sights, and sounds of Christmas, all—regardless of their origin—could experience the emotions of internationalism in their deepest, most spiritual expression.[46] His was but one of numerous accounts by visitors and patients who described the emotions they felt while at the University Sanatorium of Leysin, especially at Christmas-time. If his words cannot be taken at face value, they nonetheless demonstrate that Dr. Vauthier had successfully achieved his objective of making shared experiences and emotions a central part of life at his establishment.

5.3 Failed Feelings as Evidence of Success

While photographs and descriptions convey an idyllic view of the University Sanatorium, other sources reveal the many frictions that characterized its communal life. Sometimes people failed at feeling the emotions that Dr. Vauthier tried so hard to instill in them, or expressed that either they or somebody else felt a particular emotion while providing evidence to the contrary at the same time.[47] These moments of subversion and deviation serve as a useful window onto what people actually felt; the fact that they stood as an exception only confirms that the majority normally complied with Vauthier's wishes. Also, the measures taken against those who did not (including not only punishment but also acts of conciliation or the downplaying of their positions) reveal the many ways in which emotions could be managed. Mentioning—and sometimes overtly displaying—people whose feelings were clearly at odds with others' conveyed a sense of inclusion and gave authenticity to moments when emotions were tested and shared. Finally, openly denouncing that somebody failed at feeling certain emotions reinforced the notion that feelings were of paramount importance at this institution.

---

[46] Archives Cantonales Vaudoises, PP 911/242. Claude Aveline, *Devant un arbre de Noël: pour les étudiants du sanatorium universitaire de Leysin, 24 décembre 1937*.

[47] I thank Pascal Eitler and Uffa Jensen for stimulating the line of inquiry developed in this section at an international conference on the theme "Failing at Feelings. Historical Perspectives (1800–2000)," which was held at the Max Planck Institute for Human Development on December 15–16, 2016.

More than once in his annual reports Dr. Vauthier referred to the "negative elements" he had to kick out of the institution. He acknowledged openly his frequent and deliberate interferences to ensure that the atmosphere at the sanatorium remained amicable. In a report for 1928, he explained how the positive atmosphere of international friendship "did not create or maintain itself simply by grouping students under the same roof." At times, he had to intervene to neutralize negative elements to prevent them from poisoning the atmosphere for all. Along with his wife, he participated in all of the students' functions and administrated what he saw as necessary "cures of the soul" (*cures d'âmes*).[48] Any variation in the house's general feel concerned him deeply. In 1929, when some of the older patients left, others died, and the overall mood of the house changed for the worse, Vauthier regretted the loss of the old atmosphere. He spoke of a bygone *Stimmung*, referring to this seminal philosophical and aesthetic concept to emphasize the depth and significance of such loss.[49]

Vauthier took note of the "good" and "bad" moods that permeated the Sanatorium each year, and reflected on how he could affect them. A report by the President of the Direction Committee confirms that the moral character of the community not always corresponded to the one described in the *Règlement*. In the year 1934, "the discipline of the students at certain times had left something to be desired and redress [*redressement*] had been necessary."[50] The fact that Dr. Vauthier isolated a few individuals, labeled them as unfit for his experiment, and succeeded in kicking them out only confirmed the validity of his model. As exceptions that confirmed the rule, these cases served as evidence that the majority of people were feeling what they were supposed to.

Patients regularly broke the sanatorium's rules, especially the ones meant at safeguarding the moral standards of the place; but these instances only helped Dr. Vauthier in the realization of his overall endeavors. A 1935 document dealing with the sanatorium's management reveals that there was an issue with male and female students spending time in each other's rooms. If some considered this behavior "natural" and suggested not doing anything since there could be no way to prevent secret encounters anyway, others disagreed—contending that "if the patients were like kids they needed to be treated as such"—and insisted that under no circumstance should visits among the sexes be tolerated. Furthermore, in a medical establishment where all unhealthy habits had been outlawed, the committee debated over how to deal with smokers. They blamed the Director for such breaches of the regulations, remarking that Dr. Vauthier himself had given an

---

[48] Archives Cantonales Vaudoises PP 911/197, sixth annual report of the Director and Chief Doctor, year 1928, 3–4.

[49] Archives Cantonales Vaudoises PP 911/197, seventh annual report of the Director and Chief Doctor, year 1929, 2.

[50] Archives Cantonales Vaudoises PP 911/197, report by the President of the Direction Committee (L. Michaud), year 1934, 8–9.

ashtray as a Christmas gift to one of the people known for breaking the rules.[51] They also reprimanded the Library committee for having bought beer with part of their funds, confirming that the University Sanatorium's strict rules were merely nominal and often disregarded.[52] The fact that Dr. Vauthier seemed to enable the breaching of his own rules suggests that the doctor might have chosen a less direct approach to emotional management. He showed himself lenient and benevolent, as well as complicit and gregarious (as in the ash-tray example), ultimately reinforcing his own standing. In the end, emotions such as complicity in the relationship between doctor and patients only strengthened Dr. Vauthier's position.

Sometimes negotiating tensions to the advantage of an internationalist agenda was not easy. At the sanatorium there were frequent conflicts between German and French-speaking patients. At one point, a group of Germans tried to get Dr. Vauthier removed while the French wrote to the administration to defend him. In his accounts, Vauthier only mentioned this question in passing but the records survive on how the matter was handled by the sanatorium's higher governing bodies. For its part, the administration sought conciliation: they kept the doctor in his post but added a supervising body. They re-adjusted the course, and later monitored their success by commenting on the fact that the "good atmosphere" had been restored.[53] Dr. Vauthier emerged as the winner, though not without great struggles.

Naturally, the University Sanatorium was not immune to the political tensions that were ripping the continent apart in the 1930s. A 1939 report by the Direction Committee well illustrates the multiple strains that the war placed on the community. Most of the staff, including Dr. Vauthier, had been mobilized multiple times. Among the patients were now refugees from countries recently invaded by the German army, whom the Administration had decided to admit despite their inability to pay for their fees. Moreover, in solidarity with the victim of the Soviet-Finnish war, the sanatorium's patients decided to give up meat once a week and to donate the amount of money thus saved to the Finnish Red Cross. After a few months, however, some students complained and this initiative was interrupted.

---

[51] Archives Cantonales Vaudoises PP 911/25, *Protokoll der Ordentlichen Sitzung des Stiftungsrates des Schweizerischen Hochschulsanatoriums*, 2 March 1935 in Leysin, 7–8. Illegal smoking was common in sanatoria. In a work about his experience at the Beau-Site, also in Leysin, Jean Houriet included a humorous alphabet meant to provide an insider's view: the letters W.C. did not refer to "water closet" but to "*petit fumoir*"—or "small smoking room." Jean H. Houriet, *Années perdues, années retrouvées: sous un toit sanatorial* (Neuchâtel: Messeiller, 1974), 63.

[52] Archives Cantonales Vaudoises PP 911/25, *Protokoll der Ordentlichen Sitzung des Stiftungsrates des Schweizerischen Hochschulsanatoriums*, 2 March 1935 in Leysin, 8.

[53] L'association générale des étudiants des universités de Suisse romande and others wrote a long memo in defense of Dr. Louis Vauthier. They referred negatively to some students who unjustly tried to oust him, and often implied an underlying tension between German and French speaking people at the sanatorium. See Swiss Federal Archives, E3001A#1000/728#260, Sanatorium universitaire international Leysin, 1930–9.

Furthermore, rumors circulated that the sanatorium had become home to communist and Nazi groups. The Direction Committee conducted an investigation in this regard and dismissed such concerns. The committee concluded that the communist elements, if they had ever existed, by then had departed. As for the Nazi, they deemed students who read fascist papers and distributed propaganda to be "inoffensive"; in their view, they were simply clashing with the "patriotic and healthy convictions of the majority of our students" and the sanatorium "could not be suspected to host neither communists nor members of the V column!"[54]

To be sure, the fact that this investigation was conducted and such clashes existed demonstrates that Vauthier's descriptions mirrored his vision more than the reality of its implementation.[55] Yet, the administration intervened to ease ongoing tensions. In an internal report written in 1940, Dr. Vauthier commented that despite "nefarious external influences," a "calm abandonment (*abandon confiante*), a complete harmony, a general good mood characterized the rest of the year."[56] And in the midst of the Second World War, he remarked how the years 1943 and 1944 flowed in "an atmosphere of peace."[57] If there is no way of knowing if Dr. Vauthier's descriptions were accurate, it is clear that an "atmosphere of peace" was yearned for and promoted at his institution.

On other occasions, examples of people clearly not feeling the right emotions occupy a central place in Dr. Vauthier's accounts and even in some of the materials that his institution published for a broader audience. The inclusion of this contradictory evidence gave authenticity to moments of international encounter and only reinforced Dr. Vauthier's work and message. This dynamic is illustrated well by a series of "conferences of international understanding" (*conferences d' entente internationale*), which Dr. Vauthier enthusiastically supported.[58] Though he had invited numerous speakers to discuss current events in an atmosphere of mutual respect, preserving such feel must not have been easy. In general, Dr. Vauthier tended to downplay the conflicts among people from different countries. He frequently praised the foreign patients for their "excellent spirit." And if he acknowledged the advantage of having a growing international population ("should I add that their financial contribution...is not negligible?," he once noted in this regard), he most often emphasized diversity as one of the "riches"

---

[54] Archives Cantonales Vaudoises PP 911/197, report by the President of the Direction Committee (L. Michaud), year 1939.

[55] Archives Cantonales Vaudoises PP 911/197, report by the President of the Direction Committee (L. Michaud), year 1939. In the 1950s, there would be another inquiry into suspicious communist propaganda. Vancampenhout, *La tuberculose et le sanatorium universitaire de Leysin, 1922–1961*, 148.

[56] Archives Cantonales Vaudoises PP 911/197, eighteenth annual report of the Director and Chief Doctor, year 1940, 1–2.

[57] Archives Cantonales Vaudoises PP 911/197, twenty-first annual report of the Director and Chief Doctor, years 1943–4, 2.

[58] Archives Cantonales Vaudoises PP 911/197, eight annual report of the Director and Chief Doctor, year 1930, 2.

and "greatest charms" of the place.[59] In contrast to this trend, the account of the "conferences of international understanding" included the texts of addresses that openly questioned—if not berated—internationalism and the actions of the League of Nations, which was the quintessential internationalist body in this period and a natural reference point for the University Sanatorium.[60]

The most striking case was that of Nino-Severino Siffredi, a professor of economics at the University of Genoa who gave a lecture entitled "Italy." He began his talk by promising that "despite belonging to the National Fascist Party, he would provide an exposition of maximum objectivity" on "the historical precedents of Fascism in Italy, the political and historical achievements of the Fascist Government," and on Italian foreign policy. He then attacked the decisions taken in Paris, which determined that Italy would receive only "crumbs" of the "abundant meal" enjoyed by others. Next he listed the many successes that the Duce had been able to obtain thanks to a diplomacy characterized by "sincerity without any subterfuge or loophole," one which had scored Italy territorial gains in Corfu, Yugoslavia, and Greece. He praised the many treaties that Mussolini had signed with Spain, Albania, and Hungary, as well as the 1929 Lateran Pacts that had normalized Italian relations with the Vatican. Siffredi did not shy away from talking about Italy's demographic need to expand—tellingly, he concluded his address by stating that "naturally, when all of our efforts will have been vain, 'we will remain alone with Rome and for Rome'"—and unapologetically negated many of the principles on which the University Sanatorium had been founded.[61]

The fact that Dr. Vauthier decided to include fascist views in a published report of this event only confirms that he thought they could help his cause. The preface was written by essayist Robert de Traz, the author of a 1929 piece on the "spirit of Geneva" that had made him an authoritative voice within the internationalist movement.[62] While introducing the Leysin conference report, de Traz explained that the open exchanges on current events that Dr. Vauthier had initiated were meant to build real and concrete understanding. "We do not make theoretical pacifism," de Traz declared, defending the idea behind a series of events such as this. Along similar lines, in his "Avant-propos," Belgian professor Henri Laurent also emphasized the importance of discussing contentious issues freely. Reasoning (*rayonner*) ultimately would have ensured a constructive and peaceful atmosphere.[63]

---

[59] Archives Cantonales Vaudoises PP 911/197, fifth annual report of the Director and Chief Doctor, year 1927, 5.

[60] Archives Cantonales Vaudoises PP 911/197, eight annual report of the Director and Chief Doctor, year 1930, 2. Archives Cantonales Vaudoises, PP 911/241, Cahier du Sanatorium Universitaire Suisse, *Tableau politique de l'Europe 1931/32* (Zürich, 1932).

[61] Nino-Severino Siffredi, "L'Italia," in *Tableau politique de l'Europe 1931/32*, 93–7.

[62] Robert de Traz, *L'esprit de Genève* (Paris: Grasset, 1929).

[63] Henri Laurent, "Avant-propos," in *Tableau politique de l'Europe 1931/32*, 15.

These texts framed moments such as Siffredi's address as opportunities for students to be exposed to various points of view. Lectures had been broadcast via radio in each room so that all patients could hear regardless of their health conditions. After each talk, speakers had continued their discussions, "establishing extremely fecund (*fécondes*) relations and contacts perhaps more intimate (*intime*) and lasting than in regular academic life."[64] The fact that the booklet had been published in both German and French bore witness to the reality of discussing conflicting points of view in a peaceful and constructive manner. The presence of speakers who clearly failed at feeling the emotions of internationalism only confirmed the inclusive character of this event and gave it authenticity. Artfully mixed in with others, these moments of dissonance fostered—rather than hindered—the overall internationalist mood, message, and emotions of the establishment.

The case of Siffredi serves as a reminder that fascist internationalism—a set of ideas and practices through which extreme nationalists sought to create a unified, international movement—sometimes developed in the same spaces and within the same people involved in other forms of international cooperation. The fact that "good" internationalists ultimately gave him a platform to disseminate his ideas challenges historians not to fall into easy characterizations of internationalism as benevolent by default. If internationalist rhetoric and emotions must be studied seriously, they cannot be taken at face value. Much effort went into shaping them, and the process through which these were made can tell us more about the past than how much—or how little—these reflected what people authentically felt.

5.4 Witnesses and Makers of "Authentic" Emotions

Numerous patients and visitors devoted much energy to fueling the idea that the University Sanatorium successfully engendered the emotions of internationalism, and that these would serve the internationalist cause of fostering peaceful relations among people from various nations. Their voices not only described Dr. Vauthier's message and lent it authenticity but also amplified it and gave it an emotive value it would have not otherwise had.

The Sanatorium's most celebrated visitor, the leader of the Indian independence movement Mahatma Gandhi (1869–1948), gave Leysin a higher spiritual meaning and inspired strong feelings in those who followed in his steps. From December 6 to December 11, 1931, he stayed at Leysin while calling on a friend, the renowned French writer Romain Rolland (1866–1944) who had written a book about him in

---

[64] Laurent, "Avant-propos," 16.

1924; and one day, he spoke at the University Sanatorium.[65] Released from prison in January of the same year, Gandhi had been in Europe since September to participate in the Second Round-Table Conference in London on constitutional reforms in India. His visit to Leysin—though brief and private in character—is still remembered, and its 80th anniversary was fervently celebrated. As Narayani Ganesh remarked in a newspaper article written for *The Economic Times* of New Delhi, "It may be 80 years since the unusual visit of a shawl-clad Gandhi in the region surrounded by snow, ice and political ferment but the impact of those five days in 1931 is still alive, as fresh as the Alpine air, reminding the people here of another world, one of spiritualism and affection, free of greed and rancour."[66] Asked what he thought about disease, Gandhi replied that illness had been turned into a "fetish." People needed to have the courage to face it not by building more sanatoria but by living frugal and healthy lives, and by remembering that if humans can bear physical ills, the ones they cannot survive are the spiritual ones.[67]

Gandhi interacted with the Sanatorium's patients, fully immersing himself in the friendly atmosphere of the place. One photograph captured him surrounded by students and doctors; another showed him on a walk (see Figures 5.4 and 5.5).[68] Gandhi's presence, images, and words strengthened the Sanatorium's emotional character, enriching it with spiritual and moral values it would have otherwise lacked. His non-violent "spiritualism" evoked profound critiques of modernization and colonial exploitations; his embodiment of strength and frugality exuded these qualities onto those who surrounded him; and his passage—albeit brief and coincidental—continued to resonate through the years, giving Leysin a lasting emotional quality that commentators like the ones quoted above tried to capture.

Other illustrious visitors played an active role in creating an imagined "emotional community" with the University Sanatorium at its center.[69] Claude Aveline wrote extensively on this point. He contended that "the position of the intellectual in regard to disease is of a particular order." Stricken with disease, the intellectual's "reflection" quickly turned into a "monument of deductions" that resembled a "prison," or even a "tomb." While industrialists or workers were preoccupied exclusively with supporting their trade, and "once the problem of their [financial] fortune had been solved, everything had been solved," for intellectuals "the spirit" was all that mattered. If the body failed, the spirit failed with it. Aveline drove his

---

[65] Romain Rolland was an internationalist in his own right. See David James Fisher, *Romain Rolland and the Politics of Intellectual Engagement* (Berkeley: University of California Press, 1988).

[66] Narayani Ganesh, "Vaud prepares to celebrate Romain Rolland–Gandhi meet 80th anniversary," *The Economic Times* (Online) [New Delhi], November 8, 2011. https://economictimes.indiatimes.com/vaud-prepares-to-celebrate-romain-rolland-gandhi-meet-80th-anniversary/articleshow/10648160.cms (accessed on September 4, 2018).

[67] D. G. Chatenay, "La Visite du Mahatma: l'opinion de l'Eglise nationale vaudoise," *La Sentinelle*, December 29, 1931.

[68] Archives Cantonales Vaudoises, PP 911/16, photographs 10 and 47.

[69] On the notion of "emotional communities" see Barbara H. Rosenwein, *Emotional Communities in the Early Middle Ages* (Ithaca, NY: Cornell University Press, 2007).

Fig. 5.4 University Sanatorium. Gandhi's visit (1931). ©Archives cantonales vaudoises, PP 911/16, photograph 10.

Fig. 5.5 27 University Sanatorium. Gandhi's visit (1931). ©Archives cantonales vaudoises, PP 911/16, photograph, 47.

point through with a simile: this would be as if "in the moment in which the industrialist fell sick, the factory became sick with him." As everything collapsed at the same time, the intellectual was then overtaken by disease. "Time is then suspended, almost stopped" as hours, months, and years click by, and deep questions torture his soul: "The spirit fights the ghosts (*fantômes*) it engenders and takes pleasure in letting itself being defeated by them." All around, "the mountains…in their immobile appearance seem to mock his life as it is falling apart and his thoughts as they die." Such suffering is evident in the "young faces" that populate the galleries of ordinary sanatoria and in the "painful obsession" (*obsession douloureuse*) they convey.[70]

Aveline drew heavily on contemporary discourses regarding intellectuals and the *mal du siècle* that afflicted them. Concerns about "inquietude" and "malaise" had grown deeper after the First World War, and many interpreted the sickly status of young, intelligent men as a sign of the worsening state of society as a whole.[71] Melancholy too was a prominent theme in interwar art, reminding all of the sad condition plaguing the deepest, most educated members of society.[72] By describing the patients of the University Sanatorium as a community of young intellectuals in a state of depression, and by implying that their state would affect negatively society as a whole, Aveline thus reinforced many of the anxieties of his time while also asserting the existence of a link among them.

Speaking both as a former patient and as a visitor, Aveline insisted that the University Sanatorium had succeeded in healing the intellectuals' emotional ills. In enthusiastic terms, he described how Dr. Vauthier and his University Sanatorium came as a "dream" with the power of dispelling negative feelings, and, for this reason, patients like himself celebrated them. He painted a vivid picture of the atmosphere that such a "dream" had created, one which he had the opportunity to witness multiple times as he walked through the galleries himself. He spoke of the sun that illuminated all corners of the dwelling and of the sound of students debating and laughing among themselves and with their professors. "One has to attend one of the conferences, one has to have seen those young faces tanned by the sun, their gaze lively (*vivant*), their expressions relaxed (*les traits detendus*), to understand that they are simply happy." As they "have forgotten the disease," they now heal, and later remember their time there as a good one in which both their physical and their intellectual needs had been met.[73] Aveline used the mountains features (e.g., its air and sun), the aesthetic appearance of the patients' bodies,

[70] UNESCO Archives, IICI CVII 7, Aveline, *Le sanatorium universitaire de Leysin* (1928), 1–4.

[71] Nicholas Hewitt, *Les maladies du siècle: The Image of Malaise in French Fiction and Thought in the Inter-war Years* (Hull: Hull University Press, 1988), 22–4; 74. See also Georges Minois, *Histoire du mal de vivre: de la mélancolie à la dépression* (Paris: Martinière, 2003), in particular chapter XI "Une culture du mal de vivre: modernité et anxieté au XX e siècle," 357–94.

[72] Jean Clair, *Malinconia: motifs saturniens dans l'art de l'entre-deux-guerres* (Paris: Gallimard, 1996).

[73] Aveline, *Le sanatorium universitaire de Leysin*, 7.

and their physical expressions as proof of the success of Vauthier's approach. Moreover, by presenting the sanatorium as the result of both individual and societal regeneration, Aveline contributed to the construction of a new, generative vision, one in which the sanatorium represented a new set of aesthetics and emotions embodied by the mountains.

Catholic writer Henry Petiot, also known under the pseudonym Daniel-Rops (1901–65) also aided in the creation of a special metaphorical space for the "intellectual in front of the disease." In 1930, he wrote a piece in which, like Aveline, he drew a distinction between the ordinary patient (what he called the *malade ordinaire*, who could be a worker, an employee, or a merchant) and intellectuals such as academics, journalists, lawyers and doctors, "and all those who form the tribe of 'liberal professions.'" In contrast to Aveline, Petiot spoke of physical distinctions that set intellectuals apart, asserting that "because of the very constitution of its being," a member of such "tribe" naturally tended to worsen his situation from a psychological standpoint and, from a social point of view, tended to be isolated.[74] The intellectual would "create monsters" (*monstres*) who would slow down his recovery. For this reason "he suffers more pain (*a plus mal*) than another man," or is more prone to disease than others. Petiot did not consider these physical differences innate but contended that they derived from lifestyle choices and conditions. He believed that intellectuals were more likely to fall sick than people in other trades, as "brain work" (*travail cérébral*) was especially draining. The posture imposed by their intellectual work also hurt them, as sitting in front of a blank page while trying to write or grading endless stacks of papers placed a great burden on people's health. Moreover, young students and researchers were grossly underpaid and often under financial duress. As a consequence, they would be more likely to end up in depressing environments that led them to get sick.[75]

Petiot pointed out that the University Sanatorium in Leysin had been designed to address all of these problems, tackling the particular situation of the intellectual and providing concrete answers to his plight. By pronouncing the physical and emotional strains of the people he described, he made them aware of their conditions and inspired their improvement in a mountainous setting. The fact that Petiot praised the University Sanatorium as the epitome of successful physical and societal regeneration emphasized the emotional issues it addressed while providing recourses that others could follow.

A similar dynamic shaped the perception and the experience of the University Sanatorium as a place for international encounter. More than one visitor described how they had witnessed concrete examples of amicable atmosphere and international friendships developing right in front of their eyes. Offering themselves as living proof, they turned the internationalist project into a self-fulfilling

[74] UNESCO Archives, IICI CVII 7, Henry Petiot, *Les sanatoria universitaires* (1930), 1–2.
[75] Petiot, *Les sanatoria universitaires*, 3.

prophecy. In an article published on *Le Journal* of Paris on July 12, 1927, French doctor and writer Georges Duhamel pondered how among those students "saved" at Leysin there might be someday "a Pascal, a Descartes, a Pasteur"; and he was already certain that those educated there, "who came from twenty different countries," had already engaged in exchanges "in a spirit of mutual curiosity and harmony."[76]

Such descriptions informed practice: Swiss professor Marcel du Pasquier (1883–1976) commented on how each guest was introduced to a patient whose language might be different from his or her own, and conversation would easily ensue regardless. At mealtime, "a German student next to a Polish one: they are a pair of friends. The Swiss cantons fraternize; medicine and law share bread and cheese," he noted in one of his writings, pointing out that "these meals in common are symbolic of the breadth of inspiration at once academic and Christian" and defining this the 'genius of the place'" (*génie du lieu*). Declaring the University Sanatorium of Leysin a space for amicable exchange made it one, guiding the norms and behaviors of those who populated it to the point that prescription turned into a reality.

These descriptions built expectations among readers: "Since a smile of gratitude houses the most ineffable of presents, in the end it is you who is in debt," du Pasquier wrote to readers whom he imagined as prospective guests.[77] If expectations alter experience, these writings must have affected how people travelling to Leysin approached these encounters from the outside. The fact that many visitors later published written accounts of their experiences added purpose to their time there, thus shaping what the University Sanatorium felt like for both patients and guests. The first knew they might become literary subjects, while the second looked for evidence to include in their narratives. Moreover, the spiritualism that characterized these descriptions must have influenced how these encounters played out, although it is difficult to know exactly how. Marcel du Pasquier commented how if this kind of interaction were to be all that survived of the League of Nations, it would be worthwhile, since "nothing definitive can be built...outside of love." It is only while looking at the mountains "while listening to the great silence whose secret our agitated lives have lost," that such spiritual understanding of international cooperation could arise.[78] The Alps, with their sights, sounds, and silences thus represented the answer to humanities' many ills.

Along similar lines, another visitor, Swiss professor of literature Giuseppe Zoppi, praised Vauthier's enthusiasm and the beautiful work (*opera bella*) he accomplished. He recounted his encounter with two French students. The first,

[76] League of Nations Archives, Box R 1056, folder 13C/58839/28370. Georges Duhamel, "Le Sanatorium Universitaire de Leysin, Suisse."
[77] Marcel du Pasquier, *Le Sanatorium Universitaire du Dr. Vauthier à Leysin* (Montreux: Journal de Montreux, 1936), 3. One copy is available at the Swiss National Library.
[78] Du Pasquier, *Le Sanatorium Universitaire*, 4–7.

who had surgery the day before, had already returned to his studies; the other helped him. Zoppi noted how in their country of origin "they had never met, while here they are like brothers." But Leysin served as more than a ground for international encounters: "in their discourse, and in their questions and answers, one feels a rare elevation (un'elevazione rara), an angst never quenched for new conquests (un'ansia non placata da nuove conquiste), a sincere interest in the greatest problems of the spirit (massimi problemi dello spirito)." If there is no way to know for sure if these emotions were actually felt, there is plenty of evidence to suggest that feelings were expressed and communicated in vivid terms, and that the alpine "elevation" was imagined to extend to all realms of life. In the background of this article, photographs of interactions between students and professors and scenes of alpine views and promenades seem to convey an intensity that must have resonated with its visitors, and their unsolicited descriptions of these experiences suggest that they experienced an irresistible urge to outpour their feelings.[79]

To be sure, not all visitors left Leysin uplifted. The aforementioned essayist Robert de Traz, for instance, wrote a book entitled Les heures de silence (The Hours of Silence) in which he fully conveyed the sadness and despair he encountered at Leysin. To him, the patients' hilarity seemed artificial. In fact, he interpreted one's laughter as a means "to save the integrity of his secret sadness"; and he quoted another patient saying: "that gaiety you like, make no mistake, it's a parody."[80] Yet, denouncing examples of people failing at feeling the right emotions strengthened the notion that these actually existed. Robert de Traz mentioned how patients showed the flags of their country of origin—if only to express their nostalgia for home—while also finding themselves united across national borders by the common experience of disease. He described them discussing theories for international rapprochement. Most strikingly, he glorified pain as a unifying experience. In lieu of a dedication, his book opened with a quote from Vinet proclaiming that, "Peut-être que souffrir / n'est autre chose que vivre / plus profondément" (Perhaps suffering / is nothing but living / more deeply); and later in the book, he cited a patient who called himself "blessed" because suffering had revealed to him "the truth."[81]

In the end, for Robert de Traz, communal "suffering" united people across borders. The fact his writings were reproduced, disseminated, and even cited in other sanatoria's publications suggest that they piqued the attention of their readers. This is not surprising, as this was a time—the aftermath of the "Great War"— when internationalists often presented hurting as a feeling that all of humanity shared and needed to overcome.[82] As seen in many cases examined in previous

---

[79] Giuseppe Zoppi, Il Sanatorio Universitario di Leysin (1930). One copy of this document is available at the Swiss National Library.

[80] Robert de Traz, Les heures de silence (Paris: Grasset, 1934), 26; 36–7.

[81] De Traz, Les heures de silence, 6; 26; 58; 216.   [82] On this rhetoric, see also Chapter 2.

chapters, and most poignantly in Robert de Traz's words, the emotions of internationalism included pain. Perhaps because of it, they were shared so widely by people whose life had been devastated by the "Great War."

To many contemporaries, Leysin's internationalism eased anxieties about what the future had in store by drawing a connection between physical and political healing. In 1936, world traveller and member of the Société de Géographie René Gouzy (1877–1952) published *Le Sanatorium universitaire de Leysin refuge de la bonne humeur* (The University Sanatorium of Leysin as a Refuge of Good Mood). After going to the University Sanatorium to share his impressions of his latest trip to Polynesia, he spoke of Leysin as a place of "moral health," "gaiety" (*gaîté*), and "joyous animation (*joyeuse animation*)." He described the comforting and "tonic" effect the visit had had on him, further reinforcing the notion that Leysin exuded a positive energy on the world that surrounded it. Gouzy portrayed the University Sanatorium of Leysin as a place that fostered "corporative solidarity" (*solidarité corporative*). He praised the Sanatorium's funding system, which relied on a fee that Swiss students and professors had imposed on themselves to further the prosperity of this international establishment. To him, such an arrangement embodied cooperation (*entr'aide*) at its best, implying that corporative links needed to be strengthened. Although implicit, the message was that liberal models that neglected such links ought to be abandoned, and emotions should be considered indispensable ingredients for any project to succeed.[83] His endorsement must have strengthened the associations among physical, social, and political health.

In a booklet published in Italian in 1933, Jean Borel also reinforced the notion that the emotional connections established at Leysin extended to the political realm.[84] An enthusiastic supporter of the Fascist regime, Borel nonetheless praised the sanatorium for its political values and what they represented. During a visit there, he was struck by the "healthy gaiety" (*gaiezza sana*) of the youth he encountered. He recalled how, as early as 1927, Benito Mussolini had given a "vigorous encouragement" (*possente incoraggiamento*) to Dr. Vauthier when he met him in Rome and granted him a "long interview" at Palazzo Venezia.[85] Borel also rejoiced in learning that many students at the sanatorium were aware of recent changes in the "new Italy" and followed them with great interest. During his visit, he did his best to reinforce positive images of the Fascist regime. "Very modestly, in a little familiar chat illustrated with projections, I paid my tribute of admiration to the work of the Duce," he recounted. He also spoke about the recent

---

[83] René Gouzy, *Le Sanatorium universitaire de Leysin refuge de la bonne humeur* (1936). One copy is available at the Swiss National Library.
[84] Jean Borel, *Il sanatorio universitario internazionale di Leysin e l'Italia* (Rome, 1933). One copy is available at the Swiss National Library.
[85] Tuberculosis represented a central concern for the fascist government. See Silvano Franco, *Legislazione e politica sanitaria del fascismo* (Rome: APES, 2001), 106.

archeological discoveries in the Roman city of Ercolano and the land reclamations of the Pontine Marshes that had led to the founding of the city of Littoria. He then effectively connected the Sanatorium's healing mission with the story of Mussolini (who had once worked as "a mason not far from Leysin") and what he saw as an unprecedented recovery of the Italian land and country. If the students already knew about "the corporative system that Fascist Italy had put forth to the world," they also lived it in their community.[86]

Borel's account emphasized that nationalist and internationalist notions of health were not at odds with one another. It also demonstrated that many people thought that public health could be achieved only through a corporative model; thus, for them, supporting an establishment such as the University Sanatorium in Leysin served as an endorsement of those who encouraged corporative approaches (the Fascist regime in Italy, for example). Far from weakening the sanatorium's internationalist message, his endorsement confirmed its versatility and inclusiveness, arguably eliciting the emotions that it implied. To many, his words might have sounded reassuring, as they presented Fascism not as a threat to peace but as a key ally to maintaining it.

The patients themselves played an active role in producing materials that would breed internationalist feelings. In 1930 a group of students crafted *Éphémère,* a collection of short stories and poems published to raise money for a new T.S.F. electrophone, a machine that could distract and bring "voices and songs" from the plains to those confined to their bed up in the mountains. The preface, written on two adjacent pages in both French and German, immediately com-municated how in Leysin both linguistic groups coexisted peacefully. The many languages in which the works were written (French, German, English, and Italian) underscored the international (and internationalist) character of the place. And the wide spectrum of feelings expressed in each piece—ranging from sadness, to happiness, to humor, to despair—effectively conveyed the importance of shared emotions at Leysin. A line from one of Goethe's poems, *Der Bräutigam* ("The Bridegroom"), placed in lieu of a formal dedication, portrayed the complex mixture of feelings that permeated life at the Sanatorium. On a blank page, printed on two lines, the German words: *"wie es auch sei / das leben— ist gut"* (literally, "whatever may be / life—it is good") evoked the longing and hope expressed in this famous poem, one that was often conjured by the internation-alist movement as a whole. If literary references affect the mood of a place and the emotions that permeate it, then these writings did much to shape the University Sanatorium's feel.[87]

---

[86] Borel, *Il sanatorio universitario internazionale di Leysin e l'Italia,* 5–8.
[87] *Éphémère: cahier des étudiants du sanatorium universitaire suisse, Leysin,* avec des bois originaux dessinés par E. Andreazzi et gravés par R. Guiart (Berne: Büchler & Cie, 1930). A copy is available at the Swiss National Library.

In 1932 the students of the University Sanatorium produced another volume, *Variétés*, a notebook featuring their own literary and artistic production, one which must have engendered the emotions of internationalism. Compared to *Éphémère*, which had been published by a commercial press, *Variétés* represented a more artisanal endeavor. The patients themselves printed 110 copies by hand and sold them to raise money to sponsor the Sanatorium's future cultural activities. The booklet contained a large number of prints, as well as a poem, a short story, and a play, whose handcrafted quality gave authenticity to their internationalist message and emotions. While a note at the beginning attributed all works to a "group of students," the author of each was not specified to stress the communal character of the place.[88]

Another material object that at once expressed and generated the emotions of internationalism was the *Livre d'or*, a set of three large, leather-bound, metal-sealed "Golden Books" in which visitors and patients outpoured their feelings at the end of their stay. Many of their comments captured shared experiences: some people conveyed their memories through art, others through musical notes, others still through words artfully written in countless languages and alphabets. Many outlined the mountains' profile or reminisced about the fondue meals they enjoyed during their stay in the mountains. The sheer creativity and the amount of time each person devoted to crafting their last message reveals the great emotional experience this object drew out. As the last act to be formally required, this written expression of feelings drove authors to confront their emotions and also forced readers to come to terms with other people's. The overall message was that the University Sanatorium of Leysin represented internationalism in its most authentic and tangible expression, as people voiced how they felt as members of a larger world community. Their expression reified internationalism, turning ideas of an international emotional community into a reality.[89] With time, the emotions that accompanied their international experience at Leysin proved to be their most enduring legacy.

5.5 A New International University Sanatorium

The history of the project for a new International University Sanatorium best conveys how emotions, which were central to internationalism in the 1920s and 1930s, gained further value and came to constitute one of the main justifications for internationalist ideas and practices after 1945. The proposed New International

---

[88] *Variétés: cahier rédigé par un groupe d'étudiants du sanatorium universitaire* (Leysin, 1932). A copy is available at the Bibliothèque cantonale et universitaire BCU in Lausanne, site Unithèque.
[89] Archives Cantonales Vaudoises PP 911/18–20, *Livre d'or* (3 vols).

Fig. 5.6 Postcard of Leysin, undated. Marked in pencil are the sites of the existing University Sanatorium (SU) and the proposed International University Sanatorium (SUI). League of Nations Archives, R 2335, loose postcard. ©Editions Perrochet/ Archives de la construction moderne—EPFL.

Sanatorium, to be built near the old one, would not have been limited to students already enrolled in Swiss universities (Figure 5.6). It would have operated under the auspices of international organizations (namely, the League of Nations), and it would have been administered by a number of international groups, fully implementing Vauthier's original vision of a body dedicated to both physical and political healing. Even though this particular project did not turn into reality, for decades it received significant endorsements by a wide variety of state and non-state actors and thus well illustrates the argument and the assumptions that guided their decisions.

The idea for an enlarged international institution in the Alps to foster the emotions of internationalism continued to be debated for decades, from the 1920s to the 1960s and beyond. As early as 1926, Dr. Vauthier met with representatives of the newly opened International Institute of Intellectual Cooperation in Paris several times to secure the Institute's support for their initiative.[90] In the meantime, a group of patients wrote a formal letter to the Assembly of Representatives of the Associations internationales d'étudiants in support of the project. Talking

---

[90] UNESCO Archives, FR PUNES AG 1-IICI-C-VII-7, "Note pour M. Le Directeur" dated 22 novembre 1926 by F. Micheli (later marked Ca.I.22).

directly to the League of Nations and referring to the proposed plan as the "germ of a great work inspired by the high ideal of intellectual cooperation in the name of which you have gathered," they asked for the International University Sanatorium to be pursued "for the health of our comrades, the young intellectuals of tomorrow."[91] They then proceeded to sign their names, each followed by their own nationality. Acting as representatives of their country of origin, they presented themselves as a visible proof of the emotions of internationalism at work in a concrete setting and as an authoritative voice committed to fostering its expansion.

In April 1927, the Committee of the Representatives of International Student Organizations (*Comité des représentants des organisations internationales d'étudiants*) decided to recommence work on the project and, on July 21, 1927, they organized a meeting with the International Committee on Intellectual Cooperation (ICIC) of the League of Nations to ask for support.[92] A committee was formed, presided over by Swiss historian Gonzague de Reynold who represented the ICIC. The other members included Jan Balinski-Jundzill for the International Confederation of Students (*Confédération internationale des étudiants*) and the International University Federation for the League of Nations; Walter Kotschnig of the International Student Service (*Entr'aide universitaire*); renowned pathologist Leonore Gourfein-Welt of the International Federation of University Women (*Fédération Internationale des Femmes Diplômées des Universités*); Francis Pickens Miller of the World Student Christian Federation (*Fédération universelle des associations chrétiennes d'étudiants*); and Léon Steinig of the World Union of Jewish Students (*Union universelle des étudiants juifs*). Invited to attend the first meeting were also Dr. Vauthier of the University Sanatorium of Leysin; architect George Epitaux, who had just completed a new building for the International Labor Office (BIT) in Geneva;[93] G.A. Johnston of the International Labor Office, and the secretary of the Committee of Representatives, Hallsten Kallia.[94] In addition, Pax Romana, an international federation of Catholic students, though absent at the first meeting, asked to be represented by Gonzague de Reynold.[95] All of the associations present at this meeting expressed enthusiastic

[91] The letter was signed by Ernst Michaelis (Germany), Douglas Chandler (England), M. Stoiloff (Bulgaria), Jean Bresch, R. Guiart, and Jacques Momméja (France), Professor T. Iguchi (Japan), Sruoga (Lithuania), Ed. Lichtenstern (Czechoslovakia), and S. Emin (Turkey). Frank Abauzit, *Projet d'un sanatorium universitaire international à Leysin* (Lausanne: La Concorde, 1928), 53–4.

[92] Archives Cantonales Vaudoises PP 911/197, fifth annual report of the Director and Chief Doctor, year 1927, 3.

[93] This building, known as the Centre William Rappard, was later incorporated by the World Trade Organization. An online exhibit of its history is available in "The WTO building: Centre William Rappard" https://www.wto.org/english/thewto_e/cwr_e/cwr_e.htm (accessed on March 30, 2016).

[94] UNESCO Archives, FR PUNES AG 1-IICI-C-VII-7, Comité des représentants des organisations internationales d'étudiants, sous les auspices du CICI, session extraordinaire tenue à Genève le 21 juillet 1927, Rapport du Comité.

[95] As such it was listed in the letterhead of the committee; see UNESCO Archives, FR PUNES AG 1-IICI-C-VII-7, Letter dated February 2, 1929, from Louis C. Vauthier to F. Micheli (IICI).

support for a structure that would foster the emotional and internationalist goals they all shared.[96]

Emotions and aesthetics represented the core of these groups' concerns and their value was so widely recognized that it was not even the subject of discussion. At this meeting, Vauthier proposed a structure for 200 beds at an estimated cost between 2.750.000 and 3.000.000 Swiss francs (20.000 Swiss francs per bed). George Epitaux's design was dominated by horizontal lines to balance the mountains' verticality, resulting in a building that blended in with the Alps in a harmonious fashion.[97] Every detail had been taken into account to maximize the view and to welcome sunlight.

As in the designs for the Palais des Nations in Geneva, the shape and the size of the nearby mountains was emphasized to convey the centrality of their presence.[98] Rooms all of the same size would eliminate class differences and jealousies. Carefully-designed common spaces would foster sociability and shared recreation. As the architect explained, special care had been put into ensuring that the veranda, where the patients would have spent most of their time, would be "intimate" (*intime*) in order to create bonds among them.[99] This project and the discussion that ensued left no doubt that all agreed on the significance of aesthetics and of the emotions of those who would inhabit this space once completed.

Despite the projected high cost, there was no proposal to change the aesthetic features of the design. Instead, the committee debated the option of building a structure half the size and emphasized the imperative of keeping the price as low as possible by reducing the number of beds (without touching plans for large and shared common areas). A questionnaire by the International Student Service had

[96] On the relevance of these student organizations, especially since they involved many future leaders, see Daniel Laqua, "Activism in the 'Students' League of Nations': International Student Politics and the Confédération Internationale des Étudiants, 1919–1939," *The English Historical Review* 132, no. 556 (June 2017), 605–37.

[97] On the conflicting tendencies (return to nature vs. modernism) in sanatoria's architectural designs see Sarah Schrank and Didem Ekici, eds., *Healing Spaces, Modern Architecture, and the Body* (New York: Taylor and Francis, 2016).

[98] UNESCO Archives, FR PUNES AG 1-IICI-C-VII-7, Le Sanatorium Universitaire International, Leysin, Suisse, undated, 13 (pages are not numbered in the original). Dave Lüthi also noticed similarities between Epitaux's project and the Palais des Nations in Geneva in terms of their use of "monumental classicism." Dave Lüthi, *Le compas & le bistouri: architectures de la médecine et du tourisme curatif. L'exemple vaudois (1760–1940)* (Lausanne: BHMS, 2012), 464.

[99] UNESCO Archives, FR PUNES AG 1-IICI-C-VII-7, Avant-projet du Dr. Vauthier (undated), Annexe de l'architecte G. Epitaux, 3. See also League of Nations Archives, R 2235, 5 B/8409/4533, Avant-projet du Sanatorium Universitaire International à Leysin dressé par l'Architecte Epitaux, de Lausanne. In contrast, older sanatoria had individual balconies to ensure the patients' privacy. See Lüthi, *Le compas & le bistouri*, 348. The change was also justified by a shift in medical standards, as enclosed balconies came to be criticized for not allowing the air to circulate and open veranda were therefore preferred. Margaret Campbell, "What Tuberculosis Did for Modernism: The Influence of a Curative Environment on Modernist Design and Architecture," *Medical History* 49, no. 1 (October 2005), 476–8. On Leysin's architectural styles, and specifically on the distribution of utilitarian, Belle Époque and alpine, see Andrew W. Gilg, "Settlement Design in the Alps: The Case of Leysin," *Landscape Research* 8, no. 1 (June 1983), 2–12.

shown that members were interested in the idea, with Norway, Sweden, Great Britain, Poland, Belgium, and Japan in favor of the project and Denmark only standing in opposition.[100] Also, at a Course of Study on Methods of Self-Help held in Dresden, representatives from twenty nations had expressed unanimous approval of the project. Clearly, Dr. Vauthier's aesthetic and emotional approach received wide support.

The organizational aspects of this project were also presented as a crucial component of Dr. Vauthier's internationalist plan. After establishing a preparatory committee with Dr. Vauthier as its General Secretary, each organization committed to sponsor this committee's activities with an initial small—yet highly symbolic—contribution of 2.000 Swiss francs. As emphasized in the conclusion of the committee's report, each member rejoiced at the fact that for "the first time in history" international students organizations had all united "for a common enterprise, abandoning all misunderstandings and prejudices." Together, they were now hoping for "the full success of the initiative."[101] In their rhetoric, the simple act of discussing this plan had already created an emotional bond. The implication was that this was only the first of many more in the new, enlarged International Sanatorium of Leysin they had committed to found.

In principle, Dr. Vauthier's emotional and aesthetic approach to international cooperation was supported also by the International Committee on Intellectual Cooperation of the League of Nations, which discussed the matter at its tenth session held in Geneva on July 25–30, 1928. Renowned internationalist Alfred Zimmern (1879–1957), who represented the International Institute of Intellectual Cooperation in Paris, endorsed the plan enthusiastically while expressing the hope that this would be "only one of a series."[102] His enthusiasm, however, was not matched by all. Dr. Ludwik Rajchman (1881–1965), who was at the head of the Health Organization of the League of Nations, declined to participate in the meeting and did not support the project. No document survived to explain the reasons for his position, although archival evidence shows that when similar proposals had been put forth in the past he had opposed them as well. For instance, in 1926, American Dr. Conrad Hoffmann (1884–1958) of the International Student Service had proposed an International Tuberculosis Sanatorium for students to be established in Arosa, also in the Alps.[103] The Health Office rejected the idea on the grounds that teaching in various languages would have proven too

---

[100] UNESCO Archives, FR PUNES AG 1-IICI-C-VII-7, Comité des représentants des organisations internationales d'étudiants, sous les auspices du CICI, session extraordinaire tenue à Genève le 21 juillet 1927, Rapport du Comité, 5.

[101] UNESCO Archives, FR PUNES AG 1-IICI-C-VII-7, Comité des représentants des organisations internationales d'étudiants, sous les auspices du CICI, session extraordinaire tenue à Genève le 21 juillet 1927, Rapport du Comité, 7–8.

[102] See League of Nations Archives, C.533.M.160.1928.XII (Publications of the League of Nations 1928.XII.A.7), 92.

[103] See correspondence in League of Nations Archives, R 883, 12B/55384/28795.

complicated and offering classes in all majors too expensive.[104] Rajchman himself often postponed or neglected to reply to invitations and requests related to the project.[105] In the case of the International Sanatorium in Leysin, however, the Committee of International Cooperation proceeded without the Health Organization's endorsement. The committee of International Cooperation passed a resolution to approve the project, and, from then on, the League of Nations' endorsement was widely publicized in the Sanatorium's literature.[106]

In 1928, in Chartres, a formal "Acte de Fondation" was signed for an international institution that—according to article 2—would provide medical treatments and opportunities for pursuing intellectual work "in an atmosphere of international collaboration." Sponsored by the founding student organizations together with a number of governments and educational institutions, the International University Sanatorium would also receive regular subventions by students and faculty. Seats on the administrative bodies would be allotted to each state in proportion to the funding provided (one representative for sponsoring two beds; two for five, and three for funding the equivalent of ten beds). Any other "physical or moral person" sponsoring at least two beds could also sit on the Board, together with representatives from all founding organizations.[107] National representation was not the only criteria for allocating seats and power. Instead, financial contributions dictated the weight that each group would have in the institution as a whole.

National governments would also play a major role in backing Dr. Vauthier's plan. As announced at a meeting held in 1928 at the International Institute of Intellectual Cooperation in Paris, Mussolini was in favor, the Hungarian government and universities were particularly keen to the idea, "and in Germany interest was no less great." In fact, the head of the German legation in Bern, Adolf Müller, had already given Dr. Vauthier 5.000 Swiss francs to support secretarial and printing costs, and Dr. Schairer had assured him that the major German association for student financial assistance (the *Wirtschaftshilfe der Deutschen Studentenschaft*) would take forty beds. In France, "Poincaré and Briand had promised him the collaboration of the French government." Moreover, fundraisers had been organized in Belgium, and a committee had already formed in Great Britain. The members of the committee of action now included not only members of League's International Committee on Intellectual Cooperation but also Dr. Ludwik Rajchman of the Health Organization. Finally, Stephen Duggan represented the Institute of International Education in New York, confirming that

---

[104] See League of Nations Archives, R 883, 12B/55384/28795, note dated November 11, 1926, by Dr. Yves Biraud of the Health Office.
[105] See correspondence in League of Nations Archive, R 1056, 13C/58839/28370 and R 2335, 5B/8409/4533.
[106] See for instance Abauzit, *Projet d'un sanatorium universitaire international à Leysin*, 55–8.
[107] UNESCO Archives, FR PUNES AG 1-IICI-C-VII-7, "Acte de Fondation."

additional support for the International University Sanatorium could come from countries that were not members of the League of Nations.

Such extensive support was due to the tireless work of the Secretary General of the International Student Service, who had travelled far and wide to advertise the initiative in Germany, England, Austria, Bulgaria, the Netherlands, Hungary, Greece, Czechoslovakia, Turkey, and Yugoslavia. Delegates had taken it upon themselves to spread the word too. Encouraged by these successes, the Committee now aimed to raise 5.000.000 Swiss francs to turn the project into a reality.[108] Such endorsements and investments reveal that all agreed on the potential of an international institution aimed at engendering emotions in people from various nations.

Because of the economic downturn and the international tensions that ensued in the 1930s, the optimism and enthusiasm expressed at this meeting soon dampened: as Vauthier noted in 1938, little progress had been made in the previous ten years. Yet, the correspondence between Vauthier, the International Student Service, and the International Committee on Intellectual Cooperation never ceased. The doctor continued to believe that "in spite of all obstacles, the [same] enthusiasm that created the University Sanatorium will create someday an International University Sanatorium for the honor of Switzerland and to serve in its spirit, even if in small measure, international cooperation."[109]

On November 17, 1938, a radio address by Claude Aveline and Dr. Louis Vauthier was broadcast on Swiss radio, presenting the project as alive and well.[110] Aveline emphasized that the Swiss government had agreed to sponsor this initiative, at least in part. He reiterated the points he had made in his past publications about the particular condition of intellectuals facing disease. He then described the life and successes of the University Sanatorium at Leysin, a place where "youth from different lands (*patries*) and races gathered under one roof, united by the threefold bonds (*liens*) of disease, intellectual preoccupations, and an attentive affection (*affection attentive*) that considers them children of the same family. The human family!" By framing the physical and emotional aspects of their experience at Leysin in universalistic terms, he remarked that the patients' laments of suffering sound the same in every language, just as "all tears are salty."[111]

---

[108] UNESCO Archives, FR PUNES AG 1-IICI-C-VII-7, Comité d'initiative en faveur d'un Sanatorium Universitaire International. Procès–verbal de la séance du 4 décembre 1928, tenue à Paris à l'Institut International de Coopération Intellectuelle.

[109] Archives Cantonales Vaudoises PP 911/197, sixteenth annual report of the Director and Chief Doctor, year 1938, 4.

[110] "Le Sanatorium Universitaire Suisse et le Sanatorium Universitaire International de Leysin par Claude Aveline et le Dr. Louis Vauthier," in Claude Aveline, *Le sanatorium universitaire suisse et le sanatorium universitaire international de Leysin: causeries radiophoniques* (Leysin: Impr. nouvelle, 1938). One copy is held at the Swiss National Library.

[111] "Le Sanatorium Universitaire Suisse et le Sanatorium Universitaire International de Leysin," 7–15.

Aveline then continued by talking about the "legend" of the International University Sanatorium and by recounting its long and tormented history. After substantial endorsements had been obtained, the economic crisis had prevented the project from coming to fruition. But inspired by the youth that surrounded him, Dr. Vauthier had remained persistent in his work. The French writer now called on all listeners to envision the many "masters" that some day would come out of Leysin healed in body and mind, exclaiming: "Together and everywhere at the same time, they will work for peace in the world!"[112] At a time when international tensions were raising, Aveline employed familialism as a tool to convince his listeners to support Dr. Vauthier's plan. More than rational arguments about the imperative of healing disease, he thought that emotions could move various audiences to support this new internationalist project.

In his address, Dr. Vauthier also used emotions to elicit support for his initiative. "Asked to be very personal," he accepted to share his most intimate thoughts in the hope of achieving an even "deeper communion" with his audience. He spoke of the love he received throughout his life, and of how it was "with gladness" (*allegresse*) that he was now returning some of the riches had come to him "from all sides." He then spoke of the University Sanatorium as his "big family" (*grande famille*), and of how he "suffered" with his patients as they endured physical pains as well as financial duress. He then explained how he trusted that his listeners, after hearing what he had just confided to them, would surely understand why he did everything he could to ensure that the new International University Sanatorium would not be open only to those "favored by wealth." He continued by referring to his two projects (the University Sanatorium and its International counterpart), as his "two children." He likened them to the left and the right side of the heart, as inseparable.

After a long sequence of physical and emotional images, Vauthier then articulated why it was imperative that the project continue despite ongoing international tensions. He insisted that "it has to happen *now* [italics in the original] precisely because the times are bad [*mauvais*], to remember what there should be, to greet (*saluer*) what will return and to prepare it." He then added one more string of metaphors: "It is during the night that one needs to believe in the light, that one has to manifest light." He saw the Swiss government's support for a major internationalist endeavor such as the International University Sanatorium as a true "spiritual offensive" by all "realists for a better world." Rich or poor, future sponsors or mere sympathizers, all could "save the wounded of the University, save science, promote rapprochement among nations, put more beauty and fraternity among men."[113] In this case, too, Vauthier's use of metaphors associated with emotions suggests that he believed such arguments would be effective.

---

[112] "Le Sanatorium Universitaire Suisse et le Sanatorium Universitaire International de Leysin," 17.
[113] "Le Sanatorium Universitaire Suisse et le Sanatorium Universitaire International de Leysin," 21–6.

Vauthier was right. His arguments did not go unheard, and many continued to share his contention that engendering the emotions of internationalism was not only possible but also necessary. In 1941, a small room at the University Sanatorium was placed at the disposal of the new International University Sanatorium as the site for its Secretariat.[114] If the war slowed down further planning, it also reaffirmed the need for it. Between February 1945 and September 1947, the University Sanatorium of Leysin hosted a Centre d'Accueil Provisoire (Temporary Welcoming Center) which housed 345 students and professors from various nationalities. After major restructuring and modifications, in 1952 the Swiss government established a new foundation and in 1953 adopted and refinanced the project.[115] International student organizations were no longer part of the initiative, as representatives of Swiss governmental or financial institutions would sit on the Board together with Dr. Louis Vauthier. Even if rooted in only one country, the project would remain international in scope and keep emotions at its center.

As time went on, the importance of the aesthetic and emotional aspects of Dr. Vauthier's plan increased. In 1955, at the III International Conference of University Sanatoria held in the Dutch city of Laren, Vauthier presented his most passionate set of remarks.[116] In what he called his "spiritual testament," he summarized what he saw as the principles that guided his entire life and work. Beginning with a "confession," he quoted Montaigne's famous saying that "a strong imagination creates the event" and vividly described how he had experienced such wisdom in his own life. "What passionate experiences one has when launched completely in such an adventure!" he exclaimed, while also pointing out that the "human and spiritual enrichment" that derived from them had been well worth any failure that may have accompanied such endeavors. He also emphasized that he had been able to achieve some of his goals. He had succeeded in impressing a "solidaristic" (*solidariste*) character to the University Sanatorium that he had directed for more than three decades. More than 3000 writers and artists had visited and performed at his establishment. And after he had inaugurated the first University Sanatorium in Leysin in 1922, many more institutions of the same kind had opened in other countries: first in Zakopane, Poland (1926) and in Saint-Hilaire-du-Touvet, in France (1933); and then Greece followed in 1936, Denmark in 1943, Spain in 1946, Belgium in 1947, Czechoslovakia in 1949, the Netherlands, India, the United Kingdom, Italy, Japan, and China in 1952; and of others in Bulgaria,

---

[114] Archives Cantonales Vaudoises PP 911/197, nineteenth annual report of the Director and Chief Doctor, year 1941, 7.

[115] Swiss Federal Archives, E3001B#1984/23#14*, Fondation du Sanatorium universitaire international, Leysin, 1952–1961. On position of the Conseil Fédéral, see Vancampenhout, *La tuberculose et le sanatorium universitaire de Leysin*, 158–60.

[116] Swiss Federal Archives, E4001D#1973/125#1659 Vauthier, Dr., 1952–60.

Norway, Sweden, and the USSR he knew the existence but not the details.[117] In his view, seen as a whole, such institutions constituted a "moving ensemble" (*en émouvant ensemble*) whose worth was self-evident. He thus saw his lifelong dream of opening an International University Sanatorium in Leysin, now scheduled to become a reality, as the culmination of these efforts.[118] Dr. Vauthier did not spend any time trying to convince his audience that triggering the right emotions represented a viable and a worthwhile endeavor. The fact that he took for granted that everybody agreed on this notion suggests that this was widespread in this period.

Vauthier probably knew that his biggest challenge would not come from individual governments or from people skeptical of the importance of emotions but from fundamental changes in the way tuberculosis was treated. After streptomycin was first isolated in 1943, antibiotic therapies had gradually begun to replace lengthy stays at sanatoria such as the one he directed and the one he was proposing. To be sure, other scientific advancements had to take place for antibiotic treatments to become lasting and effective. Yet, by the mid-1950s the writing was on the wall and sanatoria had started to be seen as a fading reality in medical practice. For this reason, Vauthier made it a point to frame his vision for the new International University Sanatorium in terms that went well beyond its medical usefulness. He envisioned a place for a holistic approach to the many ills that were plaguing the people of his time. Since disease was as much psychological as it was physical, the new center would have offered "noo-therapy" (a term derived from *nous*, "mind" in Greek, to refer to a treatment consisting of intellectual activities that would nurture the mind), "hilarotherapy," a cure through happiness, as well as "spiritual healing" (*guerison spirituelle*). As the grand finale of his address, Dr. Vauthier read several pages of quotes left on the *Livre d'or* by former visitors and patients. He trusted the voice of what he referred to as the "*anciens*," the "ancient" patients, to best convey the magnitude of his project.[119]

Many thought that he had made a substantial contribution toward world peace and that his efforts deserved recognition exactly because they had made people feel the benefit of international cooperation. Most notably, Vauthier was nominated for the Nobel Peace Prize several years in a row in the early 1950s.[120] Swiss representative Albert Malche, who nominated him twice, first in 1951 and then in 1953, argued that this prestigious award would "open to Dr. Vauthier the doors he would have to knock to find the capital he needs" and allow him to coronate his

---

[117] For a list of other university sanatoria which were inspired by the University Sanatorium in Leysin, see Vancampenhout, *La tuberculose et le sanatorium universitaire de Leysin*, 189.

[118] Swiss Federal Archives, E4001D#1973/125#1659 Vauthier, Dr., 1952–60.

[119] Swiss Federal Archives, E4001D#1973/125#1659 Vauthier, Dr., 1952–60.

[120] The Nobel Prize, *Nomination Database*, http://www.nobelprize.org/nomination/archive/show_people.php?id=9571 (accessed on April 2, 2016).

life-long dream of an International University Sanatorium in Leysin.[121] In the words of Queen Elizabeth of Belgium, Vauthier had created "one of the most beautiful humanitarian works there is" and therefore needed to be celebrated and helped in every way possible.[122]

The Nobel Prize Committee, however, never awarded Vauthier its highest recognition. The alternative choices they made illuminate how the world was changing in this period, and how Vauthier's life and work more and more seemed a thing of the past. In 1950, the Peace Prize went to Ralph Bunche, Peace Negotiator in the Middle East and the first Black person to receive this honor. In 1951, French trade union leader Léon Jouhaux won for his efforts toward social equality. In 1952, medical doctor Albert Schweitzer was recognized not only for his work in Gabon but also for being a powerful voice against nuclear testing. George C. Marshall won in 1953 for his plan of economic recovery in Western Europe; and in 1954 the Office of the United Nations High Commissioner for Refugees became the first UN agency to receive Nobel's prestigious recognition. The image of a Sanatorium in Switzerland, albeit international, no longer reflected the scope of a broader world that was becoming increasingly interconnected.

The value of emotions, however, remained undisputed. The long-lasting quality of Dr. Vauthier's ideas became evident in 1956, when the Swiss Government decided to liquidate the project for a new International University Sanatorium. They believed that antibiotics had made this kind of establishments obsolete. In a letter dated July 6, 1956, Vauthier explained to all supporters that such liquidation had been necessary to allow his vision to be adapted to changing needs and realities. He now had in mind a facility where a wider range of diseases could be treated while nurturing the higher spiritual and moral values on which his lifetime work had been founded. In April 1957, he wrote a letter to the Swiss Department of Interior with a revised proposal for what was now called a "Centre Universitaire et Mondial de la Santé" (University and World Center of Health) to be established in Leysin.[123] This too, however, would not materialize. A few years later, Vauthier died with his project for a new internationalist institution left unfinished.

*   *   *

The fact that Vauthier's vision did not come fully to fruition should not overshadow the reality that the assumptions on which his institution was built continued to influence university life well after his death. When the University Sanatorium

[121] Albert Malche, *Rapport de M. Albert Malche... destiné à présenter la candidature du Dr Louis-Constant Vauthier au prix Nobel de la paix* (Geneva: 1950), 13. A copy is preserved at the Swiss National Library.

[122] Malche, *Rapport de M. Albert Malche*, 3.

[123] Swiss Federal Archives, E3001B#1984/23#14*, Fondation du Sanatorium universitaire international, Leysin, 1952–61.

closed in 1961, a proposal was discussed to turn it into an international intellectual and sport center to encourage international friendships.[124] In 1974, in an account of his life in Leysin in the 1920s, doctor Jean Houriet lamented that modern medicine, with all of its machines, had grown distant from the patients.[125] Along similar lines, in his 2001 autobiography Bertrand Hourcade described Leysin, where he had lived and taught from 1980 to 1996, as a "magic village" of unspoken tolerance and open internationalism.[126] A "cosmopolitan" atmosphere remains an essential selling point for all universities who aspire to be international in scope. The model of internationalism inaugurated by Vauthier is now mainstream. It certainly shaped the international educational experience of the author of this book, and arguably many of its readers'. As for the broader implications of recognizing these continuities, these will be explored in the Conclusion.

---

[124] Vancampenhout, *La tuberculose et le sanatorium universitaire de Leysin*, 178–83.
[125] Houriet, *Années perdues, années retrouvées*, 72.
[126] Bertrand Hourcade, *Le village magique: souvenirs de Leysin* (Pully: Ed. Les Iles Futures, 2001).

Conclusion

This book's journey through the history of a broad range of political, leisure, educational, and medical institutions in the Alps shows that emotions constituted an essential ingredient in the development of internationalist ideas and practices in the interwar period. After the First World War—a traumatic event that con- temporaries blamed on mismanaged passions—internationalists constructed the Alps—a recent battleground and the markers of national borders—as ideal sites for instilling amicable feelings among nations. The staging of large-scale inter- national events such as the 1924 Winter Olympics strengthened the image of mountains as a natural backdrop for peaceful encounters. The commercialization of "typical" convivial products such as cheese fondue and the "cup of friendship" further reinforced this association. At the same time, in an age of increasing industrialization, the Alps attracted both public and private entities interested in large infrastructure projects (including roads, electrical plants, railway lines, and tunnels like the one celebrated in *Excelsior*), which they often presented as steps towards lasting friendship among peoples. In turn, the movements for environ- mental protection that opposed these initiatives presented the objective of saving nature in internationalist, emotionalized terms. In virtually every field, feelings emerged as a central feature. As such, I argue, they should be incorporated in international history.

Strikingly, people from a wide range of social and political positions contrib- uted to the process of associating mountains with both internationalism and emotions. Along with the *haute bourgeoisie* that had been visiting the Alps in large numbers since the nineteenth century, proletarian associations organized mountain stays for workers to engender "solidarity" among them; Catholics— encouraged by the "Alpinist Pope" Achille Ratti—chose the Alps as sites for youth education and spiritual elevation; and fascist groups picked them as spaces to organize leisure and improve the "health" of the nation. Separated by politics but unified by practice, a wide range of individuals, organizations, and governments fostered the notion that mountains represented the ideal place to create emotional bonds.

Mountain people—both those who inhabited the Alps and, by appropriation, those who visited them—became romanticized as both sick and healthy, frugal and generous, primitive yet best equipped to thrive in the modern world. Mountains therefore turned into a symbol of contemporary tensions between modernity and anti-modernity, nationalism and internationalism; and contemporary political

The Emotions of Internationalism: Feeling International Cooperation in the Alps in the Interwar Period. Ilaria Scaglia, Oxford University Press (2020). © Ilaria Scaglia.
DOI: 10.1093/oso/9780198848325.001.0001

actors used them to further their own agendas and to make the case that they could be entrusted with addressing the challenges and contradictions of the post-1919 world.

Most significantly, the League of Nations used mountains and the emotions associated with them to promote itself and its own work. The speeches delivered at the Paris Peace Conference in 1919 and at the opening of the League's first Assembly in 1920 described nations as capable of feeling—like humans do—and stressed the importance of instilling emotions such as friendship to ensure lasting peace. In concrete settings, the technical branches of the League of Nations, together with the International Institute of Intellectual Cooperation in Paris, promoted a broad range of initiatives—from international travel, to school exchanges, to summer camps and vacation colonies on the mountains—whose goal was to inspire amicable feelings among the youth. Following its lead, a large number of student, women, and religious organizations advanced a model of international cooperation which monitored all aspects of the participants' experiences—from preparations, to logistical arrangements, to the ways in which single moments would be chronicled and remembered—to prevent resentments and to generate amicable feelings.

Concerns about emotions also drove the League's choices in matters of publicity and in the overall process of managing its own reputation. Virtually all decisions, from branding strategies to the building of the League's headquarters in Geneva to the relationship with the press, took into account what people might feel. A carefully crafted emotional style—emphasizing dignity, nobility, and friendship conveyed through alpine imagery—emerged as a result. As international tensions increased in the 1930s, this same style frustrated League supporters while emboldening its opponents and contributed to defining the League's image as benevolent but weak for decades to follow.

Even in the imaginary space around the League, where countless international organizations inspired by its work operated, emotions and reputation became inextricably linked. As illustrated by the case of the Union Internationale des Associations d'Alpinisme (UIAA, or International Mountaineering and Climbing Federation), emotions played an essential role in shaping the "moral economy" of internationalism, or the dynamics through which internationalists used feelings to attribute moral values to specific beliefs and behaviors. Groups such as the UIAA, which associated their work with the League's internationalist mission while remaining independent from it, charged their activities in the realm of alpinism with political meaning. They engaged in international functional cooperation in various fields—from map standardization, to environmentalism, to art—arguing that their work fostered peace. Individuals involved in such organizations (like the UIAA President Egmond d'Arcis, for example) authored books popularizing the notion that mountains triggered emotions capable of transcending class and national differences. They appropriated features stereotypically associated with "mountain people" (like frugality and authenticity) and presented them as desirable characters for promoting peaceful relations among nations. They used emotions to mitigate failures (for instance, by blaming them on "personal feelings") and they evoked "alpine friendship" to justify their relations with fascist individuals before and after the Second World War. They also designed their international congresses as shared aesthetic and emotional experiences meant to elicit emotional bonds among participants, inaugurating a set of practices many other groups would follow.

Technological innovations accelerated the emotionalization of international life. With the quicker and cheaper dissemination of photography and film, images became a preferred means to capture and immortalize emotional expressions and to prove what people actually felt. As demonstrated by the case of the international sanatoria located in the Swiss village of Leysin, carefully staged pictures attested to medical and political successes in making people feel desirable emotions. A broad range of medical experts and patients, who at a time of expanding social programs also included soldiers, children, and workers from all walks of life, served at once as subjects and producers of these images; and they actively contributed to the shaping of a form of internationalist practice in which aesthetics (what international cooperation looked and felt like) counted as much as (if not more than) its substance.

Along similar lines, "atmospheres" and "experiences" came to constitute one of the central and longest-lasting features of international cooperation. As the case of the international University Sanatorium illustrates, aesthetic and material aspects (from building "homey" facilities to organizing alpine excursions and meals) came to dominate many forms of physical, emotional, and political healing. Multiple actors influenced these developments, including governments, universities, businesses, and networks of experts from all fields, along with individual doctors, nurses, students, faculty, visitors, and their families. An even wider public learned about them in the media and in the many cultural productions of this time.

The assumptions about the value of such "atmospheres" and "experiences" outlived sanatoria and the people who shaped them. As evidenced by the project for a new International University Sanatorium, which was never completed but nonetheless continued to be supported for decades, what people might feel came to dictate decisions in all fields, from the architectural design of medical and educational institutions to the leisure activities they facilitated. For decades after the Second World War, the notion persisted that international cooperation was tied to the emotions of those who engaged in it and informed the work of major international organizations.

Most notably, the European Union built itself through programs such as the European Region Action Scheme for the Mobility of University Students (ERASMUS)—established in 1987 to foster the formation of a European identity and also of "good Europeans" who shared emotional bonds across borders.[1] According to a 2014 report by the European Commission, some of these efforts paid off: "more than 80% of the mobile students felt more European after their study" and "all three mobile groups (students, staff, alumni) had a strong affiliation to Europe."[2] Furthermore, "Erasmus alumni were nearly three times more often in a relationship" and more likely to have a "life partner of a different nationality." Also, the report found that "personal disposition towards relationships with people from other countries and cultures is much higher among people with international experience than among non-mobile alumni."[3] For many, international emotional bonds came to determine not only if and where they travelled but also their lifetime decisions and political affiliations.

But not everybody espoused Erasmus-style lifestyle and positions. As Craig Calhoun insightfully pointed out, today's internationalists—the "cosmopolitans" who "feel at home in cities (and hotels and airports)"—might lack the "wholeness" they seem to represent.[4] Yet, even the limits of internationalism—and especially its crisis with the resurgence of extreme-nationalist movements after 1989—might be best understood as the latest chapter of the longer history of emotions reconstructed in this book. A walk through the same cities and towns examined in this study might suffice to illuminate this point. Geneva's overpriced dwellings and Leysin's advertisements promising foreign students an exclusive "international atmosphere" show both the successes and failures of the internationalist emotionalist model: they speak of international encounters as a reality on a scale unimaginable in the 1920s and 1930s; and they also embody the opposite of the "authentic" idealized in the interwar period.

Surely, Egmond d'Arcis' "Lord of the Mountain"—the quintessential type that interwar internationalists liked to evoke—would not have approved of today's "international atmospheres" because he would have found them lacking in "genuineness"; many people today share this feeling and turn to localism or to

---

[1] In constructed notions of European identity, "good Europeans" not only support but also take advantage of their rights to study and travel abroad. Jonna Johansson, "Learning To Be(come) A Good European: A Critical Analysis of the Official European Union Discourse on European Identity and Higher Education," Ph.D. Dissertation, Linköpings University, 2007, 203.
[2] In contrast," all three non-mobile control groups assigned a statistically significant lower value to this." European Commission, *The Erasmus Impact Study. Effects of mobility on the Skills and Employability of Students and the Internationalisation of Higher Education Institutions* (September 2014), 141; 189. http://ec.europa.eu/dgs/education_culture/repository/education/library/study/2014/erasmus-impact_en.pdf (accessed on July 27, 2018). This result counter-balanced, without confuting, the conclusions reached by Emmanuel Sigalas in a landmark study on the decline of European identity after study abroad. Emmanuel Sigalas, "Cross-border Mobility and European Identity: The Effectiveness of Intergroup Contact during the Erasmus Year Abroad," *European Union Politics* 11, no. 2 (June 2010), 241–65.
[3] European Commission, *The Erasmus Impact Study*, 135–6; 73; 75.
[4] Craig Calhoun, "Cosmopolitanism and Its Discontents: Why Nations Still Matter," *ABC Religion and Ethics*, March 16, 2017. http://www.abc.net.au/religion/articles/2017/03/16/4637108.htm (accessed July 24, 2018).

extreme nationalism as a reaction. One reason might be because right-wing populist movements have been successful in creating a "style" that is perceived to be more "real" than the one adopted by their opponents.[5] But there are also what Mikko Salmela and Christian von Scheve called the "emotional roots of right-wing political populism," which include attachments to "authentic" landscapes and "nostalgia" for a mythical time imbued with feelings.[6] Awareness of the long history of emotional management examined in this study may prove helpful to those interested in understanding these dynamics, as well as to those who seek to change them.

We need to know more about the functions emotions performed in various settings, particularly when individuals, institutions, and governments with varying agendas engaged in similar activities at the same time and in the same place. More broadly, much remains to be learned about the history of emotions as "emotives" that continuously acquired ontological qualities while in the process of being expressed.[7] Although the result of this generative process often eludes historians—as sources do not allow us to sense "the flames" of what people actually felt but only give a glimpse of their glow and of the sparks and attritions that created them—the field of the history of emotions has provided a rich body of scholarship to help us identify the significance of the dynamics at play. If expressing emotions was inevitably connected with feeling, further historical inquiries are needed to shed light on how various movements affected how people actually felt in the twentieth century, influencing also how they interact in an international environment in the twenty-first.

Tellingly, the Alps remain an important space for political activity. The idea that "mountain people" form a distinct community is still alive.[8] In some cases, there is a direct link with the interwar story told in this book: places like Leysin simply converted old buildings to new use (most notably, by turning sanatoria into "internationalist" schools) while maintaining their previous rhetoric and adapting slightly their aesthetics; and Thomas Mann's Davos now serves as a

---

[5] Mats Ekström, Marianna Patrona, and Joanna Thornborrow, "Right-wing Populism and the Dynamics of Style: A Discourse-analytic Perspective on Mediated Political Performances," *Palgrave Communications* 4, no. 83 (2018). Available online https://doi.org/10.1057/s41599-018-0132-6 (accessed on July 25, 2018).

[6] Mikko Salmela and Christian von Scheve, "The Emotional Roots of Right-wing Political Populism," *Social Science Information* 56, no. 4 (October 12, 2017), 567–95. https://doi.org/10.1177/0539018417734419 (accessed on July 24, 2018). Diego Rubio, *The Politics Of Nostalgia* https://www.socialeurope.eu/the-politics-of-nostalgia (accessed July 24, 2018).

[7] On emotions as "emotives" that at once describe and trigger feelings see William M. Reddy, *The Navigation of Feeling: A Framework for the History of Emotions* (New York: Cambridge University Press, 2001).

[8] See for instance the "Objectives and Mission" of the World Mountain People Association (WMPA), an organization formed in 2000 in order to "meet to the concerns of mountain people who wish to redefine a new future for their territories and rethink their place in society." UNESCO, "World Mountain People Association," https://en.unesco.org/partnerships/non-governmental-organizations/world-mountain-people-association (accessed on July 25, 2018).

venue for exclusive events such as the World Economic Forum. But this research revealed that there are broader transformations at play. As Gérald Berthoud has noted, "When God as a transcendental reference is no longer acceptable, Nature can be an adequate substitute for a whole people with the deep belief to belong to the same natural mould."[9] It is perhaps for this reason that the Alps continue to host various forms of "panalpine activism" in fields as disparate as environmentalism and local governance;[10] and that for more than a century they have never ceased to epitomize at once the best and the worst of modernity and anti-modernity, nationalism and internationalism. This might also be why its inhabitants—today's *montagnards*—remain "noble and ignoble," scorned for their backwardness but hailed for their supposed moral superiority.[11]

The Alps maintain their status as preferred sites for "friendship" that internationalists worked hard to attribute to them in the interwar period, though they have most recently been appropriated by nativist and extreme nationalist movements. For example, in the 1990s, the Italian separatist movement Lega Nord gathered at the alpine sources of the river Po, on the high slopes of Mount Monviso, to proclaim the independence of the invented country of "Padania"; and chose a flower nicknamed *sole delle Alpi* ("the sun of the Alps") as one of its symbols.[12] Even after its evolution into a nationalist, anti-European, and anti-immigrant party, it continued to use the Alps, their products, and their emotions to promote its politics.[13] A glance at a poster advertising a 2015 Lega Nord event suffices to drive the point home: the party leader, Matteo Salvini, appears against a mountainous background, and the program promises the quintessential alpine experience: a lunch at the "Baita della Polenta" (literally, the "polenta cabin") with "music and songs from the Piedmont."[14] The Lega deliberately evokes the same alpine feelings, "atmospheres," and "cleansing" effects of the mountain landscape that the League of Nations once employed, though it does so in the pursuit of extreme localist and neo-fascist agendas.

[9] Gérald Berthoud, "The 'spirit of the Alps' and the Making of Political and Economic Modernity in Switzerland," *Social Anthropology* 9, no. 1 (2001), 85.
[10] Bernard Debarbieux, "Cultures and Politics in the Present-day Alps: Issues Relating to Society, Spatiality and Reflexivity," *Journal of Alpine Research* 96, no. 4 (2008), 47–8.
[11] Berthoud, "The 'spirit of the Alps'," 87.
[12] On the history of the Lega Nord, see Mario Sznajder, "Italy's Right-Wing Government: Legitimacy and Criticism," *International Affairs* 71, no. 1 (January 1995), 84–7. On the interplay of landscape and regionalist movements in the Alps see also Jaro Stacul, *The Bounded Field: Localism and Local Identity in an Italian Alpine Valley* (New York: Berghahn Books, 2004), and "Natural Time, Political Time: Contested Histories in Northern Italy," *The Journal of the Royal Anthropological Institute* 11, no. 4 (December 2005), 819–36.
[13] Valerio Renzi, *La politica della ruspa: la Lega di Salvini e le nuove destre europee* (Rome: Alegre, 2015).
[14] See poster produced by the Italian Lega Nord in 2015, available at https://www.leganord.org/qui-lega-agenda/archivio-eventi/monviso-cittadella-2015 (accessed on July 28, 2018). The slogan reads: "Liberty is thinking and consuming local." Note the lunch at the "Baita della Polenta" with "music and songs from the Piedmont." Also, the Lega Nord symbol at the bottom includes the "sun of the Alps"—in green.

The notion that the alpine terrain—along with its infrastructure projects—symbolizes larger issues has also carried over unswervingly from the interwar period. To keep with the case of Italy, since the 1990s the Alps have housed one of the most notable examples of civic activism in recent memory—the "No TAV movement"—which fights against the construction of a new tunnel and railway line to connect the Italian Val Susa with France. As Emanuele Leonardi noted, the No TAV case stands out not only because of its long duration but also because of its larger "struggles for subjectification." As it happened with the nearby Mont Cenis tunnel whose opening Luigi Manzotti celebrated in his famous 1881 ballet, the issue of excavating a passage under the Alps has become connected to larger questions of identity.[15] At stake this time are deeper critiques of the capitalist system and broader debates over citizens' rights.[16] It is no coincidence that the Italian comedian Beppe Grillo chose to support the No TAV protest very publicly, and that his arrest and sentence for breaking through a TAV construction site garnered much notoriety for his populist—and generally anti-European—Five Star Movement, which in 2018 became the largest individual party in Italy.[17] A closer look at infrastructure in emotionalized spaces like the Alps and at the meanings attributed to them since the days of *Excelsior* might help to elucidate visceral attachments to place and the challenges these currently pose to the system internationalists established over the past century.

Examining the Alps as a terrain for political experimentation might also inspire alternative models of political organization that could be modified and implemented in the future. Judith Matloff has recently suggested that the example of Switzerland—a mountainous country that for centuries has granted much autonomy to individual cantons, thus ensuring that they do not feel oppressed by a central authority—might provide a safeguard against violent reactions against international institutions.[18] Others might find stimulating the alternative formulations described in this book, which deemed emotions a crucial aspect of policy-making and identity building. Taken critically and adapted to the present, political and economic models that place people's feelings at their center might prove valuable to those in charge of organizing the international system both within and beyond the structure of the state.

This study also showed that spaces such as the Alps can serve as a useful workshop for the historian's craft, because they allow for the full appreciation of

[15] I am referring to Luigi Manzotti's 1881 ballet *Excelsior*, whose climactic scene serves as the opening of this book.

[16] Emanuele Leonardi, "Foucault in the Susa Valley: The No TAV Movement and Struggles for Subjectification," *Capitalism Nature Socialism* 24, no. 2 (2013), 27–40.

[17] In 2014, Beppe Grillo received a four-month prison sentence for trespassing the TAV construction site during a protest. See "Italy's Beppe Grillo Given Four Month Jail Sentence," BBC News, March 3, 2014. https://www.bbc.co.uk/news/world-europe-26422237 (accessed on July 28, 2018).

[18] Judith Matloff, *No Friends but the Mountains: Dispatches from the World's Violent Highlands* (New York: Basic Books, 2017), 203–21.

the aesthetic and emotional value of the places where history unfolded. Regardless of their political position, the individuals, groups, and institutions that populated this book took great care in choosing where to be, and they depicted "space" through words and art in order to express their wrangling with the larger problems of their time. Other scholars might find it helpful to approach other places and to use them as vehicles to better understand the ideas, the practices, and the emotions of times past: rivers and seas immediately come to mind, as does the sky—for instance, the League of Nations' efforts to master the airwaves in the interwar period has yet to be studied in a systematic fashion. To be sure, more research is needed to establish similarities and differences between these spaces and the Alps, especially in complex processes such as determining borders, organizing face-to-face international encounters, and employing emotions for political purposes. It is my hope that this book has succeeded in providing a useful example of one fruitful way in which this can be done and inspiring others to accompany me in the quest for locating history in concrete, transnational, and emotionalized settings such as the Alps.

As a last—but no less important—point: although writing a history of academic activism lay outside of the scope of this book, this research nonetheless shed light on a time in which great expectations were placed on "intellectuals" from various disciplines. Interwar internationalists charged students and academics with the task of forming links with others, arguing that these had the potential of being so strong that they could prevent armed conflicts. Looking at the emotions of internationalism in the Alps showed that many of our colleagues from previous generations took this duty very seriously. To be sure, historians must contribute their analytical eye to identify the assumptions and the ulterior motives that at times guided their actions. But no amount of critical insight or cynicism can hide us from the compelling case they put forth.

Regardless of how many times internationalists make us skeptical and sometimes even cringe (especially when in cultural productions like *Excelsior* they acclaim the "Genius of Humanity" and its promises to unite people "in brotherly embrace"), we might even owe it to them. After all, these are the same people who inaugurated the international travel and educational programs through which many of us came of age academically; and it is they who established the channels through which we still communicate ideas across borders at conferences and through academic monographs like this one. Moving forward, the most meaningful way to incorporate emotions and internationalism in international history might be to rekindle the conversation they dared to open about our own civic duties as historians and world citizens who, through words and deeds, still have the ability to feel and to instill emotions that transcend all kinds of borders.

Bibliography

Archival Sources

Archives Cantonales Vaudoises, Chavannes-près-Renens, Switzerland.
    PP 911, Fondation du sanatorium universitaire suisse.
    PP 1028, Rollier (Auguste).
Archives de la Ville de Genève, Geneva, Switzerland.
Archivio storico del Club Alpino Italiano (CAI), Turin, Italy.
L'Association de la Presse Etrangère en Suisse et au Liechtenstein (APES), Private Archives,
    Palais des Nations, Geneva, Switzerland.
Chamonix Municipal Archive, Chamonix, France.
International Labor Office Archives, Geneva, Switzerland.
International Olympic Committee (IOC) Archives, Lausanne, Switzerland.
    Chamonix 1924.
    St. Moritz 1928.
    Lake Placid 1932.
    Garmisch-Partenkirchen 1936.
    St. Moritz 1948.
League of Nations Archives, Geneva, Switzerland.
Manufacture Archives, Leysin.
Swiss Federal Archives, Bern, Switzerland.
Swiss National Library, Bern, Switzerland.
    Biographic Catalogue of Newspaper Articles (BioKat).
UNESCO Archives, Paris.
AG 1, International Institute of Intellectual Co-operation, Institut International de la
    Cooperation Intellectuelle, 1926–1946, C–V–7.
Union Internationale des Associations d'Alpinisme (UIAA) Archives, Bern, Switzerland.
United Nations Archives at Geneva.

Films (in chronological order by release)

Der heilige Berg (*The Holy Mountain*). Directed by Arnold Fanck (1926). Restored version.
    L'immagine Ritrovata, Bologna, 2001.
Die weiße Hölle vom Piz Palü (*The White Hell of Pitz Palu*). Directed by Arnold Fanck and
    Georg Wilhelm Pabst (1929). Restored version. Bundesarchiv-Filmarchiv, Berlin, 1997.
Heidi. Directed by Allan Dwan (1937).

Newspapers, Magazines, and Non-academic Journals

Alpine Journal
American Alpine Journal

Bulletin du Club Alpin Suisse, Section Genevoise
Bulletin of the International Union Against Tuberculosis
Die Alpen/Les Alps/Le Alpi
Gazette des Alpes
L'illustré
Journal de Genève
La Patrie Suisse
La Suisse
T'oung Pao
Tribune de Genève

Published Primary Sources

III Olympic Winter Games Committee Lake Placid, NY, USA. *III Olympic Winter Games, Lake Placid 1932: Official Report*. Lake Placid: III Olympic Winter Games Committee, 1932.

Abauzit, Frank. *Projet d'un sanatorium universitaire international à Leysin*. Lausanne: La Concorde, 1928.

Annual Report of the Health Organisation for 1925–1930, 2. C.H. 442. (A.17.1926. III)

Appel en faveur de la fondation de la Clinique-Manufacture Internationale du Dr. A. Rollier à Leysin. Neuchâtel: Paul Attinger S. A., 1929.

Aveline, Claude. *Le sanatorium universitaire suisse et le sanatorium universitaire international de Leysin: causeries radiophoniques*. Leysin: Impr. nouvelle, 1938.

Bernard, Charles. *Un projet magnifique: le Sanatorium Universitaire International de Leysin et son initiateur*. Geneva: Jent, 1930.

Bobba, Giovanni, and Francesco Mauro, eds. *Scritti alpinistici del Sacerdote Dottor Achille Ratti (ora S.S. Pio Papa XI). Raccolti e pubblicati in occasione del cinquantenario della Sezione di Milano del Club Alpino Italiano*. Milan: Bertieri & Vanzetti, 1923.

Borel, Jean. *Il sanatorio universitario internazionale di Leysin e l'Italia*. Rome, 1933.

Bossus, Pierre. *Les cinquante premières années de l'Union internationale des associations d'alpinisme*. Geneva: UIAA, 1982.

Burnand, René. *Une ville sur la montagne*. Paris: Attinger, 1936.

Chatenay, D. G. "La visite du Mahatma: l'opinion de l'Eglise nationale vaudoise." *La Sentinelle*, December 29, 1931.

Comité exécutif des IImes Jeux olympiques d'hiver St-Moritz 1928. *Rapport général du Comité exécutif des IImes Jeux olympiques d'hiver et documents officiels divers*. Lausanne: Comité Olympique Suisse, 1928.

Comité olympique français. *Les jeux de la VIIIe Olympiade. Paris 1924. Rapport officiel*. Paris: Libr. de France, 1924.

Conference for the Reduction and Limitation of Armaments. *Co-operation of the Press in the Organisation of Peace*. Geneva: League of Nations, 1932.

Corday, Michel. *Les embrasés*. Paris: Flammarion, 1902.

d'Arcis, C. Egmond. *En montagne: récits et souvenirs*. Geneva: Sonor, 1936.

de Traz, Robert. *L'esprit de Genève*. Paris: Grasset, 1929.

de Traz, Robert. *Les heures de silence*. Paris: Grasset, 1934.

La deuxième exposition suisse d'art alpin, Genève 1936. Geneva, 1936.

Du Pasquier, Marcel. *Le Sanatorium Universitaire du Dr. Vauthier à Leysin*. Montreux: Journal de Montreux, 1936.

L'entente des peuples par la jeunesse: études sur les voyages et les échanges scolaires internationaux (collection des dossiers de la coopération intellectuelle). Société des Nations, Institut International de Coopération Intellectuelle, 1933.

Éphémère: cahier des étudiants du sanatorium universitaire suisse, Leysin, avec des bois originaux dessinés par E. Andreazzi et gravés par R. Guiart. Berne: Büchler & Cie, 1930.

Erste Ausstellung Schweizerischer alpiner Kunst, im Kunstgewerbemuseum bei Hauptbanhof Zürich, 26. März bis 17. April [1933]. Zürich, 1933.

Escarra, Jean. *Le conflit sino-japonais et la Société des Nations*. Paris: Publications de la Conciliation internationale, 1933.

Escarra, Jean. *L'honorable paix japonaise*. Paris: Grasset, 1938.

Escarra, Jean. *Réflexions sur la politique du Japon à l'égard de la Chine et sur quelques aspects juridiques du conflit actuel*. Perpignan: Imprimerie de l'Indépendant, 1937.

Escarra, Jean, Henry de Sègogne, Louis Neltner, and Jean Charignon. *Karakoram. Expédition française de l'Himalaya, 1936*. Paris: Flammarion, 1938.

Frank, Regina. "Intégration d'une donation de livre français et allemands dans la bibliothèque 'Le Livre du Malade' à Leysin." Thesis, École de bibliothécaires de Genève, 1961.

Gouzy, René. *Le Sanatorium universitaire de Leysin refuge de la bonne humeur*, 1936.

Grant, Madison. *The Passing of the Great Race, or The Racial Basis of European History*. New York: Charles Scribner's Sons, 1916.

Günther, Hans F. K. *The Racial Elements of European History*, translated by G. C. Wheeler. London: Methuen and Co., 1927.

Hitchner, Dell G. "The Failure of the League: Lesson in Public Relations." *The Public Opinion Quarterly* 8, no. 1 (Spring 1944), 61–71.

Hourcade, Bertrand. *Le village magique: souvenirs de Leysin*. Pully: Ed. Les Iles Futures, 2001

Houriet, Jean H. *Années perdues, années retrouvées: sous un toit sanatorial*. Neuchâtel: Messeiller, 1974.

Hurtwood, Lord Allen of. "Public Opinion and the Idea of International Government." *International Affairs* 13, no. 2 (March–April 1934), 186–207.

Instruction of Children and Youth in the Existence and Aims of the League of Nations. Report submitted by the Secretariat to the sixth Assembly. League of Nations publications, A.10.1925.XII.

International Institute of Intellectual Co-operation. *Le rôle intellectuel de la presse*. Paris: Société des Nations, Institut international de coopération intellectuelle, 1933.

Kessel, Joseph. *Les captifs*. Paris: Gallimard, 1926.

League of Nations, *Official Journal*, 1920–1940.

Ligue Vaudoise contre la Tuberculose. *Un projet de colonie agricole maraîchère pour tuberculeux guéris*. Lausanne: La Concorde, 1919.

Malche, Albert. *Rapport de M. Albert Malche…destiné à présenter la candidature du Dr Louis-Constant Vauthier au prix Nobel de la paix*. Geneva: 1950.

Mann, Thomas. *Der Zauberberg*. Berlin: S. Fischer Verlag, 1924.

Mann, Thomas. *La montagna incantata*. Milan: Modernissima, 1932.

Mann, Thomas. *La montagne magique*. Paris: Fayard, 1931.

Mann, Thomas. *The Magic Mountain*. New York: Alfred A. Knopf, 1927.

Manzotti, Luigi. *Excelsior: azione coreografica, storica, allegorica, fantastica in 6 parti e 11 quadri*. Musica di Romualdo Marenco. Milan: Regio Stabilimento Ricordi, 1881.

Meech, Thomas Cox, Esq. *The Press and the League of Nations*. London: C.F. Roworth, undated.

Morris, Margaret. *My Life in Movement*. London: Peter Owen, 1969.

Peattie, Roderick. *Mountain Geography: A Critique and a Field of Study.* Cambridge, MA: Harvard University Press, 1936.

Poucel, J. *Le naturalisme et la vie: la joie d'être sains.* Paris: Baillère & Fils, 1933.

Première Conférence internationale de la Lumière: physique, biologie, thérapeutique; Lausanne et Leysin, 10–13 septembre 1928. Paris: L'expansion scientifique française, 1928.

Première exposition internationale de photographies alpines. Geneva, 1936.

Répertoire des organizations internationales. Geneva, Série des publications de la Société des Nations, XII, 1936.

Ripley, William Z. *The Races of Europe: A Sociological Study.* New York: D. Appleton and Company, 1899.

Rollier, Auguste. *Le bain de soleil: Pourquoi? Où? Comment?* Montreux: Nouvelle Ch. Corbaz S.A., 1936.

Rollier, Auguste. *La cure d'altitude et la cure solaire de la tuberculose chirurgicale: communication faite au Congrès International de Physiothérapie (octobre 1907).* Neuchâtel: Delachaux & Niestlé, S. A. Geneva, 1908.

Rollier, Auguste. *La cure de soleil.* Paris: Baillière & Fils, 1915.

Rollier, Auguste. *La cure de soleil et de travail à la clinique militaire suisse de Leysin.* Lausanne: Impr. Réunies S.A., 1916.

Rollier, Auguste. *L'école au soleil.* Paris: Baillière & Fils, 1915.

Rollier, Auguste. *Le pansement solaire: héliothérapie de certaines affections chirurgicales et des blessures de guerre.* Lausanne: Payot & Cie, 1916.

Rollier, Auguste. *La santé par le travail au soleil.* Montreux: Nouvelle Ch. Corbaz S. A., 1928.

Sandoz, Louis-Marcel. *Hormones: leur rôle dans la vie du corps et de l'esprit.* Neuchâtel: Attinger, 1949.

Second congrès international des écoles de plein air, Bruxelles, 6–11 avril 1931: rapports et comptes rendus. Brussels: Librairie Castaigne, 1931.

Semple, Ellen Churchill. *Influences of Geographic Environment: On the Basis of Ratzel's System of Anthropo-Geography.* New York: Henry Holt and Co., 1911.

Seydoux, Daniel. *La Manu: histoire d'espoirs, 1903–2004.* La Manufacture bernoise, Fondation du Dr Rollier, 2004.

Stoddard, Lothrop. *The Rising Tide of Color: The Threat Against White World-Supremacy.* New York: Charles Scribner's Sons, 1921.

Tonella, Guido. *50 anni di alpinismo senza frontiere. La storia dell'UIAA. Unione Internazionale delle Associazioni d'Alpinismo.* Milan, Club Alpino Italiano, 1983.

Towe, A.L. "Arbeitstherapie in Leysin." *Der Tuberkulosearzt* 8, no. 4 (April 1954), 245–50.

Une thérapeutique qui vise l'homme tout entier ou Les adjuvants de l'héliothérapie pratiquée dans les cliniques du prof. Rollier à Leysin, 1903–1953: Au prof. Auguste Rollier, hommage de ses collab. à l'occasion du jubilé cinquantenaire de son activité méd. et humanitaire. Leysin: Soc. des établissements héliothérapiques, 1953.

Variétés: cahier rédigé par un groupe d'étudiants du sanatorium universitaire. Leysin, 1932.

Zoppi, Giuseppe. *Il Sanatorio Universitario di Leysin,* 1930.

Secondary Sources

"AHR Conversation: The Historical Study of Emotions." *The American Historical Review* 117, no. 5 (December 2012), 1487–531.

"AHR Conversation: On Transnational History." *The American Historical Review* 111, no. 5 (December 2006), 1441–64.

Adams, Annmarie. *Medicine by Design: The Architect and the Modern Hospital, 1893–1943.* Minneapolis: University of Minnesota Press, 2008.

Adriaansen, Robbert-Jan. *The Rhythm of Eternity: The German Youth Movement and the Experience of the Past, 1900–1933.* New York: Berghahn Books, 2015.

Alberti, Fay Bound. *Matters of the Heart: History, Medicine, and Emotion.* Oxford: Oxford University Press, 2010.

Alberti, Fay Bound. ed. *Medicine, Emotion and Disease, 1700–1950.* New York: Palgrave Macmillan, 2006.

Allcorn, William. *The Maginot Line, 1928–45.* Oxford: Osprey, 2003.

Allovio, Stefano. "Strategie e processi di costruzione di un prodotto tipico: il caso della Fontina della Valle d'Aosta." *Annali di San Michele* 19 (2006), 201–34.

Ambrosi, Claudio, and Michael Wedekind, eds. *L'invenzione di un cosmo borghese: valori sociali e simboli culturali dell'alpinismo nei secoli XIX e XX.* Trent: Museo Storico di Trento, 2000.

Ambrosius, Lloyd E. *Woodrow Wilson and American Internationalism.* New York: Cambridge University Press, 2017.

Anastasiadou, Irene. *Constructing Iron Europe: Transnationalism and Railways in the Interbellum.* Amsterdam: Amsterdam University Press, 2011.

Anderson, Ben. "Affective Atmospheres." *Emotion, Space and Society* 2, no. 2 (December 2009), 77–81.

Anderson, Ben M. "The Construction of an Alpine Landscape: Building, Representing and Affecting the Eastern Alps, c. 1885–1914." *Journal of Cultural Geography* 29, no. 2 (June 2012), 155–83.

Anderson, Kay, and Susan J. Smith. "Editorial: Emotional Geographies." *Transactions of the Institute of British Geographers* 26, no. 1 (March 2001), 7–10.

André, Maurice. *Leysin, station médicale.* Pully: Les Iles futures, 2002.

Applegate, Celia. "AHR Forum: A Europe of Regions: Reflections on the Historiography of Sub-National Places in Modern Times." *American Historical Review* 104, no. 4 (October 1999), 1157–82.

Ariffin, Yohan, Jean-Marc Coicaud, and Vesselin Popovski, eds. *Emotions in International Politics: Beyond Mainstream International Relations.* New York: Cambridge University Press, 2016.

Arsan, Andrew, Su Lin Lewis, and Anne-Isabelle Richard. "Editorial: The Roots of Global Civil Society and the Interwar Moment." *Journal of Global History* 7, no. 2 (July 2012), 157–65.

Audisio, Aldo, and Angelica Natta-Soleri. *Film delle montagne: manifesti. Raccolte di documentazione del Museo Nazionale della Montagna.* Scarmagno: Priuli & Verlucca, 2008.

Baggio, Antonio Maria. *Il principio dimenticato: la fraternità nella riflessione politologica contemporanea.* Rome: Città Nuova, 2007.

Balestracci, Fiammetta, and Pietro Causarano, eds. *Al confine delle Alpi: culture, valori sociali e orizzonti nazionali fra mondo tedesco e italiano (secoli XIX–XX).* Milan: FrancoAngeli, 2018.

Barbalet, Jack, ed. *Emotions and Sociology.* Oxford: Blackwell, 2002.

Barnett, Michael N. *The Empire of Humanity: A History of Humanitarianism.* Ithaca, NY: Cornell University Press, 2011.

Barry, Gearóid. *The Disarmament of Hatred: Marc Sangnier, French Catholicism and the Legacy of the First World War, 1914–45.* Basingstoke: Palgrave Macmillan, 2012.

Bates, Barbara. *Bargaining for Life: A Social History of Tuberculosis, 1876–1938.* Philadelphia: University of Pennsylvania Press, 2015.

Beattie, Andrew. *The Alps: A Cultural History.* New York: Oxford University Press, 2006.

Benjamin, Walter. "The Work of Art in the Age of Mechanical Reproduction," in *Illuminations*, translated by Harry Zohn. New York: Schocken Books, 1969. Orig. *Illuminationen*, 1st (French) edition, 1936.

Bennett, Alvin Leroy. "The Development of Intellectual Cooperation under the League of Nations and United Nations." Ph.D. dissertation. University of Illinois at Urbana, 1950.

Bernard, Paul P. *Rush to the Alps: The Evolution of Vacationing in Switzerland*. Boulder, CO: East European Quarterly, 1978.

Berthoud, Gérald. "The 'spirit of the Alps' and the Making of Political and Economic Modernity in Switzerland." *Social Anthropology* 9, no. 1 (2001), 81–94.

Bertrand, Gilles, Catherine Brice, and Gilles Montègre, eds. *Fraternité: pour une histoire du concept*. Grenoble: Cahiers du CRHIPA, 2012.

Bevis, Richard. *The Road to Egdon Heath: The Aesthetics of the Great in Nature*. Montreal: McGill-Queen's University Press, 1999.

Bille, Mikkel, Peter Bjerregaard, and Tim Flohr Sørensen. "Staging Atmospheres: Materiality, Culture, and the Texture of the In-Between." *Emotion, Space and Society* 15 (May 2015), 31–8.

Biltoft, Carolyn N. "Reversing the Curse of Babel? International Language Movements and Inter-war Chasms," in Patrick Manning, ed., *World History: Global and Local Interactions*. Princeton: Markus Wiener Publishers, 2005, 179–94.

Bleiker, Roland, and Emma Hutchison. "Introduction: Emotions and World Politics." *International Theory* 6, no. 3 (November 2014), 490–1.

Bleiker, Roland, and Emma Hutchison. "Theorizing Emotions in World Politics." *International Theory* 6, no. 3 (November 2014), 491–514.

Boddice, Rob. *The History of Emotions*. Manchester: Manchester University Press, 2018.

Bonnet, Henri. "La Société des Nations et la Coopération Intellectuelle." *Cahiers d'histoire mondiale* 10, no. 1 (1966), 198–209.

Borowy, Iris. *Coming to Terms with World Health: The League of Nations Health Organisation, 1921–1946*. Frankfurt am Main: Peter Lang, 2009.

Bouchard, Carl. " 'Formons un choeur aux innombrables voix…': hymnes et chants pour la paix soumis à la Société des Nations." *Relations Internationales* 155, no. 3 (Fall 2013), 103–20.

Bourdieu, Pierre. *Distinction: A Social Critique of the Judgement of Taste*, translated by Richard Nice. Cambridge, MA: Harvard University Press, 1984.

Bourdieu, Pierre. *Outline of a Theory of Practice*, translated by Richard Nice. New York: Cambridge University Press, 1977.

Brown, Elspeth H., and Thy Phu, eds. *Feeling Photography*. Durham, NC: Duke University Press, 2014.

Brown, Philip Marshall. "The Codification of International Law." *American Journal of International Law* 29, no. 1 (January 1935), 25–39.

Bures, Eliah Matthew. "Fantasies of Friendship: Ernst Jünger and the German Right's Search for Community in Modernity." Ph.D. Dissertation. University of California, Berkeley, 2014.

Cabanes, Bruno. *The Great War and the Origins of Humanitarianism, 1918–1924*. Cambridge: Cambridge University Press, 2014.

Camanni, Enrico. *Alpi ribelli. Storie di montagna, resistenza e utopia*. Bari: Laterza, 2016.

Campbell, Joan. *Joy in Work, German Work*. Princeton: Princeton University Press, 1989.

Campbell, Margaret. "What Tuberculosis Did for Modernism: The Influence of a Curative Environment on Modernist Design and Architecture." *Medical History* 49, no. 1 (October 2005), 463–88.

Carr, E. H. *Twenty Years' Crisis, 1919–1939: An Introduction to the Study of International Relations*. London: Macmillan, 1939.

Carter, Simon. *Rise and Shine: Sunlight, Technology, and Health*. Oxford: Berg, 2007.

Cavanna, Pierangelo, ed. *"Le 'stelle' parlano al vostro cuore: la fotografia nel cinema delle montagne*. Turin: Collezioni del Museo Nazionale della Montagna, 2004.

Cayet, Thomas. *Rationaliser le travail, organiser la production: le Bureau International du Travail et la modernisation économique durant l'entre-deux-guerres*. Rennes: Presses universitaires de Rennes, 2010.

Cayleff, Susan E. *Nature's Path: A History of Naturopathic Healing in America*. Baltimore, MD: Johns Hopkins University Press, 2016.

Châtelet, Anne-Marie. *Le souffle du plein air*. Geneva: MétisPress, 2011.

Châtelet, Anne-Marie, Dominique Lerch, and Jean-Noël Luc, eds. *L'école de plein air. Une expérience pédagogique et architecturale dans l'Europe du XXe siècle*. Paris: Éditions Recherches, 2003.

Chowdhury, Elora Halim, and Liz Philipose, eds. *Dissident Friendships: Feminism, Imperialism, and Transnational Solidarity*. Urbana: University of Illinois Press, 2016.

Cicchelli, Vincenzo, and Sylvie Octobre. *Aesthetico-Cultural Cosmopolitanism and French Youth: the Taste of the World*. London: Palgrave Macmillan, 2018.

Clair, Jean. *Malinconia: motifs saturniens dans l'art de l'entre-deux-guerres*. Paris: Gallimard, 1996.

Clavin, Patricia. "Defining Transnationalism." *Contemporary European History* 14, no. 4 (November 2005), 421–39.

Clavin, Patricia. "Europe and the League of Nations," in Robert Gerwarth, ed., *Twisted Paths: Europe, 1914–1945*. Oxford: Oxford University Press, 2007, 325–54.

Clavin, Patricia. *Securing the World Economy: The Reinvention of the League of Nations, 1920–1946*. Oxford: Oxford University Press, 2013.

Colley, Ann C. *Victorians in the Mountains: Sinking the Sublime*. Burlington, VT: Ashgate, 2010.

Condrau, Flurin. "Urban Tuberculosis and Sanatorium Treatment in the Early Twentieth Century," in Anne Borsay and Peter Shapely, eds., *Medicine, Charity and Mutual Aid: The Consumption of Health and Welfare in Britain, c.1550–1950*. London: Routledge, 2016, 183–205.

Condrau, Flurin, and Michael Worboys, eds. *Tuberculosis Then and Now: Perspectives on the History of an Infectious Disease*. Montreal: McGill-Queen's University Press, 2010.

Costigliola, Frank, and Michael J. Hogan, eds., *Explaining the History of American Foreign Relations*, 3rd edition. New York: Cambridge University Press, 2016.

Cuaz, Marco. "Catholic Alpinism and Social Discipline in 19th and 20th-century Italy." *Mountain Research and Development* 26, no. 4 (November 2006), 358–63.

Cubero Izquierdo, Carmen. *La pérdida del pudor: el naturismo libertario español (1900–1936)*. Madrid: LaMalatesta editorial, 2015.

Daston, Lorraine. "The Moral Economy of Science." *Osiris* 10 (1995), 2–24.

Daston, Lorraine, and Peter Galison. *Objectivity*. New York: Zone Books, 2010.

Davidson, Joyce, and Christine Milligan. "Editorial: Embodying Emotion Sensing Space: Introducing Emotional Geographies." *Social & Cultural Geography* 5, no. 4 (December 2004), 523–32.

Davidson, Joyce, Liz Bondi, and Mick Smith, eds. *Emotional Geographies*. Burlington, VT: Ashgate, 2005.

Davies, Thomas. *NGOs: A New History of Transnational Civil Society*. New York: Oxford University Press, 2014.

De Baecque, Antoine. *Histoires des crétins des Alpes*. Paris: Vuibert, 2018.

De Grazia, Victoria. *The Culture of Consent: Mass Organization of Leisure in Fascist Italy*. Cambridge: Cambridge University Press, 1981.

Debarbieux, Bernard. "Cultures and Politics in the Present-day Alps: Issues Relating to Society, Spatiality and Reflexivity." *Journal of Alpine Research* 96, no. 4 (2008), 45–52.

Debarbieux, Bernard, and Gilles Rudaz. *Les faiseurs de montagne: imaginaires politiques et territorialités: XVIIIe–XXIe siècle*. Paris: CNRS, 2010.

Debarbieux, Bernard, and Gilles Rudaz. *The Mountain: A Political History from the Enlightenment to the Present*. Chicago, IL: University of Chicago Press, 2015.

Del Curto, Davide. *Il sanatorio alpino: architetture per la cura della tubercolosi dall'Europa alla Valtellina*. Rome: Aracne editrice, 2010.

Delizia, Ilia, and Fabio Mangone. *Architettura e politica: Ginevra e la Società delle Nazioni, 1925–1929*. Rome: Officina Edizioni, 1992.

Dellamonica, Davide, et al., eds. *Heidi: oltre la storia*. Lugano: Biblioteca Cantonale di Lugano, 2013.

Denning, Andrew. "From Sublime Landscapes to 'White Gold': How Skiing Transformed the Alps after 1930." *Environmental History* 19, no. 1 (January 2014), 78–108.

Denning, Andrew. *Skiing into Modernity: A Cultural and Environmental History*. Berkeley: University of California Press, 2015.

De Rossi, Antonio. *La costruzione delle Alpi: il Novecento e il modernismo alpino (1917–2017)*. Rome: Donzelli, 2016.

Didi-Huberman, Georges. *Invention of Hysteria: Charcot and the Photographic Iconography of the Salpetrière*, translated by Alisa Hartz. Cambridge, MA: MIT Press, 2003.

Dixon, Thomas. "'Emotion': The History of a Keyword in Crisis." *Emotion Review* 4, no. 4 (October 2012), 338–44.

Dixon, Thomas. *From Passions to Emotions: The Creation of a Secular Psychological Category*. Cambridge: Cambridge University Press, 2003.

Dormandy, Thomas. *The White Death: A History of Tuberculosis*. London: Hambledon Press, 1999.

Doveling, Katrin, Christian von Scheve, and Elly A. Konijn, eds. *The Routledge Handbook of Emotions and Mass Media*. New York: Routledge, 2011.

Downs, Laura Lee. *Childhood in the Promised Land: Working-Class Movements and the Colonies de Vacances in France, 1880–1960*. Durham, NC: Duke University Press, 2002.

Dubin, Martin David. "Transgovernmental Processes in the League of Nations." *International Organization* 37, no. 3 (Summer 1983), 469–93.

Edwards, Siân. *Youth Movements, Citizenship and the English Countryside: Creating Good Citizens, 1930–1960*. Cham: Palgrave Macmillan, 2018.

Eghigian, Greg, ed. *From Madness to Mental Health: Psychiatric Disorder and Its Treatment in Western Civilization*. New Brunswick, NJ: Rutgers University Press, 2010.

Ellis, Reuben. *Vertical Margins: Mountaineering and the Landscapes of Neoimperialism*. Madison: University of Wisconsin Press, 2001.

Eriksen, Thomas Hylland, and Richard Jenkins, eds. *Flag, Nation and Symbolism in Europe and America*. London: Routledge, 2007.

Ernst, Waltraud, and Thomas Mueller, eds. *Transnational Psychiatries: Social and Cultural Histories of Psychiatry in Comparative Perspective, c. 1800–2000*. Newcastle upon Tyne: Cambridge Scholars Publishing, 2010.

Esson, Dylan Jim. "Selling the Alpine Frontier: The Development of Winter Resorts, Sports, and Tourism in Europe and America, 1865–1941." Ph.D. Dissertation. University of California, Berkeley, 2011.

Falasca-Zamponi, Simonetta. *Fascist Spectacle: The Aesthetics of Power in Mussolini's Italy*. Berkeley: University of California Press, 2000.

Fassin, Didier. "Les économies morales revisitées." *Annales HSS* 64, no. 6 (2009), 1237–66.

Fehrenbach, Heide, and Davide Rodogno, eds. *Humanitarian Photography: A History*. New York: Cambridge University Press, 2015.

Feldman Barrett, Lisa, Michael Lewis, and Jeannette M. Haviland-Jones, eds., *Handbook of Emotions*, 4th edition. New York: The Guildford Press, 2016.

Fenoglio, Alberto. *Il Vallo Alpino: le fortificazioni delle alpi occidentali durante la seconda guerra mondiale*. Sant'Ambrogio di Torino: Susalibri, 1992.

Fernández Pardo, Carlos A. *Régimen internacional del trabajo: la OIT en la política mundial*. Buenos Aires: AD-HOC, 2001.

Fine, Robert. *Cosmopolitanism*. London: Routledge, 2007.

Fischer-Tiné, Harald. "The Other Side of Internationalism: Switzerland as a Hub of Militant Anti-colonialism c. 1910–1920," in Patricia Purtschert and Harald Fischer-Tiné, eds., *Colonial Switzerland: Rethinking Colonialism from the Margins*. Basingstoke: Palgrave Macmillan, 2015, 221–58.

Fisher, David James. *Romain Rolland and the Politics of Intellectual Engagement*. Berkeley: University of California Press, 1988.

Foucault, Michel. *The Birth of the Clinic: An Archaeology of Medical Perception*, translated by Alan Sheridan. New York: Pantheon Books, 1973.

Foucault, Michel. *Discipline and Punish: The Birth of the Prison*, translated by Alan Sheridan. New York: Random House, 1975.

Franco, Silvano. *Legislazione e politica sanitaria del fascismo*. Rome: APES, 2001.

Frei, Philippe. *Transferprozesse der Moderne: Die Nachbenennungen 'Alpen' und 'Schweiz' im 18. bis 20. Jahrhundert*. Bern: Peter Lang, 2017.

Freund, Daniel. *American Sunshine: Diseases of Darkness and the Quest for Natural Light*. Chicago, IL: University of Chicago Press, 2012.

Frevert, Ute. *Emotions in History: Lost and Found*. Budapest: Central European University Press, 2011.

Frevert, Ute. *The Moral Economy of Trust: Modern Trajectories*. London: German Historical Institute, 2014.

Frevert, Ute, et al. *Emotional Lexicons: Continuity and Change in the Vocabulary of Feeling 1700–2000*. Oxford: Oxford University Press, 2014.

Fussell, Paul. *The Great War and Modern Memory*, 3rd edition. Oxford: Oxford University Press, 2013.

Gammerl, Benno. "Emotional Styles: Concepts and Challenges." *Rethinking History* 16, no. 2 (May 2012), 161–75.

Gaynor, Jennifer L. *Intertidal History in Island Southeast Asia: Submerged Genealogy and the Legacy of Coastal Capture*. Ithaca, NY: Cornell University Press, 2016.

Geyer, Martin H., and Johannes Paulmann, eds. *The Mechanics of Internationalism: Culture, Society, and Politics from the 1840s to the First World War*. London: German Historical Institute, 2001.

Giacomoni, Paola. *Il laboratorio della natura. Paesaggio montano e sublime naturale in età moderna*. Milan: FrancoAngeli, 2001.

Giddens, Anthony. *The Constitution of Society: Outline of the Theory of Structuration* Berkeley: University of California Press, 1984.

Gienow-Hecht, Jessica C. E., ed. *Emotions in American History: An International Assessment*. New York: Berghahn Books, 2010.

Gienow-Hecht, Jessica C. E., ed. *Sound Diplomacy: Music, Emotions, and Politics in Transatlantic Relations, 1850–1920*. Chicago, IL: University of Chicago Press, 2009.

Gilg, Andrew W. "Settlement Design in the Alps: The Case of Leysin." *Landscape Research* 8, no. 1 (June 1983), 2–12.

Gilman, Sander L. *Picturing Health and Illness: Images of Identity and Difference*. Baltimore, MD: Johns Hopkins University Press, 1995.

Gissibl, Bernhard, Sabine Höhler, and Patrick Kupper, eds. *Civilizing Nature: National Parks in Global Historical Perspective*. New York: Berghahn, 2012.

Goffman, Erving. *Asylums: Essays on the Social Situation of Mental Patients and Other Inmates*. New York: Anchor Books, 1961.

Goffman, Erving. *Interaction Ritual: Essays on Face-to-face Behavior*. New York: Anchor Books, 1967.

Goffman, Erving. *The Presentation of Self in Everyday Life*. New York: Anchor Books, 1959.

Goffman, Erving. *Stigma: Notes on the Management of Spoiled Identity*. New York: Simon & Schuster, 1963.

Gorman, Daniel. *The Emergence of International Society in the 1920s*. New York: Cambridge University Press, 2012.

Gorman, Daniel. *International Cooperation in the Early Twentieth Century*. London: Bloomsbury Academic, 2017.

Götz, Norbert. "'Moral Economy': Its Conceptual History and Analytical Prospects." *Journal of Global Ethics* 11, no. 2 (May 2015), 147–62.

Graevenitz, Fritz Georg von. *Argument Europa. Internationalismus in der globalen Agrarkrise der Zwischenkriegszeit (1927–1937)*. Frankfurt am Main: Campus Verlag, 2017.

Grasseni, Cristina. *La reinvenzione del cibo. Culture del gusto fra tradizione e globalizzazione ai piedi delle Alpi*. Verona: QuiEdit, 2007.

Graziano, Manlio. *What Is a Border?* Stanford: Stanford Briefs, 2018.

Groom, A. J. R., and Paul Taylor, eds. *Functionalism: Theory and Practice in International Relations*. London: University of London Press, 1975.

Günther, Dagmar. *Alpine Quergänge: Kulturgeschichte des bürgerlichen Alpinismus (1870–1930)*. Frankfurt am Main: Campus Verlag, 1998.

Gutek, Gerald L., and Patricia A. Gutek. *Bringing Montessori to America: S. S. McClure, Maria Montessori, and the Campaign to Publicize Montessori Education*. Tuscaloosa: The University of Alabama Press, 2016.

Hall, Todd H. *Emotional Diplomacy: Official Emotion on the International Stage*. Ithaca, NY: Cornell University Press, 2015.

Hansen, Peter H. *The Summits of Modern Man: Mountaineering after the Enlightenment*. Cambridge, MA: Harvard University Press, 2013.

Harp, Stephen L. *Au naturel: Naturism, Nudism, and Tourism in Twentieth-century France*. Baton Rouge: Louisiana State University Press, 2013.

Heller, Geneviève. "Leysin et son passé médical." *Gesnerus* 47, nos. 3–4 (1990), 329–44.

Herbreteau, Hubert. *La fraternité: entre utopie et réalité*. Paris: Atelier, 2009.

Hermitte, Guido Barbieri. *Il gozzo: storia, leggenda, aneddotica*. Venosa: Edizioni Osanna Venosa, 1996.

Herren, Madeleine, ed. *Networking the International System: Global Histories of International Organizations*. Heidelberg: Springer, 2014.

Herren, Madeleine, Martin Rüesch, and Christiane Sibille, eds. *Transcultural History: Theories, Methods, Sources*. Heidelberg: Springer, 2012.

Herren, Madeleine, and Sacha Zala, *Netzwerk Aussenpolitik. Internationale Organisationen und Kongresse als Instrumente der schweizerischen Aussenpolitik 1914–1950*. Zürich: Chronos a.

Herrmann, Anne. *Coming out Swiss: In Search of Heidi, Chocolate, and My Other Life*. Madison: The University of Wisconsin Press, 2014.

Hewitt, Nicholas. *Les maladies du siècle: The Image of Malaise in French Fiction and Thought in the Inter-war Years*. Hull: Hull University Press, 1988.

Hickman, Clare. *Therapeutic Landscapes: A History of English Hospital Gardens since 1800*. Manchester: Manchester University Press, 2013.

Hitzer, Bettina, and Pilar León Sanz. "The Feeling Body and Its Diseases: How Cancer Went Psychosomatic in Twentieth-century Germany." *OSIRIS* 31, no. 1 (2016), 67–93.

Hochschild, Arlie Russell. T*he Managed Heart: Commercialization of the Human Feeling*. Berkeley: University of California Press, 1983.

Hogan, J. Michael. *Woodrow Wilson's Western Tour: Rhetoric, Public Opinion, and the League of Nations*. College Station: Texas A&M University Press, 2006.

Hoibian, Olivier, ed. *L'invention de l'alpinisme: la montagne et l'affirmation de la bourgeoisie cultivée (1786–1914)*. Paris: Belin, 2008.

Hoibian, Olivier, and Jacques Defrance, eds. *Deux siècles d'alpinismes européens. Origines et mutations des activités de grimpe*. Paris: L'Harmattan, 2002.

Hosking, Geoffrey. *Trust: A History*. Oxford: Oxford University Press, 2014.

Hunt, Lynn. *Inventing Human Rights*. New York: W.W. Norton, 2007.

Hutchison, Emma. *Affective Communities in World Politics: Collective Emotions after Trauma*. Cambridge: Cambridge University Press, 2016.

Illouz, Eva. *Saving the Modern Soul: Therapy, Emotions and the Culture of Self-Help*. Los Angeles: University of California Press, 2008.

Imlay, Talbot C. *The Practice of Socialist Internationalism: European Socialists and International Politics, 1914–1960*. Oxford: Oxford University Press, 2018.

Ireton, Sean Moore, and Caroline Schaumann, eds. *Heights of Reflection: Mountains in the German Imagination from the Middle Ages to the Twenty-first Century*. Rochester, NY: Camden House, 2012.

Iriye, Akira. *Cultural Internationalism and World Order*. Baltimore, MD: Johns Hopkins University Press, 1997.

Isserman, Maurice, and Stewart Weaver. *Fallen Giants: A History of Himalayan Mountaineering from the Age of Empire to the Age of Extremes*. New Haven: Yale University Press, 2008.

Jantzen, René. *Montagne et symboles*. Lyon: Presses Universitaires de Lyon, 1988.

Jerónimo, Miguel Bandeira, and José Pedro Monteiro, eds. *Internationalism, Imperialism and the Formation of the Contemporary World: The Pasts of the Present*. Cham: Palgrave Macmillan, 2018.

Johansson, Jonna. "Learning To Be(come) A Good European: A Critical Analysis of the Official European Union Discourse on European Identity and Higher Education." Ph.D. Dissertation, Linköpings University, 2007.

Johnstone, Andrew. *Against Irmmediate Evil: American Internationalists and the Four Freedoms on the Eve of World War II*. Ithaca, NY: Cornell University Press, 2014.

Kaina,Viktoria, Ireneusz Paweł Karolewski, and Sebastian Kühn, eds. *European Identity Revisited: New Approaches and Recent Empirical Evidence*. New York: Routledge, 2016.

Kassab, Hanna Samir. *The Power of Emotion in Politics, Philosophy, and Ideology*. New York: Palgrave Macmillan, 2016.

Keller, Tait. *Apostles of the Alps: Mountaineering and Nation Building in Germany and Austria, 1860–1939*. Chapel Hill: The University of North Carolina Press, 2016.

Keys, Barbara J. "Emotions in Intercultural Relations," in R. D. Johnson ed. *Asia Pacific in the Age of Globalization*. New York: Palgrave Macmillan, 2015, 212–20.

Keys, Barbara J. *Globalizing Sport: National Rivalry and International Community in the 1930s*. Cambridge, MA: Harvard University Press, 2006.

Kolasa, Jan. *International Intellectual Cooperation: The League Experience and the Beginnings of UNESCO*. Wroclaw: Wroclawskie Towarzistwo Naukowe, 1962.

Koschut, Simon, and Andrea Oelsner, eds. *Friendship and International Relations*. Basingstoke: Palgrave Macmillan, 2014.

Kracauer, Siegfried. *Das Ornament der Masse: Essays*. Frankfurt am Main: Suhrkamp Verlag, l963.

Kracauer, Siegfried. *From Caligari to Hitler: A Psychological History of the German Film*. Princeton: Princeton University Press, 1947.

Kramer, Paul A. "Embedding Capital: Political-Economic History, the United States, and the World." *The Journal of the Gilded Age and Progressive Era* 15, no. 3 (July 2016), 331–62.

Kramer, Paul A. "Is the World Our Campus? International Students and U.S. Global Power in the Long Twentieth Century." *Diplomatic History* 33, no. 5 (November 2009), 775–806.

Kramer, Paul A. "Region in World History," in Douglas Northrup, ed., *A Companion to World History*. Chichester, UK: Wiley-Blackwell, 2012, 201–12.

Kühne, Thomas. *The Rise and Fall of Comradeship: Hitler's Soldiers, Male Bonding and Mass Violence in the Twentieth Century*. Cambridge: Cambridge University Press, 2017.

Labanyi, Jo. "Doing Things: Emotion, Affect, and Materiality." *Journal of Spanish Cultural Studies* 11, nos. 3–4 (September 2010), 223–33.

Laffan, Michael, and Max Weiss, eds. *Facing Fear: The History of an Emotion in Global Perspective*. Princeton: Princeton University Press, 2012.

Landry II, Marc D. "Europe's Battery: The Making of the Alpinex Energy Landscape, 1870–1955." Ph.D. Dissertation. Georgetown University, 2013.

Laqua, Daniel. "Activism in the 'Students' League of Nations': International Student Politics and the Confédération Internationale des Étudiants, 1919–1939." *The English Historical Review* 132, no. 556 (June 2017), 605–37.

Laqua, Daniel. ed. *Internationalism Reconfigured: Transnational Ideas and Movements Between the World Wars*. New York: I.B. Tauris, 2011.

Laqua, Daniel. "Internationalisme ou affirmation de la nation? La coopération intellectuelle transnationale dans l'entre-deux-guerres." *Critique Internationale* 52, no. 3 (2011), 51–67.

Laqua, Daniel. *The Age of Internationalism and Belgium, 1880–1930: Peace, Progress and Prestige*. Manchester: Manchester University Press, 2013.

Laqua, Daniel. "Transnational Intellectual Cooperation, the League of Nations, and the Problem of Order." *Journal of Global History* 6, no. 2 (July 2011), 223–247.

Laqueur, Walter. *Young Germany: A History of the German Youth Movement*. London: Transaction Books, 1984.

Lawlor, Clark. *Consumption and Literature: The Making of the Romantic Disease*. New York: Palgrave Macmillan, 2006.

Leonardi, Emanuele. "Foucault in the Susa Valley: The No TAV Movement and Struggles for Subjectification." *Capitalism Nature Socialism* 24, no. 2 (2013), 27–40.

Lespinet-Moret, Isabelle, and Vincent Viet, eds. *L'Organisation internationale du travail: origine, développement, avenir*. Rennes: Presses universitaires de Rennes, 2011.

Lewer, Nick. *Physicians and the Peace Movement*. London: Frank Cass, 1992.

Lewis, Jan, and Peter N. Stearns, eds. *An Emotional History of the Unites States*. New York: New York University Press, 1998.

Liniger-Goumaz, Max. *De l'éradication du crétinisme et autres phénomènes remarquables tels qu'on peut les observer dans la région des Alpes pennines*. Lausanne: Editions de l'Aire, 1989.

Liniger-Goumaz, Max. *Nos ancêtres les crétins des Alpes*. Geneva: Les Editions du Temps, 2002.

Long, David, and Brian C. Schmidt, eds. *Imperialism and Internationalism in the Discipline of International Relations*. Albany, NY: State University of New York Press, 2005.

Lüthi, Dave. *Le compas & le bistouri: architectures de la médecine et du tourisme curatif. L'exemple vaudois (1760–1940)*. Lausanne: BHMS, 2012.

Lyall, Francis. *International Communications: The International Telecommunication Union and the Universal Postal Union*. Burlington, VT: Ashgate, 2011.

MacMillan, Margaret. *Paris 1919: Six Months that Changed the World*. New York: Random House, 2003.

Manela, Erez. *The Wilsonian Moment: Self-Determination and the International Origins of Anticolonial Nationalism*. Oxford: Oxford University Press, 2007.

Mangan, J. A., ed. *Superman Supreme: Fascist Body as Political Icon—Aryan Fascism*. London: Frank Cass, 2000.

Mark, Peter, Peter Helman, and Penny Snyder, eds. *The Mountains in Art History*. Middletown, CT: Wesleyan University Press, 2017.

Marshall, Tim. *A Flag Worth Dying For: The Power and Politics of National Symbols*. New York: Scribner, 2017.

Mathieu, Jon. *The Alps: An Environmental History*. Oxford: Polity Press, 2019.

Mathieu, Jon. *History of the Alps, 1500–1900: Environment, Development, and Society*. Morgantown: West Virginia University Press, 2009.

Matloff, Judith. *No Friends but the Mountains: Dispatches from the World's Violent Highlands*. New York: Basic Books, 2017.

Matt, Susan J., and Peter N. Stearns, eds. *Doing Emotions History*. Urbana: University of Illinois Press, 2014.

Mazower, Mark. *No Enchanted Palace: The End of Empire and the Ideological Origins of the United Nations*. Princeton: Princeton University Press, 2009.

McMenamin, M. "A medal depicting the Palace of Nations and the Jura Mountains." *Numismatics International Bulletin* 46, nos. 3–4 (2011), 55.

McNee, Alan. *The New Mountaineer in Late Victorian Britain: Materiality, Modernity, and the Haptic Sublime*. Cham, CH: Palgrave Macmillan, 2016.

Menini, Giacomo. *Costruire in cielo: l'architettura moderna nelle Alpi italiane*. Milan: Mimesis, 2017.

Merke, Franz. *History and Iconography of Endemic Goitre and Cretinism*. Bern: Hans Huber, 1984.

Merz, Jörg Martin. "Pushing Corb: Campaigning for Le Corbusier's Project for the Palace of Nations in Geneva (1926–33)," in Shai-shu Tzeng, ed., *Agents of Modernity*, Shida Studies in Art History. Taipei: SMC, 2011, 227–84.

Minois, Georges. *Histoire du mal de vivre: de la mélancolie à la dépression*. Paris: Martinière, 2003.

Morbio, Vittoria Crespi, ed....*E guarnizioni spiccantissime. Figurini e schemi coreografici per la rappresentazione del ballo Excelsior all'Eden di Parigi*. Milan: Edizioni Amici della Scala, 1993.

Morosini, Stefano. *Sulle vette della patria: politica, guerra e nazione nel Club alpino italiano (1863–1922)*. Milan: FrancoAngeli, 2009.

Morris, Christopher. *Modernism and the Cult of Mountains: Music, Opera, Cinema*. Farnham: Ashgate, 2012.

Morris, Penelope, Francesco Ricatti, and Mark Seymour, eds. *Politica ed emozioni nella storia d'Italia dal 1848 ad oggi*. Rome: Viella, 2012.

Mosse, George L. *Fallen Soldiers: Reshaping the Memory of the World Wars*. Oxford: Oxford University Press, 1990.

Musa, Ghazali, James Higham, and Anna Thompson-Carr, eds. *Mountaineering Tourism* New York: Routledge, 2015.

Ninkovich, Frank A. *Global Dawn: The Cultural Foundation of American Internationalism, 1865–1890*. Cambridge, MA: Harvard University Press, 2009.

Nixon, Jon. *Hannah Arendt and the Politics of Friendship*. London: Bloomsbury Academic, 2015.

Nordenstreng, Kaarle, Ulf Jonas Björk, Frank Beyersdorf, Svennik Høyer, and Epp Lauk, eds. *A History of the International Movement of Journalists: Professionalism versus Politics*. Basingstoke: Palgrave Macmillan, 2016.

Nye, Joseph S., and Robert O. Keohane. "Transnational Relations and World Politics: An Introduction." *International Organization* 25, no. 3 (Summer 1971), 329–49.

Olsen, Stephanie, ed. *Childhood, Youth and Emotions in Modern History: National, Colonial and Global Perspectives*. New York: Palgrave Macmillan, 2015.

Osborne, Ken. "Creating the 'International Mind': The League of Nations Attempts to Reform History Teaching, 1920–1939." *History of Education Quarterly* 56, no. 2 (May 2016), 213–240.

O'Shea, Stephen. *The Alps: A Human History from Hannibal to Heidi and Beyond*. New York: W.W. Norton and Company, 2018.

Ostherr, Kirsten. *Medical Visions: Producing the Patient through Film, Television and Imaging Technologies*. New York: Oxford University Press, 2013.

Overy, Richard J. *The Inter-war Crisis*, 3rd edition. London: Routledge, 2017.

Pallas, Jean-Claude. *Histoire et architecture du Palais des Nations (1924–2001): l'art déco au service des relations internationales*. Geneva: Nations Unies, 2001.

Parfitt, Steven, Lorenzo Costaguta, Matthew Kidd, and John Tiplady, eds. *Working-class Nationalism and Internationalism until 1945: Essays in Global Labour History*. Newcastle upon Tyne: Cambridge Scholars Publishing, 2018.

Passerini, Luisa. *Love and the Idea of Europe*, translated by Juliet Haydock and Allan Cameron. New York: Berghahn Books, 2009.

Pastore, Alessandro. *Alpinismo e storia d'Italia. Dall'Unità alla Resistenza*. Bologna: Il Mulino, 2003.

Paulmann, Johannes, ed. *Dilemmas of Humanitarian Aid in the Twentieth Century*. London: OUP/German Historical Institute, 2016.

Pedersen, Susan. "Back to the League of Nations: Review Essay." *American Historical Review* 112, no. 4 (October 2007), 1091–117.

Pedersen, Susan. *The Guardians: The League of Nations and the Crisis of Empire*. Oxford: Oxford University Press, 2015.

Perlik, Manfred. *The Spatial and Economic Transformation of Mountain Regions*. New York: Routledge, 2019.

Pernau, Margrit. "Space and Emotion: Building to Feel." *History Compass* 12, no. 7 (July 2014), 541–49.

Perraton, Hilary. "Foreign Students in the Twentieth Century: A Comparative Study of Patterns and Policies in Britain, France, Russia and the United States." *Policy Reviews in Higher Education* 1, no. 2 (2017), 161–86.

Pietsch, Tamson. *Empire of Scholars: Universities, Networks and the British Academic World, 1850–1939.* New York: Manchester University Press, 2013.

Pietsch, Tamson. "Many Rhodes: Travelling Scholarships and Imperial Citizenship in the British Academic World, 1880–1940." *History of Education* 40, no. 6 (2011), 723–39.

Ponzio, Alessio. *Shaping the New Man: Youth Training Regimes in Fascist Italy and Nazi Germany.* Madison: University of Wisconsin Press, 2015.

Preston, Andrew, and Douglas C. Rossinow, eds. *Outside In: The Transnational Circuitry of US History.* New York: Oxford University Press, 2017.

Reddy, William M. *The Navigation of Feeling: A Framework for the History of Emotions.* New York: Cambridge University Press, 2001.

Redlin, Jane, and Dagmar Neuland-Kitzerow, eds. *Der gefühlte Krieg/Feeling War: Emotionen im Ersten Weltkrieg.* Berlin: Verlag der Kunst, 2014.

Renoliet, Jean-Jacques. *L'Unesco oubliée: la Société des Nations et la coopération intellectuelle, 1919–1946.* Paris: Publications de la Sorbonne, 1999.

Renzi, Valerio. *La politica della ruspa: la Lega di Salvini e le nuove destre europee.* Rome: Alegre, 2015.

Rodogno, Davide. *Fascism's European Empire: Italian Occupation during the Second World War,* translated by Adrian Belton. Cambridge: Cambridge University Press, 2004.

Rodogno, Davide, Bernhard Struck, and Jakob Vogel, eds. *Shaping the Transnational Sphere: Experts, Networks, and Issues from the 1840s to the 1930s.* New York: Berghahn Books, 2014.

Ronzoni, Domenico Flavio. *Achille Ratti. Il prete alpinista che diventò Papa.* Missaglia: Bellavite, 2009.

Rosenberg, Emily S. *Transnational Currents in a Shrinking World, 1870–1945.* Cambridge, MA: The Belknap Press of Harvard University Press, 2012.

Rosenwein, Barbara H. *Emotional Communities in the Early Middle Ages.* Ithaca, NY: Cornell University Press, 2007.

Ross, Chad. *Naked Germany: Health, Race and the Nation.* New York: Berg, 2005.

Rothman, Sheila M. *Living in the Shadow of Death: Tuberculosis and the Social Experience of Illness in American History.* Baltimore, MD: Johns Hopkins University Press, 1995.

Rozenblatt, Daphne. "Work: Disease, Cure, and National Ethos in Modern Italy." *Social History of Medicine* 31, no. 2 (May 2018), 348–72.

Saunier, Pierre-Yves, and Shane Ewen, eds. *Another Global City: Historical Explorations into the Transnational Municipal Moment 1850–2000.* New York: Palgrave Macmillan, 2008.

Scaglia, Ilaria. "The Aesthetics of Internationalism: Culture and Politics on Display at the 1935–1936 International Exhibition of Chinese Art." *Journal of World History* 26, no. 1 (March 2015), 105–37.

Scaglia, Ilaria. "Branding Internationalism: Displaying Art and International Cooperation in the Interwar Period," in Carolin Viktorin, Jessica C. E. Gienow-Hecht, Annika Estner, and Marcel K. Will, eds., *Nation Branding in Modern History.* New York: Berghahn Books, 2018, 79–100.

Scaglia, Ilaria. "The 'Hydrologist's Weapons': Emotions and the Moral Economy of Internationalism, 1921–1952," in Sara Graça Da Silva, ed., *New Interdisciplinary Landscapes in Morality and Emotion.* London: Routledge, 2018, 140–52.

Scheer, Monique. "Are Emotions a Kind of Practice (and Is That What Makes Them Have a History)? A Bourdieuian Approach to Understanding Emotion." *History and Theory* 51, no. 2 (May 2012), 193–220.

Schmitz, David F. *The Triumph of Internationalism: Franklin D. Roosevelt and a World in Crisis, 1933–1941*. Washington, DC: Potomac Books Inc., 2007.

Schrank, Sarah, and Didem Ekici, eds. *Healing Spaces, Modern Architecture, and the Body*. New York: Taylor and Francis, 2016.

Schueler, Judith. *Materialising Identity: The Co-construction of the Gotthard Railway and Swiss National Identity*. Amsterdam: Aksant, 2008.

Scott, James C. *The Art of Not Being Governed: An Anarchist History of Upland Southeast Asia*. New Haven: Yale University Press, 2009.

Segel, Harold B. *Body Ascendant: Modernism and the Physical Imperative*. Baltimore, MD: Johns Hopkins University Press, 1998.

Seiler, Michael P. *Kommandosache "Sonnengott": Geschichte der deutschen Sonnenforschung im Dritten Reich und unter alliierter Besatzung*. Frankfurt am Main: Deutsch, 2007.

Senatori, Luciano. *Compagni di cordata: associazionismo proletario, alpinisti sovversivi, sport popolare in Italia*. Rome: Ediesse, 2010.

Sheehan, Tanya. *Doctored: The Medicine of Photography in Nineteenth-century America*. University Park: Pennsylvania State University Press, 2011.

Shorter, Edward. *A History of Psychiatry: From the Era of the Asylum to the Age of Prozac*. New York: John Wiley & Sons, 1997.

Siegel, Mona L. *The Moral Disarmament of France: Education, Pacifism, and Patriotism, 1914–1940*. Cambridge: Cambridge University Press, 2011.

Sigalas, Emmanuel. "Cross-border Mobility and European Identity: The Effectiveness of Intergroup Contact during the Erasmus Year Abroad." *European Union Politics* 11, no. 2 (June 2010), 241–65.

Simms, Brendan, and D. J. B. Trim, eds. *Humanitarian Intervention: A History*. Cambridge: Cambridge University Press, 2011.

Sluga, Glenda. *Internationalism in the Age of Nationalism*. Philadelphia: University of Pennsylvania Press, 2013.

Sluga, Glenda, and Patricia Clavin, eds. *Internationalisms: A Twentieth-Century History*. New York: Cambridge University Press, 2016.

Smith, Graham M. *Friendship and the Political: Kierkegaard, Nietzsche, Schmitt*. Charlottesville, VA: Imprint Academic, 2011.

Smith, Mick, Joyce Davidson, Laura Cameron, and Liz Bondi, eds. *Emotion, Place and Culture*. London: Routledge, 2009.

Soëtard, Michel. *Méthode et philosophie: la descendance éducative de l'Émile*. Paris: L'Harmattan, 2012.

Sontag, Susan. *Illness as Metaphor*. New York: Farrar, Straus and Giroux, 1978.

Stacul, Jaro. *The Bounded Field: Localism and Local Identity in an Italian Alpine Valley*. New York: Berghahn Books, 2004.

Stacul, Jaro. "Natural Time, Political Time: Contested Histories in Northern Italy." *The Journal of the Royal Anthropological Institute* 11, no. 4 (December 2005), 819–36.

Stets, Jan, and Jonathan H. Turner, eds. *Handbook of the Sociology of Emotions*, vol. II. New York: Springer, 2014.

Sznajder, Mario. "Italy's Right-Wing Government: Legitimacy and Criticism." *International Affairs* 71, no. 1 (January 1995), 83–102.

Tavenrath, Simone. *So wundervoll sonnengebräunt: kleine Kulturgeschichte des Sonnenbadens*. Marburg: Jonas, 2000.

Thomas, Gregory M. *Treating the Trauma of the Great War: Soldiers, Civilians, and Psychiatry in France, 1914–1940.* Baton Rouge: Louisiana State University Press, 2009.

Thompson, E. P. "The Moral Economy of the English Crowd in the Eighteenth Century." *Past & Present* 50, no. 1 (February 1971), 76–136.

Thompson, Mark. *The White War: Life and Death on the Italian Front, 1915–1919.* London: Faber and Faber, 2008.

Thompson, Maximillian. "Making Friends: Amity in American Foreign Policy." Ph.D. Dissertation. University of Oxford, 2015.

Timpe, Julia. *Nazi-Organized Recreation and Entertainment in the Third Reich.* London: Palgrave Macmillan, 2017.

Tollardo, Elisabetta. *Fascist Italy and the League of Nations, 1922–1935.* Basingstoke: Palgrave Macmillan, 2016.

Tönnies, Ferdinand. *Gemeinschaft und Gesellschaft.* Leipzig: Fuess Verlag, 1887.

Travers, Alice. *Politique et représentation de la montagne sous Vichy: la montagne éducatrice, 1940–1944.* Paris: L'Harmattan, 2001.

Tröhler, Daniel. *Pestalozzi and the Educationalization of the World.* New York: Palgrave Macmillan, 2013.

Tworek, Heidi J. S. "Peace through Truth? The Press and Moral Disarmament through the League of Nations." *Medien & Zeit* 25, no. 4 (2010), 16–28.

Vallory, Eduard. *World Scouting: Educating for Global Citizenship.* New York: Palgrave Macmillan, 2012.

van Mol, Christof. "Intra-European Student Mobility and European Identity: A Successful Marriage?" *Population, Space and Place* 19, no. 2 (March/April 2013), 209–22.

Vancampenhout, Annick. "La tuberculose et le sanatorium universitaire de Leysin, 1922–1961," Mémoire de licence, Université de Fribourg, 1990.

Varotto, Mauro. *Montagne del Novecento: il volto della modernità nelle Alpi e Prealpi venete.* Verona: Cierre edizioni, 2017.

Viazzo, Pier Paolo. *Upland Communities: Environment, Population and Social Structure in the Alps since the Sixteenth Century.* Cambridge: Cambridge University Press, 1989.

Vidor, Gian Marco. "Fotografia e approcci storiografici alle emozioni." *Rivista Storica Italiana* 128, no. 2 (2016), 669–85.

Villaret, Sylvain. *Histoire du naturisme en France depuis le siècle des Lumières.* Paris: Vuibert, 2005.

Wehrli, Yannick. "Du pavillon de Leticia au 'non drapeau' de la Société des Nations. Échec de représentation symbolique d'une organisation internationale," in F. Briegel & S. Farré, eds., *Rites, hiérarchies.* Chêne-Bourg: Georg, 2010, 102–16.

Weiss, Thomas G., Tatiana Carayannis, and Richard Jolly. "The 'Third' United Nations." *Global Governance* 15, no. 1 (January–March 2009), 123–42.

Williams, John Alexander. *Turning to Nature in Germany: Hiking, Nudism, and Conservation, 1900–1940.* Stanford: Stanford University Press, 2007.

Williams, Raymond. *Marxism and Literature.* Oxford: Oxford University Press, 1977.

Wissmer, Jean-Michel. *Heidi: enquête sur un mythe suisse qui a conquis le monde.* Geneva: Métropolis, 2012.

Wöbse, Anna-Katharina. "Separating Spheres: Paul Sarasin and his Global Nature Protection Scheme." *Australian Journal of Politics and History* 61, no. 3 (September 2015), 339–51.

Wöbse, Anna-Katharina. "'To Cultivate the International Mind': Der Völkerbund und die Förderung der globalen Zivilgesellschaft." *Zeitschrift für Geschichtswissenschaft* 54, no. 10 (2006), 852–64.

Woloshyn, Tania. "Le Pays du Soleil: The Art of Heliotherapy on the Côte d'Azur." *Social History of Medicine* 26, no. 1 (February 2013), 74–93.

Woloshyn, Tania Anne. "Patients Rebuilt: Dr Auguste Rollier's Heliotherapeutic Portraits, c.1903–1944." *Medical Humanities* 39, no. 1 (June 2013), 38–46.

Zannini, Andrea. *Tonache e piccozze. Il clero e la nascita dell'alpinismo.* Turin: CDA&VIVALDA Editori, 2004.

Zweiniger-Bargielowska, Ina. *Managing the Body: Beauty, Health, and Fitness in Britain 1880–1939.* New York: Oxford University Press, 2010.

Websites and Electronic Sources

Association de la Presse Etrangère en Suisse (APES), http://www.apes-presse.org/en/ accessed on July 17, 2018.

"Italy's Beppe Grillo Given Four Month Jail Sentence," BBC News, March 3, 2014. https://www.bbc.co.uk/news/world-europe-26422237, accessed on July 28, 2018.

CAI Torino, http://www.caitorino.it/centro-alpinistico/ accessed on July 25, 2016.

Calhoun, Craig. "Cosmopolitanism and Its Discontents: Why Nations Still Matter." *ABC Religion and Ethics,* March 16, 2017. http://www.abc.net.au/religion/articles/2017/03/16/4637108.htm, accessed July 24, 2018.

Le Cercle des Amitiés Internationales, http://www.cai-geneve.org/le-cercle/historique/ (accessed on June 27, 2019).

The Covenant of the League of Nations. http://avalon.law.yale.edu/20th_century/leagcov.asp, accessed on July 30, 2018.

Dizionario Cinema delle Montagne, http://www.museomontagna.org/it/area-documentazione/dizionario.php, accessed on January 16, 2017.

Ekström, Mats, Marianna Patrona, and Joanna Thornborrow, "Right-wing Populism and the Dynamics of Style: A Discourse-analytic Perspective on Mediated Political Performances." *Palgrave Communications* 4, no. 83 (2018). Available online https://doi.org/10.1057/s41599-018-0132-6, accessed on July 25, 2018.

European Commission. *The Erasmus Impact Study: Effects of Mobility on the Skills and Employability of Students and the Internationalisation of Higher Education Institutions* (September 2014). http://ec.europa.eu/dgs/education_culture/repository/education/library/study/2014/erasmus-impact_en.pdf, accessed on July 27, 2018.

Frevert, Ute. "Wartime Emotions: Honour, Shame, and the Ecstasy of Sacrifice," in Ute Daniel, Peter Gatrell, Oliver Janz, Heather Jones, Jennifer Keene, Alan Kramer, and Bill Nasson, eds., *1914–1918-online. International Encyclopedia of the First World War.* https://encyclopedia.1914-1918-online.net/article/wartime_emotions_honour_shame_and_the_ecstasy_of_sacrifice, accessed on August 1, 2018.

Ganesh, Narayani. "Vaud prepares to celebrate Romain Rolland-Gandhi meet 80th anniversary." *The Economic Times* (Online) [New Delhi], November 8, 2011. https://economictimes.indiatimes.com/vaud-prepares-to-celebrate-romain-rolland-gandhi-meet-80th-anniversary/articleshow/10648160.cms, accessed on September 4, 2018.

"Georges Clemenceau's Opening Address as Conference President, 18 January 1919." http://www.firstworldwar.com/source/parispeaceconf_clemenceau.htm, accessed on February 21, 2017.

International Max Planck Research School for Moral Economies of Modern Societies, https://www.mpib-berlin.mpg.de/en/research/research-schools/imprs-mems/research/research-statement accessed on July 17, 2018.

"League of Nations Search Engine," www.Lonsea.de, accessed on July 26, 2016.

Leysin American School, https://www.las.ch/about/welcome/ accessed on June 29, 2017.

"Leysin Tourist Office: Presentation," http://www.leysin.ch/en/resort/presentation-leysin, accessed on September 12, 2016.

La Manufacture, "La Manufacture: accueil," http://www.lamanufacture.ch/wq_pages/fr/manufacture/accueil.php, accessed on July 18, 2016.

Margaret Morris Movement, http://www.margaretmorrismovement.com/welcome, accessed on July 17, 2018.

The Nobel Prize. http://www.nobelprize.org, accessed on April 8, 2016.

Nobelprize.org, *Nomination Database*, http://www.nobelprize.org/nomination/archive/show_people.php?id=9571, accessed on April 2, 2016.

Nordenstreng, Kaarle and Tarja Seppä, "The League of Nations and the Mass Media: A Forgotten Story." XV Conference of the International Association for Mass Communication Research (IAMCR/AIERI), Section of International Communication session on "Communication and Peace; The Role of the Media in International Relations," New Delhi, 27 August 1986, http://www.uta.fi/cmt/en/contact/staff/kaarlenordenstreng/publications/The_League_of_Nations_and_the_Mass_Media.pdf_1, accessed on February 23, 2017.

"Raymond Poincare's Welcoming Address, 18 January 1919." http://www.firstworldwar.com/source/parispeaceconf_poincare.htm, accessed on February 21, 2017.

Rubio, Diego. "The Politics Of Nostalgia." https://www.socialeurope.eu/the-politics-of-nostalgia, accessed July 24, 2018.

Salmela, Mikko, and Christian von Scheve. "The Emotional Roots of Right-wing Political Populism." *Social Science Information* 56, no. 4 (October 12, 2017), 567–95. https://doi.org/10.1177/0539018417734419, accessed on July 24, 2018.

Swiss Hotel Management School, http://www.shms.com, accessed on June 29, 2017.

UIAA, http://www.theuiaa.org, accessed on March 18, 2019.

UNESCO, "World Mountain People Association." https://en.unesco.org/partnerships/non-governmental-organizations/world-mountain-people-association, accessed on July 25, 2018.

Wilson, Woodrow. "Address at the City Hall Auditorium in Pueblo, Colorado, September 25, 1919." http://www.presidency.ucsb.edu/ws/index.php?pid=117400, accessed March 1, 2018.

Wilson, Woodrow. "Address to the Peace Conference in Paris, France, January 25, 1919." http://www.presidency.ucsb.edu/ws/index.php?pid=117770, accessed on November 29, 2016.

Wilson, Woodrow. "Address to the Senate on the Versailles Peace Treaty, July 10, 1919." http://www.presidency.ucsb.edu/ws/index.php?pid=110490, accessed March 1, 2018.

World Health Organization, "Micronutrient Deficiencies." http://www.who.int/nutrition/topics/idd/en/ accessed on January 17, 2017.

"The WTO building: Centre William Rappard." https://www.wto.org/english/thewto_e/cwr_e/cwr_e.htm, accessed on March 30, 2016.

Index